Bundeswehr Academy for Information
and Communication Series

Volume 30

Schriften der Akademie der Bundeswehr
für Information und Kommunikation

Band 30

Ina Wiesner (ed.)

German Defence Politics

Nomos

Die Deutsche Nationalbibliothek lists this publication in the Deutsche Nationalbibliografie; detailed bibliographic data is available in the Internet at http://dnb.d-nb.de.

ISBN 978-3-8487-0824-6

1. Edition 2013

Contents

Foreword

Stéphane Beemelmans

The fundamental changes that have taken place in the international security environment since the end of the Cold War have had a significant impact on German security and defence policy over the past two decades. The Bundeswehr, as one of Germany's main instruments for implementing its security policy, can only fulfil this role credibly and effectively if the personnel and materiel it is provided and the way it is organised afford it the necessary capabilities and flexibility.

The reorientation of the Bundeswehr is creating capabilities that are derived from Germany's security policy, adaptable to demographic change and sustainably funded, so as to enable it to tackle a wide range of and often unforeseen challenges. Only in this way can the Bundeswehr show the political authorities the actual options they have for mastering the security challenges of today and tomorrow.

With this in mind, I very much welcome the fact that general reference books like this one offer guidance on the complex subject of German defence policy. This volume eloquently places Germany's security policy activities within the context of the global security environment.

Many aspects of the reorientation are discussed in the following contributions. The Federal Ministry of Defence and the major military and civilian organisational elements of the Bundeswehr are described, along with their new structures and new functions. This gives the reader a better understanding of the implications and circumstances of the reorientation, which is far more than just an organisational reform. The Federal Ministry of Defence is used as an example to impressively demonstrate how the new Bundeswehr is focusing on the capabilities of each individual member. The result of this personnel-based approach is the creation of large, stringent and joint major resource elements that truly span the entire Bundeswehr – a sign that the Bundeswehr is not burdened by a hierarchical mindset when it comes to its basic organisational principles. In addition, critical thought is expressed, for instance, on legal aspects of operations abroad, and further fields in which the Bundeswehr could operate are addressed.

As a result of the reorientation, the Bundeswehr today depends even more on being seen and supported by society, not least because of the suspension of compulsory basic military service. This presupposes a broad understanding of its tasks and of the circumstances that shape Germany's defence policy.

I would like to express my thanks to the authors of this collective volume for having created a stimulating basis for further public debate on defence and security topics. Above all in the interest of the Bundeswehr and its members, I hope it will be widely read and will find an open-minded, international audience.

Stéphane Beemelmans | Berlin, December 2012

State Secretary
Federal Ministry of Defence

Preface

Axel Hecht

Germany, December 2012. The festive mood in the run-up to Christmas is shattered by the shocking news that a bomb attack was narrowly prevented at the central railway station in Bonn. The investigation by the Federal Public Prosecutor's Office is ongoing, but more and more evidence points to the work of Islamist fundamentalists.

With a view to the state's functions, this incident must be classified as an internal security matter. Yet it goes far beyond that. For it once again highlights how difficult it has become to pinpoint threats directed at the state and society, and how likely these are to have an international or even global dimension. So the external security domain is also affected.

In terms of public opinion, external security has become less and less important in the Federal Republic of Germany since the end of the Cold War. Here in the centre of Europe, people today feel highly secure in everyday life. Most anxiety focuses on financial and economic developments, the personal implications of which are for many more direct and tangible. This gives rise to a remarkable paradox. For our world has not become safer over the past two decades. In fact, new national and international conflicts have emerged, whether this be in Afghanistan, in various regions of Central Africa, the nuclear arms programmes of North Korea and Iran, the struggle of North African states for social and government reforms, the civil war in Syria or piracy on the high seas.

As a state institution with the mission to protect the territory and constitution of the Federal Republic of Germany against external threats, the Bundeswehr must face up to this situation. It is currently undergoing an extensive process of restructuring and reorganisation, all of which is geared towards it acquiring and maintaining the capability to take action in response to present and possible future threats.

This process, and the motivations driving it, are receiving only limited attention in the media. Experience has shown that for more than two decades, security and defence have not been high-profile topics in international or national debate. One reason for this may be that the two fields – as outlined above – hardly affect the lives of many people. Another is that security and defence topics, procedures and processes are usually very complex. They therefore cannot easily be reduced to simple formulae, and a good deal of time and effort is often required to gain a better grasp of these issues.

It is not all that easy for someone who would like to study Germany's security and defence policy in more detail to gain direct insight into the organisation and structures behind it. Parliamentary committee meetings at which such issues are dealt with are usually held behind closed doors; the way in which the Federal Foreign Office and the Federal Ministry of Defence divide tasks and interact is rarely explained to the general public; and reports on international conferences and decisions made at a high level, for instance, within NATO, are mostly brief and fairly abstract. Moreover, the suspension of compulsory military service last year has made it even more difficult for broad sections of the population to get an idea of what goes on behind the fences and walls of restricted military areas and at Bundeswehr agencies. The ongoing reorganisation and reduction in the number of garrisons across the country are greatly lowering the general visibility of the Bundeswehr and what it does.

At the same time, the Bundeswehr, as an institution of our democratic state, is obliged to disclose the reasons behind its activities and aims, and to maintain this transparency.

This volume is an attempt by the Bundeswehr Academy for Information and Communication to meet this obligation. Light must also be cast on the reasons for current developments and appraisals, some of which date back a considerable time. The editor has succeeded in compiling coverage by a number of renowned authors who excel in their fields, coverage that addresses a broad spectrum of issues in connection with German defence policy. We are pleased that, with this publication, we are able to add a further volume to the series entitled *Schriften der Akademie der Bundeswehr für Information und Kommunikation*.

Finally, we hope this volume will give its readers a helpful overview and illuminating insight into a complex subject that, ultimately, concerns us all.

Colonel Axel Hecht — Strausberg, December 2012

Commandant
Bundeswehr Academy for Information and Communication

German defence politics – an introduction

Ina Wiesner

The idea of publishing a book on how defence in Germany is structured and how it functions came about during a series of research trips in Europe in 2009 and 2010. On a number of occasions, British colleagues at the UK Defence Academy asked the editor to talk about the institutional settings within which decisions on security and defence issues are taken in Germany. They asked for information about the competencies within the portfolio of the Federal Ministry of Defence (FMOD) or about the special features of the armament sector in Germany. During the preparations for these lectures, however, it became apparent that there was no comprehensive account either in German or in English that attempted to cover German defence politics in its entirety.

Security and defence experts may be tempted to object by referring to the wide variety of relatively recent publications on Germany's foreign, security and defence policy (Böckenförde/Gareis, 2009; von Bredow, 2007), on issues concerning the ISAF operation in Afghanistan (Seiffert et al. 2012) or on the transformation of the armed forces (Jäger/Thiele, 2011; Terriff et al., 2010). No one disputes the fact that a number of outstanding analyses of German security and defence policy have been published. Nevertheless, this book breaks new ground in that, unlike publications about German defence policy, it is dedicated to German defence *politics*.

Defence policy and defence politics

Like any other political topic – be it social policy or agricultural policy – defence has more than just one dimension. While there is only one word in German for describing topics concerning social control – *Politik* – the English language has three (see Schmidt, 2010: 604 et seq.). *Polity* describes the institutional dimension of the state, which, depending on its specific character, channels the other two political dimensions, process and content. The process-related aspects of political negotiation and decision-making are covered in academic discourse by the term *politics*. Finally, all content-related aspects focus on the different perspectives and interests in the political process and concern the content of political decisions. In this context, the term *policy* refers to the object of political action in its concrete form and is mostly visible in political decisions about factual issues or in laws. Polity, politics and policy – these three political dimensions interrelate, and to some extent even determine one another.

Despite this interweaving of the three political terms, political scientists often concentrate on one dimension or another, depending on the subject of their research. It is thus noticeable that in many academic publications on issues concerning the Bundeswehr, the use of Germany's armed forces and the development of German security policy tend to refer more to the policy dimension when it comes to explaining, for instance, the operation in Afghanistan or Germany's abstention during the UN Security Council vote in March 2011 on the mandate for a military operation in Libya. Currently, no general piece of work exists that consistently and systematically deals with the institutional foundations and specific process-related aspects in the area of German defence politics.

The present publication therefore aims to close this gap in academic literature. The texts contained in this volume focus on structures, processes and competencies relating to what is understood here as German defence politics, in accordance with the distinction between the terms polity, politics and policy. This particular focus is based on the idea that a deeper understanding of how the field of defence is organised is required to appreciate current political decisions, such as those on the Bundeswehr's armed operations abroad, procurement decisions or institutional reform attempts. The institutional setting and the regulations governing the various remits may not ultimately *determine* decision-making in security and defence matters – but they do significantly influence such decision-making.

This volume is therefore intended not only for people who are interested in understanding the structures in which decisions on security are taken and implemented in Germany, but also for anyone who is seeking a comprehensive overview that goes beyond the content-related debate on how German defence measures come about.

Compared with the US, the United Kingdom and France, social science research in Germany is known to focus less on aspects of defence, and this fact is discussed (and criticised) both by circles of experts on security (von Bredow, 2007: Chap.1) as well as increasingly by the wider public (Bigalke, 2012; Deutschlandfunk, 2012). The community of researchers on defence topics is still very small in Germany. Even though the social significance of German defence politics is apparently not reflected by the public's perception of it, it must still be considered high – after all, the Bundeswehr employs more than 200,000 Germans, and military personnel risk life and limb in operations mandated by the German parliament, the Bundestag, and hence the German people. Germany's defence policy is an element of its foreign policy and has a direct influence on how the Federal Republic of Germany is seen around the world. Not least, the defence budget, which makes up ten per cent of the annual federal budget, constitutes a substantial share of public spending. For these reasons and undoubtedly others as well, it is important to devote attention to the Bundeswehr and to the politics of defence.

The essays in this volume convey sound and up-to-date expert knowledge about defence topics such as the German acquisition process and the development of jointness. Ideally, they could form a basis on which more in-depth social science research could be conducted to discover how the institutional setting influences defence outcomes.

The structure of the book

This volume is divided into five parts that build on one another and together form a whole. The first part takes a look at the foundations of defence policy in Germany. Stephan Böckenförde provides an introduction to the subject by locating defence policy as a subarea of foreign and security policy in Germany. The author provides an overview of the development of Germany's security policy from the Cold War era to the challenges of today. Sven Gareis then traces the complex decision-making processes in the fields of security and defence in Germany by taking a close look at the Federal Chancellery, the Bundestag, the Federal Foreign Office and the Federal Ministry of Defence in order to establish where the authority for making decisions on security and defence issues mainly lies. Hans-Werner Wiermann takes the subject a step further by describing Germany's military involvement in the multinational context of the United Nations, NATO and the European Union.

The second part of the present publication addresses how the Bundeswehr and the Federal Ministry of Defence are structured and function. The Bundeswehr – under the civilian leadership of the Federal Minister of Defence – is divided into military and civilian organisational elements (see Figure 1). This means that not everyone who is "in the Bundeswehr" necessarily serves as a soldier. In the summer of 2013, the Bundeswehr had 185,500 active duty military personnel. However, the Bundeswehr also employs civilian personnel (employees and civil servants) who currently occupy 72,000 non-military posts. As in many other militaries around the world, the major organisational elements comprise the usual three armed services: the Army (62,300 military personnel), the Air Force (32,100 military personnel) and the Navy (15,300 military personnel).

Then there are the Joint Support Service, which at present has 46,800 military personnel, and the Bundeswehr Joint Medical Service with around 19,100 men and women in uniform. These two services do not have their own personnel. Civilian staff and military personnel from the Army, Navy and Air Force work in them. They perform the common tasks of the armed services such as those associated with logistics, transport and medical support. The major civilian organisational elements consist of the Federal Defence Administration, which is divided into the areas of Personnel, of Equipment, IT and In-Service Support and of Infrastructure, Environmental Protection and Services, the Administration of Justice Service and the Chaplain Service.

Figure 1: The institutional structure of German defence

<table>
<tr><td colspan="5">Federal Ministry of Defence</td></tr>
</table>

<table>
<tr><td rowspan="10">Bundeswehr</td><td rowspan="5">Military Organisational Elements</td><td rowspan="5">Armed Forces</td><td rowspan="3">Armed Services</td><td>Army</td></tr>
<tr><td>Air Force</td></tr>
<tr><td>Navy</td></tr>
<tr><td colspan="2">Joint Support Service</td></tr>
<tr><td colspan="2">Joint Medical Service</td></tr>
<tr><td rowspan="5">Civilian Organisational Elements</td><td rowspan="3">Federal Defence Administration</td><td colspan="2">Personnel</td></tr>
<tr><td colspan="2">Equipment, IT and In-Service Support</td></tr>
<tr><td colspan="2">Infrastructure, Environmental Protection and Services</td></tr>
<tr><td colspan="3">Administration of Justice Service</td></tr>
<tr><td colspan="3">Chaplain Service</td></tr>
</table>

Source: FMOD, 2012.

Christoph Reifferscheid and Ulf Bednarz offer the reader a brief outline of the development of the Federal Ministry of Defence from the *Amt Blank* to the *Bundesministerium für Verteidigung* up to the *Bundesministerium der Verteidigung*. They describe its present structure and explain the reasons for the reorganisation of the Ministry that is taking place alongside the reorientation of the Bundeswehr, which began in 2011. They make repeated reference to the strong continuity in the practice of keeping separate the Bundeswehr's civilian and military task areas or areas of responsibility, and they highlight how consistently final decision-making authority is concentrated on the civilian side.

In the essay that follows, the focus shifts from the ministerial level to the armed services. Dietmar Klos, Heiner Möllers and Dieter Stockfisch, experts on issues concerning the German Army, Air Force and Navy, respectively, have written an essay that can truly be called a joint contribution. In addition to systematically describing of the development of the structure and mission of each service, the article addresses the important issue of the way in which negotiations are conducted between the services and with the FMOD. The keyword jointness is taken up in the next essay. The goal of jointness is to pool the capabilities of the Army, Air Force and Navy in order to achieve efficiency gains. Manfred Engelhardt considers this relatively new practice of coordinating common tasks on a cross-service basis, focusing on the organisational level, but also looking at jointness in operations at the operational and tactical level.

The Bundeswehr reserve is an essential element when it comes to providing for Germany's security – more than ever since compulsory military service was suspended in 2011. Reservists not only supplement and reinforce personnel on operational deployment, but also perform a key function in mediating between the Bundeswehr and society. The significance of reservists has increased in recent years as they have seen a considerable expansion in their tasks, above all concerning homeland security. In his essay, Armin Müller describes the development of the reserve, which has undergone a substantial change that is no less fascinating than that of the active force component, which has developed from a defence army into an expeditionary army.

The strict constitutional distinction made between the military and civilian sectors of the Bundeswehr in Germany is a peculiar feature of the institution and has led to the development of the Defence Administration, which supports the armed forces, that is, the military elements of the Bundeswehr. Dieter Heuer concludes the second part of the book with an essay on the Defence Administration in which he describes its development, explains its current structure and tasks and ventures a look at the future of the civilian arm of the Bundeswehr.

The essays in the third part of this book centre upon the economic aspects of German defence policy. Stefan Bayer explains how the federal budget is drawn up, which incorporates Departmental Budget 14, the defence budget. He makes it clear that the decision on funds for the defence budget is a political one, that defence is only one of many categories of public spending and that the defence department has to compete for the Federal Government's financial resources. Hellmut Heumann then discusses the armament process in Germany. He first provides an overview of the development of the institutional foundations of armament, for which the civilian sector of the Bundeswehr is responsible. He illustrates to the reader how lessons learned from the business world, for example on the further development of management procedures, also has an influence on the procedures governing the development and procurement of defence materiel. In the last section of his essay, Heumann provides an analysis of the armament sector in Germany, pointing to those areas which in his view require optimisation, and concludes by considering various possibilities for making the complex relationship between the user (the armed forces), the supplier (the armament organisation) and the enabler (industry) more efficient.

Gregor Richter provides an overview of the reform steps that the Bundeswehr has taken in recent years with a view to managing its budget. While there has been a rapid succession of reform, transformation and reorientation in the structures of the armed forces, for example, there has been an astonishing degree of continuity in the modernisation of the Bundeswehr from the economic point of view.

The next part of the volume takes a look at current debates. In the first essay, Jörg Jacobs considers how the German public sees the Bundeswehr. The approach he has adopted involves both an analysis of how the German people perceive the Bundeswehr and a description of the PR work done by the Bundeswehr and the FMOD. Gerhard Kümmel dedicates the next essay to the German public's altered attitude towards the operations the Bundeswehr has conducted since the 1990s. From its beginnings, during which it was purely defence-oriented, the Bundeswehr has evolved into an expeditionary army. These changes have not only had repercussions for its structure and materiel. They have also given rise to a number of legal issues – ranging from rights regarding the use of the Bundeswehr to rights during operational deployment. In his essay on the legal aspects of Bundeswehr operations, Dieter Weingärtner provides an overview of the legal dimensions of military action and traces the current legal challenges regarding operations abroad. Christian Mölling addresses the equally topical issue of how strained public finances are having an impact on the defence budget, and how these effects may be contained by placing greater emphasis on European defence cooperation.

The final part of the present publication is reserved for closing comments. Tom Dyson compares Germany's defence policy with recent developments in France and the United Kingdom. Although Dyson's diagnosis is that, at the political level, the Bundeswehr's force structure, military capabilities and operational concepts are still not sufficiently seen in an international context, he also notes that Germany has in recent years increasingly improved its reform efforts in the field of defence policy.

Acknowledgements

This book could not have been written without the support of many excellent minds and diligent hands. The authors who have contributed essays to this volume have conveyed their expert knowledge with patience, creativity and critical reflection. While working on their contributions, they have kept the reader in mind and thus manage to present complicated defence matters, of which many only have a thorough grasp after spending their working lives in the "Bundeswehr system", in a comprehensible way.

Special thanks go to the Federal Ministry of Defence, above all to its Press and Information Office, for making this publication possible and for providing organisational support. The support of the Press and Information Centres of the Navy and the Air Force, the Military History Research Institute, the Bundeswehr Scientific and Technical Information Centre and the technical information office and media production department of the Bundeswehr Academy for Information and Communication has been very helpful, particularly for producing the diagrams used in this book.

A large share of the success of the publication is due to the work done on it by a group of translators from the Federal Office of Languages in Hürth. They have put in a huge amount of effort to enable the publication of this English edition of *Deutsche Verteidigungspolitik* shortly after the German edition went to press. Eric Hess, head of the Language Support Section at the German Delegation to NATO, assiduously revised the complete English manuscript, turning it into a coherent work.

Kai Mürlebach, M.A., was attentive and constructive in the assistance he provided for the typesetting of the book and for the production of its graphics. He also helped with editing. The support of my colleagues from the Bundeswehr Academy of Information and Communication was invaluable for the success of this project. In this regard, special thanks go to Anne Schulz, who not only literally stood by the editor, but also gave her advice and support. To start with, she was open to the idea of producing such a book, discussed the project with the editor, worked with her on developing and revising the plans, and finally helped to get it published.

After so many minds have contributed to the production of this comprehensive work on current German defence politics, all that remains to be done is to hope it provides its audience with a stimulating read.

Bibliography

Bigalke, Silke (2012): Ungeliebte Kriegsforschung. In: Süddeutsche Zeitung, 27.02.2012, 6.

Böckenförde, Stephan/Gareis, Sven Bernhard (Eds.) (2009): Deutsche Sicherheitspolitik. Opladen/Farmington Hills, Verlag Barbara Budrich.

Bredow, Wilfried von (2007): Militär und Demokratie in Deutschland. Eine Einführung. Wiesbaden: VS Verlag für Sozialwissenschaften.

Deutschlandfunk (2012): Peace researchers contribute to the security debate. An academic contradicts criticism from the Ministry of Defence. Transcript of a radio interview with Harald Müller, Deutschlandfunk, 27.02.2012, http://www.dradio.de/dlf/sendungen/campus/1688228/ (Website visited on 01.03.2012).

Jäger, Thomas/Thiele, Ralph (2011): Transformation der Sicherheitspolitik: Deutschland, Österreich, Schweiz im Vergleich. (Globale Gesellschaft und internationale Beziehungen), Wiesbaden: VS, Verlag für Sozialwissenschaften.

Schmidt, Manfred G. (2010): Wörterbuch zur Politik, Stuttgart: Kröner.

Seiffert, Anja/Langer, Phil C./Pietsch, Carsten (Eds.) (2012): Der Einsatz der Bundeswehr in Afghanistan, Schriftenreihe des Sozialwissenschaftlichen Instituts der Bundeswehr. Wiesbaden, Verlag für Sozialwissenschaften.

Terriff, Terry/Osinga, Frans P. B./Farrell, Theo (Eds.) (2010): A transformation gap? American innovations and European military change. Stanford, Calif.: Stanford University Press.

Part I

The foundations of German defence

German security policy

Stephan Böckenförde

Introduction

The security policy of the Federal Republic of Germany is characterised by the sharp paradigm shift that took place during the three years between 1989 and 1991 as a result of the fall of the Berlin Wall, German unification and, ultimately, the dissolution of the Soviet Union.

The intensity of this shift was, however, diminished by a number of factors. Firstly, the security forces – the principal large organisations of which are the Bundeswehr and the police forces (border and state police) – took a long time to actually put the transformation into effect. This was not least due to their equipment, tailored as it was to the old paradigm and for which in some cases the procurement process extended far into the transformation period (e.g. the Eurofighter Typhoon). Secondly, numerous key elements of the old paradigm extended into this new phase as well (some of which, e.g. nuclear sharing or the framework conditions set in the German constitution regarding deployment of the Bundeswehr, still exist today). Thirdly, the public seems to be struggling with its views on security policy, or unwilling to adapt these views to the new security policy paradigm.

For the Federal Republic of Germany, the old paradigm was characterised by an underlying international structure of territorial states, which essentially confined security policy challenges to one-dimensional – territorial – and mainly military conflicts between countries. This considerably reduced the complexity of the constellations that were encountered in terms of security policy. Inherent in the above-mentioned international structure, this narrowed view was further reinforced by the fact that the international system of territorial states was overarched by the bipolar structure of the East-West conflict, and by the fact that East and West Germany were situated precisely on the dividing line between the blocs.

In accordance with this high level of significance of and emphasis on the principle of 'territoriality', the main challenge was protecting oneself against an opponent with a strong military force. Efforts were made to achieve this by establishing a strong military deterrence capability within an alliance.

This function was originally intended to be performed by a European Defence Community (EDC) (Eekelen, 1998; Haftendorn, 2001). The failure of this project in 1954 became the catalyst for NATO as a transatlantic alliance responsible for defending Europe against external threats, while the various strands of the

European communities became an integrating bracket that partly did away with sovereignty and brought about cooperation and equalisation amongst the (West) European nations themselves.

The Federal Republic of Germany, whose foundation and mere existence may essentially be understood as a product of security conditions in the political world (Bresson, 1970: 27, as cited by Bredow, 2008: 135), was in a historically unique position: Particularly during the initial phase after 1949, the Federal Government had to strive to obtain international equality and capability of action for a Germany that was only partly sovereign. By 1955, this aim had largely been achieved with 'total integration' in the Western block (Schöllgen, 2004: 41). At the same time, the 'German question', i.e. the issue of possible unification, had to be kept open politically. However, in this regard, Germany's orientation towards the West, which was necessary in terms of security policy, de facto led to an inevitable departure from the proclaimed 'priority of unity' (Janning, 2007: 752). In any case, the dominance of the East-West conflict meant that in a nuclear age the 'German question' became sidelined (Schöllgen, 2004: 57) in international politics. Generally speaking, the room for manoeuvre in terms of "innerdeutsche Beziehungen" (intra-German relations), so-called because it was positioned between domestic and foreign policy, was restricted by the framework of the Cold War.

With the fall of the Berlin Wall, German unification and the Treaty on the Final Settlement with respect to Germany ('Two Plus Four Agreement', Auswärtiges Amt, 1990) entering into force, Germany left these special circumstances behind. At the same time, following the end of the East-West conflict and the dissolution of the Soviet Union, global security policy was no longer dominated or limited in its complexity by bipolarity.

For Germany, this marked the beginning of a period of redefinition in terms of security policy: While Germany had been a European problem and an agitator until 1945, it became the object of, or a partner in, the all-dominating East-West conflict as well as the main setting for a potential hot war. From 1990 onwards, it gradually developed into a (fringe) actor within the new global security policy structure.

From then on, this step became even more complicated, since it was no longer possible to simply adopt traditional security policy patterns. Instead, it became necessary to break new ground. There were two reasons for this necessity. For one thing, a global structure supported by non-state actors had developed in parallel to the international ('post-Westphalian', Schneckener, 2005) system. This involved a loss of control on the part of the central player, the 'territorial state', which unfolded quite dramatically in some parts of the world (as well as the emergence of failing and even failed states). Furthermore, knowledge and technologies have proliferated and new vulnerabilities of highly complex and networked societies and national economies on the threshold of post-industrial systems have emerged, leading to entirely new security challenges.

Against this background, it has become necessary to restructure the state architecture of security policy actors from a traditional form tailored towards territorial state issues towards a new functional design capable of meeting the multitude of diffuse challenges. In a complex and multi-dimensional environment, it is also necessary to constantly compile and update threat analyses and adapt the security architecture if required.

The following pages provide a broad overview of the fundamental security policy issues that Germany is faced with. This overview begins with a general discussion of the concept of security, followed by an outline of security policy during the Cold War, and finally gives an account of the current security policy situation. The next section explains how the Federal Republic of Germany has met these challenges over the years since the late 1940s. In this context, the above-mentioned paradigm shift at the beginning of the 1990s represents a break that was indeed sharp in terms of the security policy situation but more gradual in terms of institutional, organisational and social aspects.

The main features of security policy

Security and security policy can take three different forms: In their most general form, they relate to the individual, who must be protected against any disastrous or destructive force and all existential dangers (cf. Böckenförde, 2009: 11-14). In their most abstract form, security and security policy extend to the preservation of a certain way of life of individuals and societies. In their most concrete form – and this is the one that evidently still dominates public understanding of the term – security and security policy refer to the protection of a political system, the ability of that system to survive and, above all, its ability to defend its territorial integrity on its external borders. However, which definition really dominates depends on the social system. Apparently, societies that are transitioning from industrial to post-industrial systems, from the 'large numbers" of the industrial age to possibly individualised societies (the German term *Gelöstschaften* adopted from Papcke, 1996: 755) within formal societies, tend to shift their understanding of security more clearly towards individualised forms, i.e. to place the individual at the centre of their concept of security.

The possibility of largely reducing security to a defence dimension – which, until recently, was the largely uncontested and most common understanding of the concept in Germany – is the result of a narrowed and history-based view. This narrowed view is connected with the emergence of territorial states in the early modern age and the spread of the territorial state as the globally dominant system of organising societies – a spread that originated in Europe and occurred in long waves between the end of the 18th century and the 1960s. The success of the territorial state (which, according to Jellinek's 'doctrine of the three elements' (Jellinek, 1903), is characterised by state authority, people and state territory, as well as by international recognition) is due to the fact that – at least during the pre-industrial and industrial phases – it was obviously the most likely form of state to be in a position to fulfil functions of social order (by forming structures of coercion on the one hand and structures of loyalty on the other) together with protective functions at its external borders, including the ability to defend itself and to pursue interests beyond its external borders and, above all, to allocate the resources needed to do this. The most important factor is that of territoriality, which determines the remit of the state's functions. The nation-state is a special form of territorial state that is characterised by a specific type of loyalty and identity formation on the part of its citizens, the nation.

Security and security precautions are two of the key tasks of the territorial state. Within the state, individual use of force in self-defence ('gewaltsames Selbsthelfertum', v. Trotha, 1995: 133) was abrogated and replaced by the state's monopoly on the legitimate use of force. Later on, however – by choice and most commonly in the form of the European social state that developed from the 19th century onwards – it also provided various aspects of economic and social security for the members of the state community.

Externally – in addition to safeguarding national interests, and in certain circumstances particular – the territorial state also exercises a protective function by securing its territorial integrity at its external borders and providing active defence, usually with the help of armed forces. It thus provides a fundamental precondition for security in the territorial state system. This precondition can be defined as the potential for a society to develop politically and socially without direct pressure from the outside (Löwenthal as cited in Meyers, 2004: 30). In terms of security policy, the external border of the territorial state thus becomes the 'hard shell' (Herz, 1961: 15) of societies.

While territorial states seek to inwardly replace the individual use of force in self-defence with a state monopoly on the legitimate use of force, the international system has, with regard to the security problem, long been an egalitarian anarchic system in which force has been the generally accepted method of accomplishing interests. States thus had to be in a position to protect themselves against attacks from the outside or, as a precaution, they pursued a strategy of demoralisation through (credible) deterrence by ensuring that the adversary considered the price of a potential attack so high or at least so incalculable that it was never launched.

In effect, the establishment of the territorial state system goes hand in hand with the reduced complexity of security policy, with threats related to the area of internal security being the main source of dangers for the individual while acts of violence perpetrated by an external agent are the main dangers to the community. The state assumes responsibility for minimising both types of threats.

A further reduction in complexity began in the late 1940s in the wake of the Cold War, or rather the East-West conflict. Numerous violent conflicts between countries could now, as 'proxy wars', very plausibly be placed in the simple context of bloc antagonism. At the heavily armed borders between the two blocs – especially on the territory of the divided states of Korea and Germany – the concept of security became extremely one-dimensional over a long time. This period was characterised by the possibility that the other side could launch a massively destructive military operation if the Cold War was to turn *hot*. Accordingly, national security was understood as the ability to successfully deter the enemy from carrying out an attack on one's own territory – in this case German territory. Viewed from to this narrowed perspective, even the contribution of Alpha Jets for the potential defence of NATO partner Turkey during the first Iraq war in 1991 sparked controversy.

Paradoxically, however, at the hotspots of the Cold War, this highly confrontational system had a distinctly stabilising effect. This stability was increased even further when, at the beginning of the 1970s, the *Anti-Ballistic Missile Treaty* (ABM), signed in 1972 by the US and the Soviet Union, came into force. This treaty marked the beginning of the period of deterrence architecture described as mutually assured destruction (MAD). In this treaty, both superpowers assured each other that they would largely refrain from developing and deploying anti-ballistic missile systems. They thus mutually assured their second-strike capability. As a result, it became possible to limit (*Strategic Arms Limitation Talks*, SALT I and SALT II), and later reduce (*Strategic Arms Reduction Treaty*, START I, START II, New START, *Strategic Offensive Reductions Treaty*, SORT) the number of missiles and warheads and, with the elimination of medium-range missiles in the *Intermediate Nuclear Forces Treaty* (INF), even to remove an entire class of weapons from the equation during the second half of the 1980s.

It is safe to say that the East-West conflict as a global structure-forming element characterised the conduct of nations towards each other (a view that political neorealism would support) and that the prevailing state of this global conflict played a substantial (co)determining role in all matters of war and peace.

In view of this structural factor, the institutional element in the international system, i.e. the United Nations and most importantly its Security Council – which were originally intended to decide on the use and prevention of violence – considerably declined in significance, at least up until the late 1980s. After the Kellogg-Briand Pact of 1928 – the first, albeit failed, attempt to ban wars of aggression under international law and, by means of a mutual self-commitment, to eliminate them as a an instrument of politics and international relations – the UN Charter of 1945 imposed a limited ban on the threat and use of force. It was limited in that states were granted the right to individual and, above all, collective self-defence. Furthermore, the Security Council has the option to authorise the use of force with a majority of at least nine votes, provided none of the five permanent members puts in a veto.

So, on the one hand, the United Nations has an egalitarian structure complemented by representative elements (changing membership in the Security Council determined by regional group and voting decisions). On the other hand, however, it has a central body that features a selective hierarchical factor (i.e. the five permanent Security Council members that have the power to veto decisions of the Security Council). Against this structural background, until the late 1980s the United Nations and its Security Council were not able to step out of the shadow of the East-West conflict and to assume their intended function of preventing wars. Only when the Cold War abated in the late 1980s could the United Nations once again assume a more important role. Of particular significance in this context is the 'annus mirabilis' 1988 (Berridge, 1991:108), which, with the changes it brought, ushered in the year of transformation: the Soviet Union withdrew from Afghanistan, the war between Iraq and Iran came to an end, termination of the Cambodian-Vietnamese War drew closer with a four-party meeting in Jakarta, and South Africa announced its withdrawal from Namibia; what is more, with the signing of the Esquipulas II Accord the previous year, an important step was taken towards ending the wars in Nicaragua and Honduras.

In the area of security policy, three phenomena occurred as a result of, or at the same time as, the end of the East-West conflict that continue to shape the future of international security. Firstly, conflicts between states were autonomised, that is separated from the context of a global major conflict, and converted or reduced to regional or local contexts, as was the case in Central America as well as in the Middle East. Secondly, 'new wars' emerged (see Kaldor, 1999; Münkler, 2002), which were no longer fought between states alone. And thirdly, established states were drawn into what were essentially asymmetric wars by non-state actors.

The end of the East-West conflict thus gave rise to a dual development. Firstly, light was thrown on regional or even local causes of violent clashes between states. The old rivalry between the superpowers, which had sometimes even worked to prevent war, had ceased to exist, and states – seemingly unregulated and unsanctioned by the superpowers – were now free to pursue their individual interests, for example irredentism, as was the case between Iraq and Kuwait. Secondly, 'new' and especially 'asymmetric' wars also led to new phenomena of violence – a kind of 'return to history' from the previously stabilising bracket of the East-West conflict, so to speak.

The main cause of 'new wars', which for territorial states constitute multifaceted challenges, is the emergence of a 'parallel and opposing world' populated by non-state power players and conflicting with the established structures of territorial statehood. The outbreak of 'new wars', and possibly even the preliminary stages of such conflicts, are a result of the failure of states or the breakdown of essential state functions – in particular the undermining of the state monopoly on the legitimate use of force. In individual cases, there might be further causes that contribute to the destabilisation of the community, such as a dysfunctional allocation of resources in the state system, lack of representation, the formation of new and perhaps even transnational identities, and hence communities, as well as related potential minority problems or issues of immigration. Additionally, economic factors such as impoverishment or uneven distribution of wealth can contribute to the undermining of statehood, as can 'natural' causes such as epidemics or the consequences of climate change.

In fragile or failed states, the non-existence of a monopoly on the legitimate use of force can lead to a 'renaissance' of the individual use of force in pursuit of personal interests, in 'spaces open to violence', and to the emergence of markets of violence (Elwert, 1997; on 'spaces open to violence' Elwert, 1997: 86) as well as to the formation of *Gewaltunternehmen* (violent entrepreneurship). While the national economies of failing states deteriorate further and further, violent entrepreneurship benefits from the perpetuation of a high level of violence, not least through the inflow of money and weapons from the global market in exchange for raw materials (e.g. 'blood diamonds'), as well as from the support of expatriate communities. Even if these *Gewaltunternehmer* (violent entrepreneurs) have close ties to global markets, their interests mainly have a local focus that is rarely even regional. Violent entrepreneurs benefit from the reduced cost of warfare – investment costs are low because of the kinds of weapons used in these wars, and materiel is often 'off the shelf'. 'Operating costs' are also low, and 'human capital' is cheap, with combatants living off the spoils of war, as in the Middle Ages. Last but not least, violent entrepreneurs in some regions conscript and use child soldiers.

In these 'new wars', which differ from pre-territorial state wars mainly in their link to a now global market – allowing them to go on *ad infinitum* – the old framework of time and space of territorial state wars becomes malleable. Clearly defined and limited territoriality is replaced by unspecific 'space', and 'new wars' usually do not have a clear beginning (and certainly not a formal declaration of war), nor do they end with a peace agreement. Instead, they oscillate between abating and flaring up and, at best, end in a 'reconciliation process'.

'New wars' have a direct violent threat potential for the affected local or regional environment. They threaten human lives and destroy social and material infrastructure as well as political and economic systems. Beyond their direct surroundings, however, the primary disruptive potential of 'new wars' is due to indirect effects that vary in their form and severity. Such effects could include hindered access to areas that are economically important to individual states or to the world economy (directly or only within their capacity as a transit region).

Likewise, the inflow of refugees or similar phenomena may put a strain on the social systems of third states.

Soon after 1990, references to this form of security challenge for the period following the Cold War began to crop up. NATO's 1991 Strategic Concept, for example, refers to new risks – 'multi-faceted in nature and multi-directional' – now facing NATO, including the negative consequences of instabilities:

> the adverse consequences of instabilities that may arise from the serious economic, social and political difficulties, including ethnic rivalries and territorial disputes, which are faced by many countries in central and eastern Europe.

While these risks were deemed not to pose a direct threat to NATO countries, it was thought that they may spill over into NATO countries or may involve other countries (NATO, 1991). These considerations are addressed again in NATO's 1999 *Strategic Concept* (NATO, 1999):

> Some countries in and around the Euro-Atlantic area face serious economic, social and political difficulties. Ethnic and religious rivalries, territorial disputes, inadequate or failed efforts at reform, the abuse of human rights, and the dissolution of states can lead to local and even regional instability. The resulting tensions could lead to crises affecting Euro-Atlantic stability, to human suffering, and to armed conflicts. Such conflicts could affect the security of the Alliance by spilling over into neighbouring countries, including NATO countries, or in other ways, and could also affect the security of other states.

The 1992 *Agenda for Peace* of the then UN Secretary-General Boutros Boutros-Ghali contains clear references to the dangers that may arise from instabilities (see Boutros-Ghali 1992), as does the European Security Strategy (see the European Security Strategy, European Union, 2003).

As multidimensional as the causes of the 'new wars' and the resulting instabilities are – after the abrupt end in the early 1990s of an era of stability engendered by the international structures resulting from the East-West conflict – so too are the security challenges that force both directly and indirectly affected states to adapt. Central to both cases, however, is that directly affected states and especially indirectly affected states aim to ultimately achieve a reconstitution of stable state structures or para-state/state-like structures in unstable regions. To this end, particularly in Western states that are at most indirectly affected, strategies for action are conforming less and less to the classic one-dimensionality of the military that is common in territorial statehood. Instead, security policy is now being reorganised across all (government) departments – if possible in a nationwide approach and from a functional perspective.

What is more, since the early 2000s, the much-debated responsibility to protect ('R2P'), which has been a controversial concept in the international community, has formed a further basis for action beyond an interest in international stability. In the R2P concept, the security of individual, or 'human security', supplants that of the state. This follows a general trend of turning away from the major collective actors in favour of 'individualisation' and a focus on smaller groups. According to the reasoning behind the R2P concept, states that fail to provide security functions for their own citizens may be held accountable by the international community – even by the use of military force if necessary.

This concept does not, however, grant states a carte blanche to intervene. Led by Gareth Evans und Mohamed Sahnoun, the International Commission on Intervention and State Sovereignty (ICISS) in its 2001 report proposes a new order of responsibilities: *first, the responsibility to prevent, second, the responsibility to react and, third, the responsibility to rebuild.* Furthermore, an intervention based on the responsibility to protect requires a UN resolution. Such a resolution must ideally be passed by the UN Security Council but in the event that the Security Council becomes gridlocked, it could, in exceptional cases, also be passed by the General Assembly (within the meaning of the *Uniting For Peace Resolution*). Fundamentally speaking, additional conditions must be met to justify a possible intervention in terms of the R2P:

- there must be evidence that gross violations of human rights are occurring or imminent;
- the purpose of any intervention must be to prevent or end these human rights violations;
- violent intervention is only permitted as a final resort if all other options have been exhausted or seem futile;
- the intervention method must be appropriate and, its purpose being to protect the people, must claim as few victims as possible;
- in accordance with the 'do no harm' principle, there must be realistic and reasonable prospects for a successful intervention;
- in addition, interventions in accordance with the R2P concept must take a comprehensive approach that creates lasting security for each individual and provides a basis for building strong political structures that enable good governance and guide the state back towards 'local ownership' (ICISS, 2001).

Alongside 'new wars' came the spread of 'asymmetric wars', in which non-state actors attack territorial states or involve them in violent conflicts. In most cases, these actors use areas that, in the wake of 'new wars', are no longer under state control as their areas of retreat. They may even be in contact with parties to the 'new wars', who themselves focus primarily on local areas. In contrast to these 'new war' parties, however, they are not restricted to local or regional areas but, with their much greater radius of action, can also attack a superpower (as on 7 August 1998 with the attacks on the American embassies in Nairobi and Dar-Es-Salaam, or on 11 September 2001) or major European states (as on 11 March 2004 in Madrid or on 7 July 2005 in London). Not just because of the reduced cost of warfare and easier access to the necessary technology but above all due to the proliferation of knowledge, these actors are able to conduct operations that have war-like effects.

Currently, however, such operations are limited (and will remain so for the time being) and attackers are unable to achieve effects similar to those of high-intensity wars between states. 'Weapons of mass disruption', however, can also cause considerable damage and can have a distinct impact on the behaviour and outlook of globalised societies. The reason for this is that these societies have become more vulnerable as a result of the increasing complexity of their social and economic processes. In addition, these societies now perceive threats in a different way. The focus has shifted from the use of force against a nation state towards the maintenance of a way of life that is mainly determined by economic but also by social and political factors.

At the same time, these actors are 'de-territorialised', displaying different vulnerability patterns than states, and these are thus not impressed by classic deterrence strategies. They penetrate the permeable exterior borders of states and – no longer adhering to the old framework of time and space – elude capture by disappearing into clandestinity.

States also respond to these new challenges. First of all, they are no longer primarily guided by threat-based concepts but, to an increasing extent, by capabilities-based concepts (see for example the US Quadrennial Defense Review 2001). The latter focus primarily on capabilities irrespective of actors rather than on specific enemies with known capabilities, as was the case, for example, during the Cold War. At the same time, states 're-symmetrise' (term based on Münkler, 2006) by compensating for the advantages their enemies gain from asymmetry. They do this, for example, by loosening legal boundaries, by reallocating responsibilities and capabilities, and by procuring new weapons or introducing new tactics that can be used to imitate non-state enemies in terms of their clandestinity and their wide-ranging detachment from the old framework of space and time (through the use of intelligence assets, special forces or drones, etc.).

Such approaches are founded in various security policy documents, e.g. the US *National Security Strategy* of 2002, in which 'terrorists of global reach' are described as the gravest danger (National Security Strategy 2002), or the *European Security Strategy*, in which international terrorism is mentioned in the same breath as the proliferation of weapons of mass destruction, regional conflicts, failing states and organised crime (European Security Strategy 2003).

Finally, beyond 'new wars' and 'asymmetric wars', some states are still engaged in traditional wars (currently, for example, in the South China Sea where China, Japan and Taiwan are in conflict over their respective claims to various islands), in which renewed and increasing worldwide armament and international weapons trade also play a role. Another problem that remains is the proliferation of unconventional weapons (Iran, North Korea, etc.). There is the possibility, however, that new types of non-kinetic 'knowledge-based' weapons could also be used between states (e.g. in the form of cyber warfare) unless these are placed under an armament control regime.

The Federal Republic of Germany's security policy in historical transition

As established at the beginning of this chapter, German security policy is marked by the sharp paradigm shift of the early 1990s. While the political establishment quickly responded with policy documents, institutional and organisational change was slow and drawn-out.

Before the paradigm shift: West German security policy from 1949 to 1990

Three fundamental interests and two questions guided the Federal Republic during the establishment its security policy:

A position on equal terms with its partners on an international level; territorial integrity and political sovereignty in the face of perceived Soviet expansionism; and the unification of the two German states. These fundamental interests gave rise to two questions: how could West Germany achieve these interests with the least amount of opposition or compromise, and to what lengths would it have to go or, rather, what price would it have to pay to do so?

Up until 1990, the valid response to this fusion of policy- and security-related concerns was that West Germany would waive a portion of its national sovereignty in return for security under the aegis of an alliance. This situation brought with it the choice of either integration into a supranational alliance or into a multinational union that did not interfere with West Germany's, albeit limited, national freedom of action. These options presented themselves in the form of NATO, on the one hand, which assumed the tasks of military deterrence and defence, and the European Communities, on the other, which through their integrative function offered the framework for peaceful conflict resolution and cooperation. After the failure of the European Defence Community (EDC), it became clear that West Germany would entrust its military defence first and foremost to NATO. The price for this was self-restriction of its sovereignty on issues of security (especially with regard to military command and control, and the potential use of nuclear weapons) and assumption of a substantial portion of the conventional defence costs (which included renouncing proper nuclear capabilities).

At the same time, West Germany had to accept that its territory would become a theatre of war should the Cold War turn *hot*. Finally, it settled on temporarily deferring its claims to unification and accepting the provisional two-state solution. Intra-German policy thus became a field of politics that comprised both foreign and domestic policy. It was placed under the authority of the Ministry of Intra-German Relations, which was created especially for this purpose.

The balancing act of West German foreign policy between the political ideas of the United States and the, at times hypertrophic, notions of the French – both of which were themselves subject to the tensions of relations between the US, the United Kingdom and Germany, on the one side, and the Soviet Union, on the other – resulted in the decision to, on the one hand, defer military defence structures to NATO, with its transatlantic organisation and orientation towards international confrontation, which was tailored to the global dimensions of the Cold War. On the other hand, questions of regional security were left to the network of European structures, with the European Union at the highest level.

The European dimension of defence policy rested on the idea that gradual integration and a supranational architecture in various areas would bring peace to relations between member states and, more importantly, bind West Germany to its partners in the future. In the global theatre, this European dimension served as a defence component against the Soviet Union and gave Europe an autonomous position between the superpowers. It consisted of several elements: the Council of Europe in the area of politics, and, in the economic field, the Organisation for European Economic Co-operation (OEEC) and the European Coal and Steel Community (ECSC), later the European Economic Community (EEC) and the European Atomic Energy Community (EURATOM). The first military element was the *Treaty of Brussels*, which excluded Germany or, rather, was even meant to serve as a defence pact against a potentially renewed German aggression. However, in light of the Korean War (1950–1953), it soon became clear that military defence of Western Europe would be difficult to accomplish without a West German contribution. Consequently, talks on the rearmament of West Germany began in the fall of 1950 with such key initiatives as the Himmerod Memorandum on a national level and the Pleven Plan on an international one. The goal of these talks was to firmly incorporate German contingents into international structures as part of the European Defence Community (EDC).

After France had originally planned to use the EDC to position Europe between the US and the Soviet Union under French leadership and with German involvement (Schöllgen, 2004: 67ff), the EDC foundered in August 1954 — ironically as the result of the French National Assembly's failure to ratify it. Three developments emerged from this situation. Firstly, the Treaty of Brussels was transferred into the Western European Union (WEU), in which Germany and Italy joined the original signatory states Belgium, the Netherlands, Luxembourg, France and Great Britain, followed in the 1990s by Spain, Portugal and finally Greece. The WEU remained one of the pillars of Europe's various integrative structures until the 1998 Franco-British Summit of St. Malo set off the process of its absorption by the EU, which came to completion with the *Treaty of Lisbon* in 2009.

Secondly, the ECSC, EURATOM, and the EEC, later the EC, contributed to a gradual vertical integration in the economic area, i.e. an intensified integration among members at increasingly short intervals, but also to a horizontal integration on the continent, i.e. new memberships, that initially focused primarily on Denmark, the United Kingdom and Ireland. The European integrative community's network of cooperation had a peace-building effect beyond its own borders, which became evident with the admission of Spain, Portugal and Greece in the 1980s. These admissions proved that the EC's powers of attraction, assimilation and integration had been able to counteract the instabilities that had been looming at its southern periphery following the transitions to democracy in those countries during the 1970s.

Thirdly, after West German rearmament had been agreed and after NATO had decided in 1952 to engage in a forward strategy a involvement of West German had become indispensable, NATO assumed the function that was originally conceived for the EDC, namely defending Western Europe, including West Germany, against an attack from the Eastern bloc. As a result, the Cold War had finally reached a global dimension. Today, one can only speculate whether a more limited European solution under a French-led EDC would have contained the conflict – and whether Western Europe would have been able to resist pressure from the Eastern bloc. Western Europe on its own would probably not have been able to effectively defend itself. Aside from 'proxy wars', which were greatly determined by local factors, the epicentres of the Cold War lay in East Asia (Korea) and in Europe (especially in Germany). At the same time, West Germany had achieved partial sovereignty through the Petersberg Agreement of 1949 and the first and second General Treaty of 1951 and 1955. It had furthermore emancipated itself into semi-sovereignty by way of 'total integration' ('Totalintegration'; Schöllgen, 2004: 41) in the Council of Europe, WEU, and NATO. This, however, came at the cost of rearmament and the temporary postponement of German unification, which at best would have produced a neutral state under Soviet influence.

The integration of West Germany into NATO prompted four new questions: what burdens would the Federal Republic assume? Would it pursue its own nuclear option? And in that context: to what extent was it prepared to allow its territory to become the theatre of a *hot* war, should it come to that? And in what way would it help bear the burdens of other NATO member states (especially the US, who were becoming increasingly involved in Indochina)?

With West Germany's accession to NATO, rearmament and the formation of the Bundeswehr had been decided. It was clear from the onset – when the first soldiers enlisted in January 1956 and universal conscription was introduced in the summer of the same year – that the Bundeswehr was to become a defence force with a strength of approximately 500,000 troops, firmly rooted in civil society and integrated into international structures (through subordinating all units except the national territorial commands to the NATO supreme command SACEUR and relinquishing a national general staff). The Bundeswehr was expected to reach its target size by the 1980s (Varwick, 2007: 248). Bundeswehr units played a role in NATO's forward strategy in so far as they were expected to bind the Eastern bloc forces during a westward advance in the 'delay zone West Germany' until further defence forces became available.

At the time, how many resources could and should be allocated to the European theatre had already been discussed in the US. Besides, a significant German contribution was not expected in the long term. Indeed, it was not until the mid 1960s that the Bundeswehr became at all capable of defence (see Thoß, 2007: 24). Accordingly, deliberations regarding the incorporation of American nuclear weapons into NATO's defence strategy were already under way half a year before West German accession to NATO (MC 48, *The Most Effective Pattern of NATO Military Strength for the Next Five Years*). This step was implemented in May 1957 with MC 14/2 (*Overall Strategic Concept for the Defence of the NATO Area*), in which the doctrine of massive retaliation was first mentioned. It excluded the option of a 'limited' war against the Soviet Union, though it did not necessarily imply an automatic and immediate use of nuclear weapons. For the following years this meant that West Germany would be trading the *Scylla* of destruction by conventional defence in depth for the *Charybdis* of nuclear annihilation by tactical nuclear weapons.

For West Germany, this situation gave rise to four necessities. First, the development of a strong deterrent capability, especially by quickly increasing the strength of the Bundeswehr and at the same time binding the US to Europe. Second, the acquisition of leverage in US nuclear planning and, in the extreme case, deployment. Third, the establishment of an effective civil defence system (which, however, did not come to pass before the end of the Cold War) (on these three points, see Thos 2007: 19f). And, fourth, the adoption of a confidence-building policy of détente to complement the strategy of deterrence – which came to fruition during the late 1960s.

In 1967, this change in policy manifested itself in the shift in NATO nuclear strategy from MC 14/2 (massive retaliation) to MC 14/3 (flexible response). According to this doctrine, an attack was to be initially met with a response at the same level while escalating the conflict up to a general nuclear response as a final option was not ruled out. On the other hand, NATO approved the Harmel Report, opening the door for a policy of complementing military deterrence with diplomacy, dialogue and détente – a direction that greatly suited West German interests.

Strategists had already been considering a shift from massive retaliation towards a dual approach of flexible response and détente since 1962. Several circumstances influenced these considerations during the early 1960s. Initially, the reluctance of the US to condemn the suppression of the Hungarian Uprising by the Warsaw Pact countries in 1956 and its (weak) response to the construction of the Berlin Wall in 1961 made Europeans doubt whether – in the worst case scenario of a Soviet attack against Western Europe – the US would actually pursue a rollback strategy, if necessary with nuclear weapons, in the spirit of massive retaliation. In other words: there were fears that Western deterrence lacked credibility in the eyes of the Warsaw Pact. These doubts were further nursed by the fact that the US had lost its nuclear dominance over the Soviet Union in the course of the 1950s and 1960s. The 'Sputnik Shock' of 1957 made it clear that even the US was no longer invulnerable to a Soviet missile attack. This raised the question of whether the US would ultimately be prepared to 'sacrifice' a major American city for the defence of Western Europe. When, moreover, China conducted its first nuclear weapons test in 1964 and fears arose that more states would pursue nuclear armament, the US and the Soviet Union drafted the *Non-Proliferation Treaty* (NPT) with the aim of limiting the number of nuclear powers. However, the NPT also thwarted the nuclear ambitions of other NATO members. In 1969, Germany joined the treaty only after great hesitation, to the disappointment of certain groups, which had advocated developing a national or joint European nuclear capability. Then again, the American project of a Multilateral Nuclear Force (MLF) had failed in 1966. The objectives of this project had been to compensate for British weakness in the area of nuclear armament and France's imminent withdrawal from NATO (which occurred in 1966), while countering West German nuclear ambitions impelled by demands for equality with the option of participation in NATO nuclear planning (Schöllgen, 2004: 73f.). The gap left by the failure of the MLF was filled by the NATO Nuclear Planning Group in which West Germany was granted its long-coveted say in matters of tactical nuclear deployment and targeting in the event of the Cold War turning *hot*.

Ultimately, what conditioned the doctrinal shift from massive retaliation to flexible response were both France's withdrawal from NATO's integrated military structure as well as West Germany's reluctant approval in the face of Germany's recurring fears that it could become the theatre of a conventional war (Schöllgen, 2004: 62) if NATO did not immediately escalate.

However, flanked by clear signals of a willingness to engage in dialogue, this shift opened the door to a phase of détente between the superpowers that came with two prospective options for West Germany: a reduction of the threat through the adoption of confidence-building measures (CBM), arms control and possibly even conventional as well as nuclear disarmament, and the opportunity of developing a relatively independent intra-German policy that would no longer be able to postulate immediate unification as its consequence, but could in return nonetheless raise hopes for, as Egon Bahr had phrased it in 1963, 'change through rapprochement' ('Wandel durch Annäherung') and a reorientation in national-political cooperation towards 'relief for the people' ('Erleichterungen für die Menschen').

All this took place under the canopy of global détente, which was ultimately made possible by the combination of the *Non-Proliferation Treaty* (NPT) and the *Anti-Ballistic Missile Treaty* (ABM). While the NPT limited the number of nuclear nations to the two superpowers as well as Great Britain, France, and China (more recent nuclear powers such as Israel, India, and Pakistan have to date not joined the NPT), the ABM confirmed the principle of mutually assured destruction for the United States and the Soviet Union, the two leading nuclear nations. It was only on this basis of mutually assured deterrence that further arms control and later even disarmament treaties became negotiable.

As regards Europe, however, the concern remained that despite the phase of détente, a war, especially a nuclear war, might be fought on German territory. The possibility of the United States loosening its ties with Europe and thus upsetting the balance of deterrence continued to present a particular cause for anxiety. Such a contingency would have raised the likelihood of limited nuclear war, be it because it would undermine the credibility of Western deterrence and embolden the Soviet Union to attack or, conversely, because US reluctance to wage war at Europe's expense would have decreased if it had been able to protect itself from a Soviet retaliation strike.

These two rationales stood behind the developments in the second half of the 1970s and the first half of the 1980s. The deployment of highly accurate SS-20 intermediate-range ballistic missiles initiated by the Soviet Union in 1976 fuelled lingering fears that the Soviet Union might be inclined to conduct a surprise first strike against land-based NATO targets. The West responded with the NATO Double-Track Decision, which announced that the US would withdraw 1,000 nuclear warheads within the next years, but at the same time deploy new medium-range nuclear weapons (*Pershing* and *cruise missiles*); the interim period was to be used for negotiations between the two sides. However, once rearmament was under way, ideas began circulating even in the United States about a surprise 'decapitation strike' with high-accuracy nuclear weapons based in Europe. What made this scenario quite conceivable was that the Soviet Union would lose its capability to launch an effective counter-strike against the United States. Such considerations received further backing under US President Ronald Reagan (1981–1989), whose concept of a missile defence system would, once installed, give the United States a sense of invulnerability. This debate was stoked further by the Soviet invasion of Afghanistan — a move that was often interpreted as part of a Soviet strategic advance towards the Indian Ocean. It was not until Gorbachev launched his reform programme and, more specifically, negotiated the *Double-Zero Deal* (INF Treaty) with Reagan in late 1987, which provided for the withdrawal and dismantling of all medium-range weapons on European territory, that the debate about the feasibility or even 'winnability' of nuclear war in Europe was discontinued.

Below the nuclear threshold, the beginning of the phase of détente in the early 1970s paved the way for talks, which was entirely in Germany's interest. Negotiations were aimed at the reduction of conventional arsenals (*Mutual and Balanced Force Reduction*, MBFR) and at security and cooperation in Europe (Conference on Security and Cooperation in Europe, CSCE), which was initially particularly in the interest of the Soviet-led Eastern bloc (Schöllgen 2004: 134-137). The MBFR talks, however, dragged on until they were aborted in the spring of 1989 without tangible results apart from the fact that negotiations had taken place. The reasons for the lack of progress were manifold. First, no accord was reached on whether to reduce weapons by equal quantities or until equal ceilings were reached. Second, the weapon systems at issue were hardly comparable in terms of quality. Third, the West never stopped doubting the correctness of the numbers presented by the Warsaw Pact. The MBFR talks ended in 1989 and were superseded by negotiations on the *Treaty on Conventional Armed Forces in Europe* (CFE). Initially successful, the treaty set the terms for conventional disarmament, but then produced no further results – mostly due to Central and Eastern European countries joining the *Adapted Conventional Armed Forces in Europe Treaty* (A-CFE).

In contrast to the unsuccessful MBFR talks, the CSCE was able to draft a final act in 1975 that reflected the essential interests of all 35 Western and Eastern European participants as well as those of the United States and Canada. The central components of the final act were summarised in what were referred to as 'baskets': The second basket covered economic interests (this had been important to the Soviet Union). The third basket dealt above all with sub-national issues (the development of humanitarian cooperation had been of special interest to Western states). The first basket contained provisions for international relations, with which the Eastern bloc had hoped to freeze the *status quo* in Europe and cement the post-war order even in a situation in which no peace treaty had formally ended World War II. However, the inviolability of national borders and territorial integrity did not preclude a change in the *status quo* as a result of internal developments (as indeed happened in the late 1980s). In such a case, each state (not least the Soviet Union itself) was bound to 'respect each other's right freely to choose and develop its political, social, economic and cultural systems as well as its right to determine its laws and regulations' (Conference on Security and Co-operation in Europe, Final Act, 1975). This passage was an implicit reference to the 1953, 1956 and 1968 uprisings in East Germany, Hungary and Czechoslovakia respectively. Contrary to what the Eastern bloc had hoped for, the Conference on Security and Cooperation in Europe had left the 'German question' open by using the passage cited above to refer to a future reunified Germany.

These considerations were central to West German *Ostpolitik*, i.e. West German policy with regard to the Eastern bloc, in the late 1960s and early 1970s. Accordingly, the West German government had sent a 'Letter on German Unity' to the East German government even before the conclusion of the *Basic Treaty* in 1972, where it explicitly stated 'that this treaty does not conflict with the political objective of the Federal Republic of Germany to work for a state of peace in Europe in which the German nation will recover its unity in free self-determination'. These all-German endeavours were founded on a general policy of dialogue and détente towards the nations of the Eastern bloc that became manifest in the *Treaty of Moscow* signed in August 1970, the *Treaty of Warsaw* signed in December 1970, the *Four Power Agreement* signed in September 1971, the *Transit Agreement* signed in December 1971, and the *Treaty of Prague* signed after the *Basic Treaty* in December 1972. These treaties represented the pinnacle of West German *Ostpolitik* with which the Federal Republic of Germany had normalised its relations with the Soviet Union, Poland, and Czechoslovakia and had separated the 'German question' to the greatest extent possible from the East-West conflict. As a result, both German states were able to shape certain aspects of their relations below the threshold of bloc-against-bloc antagonism as 'relations of a special kind' (Willy Brandt, 1969), halfway between domestic and foreign policy.

It was on the foundations of these developments and helped along by Gorbachev's reform policies that the states of the Warsaw Pact achieved some extent of self-determination, and that, eventually, the Iron Curtain and the Berlin Wall were brought down. The Cold War and the East-West conflict were thus at an end, which was sealed in September of 1990 with the *Treaty on the Final Settlement with Respect to Germany (Two Plus Four Agreement)* and in November of that same year with the *CSCE Charter of Paris for a New Europe* (CSCE, 1990).

After the paradigm shift: redefining German security policy

The now reunified Germany thus entered a completely new era of security policy. It was no longer one of the centres of global conflict. To begin with, this led to the questions of how 'security' was to be defined in general, what were the security challenges facing Germany, and would Germany be involved in creating security on Europe's periphery and possibly in regions beyond. One answer to these questions was a strategy of an accelerated integration of the former enemies into NATO and the EU. Also, Germany began involving the Bundeswehr in operations abroad mandated by the United Nations, NATO and the European Union. The attacks of 11 September 2001 brought the question to the fore of whether the hitherto prevailing dichotomy of domestic versus foreign security was still sustainable. Although the old dichotomy was outdated in terms of security policy, the principle of deploying Germany's military forces abroad instead of at home was maintained, even if these new missions abroad came now very close to police operations. Actors from other areas (e.g. development cooperation) became increasingly involved in issues relating to security policy, and domestic security structures underwent a major reformation process.

As regards domestic German development, however, primary emphasis was initially placed on merging the two German societies. In the area of security policy, one of the main issues was how to handle the remaining members of the former National People's Army (NVA) following the end of the German Democratic Republic. Attempts to ease the mood in the NVA, which had heated up amid the uncertainty following the March 1990 elections, were successful (see Digutsch, 2007: 464). Regardless of this, however, all signs were pointing to German unification and the position of the NVA became untenable. In the summer of 1990 it became clear that the Soviet troops would withdraw from East Germany and that there would no longer be two German armies. Instead, the NVA would be removed from the Warsaw Pact and disbanded. After undergoing a vetting process, former members of the NVA would be admitted into the Bundeswehr (see Digutsch, 2007: 465ff.). After the NVA had been disbanded in accordance with an order of 2 October 1990, the remaining members of the NVA were placed under the command of the German Ministry of Defence as of 3 October. Suitable interested candidates were then identified for admission to the Bundeswehr for long-term careers. Of the 90,000 soldiers who had initially been admitted into the Bundeswehr in 1990, approximately 12,000 commissioned officers, 12,000 non-commissioned officers and 1,000 enlisted personnel applied during the following months. Following vetting, 3,000 commissioned officers, 7,600 non-commissioned officers and 800 enlisted personnel were eventually admitted as temporary-career volunteers and career service members (see Digutsch, 471f.). At the same time – in accordance with, among other things, the CFE Treaty – most of the NVA's materiel was destroyed or given to third parties. In addition, the strength of the new Bundeswehr was reduced to a maximum of 370,000 as specified in the *Two plus Four Agreement*.

Beyond the direct integration resulting from German unification, relations between the countries of Western and Eastern Europe during the following years shifted from confrontation to rapprochement and cooperation. NATO's structures were particularly helpful in this regard (Jacoby, 2004). In addition to its mission to defend the integrity of Alliance territory, NATO – with its North Atlantic Cooperation Council, which would later become the Euro-Atlantic Partnership Council, and the Partnership for Peace programme – gradually established numerous forums to draw the countries on the European borders of NATO, first in the east and later those bordering on the Mediterranean, as well as various Arab countries, closer to NATO. Some of these countries later became NATO members. The number of NATO members thus increased from 16 to currently 28, and many non-members entered into a dialogue with NATO.

At the same time, the Bundeswehr gradually and 'in homeopathic doses' became more involved in operations abroad. The considerations that formed a basis for these developments can be found in the 1992 *Defence Policy Guidelines*, which, in turn, were based on recommendations by the Unabhängige Kommission für die künftigen Aufgaben der Bundeswehr (*Independent Commission on the Future Tasks of the Federal Armed Forces*, also known as the *Jacobsen-Kommission)* of July 1990 (Frank, 2007: 442). In line with these recommendations, a distinction was drawn between security challenges with 'direct' and 'indirect' effects. 'Direct' referred to traditional military threats coming from the Commonwealth of Independent States (CIS) area (although the possibility of a surprise attack was not included) or from the European periphery. In addition – in particular in the wake of the collapse of Yugoslavia – the recommendations listed regional conflicts on the European periphery as well as threats to individual citizens.

'Indirect' threats were – as already formulated in the 1991 *NATO Strategic Concept* – 'multi-faceted' and 'multi-directional' (see NATO, 1991) undesirable developments that posed a threat to stability and had numerous negative consequences for the regions themselves and for their wider surroundings. These included negative impact on social and economic progress, the destruction of development opportunities, the triggering of migration movements, the elimination of resources or the promotion of radicalisation and readiness to use violence. Against this backdrop, traditional tasks of national defence faded into the background for the Bundeswehr, while tasks gained centre stage that involved active, geographically non-specific crisis and conflict management in the form of an interministerial, cause-oriented approach to risk prevention in cooperation with international organisations. As specified in the 1992 Defence Policy Guidelines, 'as a future main task, crisis management will replace the previous orientation towards defence against large-scale aggression' (BMVg, 1992: item 48).

Accordingly, the Bundeswehr gradually developed into an army geared towards operations abroad. Initially – after Germany had mainly been involved financially in the first Gulf War in 1991 – the Bundeswehr cleared mines off the coast of Kuwait. Later, medical personnel were deployed in Cambodia. Further contingents were deployed in Somalia, and, under the umbrella of the WEU and NATO, the Bundeswehr also took part in the UN-mandated embargo operations in the Adriatic. This gradual increase in operations abroad caused the SPD parliamentary group in the German Bundestag but also the FDP parliamentary group – part of the ruling coalition – to bring the matter before the German Federal Constitutional Court which reviewed the constitutionality of such operations.

The result of this review in July 1994 represented a paradigm shift for the armed forces themselves and repeated the security policy paradigm shift of the early 1990s. When the judges decided that the Bundeswehr, subject to a national mandate issued by the Bundestag as well as to an international mandate, could be employed beyond the mere territorial defence of German and Alliance territory, the German military changed, both legally and politically, from a defence army into an army for operations. Since then, its employment has ultimately been based on case-by-case considerations depending on the situation at hand, i.e. considerations of appropriateness and political decisions resulting from such considerations. Against this background, the Bundeswehr then set up specific crisis response forces flanked by a basic military organisation and the main defence forces (Varwick, 2007: 249).

Originally, the CSCE or, as of 1990, its successor organisation, the Organisation for Security and Cooperation in Europe (OSCE), was allocated the key role of ensuring cooperation between European states and maintaining security in Europe ('CSCE first', Roloff, 2007: 784). However, this organisation proved unsuitable for achieving a sustainable solution to the conflict in the Balkans. Beginning in the mid-1990s, 'NATO first' (Roloff, 2007: 786) thus became the standard in Europe. This primarily applied to the Balkans, where the Bundeswehr was involved for the first time in 1995 in enforcing the no-fly zone and conducting the stabilisation operation in Bosnia. It was later involved in the NATO-mandated air campaign against Serbia and in the ensuing UN-mandated stabilisation operation in Kosovo.

After the paradigm shift of 1990/91, NATO, for its part, had thus changed from being a confrontational but static defence organisation into a semi-confrontational/semi-cooperative integration/dialogue/enforcement organisation with strong military capabilities. On the other hand, the European Union, too, was now becoming increasingly involved in operational security. In contrast to NATO, the EU's *Common Security and Defence Policy* (CSDP) relies not only on military but first and foremost on non-military capabilities. It is thus much more than NATO aligned with the concept of a comprehensive approach, i.e. an approach that encompasses all actors involved and makes equal use of both military and civilian forces.

Following the attacks of 11 September 2001, Germany ultimately entered the era of 'asymmetric wars'. The traditional line drawn by territorial states between domestic and foreign affairs is becoming increasingly blurred because non-state actors can also achieve war-like effects by employing specific clandestine tactics. This initially led to a revision of threat catalogues in Germany. At the same time, the legal constraints that state security institutions and actors are subject to were reassessed and additionally functions were reallocated.

In the area of traditional domestic security tasks, the first response to this development was to establish 'Security Packages' I and II, which considerably broadened the powers of the authorities in the field of inner security, and to carry out an extensive restructuring process (see Möllers, 2009). Moreover, the 2003 and 2011 *Defence Policy Guidelines* (BMVg, 2003, 2011) and the 2006 *White Paper* (BMVg 2006) summarised requirements for regional stabilisation and for combating asymmetric enemies by issuing new challenge and threat catalogues.

The 2003 and 2011 *Defence Policy Guidelines* and the 2006 *White Paper* refer throughout to three main threat scenarios – international terrorism, the proliferation of weapons of mass destruction and the consequences of domestic or regional conflicts and state failure. The 2003 Defence Policy Guidelines also address the issues of organised crime, migration and the possibility of attacks against communication and information systems. They also emphasise the vulnerability of the German economy. The 2011 guidelines additionally refer to the danger of radicalisation and to the danger of destabilisation emanating from deliberate disinformation and to the possibility of attacks on what is referred to as 'critical infrastructure' such as telecommunication networks or various financial establishments.

Summary and outlook

As has been shown, German security policy has been marked by a paradigm shift that took place in the early 1990s. The period between 1949 and 1989 was characterised by three tasks: first of all there was the task of recovering political sovereignty, which was completed to a certain extent when partial sovereignty was achieved as of the middle of the 1950s. A second task was to secure territorial integrity. This was achieved for one thing through participation in a regional system of European integration. Communitisation in various areas of policy meant that wars between states in which Germany may have been involved were prevented – albeit at the cost of restricting political sovereignty. Another way of securing territorial integrity was to become a member of the Transatlantic Alliance – albeit at the price of enormous contributions paid by Germany to the Alliance and with the added complication that Germany would have inevitably become the setting of a conventional or even nuclear war if deterrence measures had failed on either side. To minimise this risk, it was essential to prevent the United States from detaching itself from Europe, the potential arena. But even in this case, Germany was caught between the *Scylla* of a conventional and the *Charybdis* of a nuclear war. An improvement only came with the policy of détente, which also accommodated Germany's third interest – the unification of the two German states, which had temporarily faded into the background.

The end of the Cold War and of the East-West conflict gave rise to two new major challenges for Germany. For one, there were indirect threats associated with the development of new regions of instability, mainly caused by the outbreak of 'new wars'. Although these wars posed a physical threat to states and their citizens, more than anything they were a threat to their way of life. One response to this is an interministerial, 'whole-government' stabilisation strategy coordinated with other states. In assuming the required functions collectively, the individual actors overcome boundaries that existed between them. The second new challenge is 'asymmetrical' conflicts between states and non-state actors – which have completely dissimilar qualities. Essentially, the main task here is to compensate for the asymmetry through a process of 're-symmetrising' in various areas by using protective as well as offensive measures.

These developments are taking place against the background of shifting global centres of power. After practising a form of 'benign hegemony' following the end of the bipolar world order, the United States is now focussing heavily on Asia, even in the field of security policy. At the same time, the '*neue Gestaltungsmächte*' ('*new players in globalization*', such as China, India, Brazil and others) are preparing to gain worldwide influence and, accordingly, are regarded by Germany as partners (see Auswärtiges Amt, 2012a). Moreover, the European Union is becoming more significant in the field of security policy, pursuing an approach that is gradually moving away from the dominance of military and increasingly involving police and civilian actors.

This is particularly significant in that great emphasis is being placed now on the issue of 'fragility', which generates instability effects (new wars) and offers safe havens to actors who operate asymmetrically (asymmetric wars). This is evidenced by a guideline on the subject issued in autumn 2012 by the German Foreign Office, the Federal Ministry of Defence and the Federal Ministry for Economic Cooperation and Development (Auswärtiges Amt, 2012b). This guideline is itself a continuation of considerations from the 2004 'Civilian Crisis Prevention, Conflict Resolution and Post Conflict Peace Building' Action Plan (Bundesregierung, 2004). Against the background of state-building efforts by the International Security Assistance Force (ISAF) in Afghanistan – a project that is controversial in terms of its 'successes' – it may also, however, represent a careful rejection of further stabilisation operations mainly carried out by the armed forces.

For the armed forces, these large-scale international operations could in future be replaced by a series of different operations. First of all, this includes conflicts between states that are, however, no longer carried out with conventional methods but clandestinely with new weapons (e.g. in the form of cyber warfare or information warfare aimed at achieving interpretation supremacy regarding global phenomena), while in other regions of the world, we may see a renaissance of 'traditional', conventional wars (e.g. between Asian states and most importantly in connection with China's increasing claim to power and influence, which may also be territorial in nature). Second, there will be operations of a 'police' nature, in which special forces and/or drones play an important role. And finally, an increase in fragile regions may mean that evacuation operations could come to play a more prominent role.

The consequences are numerous: is the Federal Republic of Germany in a position to create the political framework for meeting these security challenges? Can legal foundations be adapted accordingly, and is society willing – or rather, how far is it willing – to go along? Will it be possible to adjust the functions of institutions and equip them with personnel and material in such a way that they will be able to meet the given challenges? And finally: will the state be in a position – both politically and financially – to control these processes? Some of these questions will be addressed by other authors in this volume.

Bibliography

Auswärtiges Amt (1990): Vertrag über die abschließende Regelung in Bezug auf Deutschland vom 12. September 1990. http://www.auswaertiges-amt.de/cae/servlet/contentblob/373162/publicationFile/3828/ZweiPlusVier%20(Text).pdf (engl: Treaty on the Final Settlement with Respect to Germany).

Auswärtiges Amt (2012a): Globalisierung gestalten – Partnerschaften ausbauen – Verantwortung teilen. Konzept der Bundesregierung. Berlin: Auswärtiges Amt (engl.: Shaping Globalization – Expanding Partnerships – Sharing Responsibility: A strategy paper by the German Government).

Auswärtiges Amt (2012b): Für eine kohärente Politik der Bundesregierung gegenüber fragilen Staaten – Ressortübergreifende Leitlinien. http://www.auswaertiges-amt.de/cae/servlet/contentblob/626452/publicationFile/171912/120919_Leitlinien_Fragile_Staaten.pdf.

Berridge, Geoff R. (1991): Return to the UN UN diplomacy in regional conflicts. New York: St. Martin's Press.

BMVg (1992): Verteidigungspolitische Richtlinien für den Geschäftsbereich des Bundesministers der Verteidigung. In: Blätter für deutsche und internationale Politik 9/1993: 1137-1151.

BMVg (2003): Verteidigungspolitische Richtlinien für den Geschäftsbereich des Bundesministers der Verteidigung. http://www.bmvg.de/.

BMVg (2006): Weißbuch 2006 zur Sicherheitspolitik Deutschlands und zur Zukunft der Bundeswehr (engl.: White Paper 2006 on German Security Policy and the Future of the Bundeswehr), http://www.bmvg.de/.

BMVg (2011): Verteidigungspolitische Richtlinien für den Geschäftsbereich des Bundesministers der Verteidigung: Nationale Interessen wahren – Internationale Verantwortung übernehmen – Sicherheit gemeinsam gestalten (engl.: Defence Policy Guidelines: Safeguarding National Interests – Assuming International Responsibility – Shaping Security Together), http://www.bmvg.de/.

Böckenförde, Stephan (2009): Die Veränderung des Sicherheitsverständnisses. In: Böckenförde, Stephan/Gareis, Sven B.: Deutsche Sicherheitspolitik: Herausforderungen, Akteure und Prozesse. Opladen/Farmington Hills: Verlag Barbara Budrich: 11-44.

Boutros-Ghali, Boutros (1992): Agenda for Peace: Preventive Diplomacy, Peacemaking and Peace-Keeping. http://www.un.org/Docs/SG/agpeace.html.

Brandt, Willy (1969): Government Policy Statement by Federal Chancellor Willy Brandt of 28 October 1969. http://www.bwbs.de/UserFiles/File/PDF/Regierungserklaerung691028.pdf.

Bredow, Wilfried von (2008): Die Außenpolitik der Bundesrepublik Deutschland: Eine Einführung, 2nd revised edition. Wiesbaden: VS Verlag für Sozialwissenschaften.

Bundesregierung (2004): Aktionsplan Zivile Krisenprävention, Konfliktlösung und Friedenskonsolidierung. http://www.auswaertiges-amt.de/diplo/de/Aussenpolitik/Themen/Krisen-praevention/Aktionsplan-Volltext.pdf (engl.: Action Plan 'Civilian Crisis Prevention, Conflict Resolution and Post-Conflict Peace-Building').

Conference on Security and Co-operation in Europe 1975: Final act. http://www.osce.org/de/mc/39503.

Conference on Security and Co-operation in Eurpoe (1990): Charter of Paris for a New Europe. http://www.osce.org/de/mc/39518.

Digutsch, Gunnar (2007): Die NVA und die Armee der Einheit. In: Nägler, Frank (Eds.): Die Bundeswehr 1955 bis 2005: Rückblenden – Einsichten – Perspektiven. Munich: Oldenbourg: 452-476.

Eekelen, W. F. van (1998): Debating European Security, 1948-1998. The Hague/Brussels: Sdu Publishers; Centre for European Policy Studies.

Elwert, Georg (1997): Gewaltmärkte: Beobachtungen zur Zweckrationalität der Gewalt. In: Trotha, Trutz von (Ed.): Soziologie der Gewalt. Opladen/Wiesbaden: Westdeutscher Verlag: 86-101.

European Union (2003): A Secure Europe in a Better World – The European Security Strategy. Brussels. http://consilium.europa.eu/uedocs/cmsUpload/78367.pdf.

Frank, Hans (2007): Nur von Freunden umgeben: Die veränderte Sicherheit nach Vereinigung und Überwindung des Kalten Krieges. In: Nägler, Frank (Ed.): Die Bundeswehr 1955 bis 2005: Rückblenden – Einsichten – Perspektiven. Munich: Oldenbourg: 441-449.

Haftendorn, Helga (2001): Deutsche Außenpolitik zwischen Selbstbeschränkung und Selbstbehauptung. Stuttgart/Munich: Deutsche Verlagsanstalt.

Herz, John H. (1961): Weltpolitik im Atomzeitalter. Stuttgart: W. Kohlhammer.

International Commission on Intervention and State Sovereignty ICISS (2001): The Responsibility to Protect: Report of the International Commission on Intervention and State Sovereignty. http://www.iciss.ca/pdf/Commission-Report.pdf.

Jacoby, Wade (2004): The enlargement of the European Union and NATO: ordering from the menu in Central Europe. Cambridge, UK/New York: Cambridge University Press.

Janning, Josef (2007): Europäische Union und deutsche Europapolitik. In: Schmidt, Siegmar/Hellmann, Gunther/Wolf, Reinhard (Eds.): Handbuch zur deutschen Außenpolitik. Wiesbaden: VS Verlag für Sozialwissenschaften: 744-762.

Kaldor, Mary (1999): New and Old Wars: Organized Violence in a Global Era. Palo Alto: Stanford UP.

Meyers, Reinhard (2004): Der Wandel des Kriegsbildes. In: Ringe, Bernhard/Woyke, Wichard (Eds.): Frieden und Sicherheit im 21. Jahrhundert. Opladen: Leske + Budrich: 25-50.

Möllers, Martin H. W. (2009): Innenpolitische Dimensionen der Sicherheitspolitik in Deutschland. In: Böckenförde, Stephan; Gareis, Sven B.: Deutsche Sicherheitspolitik: Herausforderungen, Akteure und Prozesse. Opladen/Farmington Hills. Verlag Barbara Budrich: 131-172.

Münkler, Herfried (2002): Die neuen Kriege. Reinbek: Rowohlt.

Münkler, Herfried (2006): Der Wandel des Krieges: Von der Symmetrie zur Asymmetrie. Weilerswist: Velbrück.

NATO 1991: The Alliance's Strategic Concept agreed by the Heads of State and Government participating in the meeting of the North Atlantic Council. http://www.nato.int/docu/basictxt/b911108a.htm.

NATO 1999: The Alliance's Strategic Concept: Approved by the Heads of State and Government participating in the meeting of the North Atlantic Council in Washington D.C. on 23rd and 24th April 1999. http://www.nato.int/docu/pr/1999/p99-065e.htm.

Papcke, Sven (1996): Solidarität oder Sankt-Florians-Prinzip? In: Gewerkschaftliche Monatshefte 11-12/96 748-756. http://papcke.de/Texte/gmh_1996-11-a-748.pdf.

Roloff, Ralf (2007): Organisation für Sicherheit und Zusammenarbeit in Europa. In: Schmidt, Siegmar/ Hellmann, Gunther/ Wolf, Reinhard (Eds.): Handbuch zur deutschen Außenpolitik. Wiesbaden: VS Verlag für Sozialwissenschaften: 779-787.

Rumsfeld, Donald (2001): Quadrennial defense review report, U.S.Department of Defense.

Schneckener, Ulrich (2005): Post-Westfalia trifft Prä-Westfalia: Die Gleichzeitigkeit dreier Welten. In: Jahn, Egbert/Fischer, Sabine/Sahm, Astrid (Eds.): Die Zukunft des Friedens, Volume 2: Die Friedens- und Konfliktforschung aus der Perspektive der jüngeren Generationen. Wiesbaden: VS Verlag: 189-211.

Schöllgen, Gregor (2004): Die Außenpolitik der Bundesrepublik Deutschland: Von den Anfängen bis zur Gegenwart, 3rd edition, Munich: C.H. Beck.

Solana, Javier (2003): A secure Europe in a better world: European security strategy. European Council meeting.

Thoß, Bruno (2007): Bündnisintegration und nationale Verteidigungsinteressen: Der Aufbau der Bundeswehr im Spannungsfeld zwischen nuklearer Abschreckung und konventioneller Verteidigung (1955 bis 1968). In: Nägler, Frank (Ed.): Die Bundeswehr 1955 bis 2005: Rückblenden – Einsichten – Perspektiven. Munich: Oldenbourg: 13-38.

Trotha, Trutz von (1995): Ordnungsformen der Gewalt oder Aussichten auf das Ende des staatlichen Gewaltmonopols. In: Nedelmann, Birgitta (Ed.): Politische Institutionen im Wandel. Opladen: Westdeutscher Verlag: 129-166.

Varwick, Johannes (2007): Bundeswehr. In: Schmidt, Siegmar/Hellmann, Gunther/Wolf, Reinhard (Eds.): Handbuch zur deutschen Außenpolitik. Wiesbaden: VS Verlag für Sozialwissenschaften: 246-258.

White House (2002): The National Security Strategy of the United States of America. September 2002. http://www.whitehouse.gov/nsc/nss/2002/index.html.

The making of Germany's security and defence policy – actors, responsibilities, procedures, and requirements

Sven Bernhard Gareis

Averting dangers to the lives, health and property of its citizens and creating a security architecture on the basis of which freedom and prosperity can flourish are two of the basic functions of every modern state. However, not only in Germany is performing these central state functions becoming increasingly difficult. On the one hand, this is due to the concept of *security* itself: It is a highly ambiguous construct that has both personal (individual) and collective (social groups, nation) dimensions, that depends to a high degree on perceptions and subjective assessments and that is consequently difficult to grasp in a political-conceptual sense.

Under the impact of the East-West conflict, national security provision in Germany – the subject of this article – was for a long time characterised by a clear distinction: Defence of fundamental interests such as the political independence and territorial integrity of the country against the threat from the Soviet Union and its allies was the task of the Bundeswehr. In contrast, the prevention, fighting and prosecution of crime and other national security problems were the responsibility of the police and the judiciary. With the turnaround in global politics in 1989/90, the danger of a large-scale war resulting from the antagonism between Western democracies and Eastern socialist states was overcome. Since then, Germany – together with most of her partners in the Euro-Atlantic area – has faced new demands on its security and defence policy. They are characterised by three main trends:

Firstly, the scenario of an open threat from powerful, albeit known and predictable, actors has given way to an increasingly complex cluster of direct and indirect security risks in a globalized and therefore more interconnected world. This cluster includes crises and wars in a polycentric global conflict scenario, transnational terrorism and the problem of the proliferation of weapons of mass destruction, but also the challenges caused by social and economic disparities, environmental destruction, climate change and disease. Often, these new risks cannot be clearly attributed to any specific actors, and their effects are not felt where they originate, but frequently in distant countries and regions. Above all, however, they can no longer be placed in apparently distinct categories such as 'internal' and 'external'. The boundaries between crime-fighting and defence, between internal and external security are becoming increasingly blurred (see Wiefelspütz, 2007: 9 et seq.), and with that so is the traditional assignment of responsibilities to the classic state security agencies such as the military, the police and the judiciary.

Secondly, the complexity of the new security risks requires a comprehensive political approach that – in addition to the traditional fields of internal security and defence – also includes preventive policies in areas such as international development cooperation, education, poverty reduction and assistance to enable good governance. This kind of approach, however, also requires the great variety of specialized actors; their working methods and the instruments they use need to be brought together in a comprehensive system of consultation, coordination and cooperation. In Germany, the White Paper issued by the Ministry of Defence in 2006 postulates such an approach under the heading 'Networked Security' (BMVg, 2006: 29 et seq.). Very similar goals have been pursued for quite some time by the 'Aktionsplan Zivile Krisenprävention' (Civilian Crisis Prevention Action Plan; Federal Government, 2004).

Thirdly, the complexity of the security risks cited and the dissolution of their boundaries under the impact of globalisation mean that dealing with them far exceeds the capabilities of any individual state. Therefore, Germany's security and defence policy is also only conceivable if the country collaborates with its partners in the international system and works within the framework of international organisations such as the European Union (EU), NATO and the United Nations (UN). This is particularly true when it comes to countering risks where they arise in order to prevent them from developing into manifest threats to the security of Germany or Europe. As for the military, the Defence Policy Guidelines issued in 1992 already stated, based on a clear-sighted analysis of the emerging new global situation, that engagement in international crisis management had taken the place of the Bundeswehr's classic priority task of defending Germany against acts of large-scale foreign aggression (BMVg, 1992: no. 47). Traditional national defence, 'which previously solely determined the structures of the Bundeswehr, no longer corresponds with the actual security policy requirements' (BMVg, 2003: no. 12); participation in collective 'out of area' missions thus became the principal task of the German military.

For more than two decades, these trends have placed considerable demands on the decision-making processes in Germany's security and defence policy. A growing number of actors from the federal level, from the *Länder* governments as well as from international organisations or alliances need to harmonize their policy approaches and coordinate their efforts. The present article thus examines the key actors involved in the development and implementation of Germany's security policy, their functions and responsibilities, and the procedures and tools at their disposal. It also discusses possible future prospects for Germany's security and defence policy.

While analysing the internal mechanisms of this policy field, the demands of the international system are also taken into account. The interplay of German domestic provisions and constellations and the expectations of the Euro-Atlantic partners have a significant impact on what action Germany takes in her security and defence policy (see Höse/Oppermann, 2011).

In a democratic state, the making of security and defence policy is regulated by constitutional or legal norms and guidelines. However, such formal provisions can only reflect a small part of the complex reality of this policy field. Even within the Federal Government, which is primarily responsible for external politics and its security and defence implications at the national level, many ad hoc or informal factors such as the Federal Chancellor's personality, relations between the ministers, coalitions, and so on, are important for shaping policy. Then there are the parliamentary majorities, the interests of private actors such as businesses and NGOs, and last but not least, public opinion as articulated in the media and in demographic surveys. Furthermore, national security provision is a field in which a variety of complex structures exist due to Germany's federal system and the fact that there are sixteen 'parallel governments' in the *Länder*, all again very heterogeneous in their party-political composition.

It should also be mentioned at this point that, as of yet, there has been no comprehensive scientific study of the decision-making processes and procedural regulations applicable to security and defence policy in Germany. Nevertheless, it is possible to make a number of general statements about the actors involved, the responsibilities conferred on them by the constitution or by law as well as the formal and informal conditions for interaction and networking that exists between them in order to at least outline the way in which German security and defence policy is organised.

Constitutional assignment of responsibilities

If one looks at the demands on a state or government through the prism of a complex concept of security and defence policy, special attention must be devoted to Germany's federal system. On account of its Basic Law, or *Grundgesetz*, its many other laws and regulations and, last but not least, its political practice, security responsibilities, tasks and powers, as well as the instruments of power associated with them are assigned to a broad array of actors at the level of the federation and of the *Länder*. Article 30 of the Basic Law, for example, in principle confers the execution of fundamental state powers and the performance of state tasks to the *Länder* – albeit subject to other rules enshrined in the Basic Law. These can be found in numerous articles of the constitution in which exclusive powers are in turn conferred to the Federal Government. The division of powers between the federation and *Länder* is basically regulated by Articles 70 to 74 of the Basic Law, which specify the political fields in which the federation claims exclusive legislative powers (Article 73, Basic Law) or in which, within the scope of the so-called 'concurrent legislative power' (Article 72 of the Basic Law in connection with Article 74 of the Basic Law), responsibilities remain with the *Länder* as long as the federation does not raise any of its own regulatory claims (Schmidt, 2007: 181 et seq.).

In the field of state security provision, the Basic Law confers central responsibilities on the Federal Government. Under Article 73 (1) (1) of the Basic Law, for example, the Federal Government is responsible for foreign affairs and defence, including protection of the civilian population. Article 32 (1) of the Basic Law stipulates that the Federal Government is responsible for relations with foreign states. Article 87a (1) of the Basic Law states that the federation shall establish armed forces for the purpose of defence, and that apart from defence they may be employed only to the extent expressly permitted by the Basic Law (Article 87a (2)). As for domestic security provision, the federation claims exclusive legislative power for cooperation between the federation and the *Länder* concerning criminal police work, protection of the free democratic basic order, protection against activities which, due to the use of force or preparations for the use of force, endanger the external interests of Germany, the establishment of a Federal Criminal Police Office and international action to combat crime (Article 73 (1) (10)). Against the background of changes in the perception of threats after 11 September 2001, and following amendments to the constitution in the course of the Federalism Reform of 2006, item 9a was added to the catalogue of Article 73 (1). This provision confers responsibility on the Federal Government for providing 'protection against the dangers of international terrorism when a threat transcends the boundary of a *Land*, when the jurisdiction of a Land's police authorities cannot be determined, or when the highest authority of an individual Land requests the assumption of federal responsibility' (see also Lachmuth et al., 2006: 7). Exclusive legislative power thus provides the federation with a broad scope for action. If, however, as in the case of Article 73 (1) (9a), the interests and responsibilities of *Länder* are affected, they can exert considerable influence on federal legislation by invoking their rights in the *Bundesrat*, the Second Chamber of the German parliamentary system.

The institutional assignment of security tasks also corresponds with this constitutional assignment of powers at the federal and the *Länder* level. Whilst the Federal Government is responsible for national security, it is the responsibility of the *Länder* to maintain public order and security in everyday life, which above all means protecting the people from crime, disasters and other dangers that may arise within the borders of a *Land*.

In addition to this, there are functional attributions to different actors that cannot simply be explained by referring to the principle of federalism, but serve one of its most important characteristics in Germany's political system – the decentralisation of power. Article 35 of the Basic Law states that the federal and *Land* authorities shall render legal and administrative assistance to one another, although this assistance is temporary and primarily limited to specific incidents such as when the Bundeswehr is used to tackle grave accidents and natural disasters. However, continuous coordination mechanisms or regulated information and communication channels between the various federal and *Länder* institutions are still at best rudimentary.

In Germany – unlike in France, Italy or the Netherlands, for instance, where military formations such as the Gendarmerie, the Carabinieri and the Marechaussee also perform police functions – the tasks of the Bundeswehr and the police are still strictly separated from one another. However, as will be shown below, the debate on the use of the Bundeswehr for averting danger within German territory suggests that this separation may be becoming increasingly blurred.

The separation of the powers of the police and intelligence services is also basically clear. Simply put, the intelligence services have far-reaching powers that authorise them to conduct investigations even when there are no specific suspects – although without executive responsibilities. By contrast, the police have powerful enforcement tools for the purposes of criminal prosecution, but they may only conduct investigations when there are specific grounds (Möllers, 2010: 1983 et seq.; Normann, 2007: 13 et seq.). The tasks of the police and intelligence services have also been transferred to specialized agencies at federal and *Länder* level. In addition to sixteen *Länder* police authorities and sixteen State Offices for the Protection of the Constitution, there are two other federal police authorities – the Federal Police and the Federal Criminal Police Office – and three national intelligence services, namely, the Federal Intelligence Service (*Bundesnachrichtendienst*, BND), which is responsible for foreign intelligence, the Military Counterintelligence Service (*Militärischer Abschirmdienst*, MAD) and the Federal Office for the Protection of the Constitution (*Bundesamt für Verfassungschutz,* BfV), which is responsible for the protection of the democratic political order in Germany.

This decentralised security order that has developed in Germany is essentially the Basic Law's answer to Germany's negative past experience with the unlimited abuse of state power by centralist and all-embracing structures such as the ones formed by the *Reichssicherheitshauptamt* and the Gestapo during the 'Third Reich'. Since its very foundation, the Federal Republic of Germany contrasted markedly with the German Democratic Republic (GDR), which maintained an oversized and centralised 'security apparatus' right up to the end of the socialist

SED dictatorship. The division of tasks, powers and tools is intended to limit the power of the security institutions and to ensure these are kept under democratic control (Bukow, 2007: 69).

However, it must also be understood that the security sector in Germany is not only decentralised, but rather strongly fragmented, extremely difficult to oversee and, given the new risks and threats to public security in Germany, also in need of an examination with respect to its efficiency and effectiveness. The difficulties associated with coordinating the many federal and *Länder* security institutions have become all too clear after the terrorist activities of the National Socialist Underground (NSU) were uncovered in November 2011 only by mere chance. The criminal activities of this organisation included the killing of ten people in Germany between 2000 and 2006 and many other acts of violence and offences in a number of *Länder* – and a lack of communication and exchange of information and evidence between the diverse agencies prevented effective investigation and prosecution.

On the other hand, there is a trend towards closer coordination between the levels and responsibilities that were previously strictly separated – a trend that has intensified since the terrorist attacks on 11 September 2001. By means of the so-called Security Packages I and II and the Counter-Terrorism Act on which they are based, the powers of the police authorities and intelligence services have been extended (Hein, 2004). Interministerial and cross-level cooperation between the security institutions also takes place at the Joint Counter-Terrorism Centre, which was set up in Berlin in December 2004. Here the cooperation between all the federal and *Land* police authorities, intelligence services and customs authorities is coordinated in the field of counter-terrorism, and access is also available to the central anti-terrorism database, which was created in 2007 (Normann, 2007: 12 et seq.). To take account of the need for institutionalised communication and information channels that was revealed by the mistakes made during the investigations into the NSU's terrorist activities, a central Right-wing Extremism Database (RED) containing the information held by all of Germany's federal and *Länder* authorities was created in September 2012.

When it comes to averting dangers within Germany, there is increasing debate on the idea of assigning new functions to the Bundeswehr (see Knelangen, 2006) and attempts are being made to implement this (Wiefelspütz, 2007, see more references there). One example was the case of the Act on Aviation Security, even though it was declared unconstitutional by Germany's Federal Constitutional Court in 2006 on account of the main issue associated with it, namely the possible use of the Air Force against a hijacked aircraft employed for a terrorist attack. In many operations abroad German soldiers have for a long time been required to alternate between performing military and political tasks, fighting ter-

rorism, maintaining public order in cities, participating in the search for war criminals or assisting in training police forces.
Against the backdrop of these still strongly fragmented institutional responsibilities, the way German security and defence policy is organised will be analysed in the light of the question of how efficiently and effectively 'networked security' is being put into practice by a multitude of actors.

Important actors and procedures at the federal level

As already explained, Article 73 of the Basic Law assigns central tasks and responsibilities for national security to the federation by granting it exclusive legislative power. However, a distinction must be made between the powers of the various actors at federal level. Particularly along the dividing line between foreign policy and domestic policy – which is becoming increasingly blurred –, there is a considerable difference in the powers held by two of the most important constitutional bodies, namely, the Federal Government and the Federal Parliament, i.e. the *German Bundestag*.

On account of its extensive right of initiative and mandate to act on general policy matters, for instance, the Federal Government has a strong role to play in foreign, security and defence policy. The Federal Government is responsible for maintaining diplomatic relations with other states and international organisations such as the EU, NATO and the UN. It negotiates international treaties and agreements and has far-reaching powers to interpret and further develop them, as in the case of NATO's strategic concepts. It is responsible for shaping the policies Germany pursues within international organisations and decides on whether Germany will participate in collective action up to and including military operations. In this policy field, the Bundestag above all has participation rights and rights to exert indirect influence, e.g. via budget legislation.

The relationship between the two bodies is quite different in the field of domestic security. Because domestic action by the government is above all bound by legislation, the Bundestag also has far greater weight when it comes to domestic security than to provision of external security. The legislative branch also has its own rights of initiative and can therefore much more actively influence policy development.

However, since the government is usually backed by a Bundestag majority, differing positions in parliament tend to be rare. The Basic Law does not make any provision for the kind of competitive situation between a strong executive and a powerful parliament that can arise, for instance, in the US system, nor has such a constellation developed in political practice in Germany. Nevertheless, as will be shown later, in political practice the Bundestag has more leverage to influence decisions in the field of external security and defence policy than the powers formally assigned to it might lead one to expect.

The Federal Government

Within the Federal Government, the *Federal Chancellor* (Bundeskanzler) holds a dominant position, which is derived chiefly from Article 65 of the Basic Law. This article, which is fundamental to the way the Federal Government works,

- invests the Chancellor with the power to determine the general guidelines of policy (the 'Chancellor principle'), which in accordance with the explanatory provision in paragraph 1 of the Federal Government's rules of procedure applies expressly to both domestic and foreign policy,
- determines that each Federal Minister shall conduct the affairs of his department independently and under his own responsibility (the 'principle of ministerial autonomy'),
- uses the 'cabinet principle' to resolve differences of opinion between Federal Ministers, as part of the Federal Government's collective discussion and decision-making mechanism, which is presided over by the Federal Chancellor (see Thränhardt, 2003: 65).

In addition, on account of his organisational power as laid down in Article 64 of the Basic Law, the Federal Chancellor may propose that the Federal President shall appoint or dismiss Federal Ministers, while he himself, as the only member of the government elected by the Bundestag, can only be dismissed by means of a 'constructive vote of no confidence'. This means that the Bundestag 'may express its lack of confidence in the Federal Chancellor only by electing a successor by the vote of a majority of its Members' (Art. 67 of the Basic Law). Because it grants the head of government this eminent position, the political system in Germany is often referred to as a 'chancellor democracy' (Hennis, 1968; Niclauss, 2004) – this applies in particular to security and defence, the fields of politics under consideration here.

The head of government has at his disposal the *Federal Chancellery*, an important instrument for exercising his power of direction and thus also for coordinating policy. This is not only where the threads of each department's policies come together and the weekly meetings of the Federal Cabinet are prepared, at the so-called State Secretary's meeting chaired by the Head of the Federal Chancellery. It is also where the entire Federal Government is reflected in six directorates and sixteen groups, subordinated to which are the so-called 'mirror branches'. In Directorate 1 of the Chancellery (central affairs directorate, domestic and legal affairs), Group 13 contains one branch staffed by civil servants from the Federal Ministry of Justice and one branch staffed by civil servants from the Federal Ministry of the Interior. In foreign relations matters, the Chancellor is assisted by an advisor, usually a top diplomat from the Foreign Office. This advisor also oversees Directorate 2 (foreign, security and development policy), in which civil servants seconded from the Foreign Office as well as military officers and civil servants from the Federal Ministry of Defence work in Groups 21 and 22. The Secretariat of the Federal Security Council also belongs to Group 22. By establishing a separate directorate for European affairs (Directorate 5), Chancellor Gerhard Schröder (1998-2005) highlighted the importance of European policy for the head of government. Directorate 6 has particularly grown in importance due to the increased demands of counter-terrorism. This is also the directorate that exercises technical supervision over the Federal Intelligence Service (BND) and coordinates activities with the other federal intelligence services. Branches 603 and 604 deal with the international situation and the control of the procurement of information on international terrorism, extremism and organised crime. The functions and form of the Chancellery have changed little under Chancellor Angela Merkel (2005 to present) compared with the structures created by her predecessor. The concentration of a considerable amount of expertise in the Chancellery also underpins the 'chancellor principle' in the area of foreign and security policy.

Within the Federal Government, the *Federal Foreign Office* is responsible for coordinating foreign policy in general (Section 11 of the Federal Government's rules of procedure) and for security policy in particular. With its embassies in other countries and missions to international organisations, the Foreign Service plays a major part in negotiating international treaties. Its staff look after Germany's interests abroad and thus make an important contribution to maintaining peaceful relations with Germany's partners in the international system (Brandt/Buck, 2005). The Foreign Office also operates a permanent Crisis Response Centre in which staff from a variety of ministries monitor developments in the international system that may escalate into crises, if necessary convening a crisis task force and coordinating its activities. The Foreign Office also has representatives and coordinators for specific areas of policy (security policy, human rights policy and humanitarian aid) or for countries and regions (Afghanistan/Pakistan, Franco-German, German-Polish and German-Russian relations and US/Transatlantic relations) with responsibilities that also strongly influence security and defence policy matters.

While the Federal Chancellor and the Foreign Minister, who for almost fifty years have regularly belonged to different coalition partners, repeatedly find themselves competing against each other for political reasons, the head of government traditionally tends to avoid infringing all too directly on the area of responsibility of the Federal Minister of *Defence,* beyond setting budgetary caps.

In peacetime, the Defence Minister, as commander-in-chief of the Armed Forces, bears the responsibility for military policy and thus also for specifying both the mission, size and structure of the Bundeswehr (see Box 1) and the international peace missions conducted under EU, NATO or UN lead or other arrangements in which the Bundeswehr participates.

Box 1: The mission and basic structure of the Bundeswehr

The Bundeswehr

- protects Germany and its citizens,
- ensures Germany's capacity to act in the field of foreign policy,
- provides assistance in the defence of our allies,
- contributes to international stability and partnership and
- fosters multinational cooperation and European integration.

(Source: Federal Ministry of Defence 2011:11)

By 2017, the strength of the Bundeswehr, which is currently undergoing a process of reorientation, is to be reduced to 185,000 military personnel (170,000 regulars and temporary-career volunteers, 15,000 military service volunteers) as well as 55,000 civilian personnel. The armed forces are divided into the following elements:

- the Army with 55,300 military personnel
- the Air Force with 22,500 military personnel
- the Navy with 13,050 military personnel
- the Bundeswehr Joint Medical Service with 14,620 military personnel
- the Joint Support Service with 36,800 military personnel

(Source: Federal Ministry of Defence, 2012).

The ministry that is primarily responsible for domestic security is the Federal Ministry of the Interior, whose area of responsibility not only includes the Federal Police, Federal Criminal Police Office and Federal Office for the Protection of the Constitution, as mentioned earlier, but also has a permanent situation centre for dealing with major threats to domestic security. Due to the extensive powers of the *Länder* in the field of domestic security and in particular in policing, the Federal Minister of the Interior is dependent on close consultation and cooperation with his *Länder* colleagues in the Standing Conference of the Ministers and Senators of the Interior of the *Länder* (*Innenministerkonferenz,* IMK). This conference is the most important federal body within which the *Länder* can get together to form opinions and make decisions on security policy matters (Lensch,

2010: 979). The Federal Minister of the Interior has an advisory function in this conference.

Among the most important bodies for federal-level political coordination is the Cabinet, a collective body in which all the Ministries are represented and which is headed by the Federal Chancellor. However, the Cabinet's chief occupation is to achieve interministerial agreement mostly on domestic policy topics such as bills concerning social affairs, health and the economy, so that security and defence issues, which again and again arise unexpectedly, are not always on the agenda. Even so, all of the legislative initiatives concerning security and defence policy (such as the suspension of the Compulsory Military Service in 2011) require a Cabinet decision before they can be tabled in parliament. The same applies to decisions on the aims, nature and scope of the Bundeswehr's participation in international military operations and to the extension of its mandates. Bills drawn up for such a purpose by the Federal Ministry of Defence are then forwarded by the Federal Government as a motion to the German Bundestag, for final decision-making (see below).

The Federal Security Council was established in 1955 and is one of five Cabinet committees. Besides the Federal Chancellor, its members are the Federal Foreign Minister, the Ministers of Defence, the Interior, Finance, Justice and Economics and – since 1998 – the Minister for Economic Cooperation and Development. The Head of the Federal Chancellery and the Chief of Defence (*Generalinspekteur der Bundeswehr*) also sit on it, in an advisory capacity. After having played hardly any role for a long time, particularly during the Helmut Kohl government (1982-1998), the Social Democrat/Green coalition government announced in 1998 that it wanted to 'restore the Federal Security Council to its originally intended role as the body responsible for coordinating German security policy and to establish the necessary prerequisites for this' (Coalition Agreement, 1998: no. XI, 9). Even since 11 September 2001, however, hardly anything has changed in the way the Federal Security Council works. It remains essentially a body that convenes at irregular intervals, maintains strict confidentiality and is chiefly concerned with approving arms exports. Since Gerhard Schröder was Chancellor, the coordination processes in the narrower sense of security and defence policy have shifted to a somewhat smaller, more informal 'Security Cabinet' consisting of the Federal Chancellor, the Foreign Minister, the Defence Minister, the Minister of the Interior and the Head of the Federal Chancellery.

Coalition bodies have also long played a major role in coordinating security and defence policy activities, even though all of the ministers and experts responsible for foreign affairs cannot necessarily participate in them. Such discussion forums within the coalition are often of an informal and ad hoc nature, but during the Kohl, Schröder and Merkel administrations highly formal, so-called coalition committees have become established with a fixed core of participants, agendas and protocols. On the one hand, these coalition committees facilitate the processes for reaching agreement on policy issues, which would be difficult to do in the Cabinet. On the other hand, they are limited in the way they can address complex detailed issues (Siwert-Probst, 1998: 20). Without a doubt, the job of coordinating fragmented and increasingly decentralised foreign, security and defence policies within the Cabinet places high demands on the Chancellor as regards the use of the various control instruments that are available, but it in general strengthens the lead role that he has and that is anchored both in the Basic Law and in political practice.

The German Bundestag

In the previous section, reference was made to the fact that the German Bundestag, the highest legislative body of the Federal Republic of Germany, has extensive powers to shape decisions in all areas of policy regulated by law. In the area of foreign relations and the respective security and defence dimensions, a number of important rights and responsibilities have been assigned to the Bundestag by the Basic Law as well as by decisions of the Federal Constitutional Court.

- Pursuant to Article 59 (2) of the Basic Law, international treaties which are negotiated and signed by the Federal Republic of Germany to regulate the political relations of the federation require the consent of the Bundestag in the form of a federal law (ratification).
- In the area of European policy, which is increasingly linked with security issues, Article 23 of the Basic Law stipulates that changes in the EU's treaty foundations and comparable regulations that amend or supplement the Basic Law must be confirmed by a two-thirds majority of the Bundestag – as well as by two thirds of the Bundesrat.
- According to the Federal Constitutional Court decision of 12 July 1994, the Bundeswehr is a 'parliamentary army' whose deployment abroad requires a constitutive Bundestag decision (parliament's right of prior approval), a step that is not provided for in the Basic Law. The Parliamentary Participation Act passed by the Bundestag in December 2004 specifies further details of the procedure governing the participation of the Bundestag and grants it the right to withdraw the Bundeswehr at any time.
- The Bundestag and its members also have the right and the option to deal with, debate and express their views on any foreign and security policy issue. Besides the plenum, the most important parliamentary bodies that exist for this purpose are the Committee on Foreign Affairs and the Defence Committee, which are appointed pursuant to Article 45a of the Basic Law,

and a Committee on the Affairs of the European Union (Article 45 of the Basic Law). Last but not least, the Bundestag may also use its right under the budget law to influence decisions on foreign and security policy issues, for instance, in cases concerning the budget of each ministry, procurement measures for the Bundeswehr, or spending on development aid.

Account, however, must be taken of the fact that these responsibilities of the Bundestag are essentially limited rights of participation. This means that the Bundestag cannot introduce any addenda or reservations into an act ratifying an international treaty that has been negotiated by the Federal Government, but may only approve or reject it in its entirety. The same applies to the second important area of participation, namely, the deployment of German armed forces abroad: Since the Federal Constitutional Court issued its decision on this in 1994, the primary power to decide on whether and how German soldiers are to participate in international military missions rests with the Federal Government, whereas the Bundestag only has the option of permitting or preventing their deployment.

The joint responsibility of government and parliament for the deployment of German armed forces abroad

Some ten years after the Federal Constitutional Court decision, details on how joint responsibility for the German military's operations abroad was to be structured were laid down in the 'Act Governing Parliamentary Participation in Decisions on the Deployment of Armed Forces Abroad', the so-called Parliamentary Participation Act of 2004 (for more details on the act, see: Gilch 2005). This act stipulates that the deployment of German armed forces requires the consent of the Bundestag (Section 1 (2) of the Parliamentary Participation Act) and defines this as the involvement or expected involvement of German soldiers in armed operations (Section 2 (1) of the Parliamentary Participation Act). By contrast, prevention and planning measures as well as humanitarian aid services and relief operations in which no involvement in hostilities is expected are not operations and consequently do not require parliamentary consent (Section 2 (2) of the Parliamentary Participation Act).

In order to obtain the consent of the Bundestag, the Federal Government has to submit a detailed motion as specified in Section 3, which must notably contain information about the objectives and tasks of the mission, the theatre of operations and the legal basis for the operation. It must also contain statements about the maximum number of soldiers that have to be deployed and about their military capabilities. The planned duration of the deployment as well as its foreseeable costs and the financing arrangements must likewise be stated. These detailed motions bind the Federal Government for the duration of the mandate in all essential operational parameters. Any changes require the renewed consent of the Bundestag and, if needed, a separate mandate. By contrast, there are still large restrictions on parliamentary control of operations of the Special Forces Command (KSK) or of the Navy's combat divers. Only the parliamentary spokespersons in the Defence Committee and in the Committee on Foreign Affairs are informed about their missions and their exact number (Noetzel/Schreer, 2007: 2 et seq.).

In the Parliamentary Participation Act, a simplified decision-making procedure was also introduced for operations 'of limited intensity and scale' (Section 4 of the Parliamentary Participation Act). Parliamentary consent is therefore deemed to have been given when the President of the Bundestag has informed the parliamentary spokespersons in the Defence Committee and the Committee on Foreign Affairs about a corresponding motion of the Federal Government, when all Members of Parliament have been informed of this motion in writing and when no parliamentary faction or more than five per cent of the MPs have called for a plenary session within seven days.

An operation can be mounted without the Bundestag deciding on it beforehand if danger is imminent and if action must be taken quickly and covertly. The Bundestag may then approve the operation afterwards or recall the forces deployed (Section 5).

The rights of the Bundestag – at least at first blush – have been significantly strengthened by Section 8 of the Participation Act, which grants the parliament a right of withdrawal that may be exercised at any time. However, it must be borne in mind that the Bundestag does not serve as a body that keeps a check on the government, but is closely interlinked with it through the political parties and officials. A loss of a Chancellor's majority is an important security issue therefore has to be regarded as a heavy burden for a Federal Government that rests on a coalition. In political practice, however, the Chancellor has at his disposal effective means for exerting pressure on parliament. For instance, a motion tabled by the Social Democrat/Green coalition government in favour of the participation of German soldiers in the NATO Operation Essential Harvest to disarm insurgents in Macedonia on 29 August 2001 won a broad parliamentary majority. However, a total of 26 MPs of the coalition parties' parliamentary groups withheld their consent, so that the decision was finally reached due to the opposition's vote in favour of the motion. On 16 November of the same year, Chancellor Gerhard Schröder then linked the government motion for the participation of the Bundeswehr in the fight against international terrorism within the framework of Operation Enduring Freedom to the vote of confidence under Article 68 of the Basic Law. This nexus had a strong disciplinary effect on critical MPs in the coalition parties' parliamentary groups and ensured that the coalition attained its own majority (Niclauss, 2004: 332 et seq.).

Considering this, it is highly unlikely that the German Bundestag will ever make use of its right under Section 8 of the Parliamentary Participation Act to withdraw soldiers from operations against the will of the Federal Government. Such a step by parliament would be tantamount to a loss of the government's majority on an important foreign and security policy issue and would certainly indicate a serious crisis within the government. This would most probably lead to resignation by the Chancellor and give rise to new parliamentary elections.

In the Basic Law and in political practice, the executive thus has a dominance that significantly relativises the certainly intended procedures of granting both the Federal Government and the Bundestag a share of the power to decide on foreign affairs. Joachim Krause's summary conclusion (1998: 152) remains valid: considering the strong focus in parliament on party politics, it seems unlikely that the Bundestag will assume a greater role in foreign relations in the future.

The Bundesrat and the Länder

As in the case of the German Bundestag, a distinction must again be made between domestic and foreign policy when it comes to the granting of security policy powers to the *Länder*. It has already been pointed out that within their borders, the *Länder* are primarily responsible for maintaining law and order and security and have their own authority for exercising this responsibility. For example, they are largely free to determine the tasks and structures in the areas of interior affairs, the police, the judiciary and the protection of the constitution by passing laws of their own – at least within the scope of the provisions laid down in the Basic Law. At Federal level, the Bundesrat, the body that represents the *Länders'* collective interests, gives them extensive legislative powers. Since Federal legislation on domestic security regularly concerns the responsibilities of the *Länder*, it also requires the consent of the representatives of the *Länder* in the Bundesrat. In addition, the Bundesrat gives the *Länder* the possibility of setting legislative processes in motion at Federal level (Bundesrat initiatives).

Acts from the *Länder* can also assume pioneering roles or acquire the functions of an indicator for Federal-level legislation. The Act on the Protection of the Constitution passed in North Rhine-Westphalia in 2006, for example, empowered the authority responsible for the protection of the constitution to secretly observe and monitor the Internet and to secretly access IT systems (Section 5 (2) (11) of the Act on the Protection of the Constitution). This provision was declared void by the Federal Constitutional Court on 27 February 2008 on account of infringements of general personal rights (Federal Constitutional Court,

2008a). At the same time, this decision also involved setting strict limits on the encroachment of state investigation authorities on the privacy of citizens. These restrictions had to be taken into account by the 'bill on the aversion of dangers from international terrorism by the Federal Criminal Police Office' (Bundestag document 16/9588), in the first reading in the German Bundestag in June 2008.

In the field of external security policy, by contrast, the Basic Law assigns the *Länder* far more restricted participation rights. Since these rights can only be exercised through the Bundesrat as a collective body, a cooperative arrangement for the representation of the interests of the federation and the *Länder* must be attained. This construction also expressively preserves the primacy of the federation.

Again, the foundation for this is Article 59 (2) of the Basic Law, which states that the Bundesrat must be involved in the ratification of such international treaties that – as in the case of domestic security – affect the interests of the *Länder*. Like Parliament, the Bundesrat only has the possibility of approving or rejecting a ratification bill that has been submitted by the Federal Government and passed by the Bundestag in its entirety. The Bundesrat has no initiative or amendment rights. However, Article 32 (2) of the Basic Law states that before the conclusion of an international treaty, a *Land* whose special circumstances are affected by it shall be consulted in due time. In order to clarify the contents and procedure of this standard, which had been a point of controversy between the Federal Republic and *Länder* from a very early stage, the Lindau Agreement was concluded in 1957, establishing the Standing Treaty Commission of the *Länder* as a means of ensuring that the *Länder* were fully involved (Michelmann, 1990: 219 et seq.).

The Bundesrat, however, has significantly greater powers within the framework of EU policy than elsewhere in the area of foreign policy. The *Länder* have benefited from the surrendering of national sovereignty rights to the EU as a result of advances in European integration. As a result, they have successfully pressed for greater involvement in the decision-making processes in accordance with the principle of subsidiarity. In terms of the security dimensions under consideration here, these decisions in particular concern issues of freedom, security and law (Chapter V of the TFEU). A number of functions have been raised to the European level by means of agreements and treaties such as the Schengen Agreement or the Prüm Convention and offices and mechanisms such as the European Police Office EUROPOL, the Schengen Information System (SIS) and the Visa Information System (VIS). The Federal Criminal Police Office and the *Länder* police authorities (*Länder* Criminal Police Offices) are also integrated into these cooperation and information networks.

In the course of the ratification of the Treaty on European Union (Maastricht Treaty), the amendments to Articles 23 and 55 of the Basic Law raised the Bundesrat's right of participation in matters concerning the EU to constitutional status. Paragraphs (2) and (3) of Article 23 of the Basic Law, which is fundamental in this context, essentially lay down the details of the duty of the Federal Government to inform the representatives of the *Länder* about European issues in an appropriate manner. Article 23 (4) stipulates that the Bundesrat shall participate in the decision-making process of the federation insofar as it would have been competent to do so in a comparable domestic matter. Should the interests of the *Länder* be directly affected by European policy-making, paragraph (5) states that the position of the Bundesrat shall be given the 'greatest possible respect'. In the event of a dispute, the Bundesrat may enforce its position with a two-thirds majority (Hoyer, 1998: 83). Furthermore, the Bundesrat must approve any decision on European treaty law that results in an amendment or supplement to the Basic Law by a two-thirds majority (Article 23 (1) of the Basic Law).

Furthermore, *Länder* representatives in European bodies may exercise Federal rights insofar as legislative powers of the *Länder* are affected by the negotiations (Art. 23 (6) of the Basic Law). For this purpose, all the *Länder* have established ministries of European affairs that have the necessary powers and capacities for performing these tasks and that have cooperated with one another at the Conference of Ministers of European Affairs since 1992. After the Single European Act (SEA) was passed in 1986, they also opened their own information offices at the European Commission so as to ensure that the *Länder* can quickly liaise with the EU (Knodt, 1998: 158).

Even though foreign (security) policy is the responsibility of the Federal Government, the *Länder* have many more external activities of their own. For example, they have the possibility to enter into cross-border cooperation arrangements within their areas of responsibility. Bavaria, for instance, works closely with the police forces of the Czech Republic and Austria on implementing the Schengen Agreement and provides bilateral aid for building police structures in Bulgaria and Croatia. Comparable activities are undertaken by virtually all the *Länder* with borders that are also national borders.

The Federal Constitutional Court as the supervisory authority of Germany's security and defence policy

The decision-making process in the area of security policy does not formally include the Federal Constitutional Court. However, the widespread tendency in Germany to turn political issues into legal ones and then to submit them to the Federal Constitutional Court for a final decision is largely the reason why the highest German court has repeatedly had to both delimit powers between the authorities responsible for security and defence policy and specify procedures. Some recent important examples are cited here to show that the Federal Constitutional Court has become a key actor in this field in three respects: with respect to the deployment of the armed forces, the use of the military in domestic emergencies, and the interpretation and further development of international treaties of relevance to security.

Deployment of the armed forces

In the early 1990s, the Federal Government under Federal Chancellor Helmut Kohl responded to events, not least due to growing pressure from the Allies, by arranging for German soldiers to be dispatched to the Balkans to take part in international military operations (monitoring of a UN embargo with warships and air surveillance over the former Yugoslavia with NATO AWACS aircraft) and in Somalia (UNOSOM II) without first clarifying the political and legal bases for these operations (see Gareis 2012). Several parliamentary groups in the Bundestag then brought an action before the Federal Constitutional Court against the Bundeswehr's participation in these operations. The parliamentary group of the government's coalition partner, the FDP, also opposed the deployment of the AWACS. The purpose of this was to clarify whether 'out-of-area' operations were compatible with the strict attachment of the Bundeswehr's mission to national and Alliance defence pursuant to Article 87a of the Basic Law. However, the Federal Government was of the view that this deployment of the armed forces became permissible due to the provisions of Article 24 (2) of the Basic Law, according to which the federation may enter into systems of mutual collective security and, with a view to maintaining peace, consent to limitations upon its sovereign powers.

The Federal Constitutional Court decision announced on 12 July 1994 specified the statutory prerequisites and conditions for the Bundeswehr's participation in international operations in a fundamental way (see Federal Constitutional Court, 1994). The Court confirmed the view taken by the Federal Government with regard to the enabling provision of Article 24 (2) of the Basic Law. This 'empowers the Federal Government not only to enter into a system [of mutual collective security] and to agree to the resulting restrictions upon its sovereign powers. In addition, it also forms the constitutional basis for the acceptance of duties typically resulting from membership in such a system and thus also for the deployment of the Federal Armed Forces [Bundeswehr] for operations within the framework and according to the rules of that system' (Federal Constitutional Court, 1994: 226). By contrast, it was not the intention of Article 87a, which was added to the Basic Law in 1968, to limit the courses of action that could be adopted in the sphere of foreign and security policy pursuant to Article 24 (2) of the Basic Law (Federal Constitutional Court, 1994: 258). The purpose of this article, which was created as part of the work done on Germany's emergency legislation, was rather to determine and limit the ways in which the Bundeswehr could be used in internal emergency situations under the constitution (Federal Constitutional Court, 1994: 259, 260).

However, the Federal Constitutional Court also ruled that the Federal Government had failed to obtain constitutive consent from the Bundestag prior to the dispatch of military personnel (Federal Constitutional Court, 1994: 325). The right of prior approval for parliament introduced a procedure which was completely new and limited exclusively to the deployment of the armed forces. According to this, the Bundestag receives rights of its own to exercise force abroad even though it is a power that actually lies within the remit of the executive. This construction was justified by using the historical argument that since the Weimar Constitution, German armed forces have by nature been a 'parliamentary army'. Politicians were forced to obtain consent from parliament for all ongoing operations and to do the same for all subsequent operations. However, it was also stipulated that the Bundestag has no right of initiative with respect to the deployment of the Bundeswehr in an operation. As shown above, the power to decide on the nature, scope and mandate of an operation, and also to conduct the necessary consultations and planning with international partners and authorities, thus remains solely with the executive. The Bundestag may only approve or reject a corresponding motion of the Federal Government *in its entirety* by a majority vote (50 per cent of the Bundestag plus one vote), but may not make any amendments.

With its decision, the Constitutional Court at the same time enlarged the group of international organisations that come into question as systems of mutual collective security pursuant to Article 24 (2) of the Basic Law by adding collective defence systems such as NATO and (later integrated into the European Union) the WEU (Federal Constitutional Court, 1994: 237). What this means for security-policy dealings in practical terms is that there are almost no constitutional limits on the participation of the Bundeswehr in international military operations. Only go-it-alone military operations remain prohibited. Stipulating that German military operations must be embedded in an international framework, however, means that independent military rescue operations abroad (such as 'Operation Dragonfly' to evacuate German citizens from Tirana in 1997) create considerable legal problems.

Even in its subsequent jurisdiction, the Federal Constitutional Court has shown that it insists on a narrow interpretation of parliament's right of prior approval when it comes to the deployment of armed forces. In its decision of 7 May 2008, the court ruled that any participation of – even unarmed – German soldiers requires the consent of the Bundestag if such missions are in fact armed military operations (Federal Constitutional Court, 2008: Guiding Principle).

An equally far-reaching decision for German security policy was made by the Federal Constitutional Court on 15 February 2006 when it declared void a central provision of the Aviation Security Act amendments that had come into force the previous year. Section 14 (3) states: 'The direct use of armed force shall only (...) permissible in the event that circumstances suggest that the aircraft is intended to be used against human life and this is the only means to defend this human life against the current threat.' The Federal Minister of Defence would have been authorised to issue this order (Section 13 (4)). To prevent possible suicide bombers from committing a monstrous crime, German soldiers would have to kill innocent people – an irresolvable ethical dilemma. Consequently, the act was also rejected by Germany's supreme court. This decision has clarified the law with regard to the problem of weighing up human life while taking account of the right to life as well as human dignity.

While stipulating that sacrificing the lives of people not involved in an incident to protect the lives of others is not permissible, the Federal Constitutional Court also denied the Federal Government the power to employ military weapons within the framework of administrative assistance as specified in Article 35 of the Basic Law when responding to severe emergencies (Federal Constitutional Court, 2006: no. 86 et seq.). By contrast, no answer was given to the question of how Germany is to avert attacks with aircraft and ships or other grave security threats if, on the one hand, the police or civilian disaster control forces do not have the necessary means and tools at their disposal and, on the other hand, the military has the appropriate capabilities, but is not allowed to use them.

In a remarkable turnaround, Germany's supreme court has meanwhile revised its legal interpretation of the use of specifically military assets for averting extremely serious dangers in Germany. In its decision of 3 July 2012, the plenum of the Federal Constitutional Court (with one differing opinion) adopted the view that Article 35 (2), second sentence, and (3) of the Basic Law do not in principle rule out the use of specifically military weapons, but only permit it when a narrow set of preconditions are met that 'ensure in particular that the strict limitations which are imposed on the employment of the armed forces for combat purposes in domestic conflicts pursuant to Article 87a (4) of the Basic Law are not circumvented.' (Federal Constitutional Court, 2012: 24). An accident with disastrous consequences must therefore already have happened for the armed forces to be employed (ibid., 47). Such an employment is also only 'permissible as a last resort' (ibid., 48). It remains to be seen whether and, if so, in what way Bundeswehr military personnel would be employed and how they would use their specific weapons. With his dissenting opinion, however, Judge Reinhard Gaier referred to the possible damage the decision may cause with a view to the strict separation of military and police tasks: 'Nevertheless, the plenum has extended the permissibility of the employment of the armed forces in Germany for the purpose of achieving minor, nearly unattainable gains in security by using extremely vague legal terminology; as a result, military operations motivated by domestic policy cannot be ruled out' (ibid., 89).

The further development of international treaties

In the early 1990s, not only the clarification of the legitimacy of the Bundeswehr's participation in international military action was on the agenda of the Federal Constitutional Court, but also the examination of the question of whether the Federal Government had infringed the rights of the Bundestag pursuant to Article 59 (2) by consenting to the strategic concepts of NATO and the Western European Union (WEU), which extended existing treaties. While the Federal Constitutional Court rejected this view in 1994 due to the equal division of votes in the Second Senate (Federal Constitutional Court, 1994: 261 et seq.), the suit filed by the PDS parliamentary group against NATO's New Strategic Concept, which was adopted by heads of government in 1999, was unanimously dismissed by the decision of 22 November 2001 (Federal Constitutional Court, 2001: 131). In both cases, it was agreed that further developments had been made in the existing treaties, but that no changes necessitating parliamentary participation had been made to them. This gives the executive a great deal of scope for interpreting existing international treaties.

As a result of suits filed, among others, by the parliamentary faction of Die Linke the act ratifying the Treaty of Lisbon on the reform of the EU was also brought before the Federal Constitutional Court on 24 June 2008. In section IV of the suit, great emphasis was placed on the provisions of the new EU Treaty on the Common Security and Defence Policy (notably Articles 42 to 44), the erosion of parliament's right of prior approval by EU resolutions preceding a decision by the Bundestag and infringements of the requirement to secure international peace enshrined in the Basic Law (Die Linke, 2008: 56 et seq.). In its Lisbon decision of 30 June 2009, however, the Federal Constitutional Court made it clear that the Treaty of Lisbon does not confer any responsibility on the EU 'to resort to the armed forces of the Member States without the consent of each Member State affected or of its parliament' (Federal Constitutional Court, 2009: 381). Parliament's right of prior approval is also protected by the fact that any decisions on military operations have to be unanimous. In this case, the German representative in the Council would be 'bound by the Constitution to withhold consent on every draft resolution that may violate or circumvent the German parliament's right of prior approval regarding legislation on the armed forces as laid down in the Basic Law' (ibid., 388).

Due to the decisions it has made on Bundeswehr operations and the interpretation of existing international treaties in particular, the Federal Constitutional Court has also become a kind of legal supervisory authority for German security and defence policy. The court has usually hit the ball back into the political field by creating a broad legal framework that then has to be filled in politically. But the political urgency to obtain legal clarification for increasingly detailed issues such as the nature of Bundeswehr operations that require consent suggests that the Federal Constitutional Court will also in future continue to play an important role in the way decisions on foreign and security policy matters are made in Germany.

The international dimension

As outlined above, beyond acting in self-defence, the Bundeswehr may engage in armed operations abroad only within the framework of collective security systems. This fits in well with Germany's policy, which traditionally favours integration, as it does with the country's widespread aversion to going it alone on security and defence policy matters. Nevertheless, it has become apparent over the past two decades that Germany's multilateral integration and the demands this has placed on the country, on the one hand, and the sovereign decision based on a complex domestic procedure, on the other hand, have created permanent tension. This is particularly true when participation in an international operation comes anywhere close to meaning involvement in combat. The intense debates about the operations in the Democratic Republic of the Congo (2006) and the violent situation in Afghanistan make it clear how difficult it still is for German politicians and society to accept that the Bundeswehr is an active tool that Germany can use to implement its foreign policy.

Germany must continually master the difficult act of balancing between foreign policy demands and domestic policy restraint. On the one hand, NATO and the EU put pressure on Germany to pull its weight and, as the price for solidarity, to restrict the government's scope for decision-making and to consequently more or less demand parliamentary consent in support of Alliance solidarity. This however also aims to outmanoeuvre the German Bundestag as the sovereign representative and supreme source of legitimacy. On the other hand, a sensitive public applies pressure on a parliament that tends to be receptive to momentary moods with the aim of it issuing narrow mandates, which in turn limit the government's scope for multilateral action and repeatedly cause concern among Allies.

Critics of Germany's close integration into Alliance structures claim that operations abroad are undergoing a gradual 'de-parliamentarisation' and call for the legislative branch to be granted greater powers for defining the international framework within which the Bundeswehr may operate. It must be argued, however, that international integration of Germany is valuable in and of itself, and that no insurmountable hurdles in the domestic decision-making process must stand in the way of Germany reliably honouring its Alliance commitments.

Provision of military capabilities and permission for these capabilities to be used in support of multilateral alliances and missions are thus also very much in Germany's interest. Active participation in joint operations is equivalent to political capital, the value of which lies in the possibilities it offers for influencing and shaping proceedings in the Alliance's planning and decision-making bodies. On the other hand, this has led to the creation of integrated structures from which Germany cannot withdraw its forces or can only do so at the expense of weakening the operational and functional capability of the joint units and missions. For all the countries involved, and that includes Germany, integration in these multilateral structures comes with certain restrictions on sovereign and free decision-making, with regard to the employment of military assets. Since reunification, Germany, which has traditionally shown restraint in matters of military operations, has generally participated in international peacekeeping missions more for reasons of the Alliance than out of any inherent political motivation. From the Balkans to East Timor and from the Democratic Republic of the Congo to the operation in Afghanistan, pressure from partners has resulted in German military involvement in regions, countries or task areas that for a long time were categorically ruled out by German governments. At the same time, attempts have been made to keep the scope and nature of this operational involvement within bounds that are acceptable to a public that largely goes by the principle that its country is a 'civilian power' (Maull, 2007).

Multilateralism, which is held in such high esteem particularly by Germany, is an organising principle of international politics that depends both in theory and in practice on the fact that certain states are willing to give collective goals precedence over their own particular interests. What this effectively means is that the advancing multilateral integration of a state is accompanied by a reduction in its degree of freedom to make national decisions as a sovereign state – at least as long as it is willing to honour its commitments. In the case of the military operations under consideration here, this applies not only to *whether* an operation is conducted, but also to *how*.

This issue has gained relevance in light of the debate within NATO and the EU on the merging and joint use of national capacities, which has intensified since 2011, the keywords being 'smart defence' (NATO) and 'pooling and sharing' (EU). Such efforts – including formations such as the NATO Response

Force or the EU Battle Groups – can only succeed when all partners involved can rely on provision of the promised capabilities in full and in a timely manner.

Certain modifications of the current parliamentary participation procedure are thus necessary and possible. It would be conceivable, for instance, for the Bundestag to pass an anticipatory resolution, limited to the period of readiness, when German units are assigned as NATO and EU capabilities. This could empower the Federal Government to deploy the ready forces in accordance with the decisions it was involved in making in the North Atlantic Council or the European Council. Such a privileging of operations within the framework of existing alliances and organisations has already been initiated by the Federal Constitutional Court (Federal Constitutional Court, 1994: 286, 348). This could particularly allow restrictions on theatres of operation to be eased, a move that would create greater room for manoeuvre both for political leaders and for commanders on the ground, enabling them to better adapt to changing situations. If the government were under a specific obligation to inform parliament and the (admittedly weak) right of withdrawal laid down in Section 8 of the Parliamentary Participation Act were to apply, a balance could be struck between the Bundestag's powers of participation and control and the Alliance's requirements.

Future requirements

Despite the primary responsibility of the executive branch and the strong position of the Chancellor in the Cabinet, there is growing pressure to reform the decision-making structures in the field of German security and defence policy with respect to their conceptual orientation, networking, coordination and compatibility with the multilateral commitments that have been entered into. Although Germany has shown considerable commitment in taking on new security and defence challenges for more than two decades, changes made in the Bundeswehr and civilian security systems for this purpose have not yet been integrated into a full and consistent concept. Elements of such a paper could include, for instance, the criteria for deciding on objectives for which Germany, together with its partners, wants to use power and capabilities, what political price it is willing to pay and when it will refrain from committing itself. The elaboration and, above all, implementation of such a strategic concept are hardly conceivable without coherent cooperation between the various ministries. Not only coordinated and well-established procedures of horizontal interministerial cooperation would be necessary, but also a vertical control mechanism by which priorities can be set and decisions made when interministerial conflicts arise. With the creation of the Crisis Response Centre at the Federal Foreign Office, the establishment of the Interministerial Steering Group and the Advisory Board for Civilian Crisis Prevention (Federal Government 2004, 2005; Foreign Office 2008), and last but not least the establishment of a Bundestag subcommittee on 'Civilian Crisis Prevention and Integrated Conflict Management' in 2010, steps have already been taken to enlarge the network. On the international level, these efforts have already been put into practice in the Provincial Reconstruction Teams (PRT) operating in Afghanistan, which are supported by four ministries: defence, foreign affairs, the interior and economic cooperation and development.

However, experience shows that the implementation of common tasks runs counter both to the traditional decision-making processes of the German ministerial system (principle of ministerial autonomy) and to the responsibilities of the ministries for budgeting. Priority is attached to the chief tasks, and the accustomed bureaucratic procedures are followed. The effectiveness of these new structures is therefore extremely limited – further institutional consolidation of the relations for interministerial cooperation could be an appropriate solution.

There is still no political authority that could advance networking among the many security actors at Federal and *Land* level. In the political sphere, there sporadic calls are repeatedly made for the creation of such an authority in the form of a National Security Council (CDU/CSU Parliamentary Group, 2008: 12 et seq.), but they are again and again met with harsh criticism, mainly due to reservations about centralising powers in the field of security policy (an overview of the conflicting positions can be found in Staack, 2008 and Varwick, 2008). In addition, there is widespread insistence on the fundamentals of the 'principle of ministerial autonomy' and on the ministries' sovereignty claims connected with it. Finally there is the ancient maxim that everyone likes to coordinate, but greatly dislikes being coordinated.

If, as Cord Meier-Kloth (2002: 12) rightly pointed out more than ten years ago, an American-style National Security Council is too ambitious an undertaking for Germany, a possible approach could be to raise the Federal Security Council out of its current intransparency, provide it with an appropriate operational foundation, say, for coordinating intelligence service activities or internal and external security requirements, and thus make it a forum with which the debate on foreign and security policy strategies can be guided and advanced. The assignment of an even clearer coordinating role to the Federal Chancellery would also be conceivable.

On the whole, however, the formation of security and defence policy in Germany still seems more focused on the current delineation of responsibilities than on the requirements of a complex world without a firmly established order (Krause, 2005: 25). Establishing a network between the actors in the national and international security environments is easier said than done – along with the question of *how?* there remains the question of *what for?* Since the end of the East-West confrontation, Germany has been playing a new role, both in Europe and in the world. But no new consensus has yet been formed among German politicians and society on the demands resulting from this or on how Germany should react under the new conditions. An extensive debate on the interests and goals of Germany's foreign, security and defence policy and the appropriate means and tools for achieving these goals is therefore overdue. The White Papers of 1994 and 2006 (BMVg, 1994, 2006) remain extremely vague in their lists of priorities, as they do when it comes to outlining a security and defence strategy for the future. If Germany wants to avoid getting lost in ad hoc scenarios, she must energetically strive to clarify her internal and external security policies.

Bibliography

Andreae, Lisette/Kaiser, Karl (1998): Die „Außenpolitik" der Fachministerien. In: Eberwein, Wolf-Dieter/Kaiser, Karl (Eds.): Deutschlands neue Außenpolitik. Vol. 4: Institutionen und Ressourcen. Munich: Oldenbourg: 29-46.

Auswärtiges Amt (2008): Krisenprävention als gemeinsame Aufgabe. 2. Bericht der Bundesregierung über die Umsetzung des Aktionsplans „Zivile Krisenprävention, Konfliktlösung und Friedenskonsolidierung". Berlin.

Bierling, Stephan (2005): Die Außenpolitik der Bundesrepublik Deutschland. Normen, Akteure, Entscheidungen. 2nd ed.. Munich: Oldenbourg.

BMVg (1992): Defence Policy Guidelines of 26 November 1992. Bonn.

BMVg (1994): White Paper 1994. Bonn.

BMVg (2003): Defence Policy Guidelines for the Ministry of Defence. Berlin.

BMVg (2006): White Paper 2006. On German Security Policy and the Future of the Bundeswehr. Berlin.

BMVg (2011): Defence Policy Guidelines. Safeguarding National Interests – Assuming International Responsibility – Shaping Security Together. Berlin.

BMVg (2012): The Reorientation of the Bundeswehr. Berlin.

Brandt, Enrico/Buck, Christian F. (Eds.) (2005): Auswärtiges Amt. Diplomatie als Beruf. Wiesbaden: VS-Verlag für Sozialwissenschaften.

Bukow, Sebastian (2007): Politikfeld innere Sicherheit: deutsche Entwicklungen im europäischen Kontext. In Kümmel, Gerhard/Collmer, Sabine (Eds.): Die Bundeswehr heute und morgen. Baden-Baden: Nomos: 65-84.

CDU/CSU German Bundestag Parliamentary Group (2008): Eine Sicherheitsstrategie für Deutschland. Berlin. http://www.cducsu.de/

Die Linke (2008): Antrag im Organstreitverfahren gegen das Zustimmungsgesetz zum Lissaboner Vertrag. Berlin. <http://dokumente.linksfraktion.net/pdfdownloads/7751661884.pdf>

Federal Constitutional Court (1994): BVerfGE 90, 289 – Bundeswehr operation of 12.07.1994.

Federal Constitutional Court (2001): BVerfG, 2 BvE 6/99 of 22.11.2001 (New Strategic Concept of NATO).

Federal Constitutional Court (2006): BVerfG, 1 BvR 357/05 of 15.02.2006 (Aviation Security Act).

Federal Constitutional Court (2008): BVerfG, 2 BvE 1/03 of 07.05.2008 (Air Monitoring over Turkey).

Federal Constitutional Court (2008a): BVerfG, 1 BvR 370/07 of 27.02.2008 (Act on the Protection of the Constitution, North Rhine-Westphalia).

Federal Constitutional Court (2009): 2 BvE 2/08 of 30.06.2009 (Lisbon decision).

Federal Constitutional Court (2012): 2PBvU1/11 of 03.07.2012 (Use of the Bundeswehr in Germany)

Federal Government (2002): Rules of Procedure of the Federal Government of 11.05.1951 as published on 29.03.1967 (Joint Ministerial Gazette (GMBl): 130), 12.09.1967 (GMBl.: 430), 06.01.1970 (GMBl.: 14), 23.01.1970 (GMBl.: 50), 25.03.1976 (GMBl.: 174, 354), 17.07.1987 (GMBl.: 382) and 21.11.2002 (GMBl.: 848).

Federal Government (2004): Aktionsplan „Zivile Krisenprävention, Konfliktlösung und Friedenskonsolidierung". Berlin.

Federal Government (2005): Ein Jahr „Aktionsplan Zivile Krisenprävention, Konfliktlösung und Friedenskonsolidierung". Berlin.

Gareis, Sven Bernhard (2012): Neue Aufgaben und Einsätze der Bundeswehr. In: Bohrmann, Thomas/Lather, Karl-Heinz/Lohmann, Friedrich (Eds.): Handbuch Militärische Berufsethik (2012 forthcoming).

German Bundestag (1996): Menschenrechte in Tibet. Interfraktioneller Antrag, angenommen am 20. Juni 1996. BTag-Drs. 13/4445.

German Bundestag (2002): Tibet-Resolution von 2002. Interfraktioneller Antrag, angenommen am 14. März 2002. BTag-Drs. 14/8782.

Gilch, Andreas (2005): Das Parlamentsbeteiligungsgesetz. Die Auslandsentsendung der Bundeswehr und deren verfahrensrechtliche Ausgestaltung (Dissertation). Würzburg: Bayerische Julius-Maximilians-Universität.

Haftendorn, Helga (1990): Zur Theorie außenpolitischer Entscheidungsprozesse, in: Rittberger, Volker (Ed.): Theorien der Internationalen Beziehungen. Bestandsaufnahme und Forschungsperspektiven. Opladen: Westdeutscher Verlag: 401-423.

Haushaltsgesetz (Budget Act) (2012): Act on the Federal Budget Plan for the Budget Year 2012 of 22. 12. 2011. Federal Law Gazette I: 2938

Hein, Kristin (2004): Die Anti-Terrorpolitik der rot-grünen Bundesregierung, Harnisch, Sebastian; Katsioulis, Christos; Overhaus, Martin (Eds.): Deutsche Sicherheitspolitik. Eine Bilanz der Regierung Schröder. Baden-Baden: Nomos: 145-171.

Hennis, Wilhelm (1968): Politik als praktische Wissenschaft. Aufsätze zur Politischen Theorie und Regierungslehre. Munich: Piper.

Hölscheidt, Sven (2000): Mitwirkungsrechte des Deutschen Bundestages in Angelegenheiten der EU. In: Aus Politik und Zeitgeschichte. 28: 31-38.

Höse, Alexander/Oppermann, Kai (2011): Die innenpolitischen Restriktionen deutscher Außenpolitik. In: Jäger, Thomas/Höse, Alexander/Oppermann, Kai (Eds.): Deutsche Außenpolitik. Sicherheit, Wohlfahrt, Institutionen und Normen. Wiesbaden: VS-Verlag für Sozialwissenschaften. 2nd ed.: 44-76.

Hoyer, Werner (1998): Nationale Entscheidungsstrukturen deutscher Europapolitik. In: Eberwein, Wolf-Dieter/Kaiser, Karl (Eds.): Deutschlands neue Außenpolitik. http://dokumente.linksfraktion.net/pdfdownloads/7751661884.pdf. Vol. 4: Institutionen und Ressourcen. Munich: Oldenbourg: 75-86.

Knelangen, Wilhelm (2006): Einsatz der Bundeswehr im Innern: Möglichkeiten und Grenzen. In: Gareis, Sven Bernhard/Klein Paul (Eds.) (2006): Handbuch Militär und Sozialwissenschaft. 2nd ed. Wiesbaden: VS-Verlag für Sozialwissenschaften: 112-124.

Knodt, Michelle (1998): Auswärtiges handeln der deutschen Länder. In: Eberwein, Wolf-Dieter/Kaiser, Karl (Eds.): Deutschlands neue Außenpolitik. Vol. 4: Institutionen und Ressourcen. Munich: Oldenbourg: 153-166.

Koalitionsvertrag (1998): Aufbruch und Erneuerung – Deutschlands Weg ins 21. Jahrhundert. Koalitionsvereinbarung zwischen der Sozialdemokratischen Partei Deutschlands und Bündnis 90/Die Grünen vom 20. Oktober 1998. <http://www.boell.de/alt/downloads /gedaechtnis /1998_Koalitionsvertrag.pdf>.

Krause, Joachim (1998): Die Rolle des Bundestages in der Außenpolitik. In: Eberwein, Wolf-Dieter/Kaiser, Karl (Eds.): Deutschlands neue Außenpolitik. Vol. 4: Institutionen und Ressourcen. Munich: Oldenbourg: 137-152.

Krause, Joachim (2005): Auf der Suche nach einer Grand Strategy. Die deutsche Sicherheitspolitik seit der Wiedervereinigung. In: Internationale Politik. 60:8, 16-25.

Lachmuth, Annemarie/ Georgii, Harald/Borhanian, Sarab (2006): Föderalismusreform 2006. Basic Lawänderungen – Synopse (Deutscher Bundestag, Wissenschaftliche Dienste. PD1/ WD 3 –313/06). Berlin.

Lensch, Eileen (2010): Innenministerkonferenz. In: Möllers, Martin H.W. (Eds.): Wörterbuch der Polizei. Munich: C. H. Beck. 2nd ed.: 1979.

Maull, Hanns W. (2007): Deutschland als Zivilmacht, in: Schmidt, Siegmar/Hellmann, Gunther/Wolf, Reinhard (Eds.): Handbuch zur deutschen Außenpolitik. Wiesbaden.

Meier-Klodt, Cord (2002): Einsatzbereit in der Krise? Entscheidungsstrukturen der deutschen Sicherheitspolitik auf dem Prüfstand (SWP-Studie 34). Berlin: SWP.

Michelmann, Hans J. (1990): The Federal Republic of Germany. In: Michelmann, Hans J./Soldatos, Panayotis (Eds.): Federalism and International Relations: The Role of Subnational Units. Oxford: Oxford University Press: 211-244.

Michelmann, Hans J. (2004): Federalism and Paradiplomacy. In: Jäger, Thomas/Kümmel, Gerhard/Lerch, Marika/Noetzel, Thomas (Eds.): Sicherheit und Freiheit. Baden-Baden: Nomos: 188-205.

Möllers, Martin H.W. (2010): Trennungsgebot. In: Möllers, Martin H.W. (Eds.): Wörterbuch der Polizei. Munich: C. H. Beck. 2nd ed.: 1983-1984.

Niclauss, Karlheinz (2004): Kanzlerdemokratie. Paderborn.

Noetzel, Timo/Schreer, Benjamin (2007): Parlamentsvorbehalt auf dem Prüfstand. Berlin: SWP-aktuell 10 (February 2007).

Normann, Lars (2007): Neueste sicherheitspolitische Reformergebnissee zur Terrorprävention. In: Aus Politik und Zeitgeschichte, 12: 11-17.

Schmidt, Manfred G. (2007): Das politische System Deutschlands. Munich: C.H. Beck.

Siwert-Probst, Judith (1998): Die klassischen außenpolitischen Institutionen, in: Eberwein, Wolf-Dieter/Kaiser, Karl (Eds.): Deutschlands neue Außenpolitik. Vol. 4: Institutionen und Ressourcen. Munich: Oldenbourg: 13-28.

Staack, Michael (2008): Falsche Frage zur falschen Zeit. Nicht institutionelle Reformen, sondern inhaltlicher Streit gehört auf die Agenda. In: Internationale Politik. 63:6, 82-83.

Thränhardt, Dietrich (2003): Bundesregierung. In: Andersen, Uwe/Woyke, Wichard (Eds.): Handwörterbuch des politischen Systems der Bundesrepublik Deutschland, 5th ed. Opladen: Leske + Budrich. Bundeszentrale für Politische Bildung, Schriftenreihe Vol. 406: 63-69.

Varwick, Johannes (2008): Verantwortung, nicht Denkmalpflege. Sicherheitspolitik muss Notwendigkeiten definieren statt Ressorts reklamieren. In: Internationale Politik. 63:6, 80-82.

Wiefelspütz, Dieter (2007): Die Abwehr terroristischer Anschläge und das Basic Law. Polizei und Streitkräfte im Spannungsfeld neuer Herausforderungen. Frankfurt a.M.: Verlag für Polizeiwissenschaft.

German defence and military policy in the UN, NATO and the EU from the point of view of the Military Policy Division, Armed Forces Staff

Hans-Werner Wiermann

Introduction: military and defence policy

In everyday language, 'security' is commonly understood to be the absence of danger. However, in the political field in general, and in international relations in particular, the concept of security has, for decades, been the subject of controversial discussion. While advocates of the 'classic school' usually reserve the term for those kinds of threats requiring a military response, there are others who prefer a broader concept of security. They refer to a wide spectrum of assets needing protection as well as a multitude of other threats, which often sends the message that military means are either inadequate to afford protection or just one among many other instruments.

This article will use the broader concept of security, in line with an approach that the current version of the Bundeswehr's White Paper calls 'networked security' (BMVg, 2006: 25). Assuming an interagency and multilateral standpoint, it goes far beyond merely preserving national territorial integrity, and depicts scenarios where internal and external security become ever more intertwined through a multitude of threats to our society.

From a classic perspective, external security policy is part of *foreign policy*. The fields of policy associated with security are *defence policy* and *military policy*. As a result of the lessons learned during the era of National Socialism and World War II, but also due to Germany's position as a divided frontline state in the Cold War, defence and military policy in Germany rank somewhat lower than in many other states, for historical reasons. Germany's external security policy generally focuses on non-military foreign policy that is aimed at promoting national interests. However, the conclusion that foreign policy is entirely identical with security policy would only be true in a very broad sense, even though a politically-motivated policy of military restraint often creates this impression. Defence and military policy have been, and will remain, another important part of security policy. This is also highlighted in the current Defence Policy Guidelines of 27 May 2011. These Guidelines describe the strategic framework for the mission and tasks of the Bundeswehr as a part of the whole-of-government approach to national security, and formulate the security objectives and interests of the Federal Republic of Germany.

Defence policy is an integral part of a holistic interagency approach to security, and, as such, comprehensive and all-encompassing in accordance with the concept of networked security. For the Federal Ministry of Defence as the lead agency on defence policy, this means that – compared to just a few decades ago – it will in future become much more strongly involved in Germany's security policy. This new direction of German defence policy offers both opportunities and challenges, to which the Bundeswehr must gradually adapt as part of its current restructuring process. The requirement for the future will be to promote security in close cooperation with other agencies long *before* a conflict breaks out as the power of states and alliances will be a lesser threat to Germany in the future than it was in the past during the times of the Cold War. Rather, most of threats will arise from states losing their power – in some cases even bringing them to the brink of collapse. This, in turn, will provide a ready breeding ground for terrorism, illegal migration and international crime. This phenomenon of increasing state fragility, which could spread like wildfire across entire regions, must be countered in line with national and collective security objectives. The armed forces and the Ministry of Defence can make a valuable contribution in this area. Defence policy involves all actions taken by a state to provide security in the event of an attack, primarily to preserve national or Allied territorial integrity. As a last resort, this also includes war fighting capabilities, based on national and collective defence capabilities. Defence policy also includes preventive civil and social defence (Meier/Rossmanith/Schäfer, 2003: 400).

Figure 1: Interrelation of security, defence, and military policy

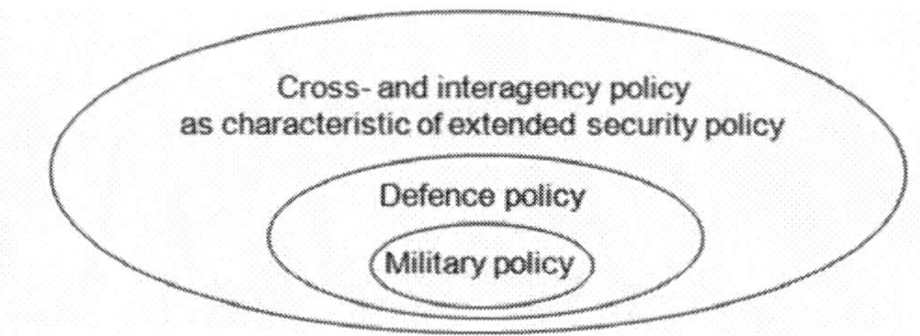

Source: image courtesy of the author

This refers to civil protection which, according to Article 73 No. 1 of Germany's Basic Law, the *Grundgesetz*, is included in the exclusive legislative competence of the federation for 'defence, including protection of the civilian population'. Civil protection is part of civil defence, and as such, the responsibility of the Federal Ministry of the Interior; it is understood to be the protection of the population in a state of emergency or defence. During the Cold War, the defence policy of the Federal Republic of Germany was primarily focused on national defence in an Alliance context as laid down in the *Grundgesetz*. Limiting German defence policy to this core task, however, would no longer suffice, either today or in the foreseeable future, in the face of the challenges of the 21st century and the national security outlook.

Military policy is an integral part of defence policy, focused primarily on military aspects of national and international importance. Military policy also takes into account armament, disarmament, and arms control issues. Military policy involves contributions to alliances such as NATO and the EU, confidence-building activities in cooperation with regional organisations such as the OSCE, and the question of how to establish, equip, organise and train German armed forces. External military policy, on the other hand, is directed at the armed forces of other nations, and designed to prevent violent conflicts from breaking out in the first place. Rather, it aims to identify conflicts early on and develop non-violent solutions that render the use of armed force unnecessary by means of co-operative, multinational crisis and conflict prevention. An integral element of national security, military policy can be used to respond to challenges which, at first glance, appear completely non-military in nature.

This essay will discuss aspects of defence and military policy considered important by the Federal Ministry of Defence. A short historical outline is followed by an overview of the different areas of application and determinants in both policy fields, with a focus on the interrelation between Germany and its partners, given the Alliance-oriented stance of German politics.

A brief overview of the development of military policy in the Federal Republic of Germany

The origins of military policy in the Federal Republic of Germany date back to the 1950s when an intensifying East-West conflict and the Soviet Union's military sabre-rattling led to the Federal Republic becoming ever more integrated into the Western community of states. In the face of a massive withdrawal of US troops from Europe following the end of World War II and the ensuing military predominance of Communist states under Soviet leadership, Western allies showed a growing willingness to rearm West Germany, while France – and, for a long time, also most of the German public – initially opposed the idea. After initial, albeit unsuccessful attempts to rearm the Federal Republic under the European Defence Community (EDC) plan (Loth, 1996: 105-112), rearmament did eventually begin in 1955 when West Germany joined the North Atlantic Treaty Organisation (NATO).

An essential criterion for West Germany's military policy was the integration of the majority of the newly-formed armed forces into NATO. In the process, equipment and procedures had to be adjusted to NATO standards, and the bulk of German troops had to be placed under NATO command. During the first ten years, another goal was to reach the target strength of approximately 500,000 that had been set in 1955/56.

The primary focus of military policy in the narrower sense of Bundeswehr policy was, and remains, armament policy. Against the backdrop of changing NATO defence doctrine (*Forward Defence*, *Massive Retaliation*, and finally, *Flexible Response*), the Federal Republic of Germany focused on strong tank units, efficient air defence capabilities, and navy units to protect convoys and conduct operations in the Baltic Sea (Thoß, 2006: 65-172, 331-370 and 513-602). The idea of adding a nuclear capability to the conventional weaponry was dropped in the face of massive public protests in Germany, and was instead limited to delivery vehicles for Allied (US) warheads.

If armament was the primary objective of West German military policy well into the 1960s, the discussion about disarmament, arms control and confidence-building began to move into the focus of military policy debate toward the end of the decade, briefly pushed aside only in the 70s and 80s by a military readjustment following the NATO dual-track decision in response to the Soviet decision to build and deploy SS-20 missiles (Rödder, 2004: 59-64). Critical milestones included the Strategic Arms Limitation Talks (SALT) and, even more important for a non-nuclear-armed West Germany, the Treaty on Conventional Armed Forces in Europe (CFE), which played a key role in reducing the number of conventional armed forces on the continent (Hartmann/Heydrich/Meyer-Landrut, 1994: 41-43).

Even though national and Alliance defence remained at the hub of West German military policy throughout the Cold War era, politicians already began to look at the Bundeswehr as an instrument of humanitarian assistance a few years after its inception. In 1960, the German Air Force and medical units came to the rescue of the earthquake-stricken Moroccan city of Agadir; disaster relief was also provided to Iran in 1962 when the country suffered a similar catastrophe.

In the following decades, German troops were repeatedly involved in humanitarian operations (e.g. in the Middle East), and while military policy measures required for warfare remained the subject of broad – and sometimes also highly critical – political debate in Germany, the humanitarian character of disaster relief operations found wide acceptance among the German population (Meiers, 2006: 53-56).

With the collapse of the Soviet Union and the Warsaw Pact in the years before and after 1990, and with the reunification of Germany, the parameters of German military policy changed completely. While it seemed much less likely now that German or NATO territory would become the target of massive military attacks, ethnic tensions arose in Eastern and, even more, in Southeastern Europe. They led to bloody conflicts that, up until then, had been suppressed by socialist dictators, so civil war and other forms of military violence now came into public view. While the political standoff between the two power blocs would have made military operations outside their respective political hemispheres quite impossible before 1990, voices demanding to 'export' the era of peace from Europe to other regions in the world grew louder. For the Bundeswehr and German military policy, it became necessary to go beyond merely providing disaster relief and to accept peacekeeping and peacemaking missions in other countries as a new form of military security policy which would call for adjustments in mindset, personnel, structures and materiel. In practice, international operations were taking priority over national defence.

In 1990, Bundeswehr troops began to participate in a number of smaller, unarmed missions, as well as in some military operations abroad. The following provides an overview of operations without giving details on mandates and missions: 1990-1991: mine detection in the Mediterranean Sea and the Persian Gulf; 1991-1993: medical support in Cambodia; 1992-1996: embargo monitoring in the Adriatic Sea; 1993-1994: logistic support in Somalia; from 1995: Croatia and Bosnia; from 1999: Kosovo; from 2002; Horn of Africa; 2006: Congo; from 2002: Afghanistan; from 2006: off the Lebanese coast (BMVg, 2010: 50-112; Naumann, 2007: 477-494). A 1994 Federal Constitutional Court decision (see Federal Constitutional Court judgement file no. 2 BvE 3/92) paved the way for an extension of the Bundeswehr's mission to include armed operations abroad which, according to the ruling, were permissible under certain circumstances (e.g. under the auspices of collective security systems such as the UN or NATO, and if approved by the German *Bundestag*).

The Federal Ministry of Defence has had to make constant adjustments to its military policy in order to accommodate the changes that occurred in 1990. Military and capability-oriented planning included aspects such as asymmetrical balances of power, the unpredictability of a large number of possible opponents and scenarios, vast geographical distances, and the increasing irrelevance of national borders. This, however, had, and still has, to be embedded in a broad whole-of-government approach to security. Military policy is also affected by other constraints such as spending cuts and the drastic reduction of personnel and materiel (Heidenkamp, 2010: 289-291). The number of active-duty personnel has dropped from 500,000 in 1990 to less than 200,000, and compulsory military service has been suspended.

Germany and the international community

The North Atlantic Treaty Organisation

When the Federal Republic of Germany joined the *North Atlantic Treaty Organisation* (NATO) in 1955, the Alliance became the mainstay of (initially West) German foreign and security policy. Today, NATO membership is still a key element in the partnership between the Federal Republic of Germany and the United States of America. West Germany's entry into NATO also heralded the beginning of reconciliation with the Western Allies, who were Germany's enemies in World War II (Wiggershaus, 2000: XI). This commitment to the West sealed West Germany's integration with the Western community of states and shared values.

The fledgling Federal Republic had opted for a cautious, considerate and heavily Alliance-oriented stance towards NATO, laying the foundation for its future role in the arena of security and military policy. To this day, Germany's role has been that of an advocate for multilateral balance, and for the concerns of smaller partners with fewer military and financial assets, while striving to trade solitary decisions for majorities and compromises. This is in Germany's own interest.

While during the Cold War West German defence policy was almost exclusively focused on preserving the integrity of national and Allied territory, a reunified Germany has proved to be a reliable partner in crisis management even beyond NATO borders since 1990. At the same time, Germany fully supported the transformation of NATO resulting from the removal of the threat posed by the Soviet Union. While internal changes included, for example, the adaptation of the Strategic Concept (most recently at the 2010 Lisbon Summit) and the creation of new capabilities and structures (e.g., cyber defence), external activities have, and still do, involve the acceptance of new members to NATO and an intensified partnership policy with non-members.

German military policy within NATO essentially breaks down into two phases: Phase One – during the years of the Cold War – was characterised by increased integration into a powerful alliance which drew its strength mostly from the military capabilities provided by the US Not only did West Germany reap a security benefit from the guarantees provided by the Allies, the country also added its troops to the overall force posture and thus increased the Alliance's deterrence capability, creating a win-win situation for both sides. Phase Two began in the 1990s and extended Germany's role in shaping the Alliance. Germany's initially reactive role in a strictly defence-oriented alliance has given way to a more proactive and self-confident stance in a NATO that increasingly sees itself also as a political organisation for regional security (Varwick, 2008: 88).

From the perspective of military policy, stronger national interests need to be coordinated with the interests of the Allies, making security policy much more complicated. In its role as political advisor, the Federal Ministry of Defence is required to assess a range of very diverse topics, from classic military risks to the proliferation of weapons of mass destruction and carrier systems, terrorism, piracy (Gareis, 2006: 65-66) and cyber attacks, just to mention a few. While the Cold War left no doubt that the enemy was in Eastern Europe, today's threats are spread across the entire globe. Current German military policy within NATO can be roughly broken down into the five following aspects:

First: Germany is an important partner in the performance of so-called 'standing operational tasks' of the Alliance such as integrated air defence or the deployment of standing maritime forces. Bundeswehr troops have, for example, contributed to the Baltic airspace surveillance mission, also known as 'Baltic air policing'.

Second: Germany is a reliable partner in supporting the NATO Command Headquarters and other Alliance facilities, including, more than anything else, the provision of continuous funding.

Third: Germany provides an indispensable contribution to the capabilities directly provided by NATO, such as the NATO Airborne Early Warning & Control Component stationed at Geilenkirchen Air Base, which is of particular importance.

Fourth: The Bundeswehr is a proactive and consistent partner when it comes to implementing political decisions within the *Partnership for Peace* (PfP) programme. Based on the resolutions adopted by the NATO foreign ministers in 2011, efforts are being made in the field of military policy to deepen existing partnerships and explore new ways of cooperation through, for example, regular multinational staff talks in the military policy arena. This, however, will be discussed in more detail at a later stage.

Fifth: Since the mid-90s, Germany has been an active partner in military Alliance operations by providing a substantial number of troops to KFOR (Kosovo), ISAF (Afghanistan), and the counter-terrorism operation *Active Endeavour* in the eastern Mediterranean.

As Germany gives impetus to NATO's military policy, and supports the extension of the Alliance's interests, changes in Alliance philosophy, in turn, have an effect on the Bundeswehr. From a military policy point of view, the most important aspect has been the conversion of military capabilities, i.e. the transition from a national defence force into an expeditionary army operating in worldwide scenarios that have little to do with classic large-scale military conflicts (Gareis, 2006: 173-190). Germany aims to provide NATO with a relevant and effective capability spectrum. It needs to be pointed out though that Germany's foreign and security policy is a product of the country's history. This is sometimes overlooked when our Allies misinterpret decisions as reluctance without putting them into a specific historical context.

Beyond the above-mentioned five fields of action, Germany also fully addresses the so-called 'new challenges' as is illustrated by a 2012 announcement by the German Minister of Defence to contribute substantial resources to the NATO Missile Defence Shield. Besides, the Bundeswehr is also a constant and reliable major contributor to the NATO Response Force.

A hierarchical structure and a series of procedures can by identified by the way in which Germany's military policy has an impact on NATO on the one hand, and draws information and stimuli from the Alliance on the other.[1] The highest panels are the summits of the Heads of State and Government, which since 2001 have mostly been convened on an annual basis, as well as the summits of the Foreign and Defence Ministers and those of the NATO Chiefs of Defence (NATO, 2006: 33-42). Coordination processes are also required inside Germany between the Federal Chancellery and the Foreign and Defence Ministries to determine Germany's positions. Delegation of responsibility to the various German ministries depends on the nature of each issue. From there, instructions will normally be sent to NATO Headquarters in Brussels, where Germany has two representations: The German Delegation to NATO is headed by an ambassador of the Federal Foreign Office who represents the Federal Republic of Germany in routine meetings of the Council and receives instructions (e.g. on voting behaviour) from the Federal Foreign Office (Theiler, 2009: 295-297). On the military side, a lieutenant general occupies the seat of German Military Representative on the NATO Military Committee as the permanent representative of the Chief of Staff, Bundeswehr. The German Military Representative receives directives from the Federal Ministry of Defence. Both offices have sufficient personnel to staff the numerous panels the Alliance runs at the working level.

Decision-making on NATO documents is a sometimes complicated and lengthy procedure often stretching over several months, since the interests of 28 member countries need to be taken into account. However, the consensus-based decisions produce strong and long-lasting signals indicating the way ahead for NATO and its members. While staff involved in analysis and panel work will take a firm stand when representing national positions, they also need to be skilled at diplomacy and must be thoroughly acquainted with the foreign-policy and security interests of the other NATO member countries, as well as in-depth knowledge of NATO's administrative workings. Ultimately, the principles of German foreign and security policy must be reflected in the decisions taken by the Alliance. The timely assessment of legal and budgetary implications is equally important. Ministerial officials will keep the responsible *Bundestag* panels abreast of current developments in NATO, supporting their parliamentary control function. Since 1955, the NATO Parliamentary Assembly has also served as a link between the now 28 national parliaments.

This network of bodies, which was established to take and articulate positions, provides the means to carefully consider even the most complex topics, with the opportunity for the German government to bring its influence to bear well in advance of decision-making within NATO.

1 For further information, visit http://www.nato.int, accessed on 15.03.2012.

The European Union

In addition to NATO, the European Union (EU) is the second important pillar of German security and defence policy, and as such it is of key importance to Germany's military policy. However, there are distinct differences between the two organisations, which, in turn, shape mutual relations. While NATO has always considered itself an organisation for joint and, above all, military crisis management, the EU has over the last decades transitioned from an organization established for economic convenience into a universal actor in all political fields, with the military component being only a small part of the overall construct of European politics. Consequently, the EU's military and civilian crisis management elements constitute an integral part of the European External Action Service (EEAS), which is responsible for all aspects of EU foreign policy. This is founded in the European and German understanding of crises as being comprehensive challenges that can only be overcome successfully by applying a broad, networked approach (for more details, see the Federal Government's 2004 Civilian Crisis Prevention Action Plan *(Aktionsplan zivile Krisenprävention)*). When Germany took over the Council presidency in 2007, highly intense efforts were made to expeditiously complement the military arm of the European Security and Defence Policy (ESDP) with a civilian component (Algieri, 2010: 391-393).

Germany's military policy interests in the EU are presented and represented through either the German Military Representative to NATO and the EU, who represents the Chief of Staff, Bundeswehr, on both the EU and NATO Military Committees, or by the Head of the Political Department of the Permanent Representation of the Federal Republic of Germany to the European Union and, who at the same time is the German Representative to the Political and Security Committee (PSC) – a (specialized) body of the Permanent Representatives. The Head of the Political Department represents Germany as Ambassador on the PSC. Among other functions, the PSC keeps track of the international situation and steers EU crisis management operations. The German PSC ambassador receives security and military policy advice from the Military and Armament Policy Branch of the Permanent Representation. The branch is headed by a brigadier general who is supported in his day-to-day responsibilities by a deputy and two desk officers.[2] German military policy interests are represented by the Federal Ministry of Defence and the Federal Foreign Office, acting in close cooperation, especially when addressing issues that go beyond technical details, such as military concepts and doctrine. German military policy in the EU (Krause, 2010: 12) focuses on two areas: first, *operations*, and, second, drafting new concepts for the *Common Security and Defence Policy* (CSDP) as laid down in the Treaty of

2 http://www.bruessel-eu.diplo.de/Vertretung/bruessel__eu/de/01/Abteilungen__und__Referate/politik/seite__pol_2003__Mil.html, accessed on 15.03.2012.

Lisbon (EU: 1-230). As for the latter, two initiatives are especially worth mentioning: The 'Ghent Initiative', launched in cooperation with Sweden, is now referred to as 'Pooling and Sharing' and has become an integral part of the European-Transatlantic debate about multinational cooperation on capability development and maintenance (Legendre, 2011: 140-141).[3] The second initiative is based on the 'Weimar Triangle' (France, Poland and Germany) and aims to provide fresh impetus for the sustained development of the CSDP after the reorganisation of EU institutions that was implemented in the wake of the Treaty of Lisbon (Hauser, 2010: 109).What both initiatives have in common is that there was, and still is, a sometimes considerable delay between political consensus building and the realisation of individual projects. However, in times of financial crisis and considering the complexity of the issues, this may not be all too surprising especially since processes often compete with other parallel activities in EU member states.

So, while Germany's impact on the EU's defence and military policy is of significant, the direct impact of the European Union and its institutions on Germany is notably less so, especially in terms of binding requirements. In contrast to NATO, for example, the EU has no binding force planning requirements that members must implement.

In 2004, establishing the *Headline Goal 2010* (HLG 2010) through the EU *Capability Development Mechanism* (CDM) marked the first attempt at force planning for EU member nations on a voluntary basis. Strategic planning assumptions were used as a basis for developing generic scenarios to identify the required military capabilities (Bono, 2006: 30-31). These requirements were then laid down in the *Requirements Catalogue 2005* (RC 05)[4], and, along the lines of the 'Petersberg Plus' tasks, a basis was created for the voluntary contribution of national forces and capabilities. The following tasks were included in the planning: humanitarian and rescue tasks, peacekeeping tasks, tasks of combat forces in crisis management including peacemaking, joint disarmament operations, support for third countries in combating terrorism, and security sector reform (Kolanoski, 2010: 49).

The defined requirements were measured against the number of forces and capabilities committed by the nations at regular intervals. The initial *Force Catalogue 2007* (FC 07) was upgraded to FC 09 as members committed additional national assets (Majchrzak, 2010: 24-25). However, there was no need for any major changes to the force and capability contributions – and the remaining

3 http://www.europarl.europa.eu/meetdocs/2009_2014/documents/sede/dv/sede260511deseinitiative_/sede260511deseinitiative_en.pdf, accessed on 16.03.2012.

4 http://www.europa-eu-un.org/articles/en/article_4735_en.htm, accessed on 12.03.2012.

shortfalls – compiled in the *Progress Catalogue 2007* (PC 07). In 2009, though, the capability gaps were re-prioritised.[5]

Since then, the focus of any subsequent measures has been on eliminating these capability gaps (especially the capability to transport forces into theatre, to protect them in theatre, and to obtain information superiority). The *European Defence Agency* (EDA) established in 2004 plays a key role in this regard, not least when it comes to drafting a *Capability Development Plan* (CDP) which will merge short-term capability requirements, medium-term national planning by the EU member states, and long-term capability requirements included in the *Initial Long Term Vision* (LTV). The National Capability Directors are responsible for preparing the CDP which will comprise the following four 'strands':

- A) Identify and prioritise capability gaps in accordance with HLG 2010 (spearheaded by the *EU Military Committee*, EUMC);
- B) Identify capability trends for the 2025 timeframe (by cooperation of EDA and EUMC);
- C) Collate a database of programmes and projects of the participating member nations (spearheaded by the EDA);
- D) Harvest lessons learned from ongoing operations to identify implications for future capabilities.[6]

The CDP is not a binding supranational EU planning directive. Responsibility for defence issues and, above all, for investments, will remain with the member states. From a German perspective, Strands A and D are of particular importance. Strand A involves a prioritisation of capability gaps by the EUMC going beyond PC 07, while Strand D not only includes the analysis of EU missions, but also those missions reported by the members on a voluntary basis.

In summary, the EU can only to a limited extent assume a role as an actor in military policy, due to the fact that this important political area is characterised by a 'culture of voluntariness'. If anything, the EU's credibility in the field of security policy can serve as a benchmark for achieving tangible and organisational progress, with the ultimate aim of providing specific requirements and identifying lessons. In the end, implementation will depend on a political evaluation of the overall system and on how much pressure such an evaluation creates.

5 http://consilium.europa.eu/uedocs/cmsUpload/090720%20Factsheet%20capacites%20militaires%20EN.pdf, accessed on 12.03.2012)

6 http://www.eda.europa.eu/Libraries/Documents/factsheet_CDP.sflb.ashx, accessed on 14.03.2012.

The United Nations

The Charter of the United Nations (UN) provides its members, and thus, virtually the whole world, with the international legal principles on which international relations are based. Peacekeeping and peacemaking are an important aspect of all UN activities. Expectations placed on the UN in this area have been growing since the end of the Cold War. Today, the UN employs more than 120,000 troops, police officers, and civilian staff in UN peace missions, who are commonly referred to as United Nations Blue Helmets.[7]

The Security Council is the highest permanent UN decision-making body at the political level. It takes decisions with the aim of settling disputes by peaceful means (Chapter VI of the UN Charter) and, in the case of breaches of the peace and acts of aggression, also on coercive measures up to and including the use of armed force (Chapter VII of the UN Charter). The Security Council is the only UN body authorised to decide on intervention in a conflict situation, and the only one whose resolutions have a binding character for the parties to the conflict. The Secretariat, headed by the Secretary-General, is responsible for supporting the Security Council in all areas of conflict prevention and crisis management. The *Department of Peacekeeping Operations* (DPKO) and the *Department of Field Support* (DFS) assist the Secretary-General in planning and directing peacekeeping missions, and in providing the required personnel and logistics.[8] If the UN chooses to assume the military lead of a mission, responsibility is shared by the DPKO and the DFS. However, with limited personnel and equipment, the Secretariat is not in a position to command any major contingents of military and police forces (Tull, 2010: 8 et seq.), so other international organisations such as NATO, the EU, the African Union or other coalitions are tasked with conducting large-scale missions. These organisations coordinate the troops, police forces, or civilian specialists provided by the member states within their own command structures (e.g. military headquarters) on behalf of the UN. However, even then, the ultimate responsibility for the mission rests with the Security Council and the Secretary-General. A Force Commander designated by the Secretary-General is responsible for operational and tactical command and control of a military UN mission; in the case of political missions, this responsibility falls to the (civilian) Head of Mission. Strategic-level political leadership is exercised not only by the Security Council and the Secretary-General, but usually also by a *Special Representative of the Secretary-General* (SRSG) (see also ZIF, 2010: esp. 28 et seq.).

7 Figures taken from http://www.unric.org/html/german/dpi1634dt.pdf, accessed on 18.02.2012.

8 For more information on organisational details and tasks, go to: http://www.un.org/en/peacekeeping/documents/dpkodfs_org_chart.pdf, accessed on 16.03.2012).

The Federal Republic of Germany has supported these peace missions from the moment it joined the UN. Germany currently contributes some 8% to the UN's regular budget for peacekeeping operations (Hüfner, 2005: 98-99). For years, Germany has also been providing a contribution of approximately 7,000 troops to UN-mandated missions, with a primary focus on peacebuilding missions such as ISAF in Afghanistan, or observer missions.

The *UN Standby Arrangements System* (UNSAS) was developed in 1993 as a planning tool to reduce the amount of time required to mount a Security Council-mandated UN mission. This tool enables UN member states to designate potential military and civilian assets and capabilities that the UN may draw on for peacekeeping purposes upon request and following national approval on a case-by-case basis (Schöndorf, 2011: 12). When the Federal Republic of Germany joined UNSAS on 24 July 1998, contributions for UN peacekeeping missions were limited to civilian resources in the form of medical and technical support only. A supplementary agreement was concluded on 1 November 2000 adding to the German UNSAS contribution military assets such as land and airlift, medical and engineering components, signal and related security elements, naval reconnaissance, surveillance and countermine components, military observers, military police units, and staff support personnel (Pleuger, 2004: 6-10). The Bundeswehr has also been deploying UN military observers (UNMO) to international missions for decades. When the military observers were pulled out of Ethiopia, Eritrea and Georgia in 2008 and 2009, Germany joined the UN military observer missions in Sudan (UNMIS), Afghanistan (UNAMA) and Darfur (UNAMID).

While it is mostly the five veto-wielding permanent members (China, France, the UK, Russia and the US) that dominate security policy in the UN Security Council, Germany does exert a certain degree of influence with the military assets and the funding it provides.

While the Federal Republic of Germany works to promote peace and strengthen the rule of law in international affairs in connection with UN efforts towards regional crisis management, it also wants to bring its commitment to the attention of an international audience. As for military policy, Germany has opted to provide specialized capabilities and expert personnel to UN-led operations, rather than large force contingents. Missions requiring a large number of personnel, such as ISAF in Afghanistan, KFOR in Kosovo and EUFOR in Bosnia and Herzegovina, are usually led by NATO or the EU on behalf of, rather than directly by, the UN.

The UN also provides a platform for several other initiatives with direct or indirect implications on the armed forces. The Federal Ministry of Defence represents its interests by delegating military advisors to the German Mission to the UN or by assigning personnel to Germany's respective negotiating delegations. Disarmament and arms control are two important issues in this context. German military policy aims to maximise humanitarian protection and political security while striving to minimise any negative impact on Germany's operational capability, and subsequently, on all those capabilities which are key to the accomplishment of military missions. Over the past years, national security and any related preventative measures have been increasingly complemented by the more human and individualised aspects of security, culminating in the concept of 'humanitarian arms control'.

International projects based on this concept – which have either already been implemented or are still being negotiated – include the multilateral *Arms Trade Treaty*, the *UN Programme of Action to Prevent, Combat, and Eradicate the Illicit Trade in Small Arms and Light Weapons in All Its Aspects*, the *UN Register of Conventional Arms*, the *Ottawa Treaty* (or Anti-Personnel Mine Ban Convention), and the *Oslo Convention on Cluster Munitions*. A healthy balance between the above principles is required in all cases, i.e. military requirements need to be weighed against humanitarian aspects. Given the complexity of the topic, achieving this balance is often quite difficult, all the more so as, with international non-governmental organisations entering the picture as a driving force, the Federal Ministry of Defence must learn how to interact with these new partners.

The Organisation for Security and Co-operation in Europe

The Organisation for Security and Co-operation in Europe (OSCE) considers itself a regional arrangement under Chapter VIII of the United Nations Charter, designed to serve as the first point of contact in the event of a regional conflict in its own sphere of influence, according to the principle of subsidiarity. German interests are represented by the Permanent Mission of the Federal Republic of Germany to the OSCE. Over time, the OSCE has grown to become an institutionalised forum for diplomacy through debate, and today, this is still the Organisation's primary focus (Ugglas, 1994: 14-32). The Organisation neither conducts nor mandates any military operations, with the one exception being the 1998/99 Kosovo Verification Mission, making it much less visible as an actor in military policy than other international organisations. The OSCE does offer a series of forums, though, which are relevant for the Federal Ministry of Defence. These forums are either an integral part of the OSCE, such as the *Permanent Council* and the *Forum for Security Co-operation*, or they act under the auspices of the OSCE, such as the CFE Joint Consultative Group (*Treaty on Conventional Armed Forces in Europe*), and the Open Skies Consultative Commission (OSCC) which is responsible for implementing the Open Skies Treaty. Another key document is the *Vienna Document 1999 of the Negotiations on Confidence- and Security-Building Measures*, a politically binding agreement concluded to increase security in Europe by creating transparency and confidence. It incorporates an information and verification regime, as well as a set of confidence-building measures and mechanisms for peaceful conflict management. The Federal Ministry of Defence provides some of the diplomatic personnel assigned to the Permanent Mission for this project to guarantee a sufficient degree of military expertise.[9]

From a German perspective, the largely civilian OSCE Missions and Offices constitute the OSCE's primary operational elements to which the Bundeswehr assigns selective staff – some of whom are military experts – as a commitment to, and in order to bring its influence to bear on, both the respective mission and the target region. Examples include the Balkans, Eastern Europe, the South Caucasus, Central Asia, and election observation missions conducted in the OSCE area. The missions cover a wide range of aspects such as the establishment of democratic structures and the rule of law, border monitoring, ceasefire and arms control (including small arms, light weapons, and ammunition management), economic and environmental cooperation, mediation in so-called 'frozen conflicts' (Caucasus and Moldova), and the establishment of functioning civil societies (Zellner, 2010: 310-318).

In spite of limited operational effectiveness, the OSCE still enjoys a near monopoly in some areas. Since military capabilities, military activities, and politico-military planning largely depend on arms control and confidence-building aimed at strategic stability, the Federal Ministry of Defence has committed to a long-term involvement in this process, and promotes a vigorous politico-military debate. The Federal Ministry of Defence considers the further development of arms control agreements for and inside Europe to be the focal point of joint efforts. While there is agreement among the majority of OSCE members that the OSCE's crisis response mechanisms – which proved largely ineffective in the Georgia crisis – need conceptual and operational improvements (Daigeler, 2005: 267-270), it is still unclear how this will be achieved in practical terms.

Bilateral cooperation

In addition to institutionalised foreign policy conducted within the framework of international organisations, the areas of defence and military policy provide the Federal Republic of Germany with a variety of further opportunities to shape bilateral relations with other states. The contributions made by the Bundeswehr lie outside the traditional military capability spectrum. In general, a distinction must be made between two types of bilateral military policy: First, Germany's efforts to exert influence on the military, the security organisations and the politics of other non-NATO, or non-EU states. The essence of such measures includes building confidence, developing a basic understanding of democratic control of

9 See http://www.wien-osze.diplo.de/Vertretung/wienosce/de/Startseite.html, accessed on 15.03.2012.

armed forces along the lines of the German principle of *Innere Führung* (Leadership Development and Civic Education) and systematically advancing capabilities in order to enable participation in common missions. Second, Germany maintains bilateral politico-military relations with classic partners inside the European and transatlantic alliances, and with states of outstanding importance outside these alliances (Federal Government, 2006: 27).

The centrepiece of politico-military cooperation with non-NATO states is *military training assistance* which may be complemented by other instruments, such as *military advice*, or *materiel support* (Federal Government, 2006: 28 - 29). In providing military training assistance, i.e. basic, advanced and follow-on training at Bundeswehr training facilities and in Bundeswehr units, Germany attempts to exert influence on the development of democratically oriented armed forces in regions whose stabilisation is of particular interest to Germany. In parallel, a second objective is to build trusting relations between Germany and the respective partner country. These efforts are in accordance with the concept of *Security Sector Reform* (for further details, see OECD, 2007: 124 - 139).

High-value training courses – such as general and admiral staff officer training, officer training, and academic education at the Bundeswehr's universities – attract the greatest interest. Every year, more than fifty states make use of these opportunities. The military training assistance programme shows its greatest effect for the respective partner country if it can be embedded into a political perspective of *Innere Führung* and the 'Citizen in Uniform' concept. With regard to Eastern and Southeastern Europe, this is certainly a success story. It stands in stark contrast to other regions in the world, such as Northern Africa prior to the 2011 uprisings, where the military training assistance programme fell well short of achieving the desired effects. While interested in acquiring specific military know-how, the partner nations showed no interest in adopting Germany's socio-political positions in the military field, such as democratic control of the armed forces, freedom of speech, or the principle of *Innere Führung.*

In the following, bilateral relations with the Allied nations – the US, France, and Great Britain – and the special relations with the non-NATO nation Russia will be portrayed, since these are of particular importance.

The *United States of America* is Germany's crucial partner on all critical security and politico-military issues. The politico-military and military network that has evolved over decades remains stable even when under strain. The close partnership between Germany and the US is symbolised by its cornerstones: American troops stationed in Germany, and the presence of German troops on US soil for training purposes. Special mention must also be made of regular meetings (to include the senior executive level), exchange programmes, troop visits, joint training, as well as staff talks and politico-military consultations. The training relations with the US form the framework for approximately forty per cent of Germany's total training conducted abroad, with up to 800 participants every year. In return, the US sends about 1,200 trainees to Germany in the same period of time. Additionally, approximately 400 soldiers attend NATO courses conducted in Germany.

From a politico-military point of view, *France* is also highly significant. Since 1988, the Franco-German Defence and Security Council has served as the institutional basis of bilateral politico-military relations, supplemented by a Strategic Dialogue agreed in 2011, which is designed to stimulate the joint defence policy debate and strengthen bilateral defence contributions to the EU and NATO. As with the US, a broad mutual exchange has given rise to significant training measures at lower levels. The depth of politico-military ties between Germany and France becomes particularly evident in the essential contributions by both states to the Eurocorps and the Franco-German Brigade.

The close partnership with the *United Kingdom*, a European actor with a global reach, is in Germany's interest. In 2011, a dialogue group was established to intensify the exchange of ideas on politico-military topics and to improve coordination on procurement and arms export issues. Similar to relations with the US and France, intensive training relations are also maintained with Great Britain, both on British and on German soil. Despite reductions, British troops continue to be stationed in Germany as a token of the bond between the two countries.

As compared to Germany's above-mentioned three Alliance partners, the *Russian Federation* as a non-NATO member is a special partner with regard to German defence and politico-military involvement. Russia is a nuclear power, a permanent member of the UN Security Council, a significant economic power, and one of the most important powers in the world both by its own account and as seen by others. Besides, it is located in relative geographic proximity to Germany. These factors alone make dialogue with Moscow one of the most important tasks of German and Euro-Atlantic politics – additionally, there are differences on to how to shape democracy, the position of the armed forces in society, and geopolitical questions touching on influence and formative power. As a bilateral instrument under the lead responsibility of the Federal Foreign Office, the *High Level Working Group on Security* deals with issues in the fields of strategic questions, weapons of mass destruction, and terrorism and organised crime. In association with the Federal Ministry of Defence, the *Stiftung Wissenschaft und Politik* (German Institute for International and Security Affairs) organises a series of seminars entitled 'Armed Forces and Democracy' that has served as a forum for dialogue between German and Russian generals since 1993. In 2011, Letters of Intent and Technical Arrangements on intensifying cooperation in different fields, such as medical service, military police matters, recruitment of new personnel, and training, were signed. In addition, establishment of a German liaison element to the Russian armed forces is planned. There are also plans for bilateral army staff talks. Training relations are maintained in the field of general staff/admiral staff officer training. Further areas of cooperation include arms control, *Innere Führung,* personnel management, logistics and military history.

Beyond the largely institutionalised bilateral contacts mentioned in the paragraphs above, another politico-military instrument at the disposal of the Federal Ministry of Defence is its currently 65 military attachés, some of whom are also accredited to other countries. They are important for maintaining regular politico-military relations between Germany and other countries. At state secretary level, the Federal Ministry of Defence has established regular dialogues with individual countries of particular politico-military interest. Further forums of dialogue exist, involving more than forty countries in staff talks at the level of Defence Policy Directors. The goal is to exchange security assessments on a permanent basis, identify common interests, as well as review and foster cooperation activities.

Summary

Since the Federal Republic of Germany was founded, German defence and military policy has followed the lines of the general security situation. Until around 1990, it was geared to meet the needs of national and Alliance defence; ever since, it has increasingly been aimed at creating the military preconditions for the Bundeswehr to deploy worldwide. At the same time, Germany's military policy has external effects on the armed forces of other, non-allied countries. Such influence is designed to draw these countries closer to the political values represented by the Federal Republic of Germany, thus contributing to conflict prevention.

In line with the tradition practised in the field of security policy over the past sixty-odd years, German defence and military policy has been subject to close coordination with key allies and treaty organisations, above all NATO, the EU and the UN. On the one hand, this is necessary to enable the Bundeswehr, which is almost exclusively employed in an Alliance context, to fulfil multilateral tasks. On the other hand, this gives Germany the opportunity to exert a certain influence on Allied countries. Certainly, coordination with partners is a complicated process – it is, however, the only option.

All in all, Germany's defence and military policy over the past decades can undoubtedly be considered a success. The Bundeswehr has adapted to new risks and threat scenarios and now has a capability profile that, while requiring continuous improvement, provides adequate and militarily backed crisis and conflict management, shoulder-to-shoulder with Germany's partners. This, however, is a key prerequisite for preserving the security of the Federal Republic of Germany and its people.

Bibliography

Algieri, Franco (2010): Die Gemeinsame Außen- und Sicherheitspolitik der EU. Vienna: UTB.

Böckenförde, Stephan/Gareis, Sven Bernhard (Eds.) (2009): Deutsche Sicherheitspolitik. Herausforderungen, Akteure und Prozesse. Opladen/Farmington Hills: Budrich.

Bono, Giovanna (2006): The impact of 11 September 2001 and the 'War on Terror' on European Foreign and Security Policy. Key issues and debates. In: (same author) (ed..) (2006): 13-36.

Bono, Giovanna (Eds.) (2006): The impact of 9/11 on European Foreign and Security Policy. Brussels: VUB Press.

Braml, Josef (Eds.) (2010): Einsatz für den Frieden. Sicherheit und Entwicklung in Räumen begrenzter Staatlichkeit. Munich: Oldenbourg.

BMVg (2006): White Paper 2006 on German Security Policy and the Future of the Bundeswehr (Weißbuch 2006 zur Sicherheitspolitik Deutschlands und zur Zukunft der Bundeswehr). www.bmvg.de.BMVg.

BMVg (2011): Defence Policy Guidelines (Verteidigungspolitische Richtlinien. Nationale Interessen wahren – Internationale Verantwortung übernehmen – Sicherheit gemeinsam gestalten). Berlin, http://www.bmvg.de/ , accessed on 08.02.2012.

Deutsche Bundesregierung (2004): Aktionsplan "Zivile Krisenprävention, Konfliktlösung und Friedenskonsolidierung". Berlin. 12 May 2004.

Deutsche Bundesregierung (2006): Sicherheit und Stabilität durch Krisenprävention gemeinsam stärken. 1. Bericht der Bundesregierung über die Umsetzung des Aktionsplans 'Zivile Krisenprävention, Konfliktlösung und Friedenskonsolidierung', covering the reporting period from May 2004 - April 2006. Berlin. 23 May 2006.

Daigeler, Fabienne (2005): Parlamentarische Kontrollrechte beim Abschluss völkerrechtlicher Verträge am Beispiel der Neubestimmung der Aufgaben der NATO und der Entwicklungen im Rahmen der OSZE. Hamburg: Kovač.

EU (Eds.) (2007): Vertrag von Lissabon zur Änderung des Vertrags über die Europäische Union und des Vertrags zur Gründung der Europäischen Gemeinschaft, signed on 13 December 2007 in Lisbon. In: Official Journal of the European Union. German edition, 50: C 306, 1–230.

Gareis, Sven Bernhard (2006): Deutschlands Außen- und Sicherheitspolitik. Eine Einführung. Opladen/Farmington Hills: Budrich.

Hartmann, Rüdiger/Heydrich, Wolfgang/Meyer-Landrut, Nikolaus (1994): Der Vertrag über Konventionelle Streitkräfte in Europa: Vertragswerk, Verhandlungsgeschichte, Kommentar, Dokumentation. Baden-Baden: Nomos.

Hauser, Gunther (2010): Europas Sicherheit und Verteidigung. Der zivil-militärische Ansatz. Frankfurt: Lang.

Heidenkamp, Henrik (2010): Der Entwicklungsprozess der Bundeswehr zu Beginn des 21. Jahrhunderts. Wandel im Spannungsfeld globaler, nationaler und bündnispolitischer Spannungsfaktoren [also: Diss. Hamburg, Universität der Bundeswehr, 2010]. Frankfurt am Main: Peter Lang.

Hüfner, Klaus (2005): Die Finanzierung des VN-Systems. 1971-2003/2005. DGVN-Texte 53. Bonn: UNO-Verlag.

Hulin, Rüdiger (Eds.) (2005): 50 Jahre Bundeswehr. Bonn: German Defense Mirror.

Kolanoski, Martina (2010): Die Entsendung der Bundeswehr ins Ausland. Zur Funktion des Parlamentsvorbehalts im Kontext bündnispolitischer Verpflichtungen. Potsdam: Universitätsverlag.

Krause, Dan (2010): Die EU. Auf dem Weg zu einer Sicherheits- und Verteidigungsunion? Integrationstheoretische Analyse ausgewählter GSVP-Strukturen. Hamburg: Diplomica.

Legendre, Thierry (2011): Military Change. Discord or Harmony? In: DIIS Report 2011 2, 137-142.

Loth, Wilfried (1996): Der Weg nach Europa. Geschichte der europäischen Integration 1939 – 1957. 3rd edition. Göttingen: Vandenhoek & Ruprecht.

Majchrzak, Katharina (2010): Die Krisenkapazität der Europäischen Union im Kontext der Petersberger Aufgaben. Unter besonderer Berücksichtigung der Kampfeinsätze bei der Krisenbewältigung einschließlich friedensschaffender Maßnahmen. Berlin: Lit.

Meier, Christoph/Rossmanith, Richard/Schäfer, Heinz-Uwe (2003): Wörterbuch zur Sicherheitspolitik. Deutschland in einem veränderten internationalen Umfeld. Hamburg: Mittler und Sohn.

Meiers, Franz-Josef (2006): Zu neuen Ufern? Die deutsche Sicherheits- und Verteidigungspolitik in einer Welt des Wandels 1990 – 2000. Paderborn: Schöningh.

Ministry for Foreign Affairs (Eds.) (1994): The Challenge of Preventive Diplomacy. The experience of the CSCE. Stockholm: Ministry for Foreign Affairs.

NATO (Eds.) (2006): NATO Handbook. Brussels: NATO Public Diplomacy Division.

Nägler, Franz (Eds.) (2007): Die Bundeswehr 1955-2005. Rückblenden, Einsichten, Perspektiven. Munich: Oldenbourg.

Naumann, Klaus (2007): Der Wandel des Einsatzes von der Katastrophenhilfe und NATO-Manöver zur Anwendung von Waffengewalt und Friedenserzwingung. In: Nägler (Eds.) 2007, 477-494.

OECD (2007): OECD DAC Handbook on Security System Reform (SSR). Supporting Security and Justice. Paris: OECD.

Pleuger, Günther (2005): Bundeswehr und Vereinte Nationen. In: Hulin (2005), 6-9.

Rödder, Andreas (2004): Die Bundesrepublik Deutschland 1969-1990. Munich: Oldenbourg.

Schöndorf, Elisabeth (2011): Die Entsendelücke im VN-Peacekeeping. Defizite, Ursachen, Handlungsoptionen. SWP-Studie 4/2011. Berlin: Stiftung Wissenschaft und Politik.

Theiler, Olaf (2009): Deutschland und die NATO. In: Böckenförde/Gareis (Eds.) (2009): 287-328.

Thoß, Bruno (2006): NATO-Strategie und nationale Verteidigungsplanung. Planung und Aufbau der Bundeswehr unter den Bedingungen der massiven atomaren Vergeltungsstrategie 1952-1960. Munich: Oldenbourg.

Tull, Dennis (2010): Die Peacekeeping-Krise der Vereinten Nationen – Ein Überblick über die Debatte. In: SWP-Studie 1/2010. Berlin: Stiftung Wissenschaft und Politik.

Ugglas, Margaretha af (1994): Conditions for Successful Preventive Diplomacy. In: Ministry for Foreign Affairs (Eds.) (1994), 11-32.

Varwick, Johannes (2008): Die NATO. Vom Verteidigungsbündnis zur Weltpolizei. Munich: Beck.

Wiggershaus, Norbert (2000): Zur Konzeption einer NATO-Geschichte. In: Wiggershaus/Heinemann (Eds.) (2000): IX-XVIII.

Wiggershaus, Norbert/Heinemann, Winfried (Eds.) (2000): Nationale Außen- und Bündnispolitik der NATO-Mitgliedstaaten. Munich: Oldenbourg.

Zellner, Wolfgang (2010): Die Leistungsbilanz von OSZE-Missionen. In: Braml (Eds.) (2010), 310–318.

Zentrum für Internationale Friedenseinsätze (2010): Glossar Friedenseinsätze. Berlin: ZIF.

Part II

Inside German defence

The Federal Ministry of Defence

Christoph Reifferscheid, Ulf Bednarz

Background

'The Minister calls the shots' (Spiegel, 1978). This phrase was coined by Hans Apel, the Federal Minister of Defence at that time, in connection with the early retirement of the then *Generalinspekteur*, General Harald Wust. In his letter of resignation, General Wust had, among other things, raised the question as to what position the Chief of Staff of the Bundeswehr was to take in the hierarchy of the Federal Ministry of Defence and who was to deputise for the Minister as the Commander-in-Chief of the Armed Forces. He wrote to Minister Apel: 'I do not question the primacy of politics. However, the Federal Minister will have to consider what part he wishes military leaders to play in the context of overall responsibility' (Spiegel, 1992). He thus reiterated a call that has already been made by the authors of the 'Himmerod Memorandum', among them Lieutenant-General Adolf Heusinger and Major Wolf von Baudissin, before the establishment of the Bundeswehr. Their ideas in 1950 for the rearmament of the Federal Republic of Germany – still a fledgling state at the time – which had been commissioned by the then Federal Chancellor, Konrad Adenauer, included the assignment of the administrative control of the Armed Forces to the 'Chief of Staff of the German Contingent' or 'Chief of the Defence Agency', who was to report to the Federal President as the Commander-in-Chief of the Armed Forces.

Initially, when the director of the Armed Forces Directorate of the then Federal Ministry *for* Defence – the so-called 'Blank Office' (*Amt Blank*) had been renamed the Federal Ministry for Defence on 7 June 1955 and subsequently, the Federal Ministry *of* Defence on 30 December 1961 – was given the official title of *Generalinspekteur*, or Chief of Staff, Bundeswehr, on 1 June 1957, the call for concentrated administrative control of the Armed Forces to be exercised by a 'supreme soldier' remained unanswered. At that time, he, the *Generalinspekteur*, was on the same level as the service chiefs of staff and was 'merely' the *primus inter pares*.

Although, with the establishment of the three ministerial directorates-general (Military Affairs, Armament Affairs and Administrative Affairs) in 1965, he was raised to the position of Director General, the service chiefs of staff were still not under his administrative control. Even after a bill was drafted in 1965 or 1966, in which Article 11 provided for the assignment of administrative powers to the Chief of Staff of the Bundeswehr in respect of territorial defence, and submitted to the other Ministries for consideration, no further action was taken (Mann, 1971: 71).

In 1966, the then *Generalinspekteur*, General Heinz Trettner, demanded that he be granted the same status as the civilian state secretary and be authorised to deputise for the Minister as the Commander-in-Chief of the Armed Forces. But he was not able to get his demands met either. In August of the same year, his successor, General Ulrich de Maizière, reiterated the demand that the *Generalinspekteur* should exercise administrative control over the Armed Forces. This time, the then Federal Minister of Defence, Kai-Uwe von Hassel, was in favour of agreeing to this demand. Von Hassel announced a 'realignment of the position of the *Generalinspekteur*'. The ministerial directive of 4 November 1966 established that the State Secretary will deputise for the Minister in his political function, the directors-general with regard to day-to-day management duties within their respective areas of responsibility, and otherwise, fundamentally, the *Generalinspekteur*, as the 'most senior director general'.

This resulted in the *Generalinspekteur*, as the 'most senior director-general' below the Minister and the state secretary, now being elevated to the third level of the ministerial hierarchy. At the same time, his 'political status was raised' as he was granted direct access to the Federal Minister of Defence (Molt 2007: 616). However, von Hassel's actual intention, i.e. to have administrative control of the Armed Forces assigned to the *Generalinspekteur*, failed because of the resignation of the then Federal Chancellor, Ludwig Erhard, on 1 December 1966 and the related reshuffling of the Federal Government.

In 1969, the *Generalinspekteur*, General Ulrich de Maizière, requested that the then Federal Minister of Defence, Gerhard Schröder, and later also his successor, Helmut Schmidt, upgrade his post to 'Chief of the General Staff of the Armed Forces' and demanded that he be given direct access to the Federal Chancellor – but it was all to no avail. While the then Federal Minister of Defence, Gerhard Schröder, was still in office, the FDP Parliamentary Group submitted a bill on 17 June 1968 which, as a constitutional amendment, was aimed at implementing an organisational arrangement governing the top-level management of all the areas (civil and military) of national defence. As far as the Federal Ministry of Defence was concerned, this bill above all provided for the command authority of the *Generalinspekteur* over the Armed Forces (Mann, 1971: 72). This bill also failed.

The first time the powers of the *Generalinspekteur* and the service chiefs of staff were precisely defined was by the then Federal Minister of Defence, Helmut Schmidt, in the 'Blankenese Directive' on the 'reorganisation of the military part of the Federal Ministry of Defence' of 21 March 1970. Again, no administrative powers were assigned to the *Generalinspekteur*, but he was confirmed as having overall responsibility for Bundeswehr planning.

Later, Schmidt wrote:

> 'In my Blankenese Directive, command of the three services, the Army, the Air Force and the Navy, was expressly not assigned to the *Generalinspekteur*, but to the Minister. The idea behind this was to rule out the possibility of a soldier ever again gaining the same degree of command authority as General von Seeckt in the days of the Reichswehr' (Schmidt, 1996: 477).

The military side or, to be more precise, the military personnel, did not achieve their aim of having administrative control of the Armed Forces assigned to the *Generalinspekteur* in the years to come either. At first glance, the distinction between military and civilian personnel seems misleading. On closer consideration, however, it is not without relevance. Section 1, Subsection 3 of the Legal Status of Military Personnel Act contains rule-making powers which allow command authority to be transferred from military to non-military personnel. This is why Section 1, Subsection 2 of the Military Penal Code expressly extends the area of application of the code to superiors of military personnel who are not themselves military personnel. The regulating authority has not (yet) made use of these powers. Hence, the Military Penal Code could at present only apply to two civilian office bearers, as superiors of military personnel without having military status themselves (non-military personnel): the Federal Minister of Defence as the Commander-in-Chief of the Armed Forces and his State Secretary, who acts as his 'alter ego' (see Hucul published in Walz, 2006: Section 1, Marginal Note 63).

The so-called 'Berlin Directive' ('Principles governing the Assignment of Tasks, Organisation and Procedures within the Top-Level Military Structure') of 21 January 2005 issued by the then Federal Minister of Defence, Dr Peter Struck, among other things assigned the *Generalinspekteur* an 'authority to issue directives to the commanders responsible for Bundeswehr operations and relief operations in response to natural disasters and emergencies. Although this further strengthened the status of the *Generalinspekteur*, it again failed to take the decisive step of assigning administrative control of the Armed Forces to him.

With the 'Dresden Directive' of 21 March 2012 ('Principles governing the Top-Level Structure, Chains of Command and the Command Organisation of the Federal Ministry of Defence and the Bundeswehr), Dr Thomas de Maizière, the current Federal Minister of Defence and son of General Ulrich de Maizière, who 46 years ago called for the administrative control of the Armed Forces to be assigned to the *Generalinspekteur*, is the first Federal Minister of Defence to assert his will politically and to stipulate that the Armed Forces are 'under the full administrative control of the *Generalinspekteur*'. This decision, the decades it has ultimately taken to come about, and the political, legal and organisational consequences arising from it will result in a truly 'new' Federal Ministry of Defence. One that, for the first time, has not only been 'slimmed down' in organisational terms, but whose organisational structures, processes and, above all, elementary concept of command and control have undergone a complete reorientation.

Anyone who today still believes that the provisions of the Dresden Directive entail 'no groundbreaking reorganisation of the competencies in the military-ministerial domain' and that it is only a case of promoting the 'personal profile' of the person responsible (Krauss, 2012) has perhaps failed to understand the implications, effects and also the historical importance of these policy decisions.

The Minister and the Ministry

'The Minister calls the shots.' – This phrase is not only the reaction of a former Federal Minister of Defence during a leadership crisis. It is also the most concise summary of the quintessence of our constitution as far as the Federal Minister of Defence, his status and his functions are concerned. It is furthermore the quintessence of what is about the only thing which will not, cannot and indeed should not change within the scope of the current reorientation of the Federal Minister of Defence and the Bundeswehr.

The Federal Minister of Defence

In accordance with Article 62 of Germany's Basic Law, the *Grundgesetz*, the Federal Minister of Defence is part of the Federal Government and hence, as such, the head of one of the five constitutional bodies. As the constitutionally legitimated head of his department, he conducts the affairs of his department independently and on his own responsibility within the scope of the general guidelines on policy defined by the Federal Chancellor in accordance with Article 65 of the Basic Law. This independence and personal responsibility fundamentally guarantee him the power to make fact-based decisions on all matters concerning his department. Neither the Federal Chancellor nor the Federal Cabinet can 'tell him what to do' with regard to these matters. However, the responsibility of the other members of the government must be observed. In accordance with Article 65, Sentence 3 of the Basic Law, the Federal Government shall resolve differences of opinion between Federal Ministers (see Oldiges, published in Sachs, 2001: Article 65 Marginal Note 21 et seq.).

Article 65a of the Basic Law expressly stipulates that the Federal Minister of Defence shall be vested with an executive function, thus giving him, as Minister, the power of command over the Armed Forces. However, in the case of a state of defence being declared (Article 115a of the *Basic Law* stipulates that the Bundestag is responsible for determining that such a state exists and the consent of the Bundesrat is required), the power of command over the Armed Forces shall pass to the Federal Chancellor in accordance with Article 115b of the Basic Law.

As the Commander-in-Chief of the Armed Forces, he is thus also the supreme administrative superior of all the military personnel in the Armed Forces and, as such, deals with all related executive tasks. However, he is precluded from holding military status. Article 66 of the Basic Law stipulates that Federal Ministers may not hold any other salaried office, thus making military status incompatible with ministerial office (see Oldiges, published in Sachs, 2001: Article 66, Marginal Note 10; Brockmeyer, published in Schmidt-Bleibtreu et al 2010: Article 66, Marginal Note 10). Conversely, this means that a soldier cannot – at least not without a constitutional amendment – become the Commander-in-Chief of the Armed Forces in the sense of being their 'exclusive top manager'.

Section 11, Subsection 1 of the Legal Status of Military Personnel Act stipulates that all military personnel are obliged to obey the Federal Minister of Defence. Violations of this duty to pay obedience may lead to disciplinary action being taken or to sanctions being imposed under military penal law.

Section 14, Subsection 1 of the Federal Government Rules of Procedure stipulates that within the Federal Government, another Federal Minister deputises for the Federal Minister of Defence. It is the currently the Federal Minister for Foreign Affairs who does so. Section 6 of the Joint Rules of Procedure of the Federal Ministries stipulates that within the Federal Ministry of Defence, a permanent state secretary deputises for the Federal Minister of Defence in his area of responsibility. This state secretary assumes the constitutional position of the Federal Minister of Defence, taking on responsibility for all associated duties, and also has the power of command over the Armed Forces (Oldiges, published in Sachs, 2011: Article 65a, Marginal Note 21; Brockmeyer, published in Schmidt-Bleibtreu et. al. 2010: Article 65a, Marginal Note 12; for more information on what was originally a very controversial debate on this topic, see also Spiegel, 1960).

This makes the command structure of the German Armed Forces very different to that of Allied nations, where power of command over the armed forces is usually vested in the head of state and not in the defence minister. In the United States of America, for example, the power of command over the armed forces is vested in the US President, in France, in the State President, in the UK, in the monarch, and in the Netherlands, in the government.

The Federal Ministry of Defence

Like every other Federal ministry, the Federal Ministry of Defence is a superior authority and is in a narrower sense at the interface between the government and the executive in the Federal Administration's structure. The Federal Ministry of Defence is not therefore part of the Bundeswehr in organisational terms and – contrary to what is often wrongly assumed –, is not a (supreme) military command. The separation of the Bundeswehr from the Ministry is only possible at a strictly *organisational* level. The very fact that the Ministry exercises management and command responsibility over the subordinate agencies makes the all-encompassing theory that the Ministry and the Bundeswehr should be regarded as separate entities appear absurd. In functional terms, they ultimately form a unit within the defence portfolio.

Section 3 of the Joint Rules of Procedure of the Federal Ministries stipulates that the Federal Ministries, including the Federal Ministry of Defence, perform duties that facilitate the exercise or support of government functions. These particularly include the strategic shaping and coordination of policies, the realisation of political objectives, priorities and programmes, international cooperation, involvement in the law-making procedure and the exercise of management and supervisory functions vis-à-vis subordinate agencies. The functional supervision of the Federal Administration is one of the key elements of the management and supervision of the Federal administration.

The Organisational Structure

Section 6 of the Joint Rules of Procedure of the Federal Ministries stipulates that the Federal Minister of Defence, together with the permanent and parliamentary state secretaries, form the executive group of the Ministry. This provision is now supplemented by the provision in Section 4.6, Subsection 1 of the 'Supplementary Rules of Procedure of the Federal Ministry of Defence', which came into effect on a provisional basis on 1 April 2012. It stipulates that the *Generalinspekteur* 'as the military advisor to the German government and as the highest military representative of the Bundeswehr, is a member of the executive group of the Federal Ministry of Defence'. At this point, it must be made explicitly clear that this does not mean that the *Generalinspekteur* assumes the status of a state secretary. He is not equal in status to a state secretary – not even de facto. The final provision of Section 6 of the Joint Rules of Procedure of the Federal Ministries is not breached by the revised version of the (explicitly only 'supplementary') Rules of Procedure of the Federal Ministry of Defence. In his speech on 18 May 2011, the Federal Minister of Defence, Dr Thomas de Maizière, explained the new status of the *Generalinspekteur*:

> In future, he [the *Generalinspekteur*] will also be the administrative superior of all the military personnel in the Bundeswehr. Nevertheless, he will continue to be subordinate to a state secretary, which I believe is a mandatory consequence of the primacy of politics.

In his speech on the occasion of the presentation of the 'Dresden Directive' on 21 March 2012, he went on to say:

> 'The *Generalinspekteur* is a member of the executive group of the Federal Ministry of Defence. He is not the deputy of the Federal Minister of Defence. He cannot be. A civilian must be. This follows from the primacy of politics.'

When established in 1955, the Federal Ministry of Defence had the following directorates below the executive group (Mann, 1971: 64):

□ Directorate I	Administration
□ Directorate II	Budget
□ Directorate III	Personnel
□ Directorate IV	Armed Forces
□ Directorate V	Army
□ Directorate VI	Air Force
□ Directorate VII	Navy
□ Directorate VIII	Legal Affairs
□ Directorate IX	Accommodation and Real Estate
□ Directorate X	Defence Industry and Technology
□ Directorate XI	Procurement (Directorate Branch Office, Koblenz)

The first major reorganisation took place only two years later, on 1 June 1957, with the military directorates being converted into the Bundeswehr, Army, Air and Naval Staffs. In order to take account of the special importance of the Medical Service, the Office of the Surgeon General, Bundeswehr, was established within the organisation at the same time. From this point on, the ministerial directorate structure was as follows (Mann, 1971: 66 et seq.):

- Administration and Legal Affairs
- Accommodation and Real Estate
- Budget
- Personnel
- Defence Industry
- Technology
- Bundeswehr Staff
- Army Staff
- Air Staff
- Naval Staff
- Office of the Surgeon General, Bundeswehr

Although the directorate structure was modified on various occasions over the years, it remained essentially unchanged for decades until 2012. Organisational measures mostly came in the form of ministerial organisational elements being merged or separated or the total number of posts being reduced. The total number of posts, for example, has continually declined since its peak in 1974 (5,426 posts).

This was not due to a lack of willingness to organise, but usually due to the structures of the Armed Forces and the Federal Defence Administration that had evolved over the years, and to the demands that the Armed Forces and the Federal Defence Administration had to meet.

Together, the Armed Forces and the Federal Defence Administration – these are separate under constitutional law as laid down in Articles 87a and 87b of the Basic Law – form the two organisational pillars on which the Bundeswehr rests. These, in turn, essentially rest on obedience to orders (Armed Forces) and on compliance with directives (Federal Defence Administration). This is why the Bundeswehr has always required a strict, top-down hierarchy that starts off with the Ministry, the highest authority. It should be mentioned at this point that the term 'Bundeswehr' is not synonymous with 'armed forces', even though the two terms are mostly used interchangeably in everyday language. To put it simply, the Armed Forces are the military component of the Bundeswehr and the Federal Defence Administration is the civilian component. The 'Military Legal System' and 'Chaplaincy Service' are two other organisational elements of the Bundeswehr, but they are not considered in detail in this article for reasons of simplicity.

So, the structure of the Bundeswehr has in the past also had a significant influence on the Ministry's directorate structure. Organisational changes in the Bundeswehr resulted in the need to make adaptations in the Ministry, which up to then had never been the actual starting point of a reform or reorientation process.

In addition to the separation of the Armed Forces and the Federal Defence Administration established by the Basic Law, these two components were in turn subdivided into military and civilian organisational elements. Sticking with the metaphor, other pillars were built within the existing pillars. Over time, the individual organisational elements or 'pillars' developed a strong tendency to drift apart in an organizational sense and pursue their own interests.

This was not a consequence of a 'hunger for power' or 'envy' on the part of certain individuals, but was often quite simply a matter of fact that resulted from the integration of the people concerned in the respective structures and hierarchies. Communication, in particular, mostly took place in vertical and parallel (command) structures, which led to an inadequate flow of information between the often separate elements. This meant that the attention of staff was almost inevitably focused consistently on their own element, with prevailing interests being pursued in each of these elements.

The Armed Forces and the Federal Defence Administration were often only united in the 'Bundeswehr corporation' in the Ministry, in the person of the Federal Minister of Defence as Commander-in-Chief of the Armed Forces and head of department, or in the persons of the state secretaries, who acted as his 'alter egos'.

The purpose of the current reorientation of the Bundeswehr is to maintain the features that have proven their worth and to harmonise aspects which seem impossible to harmonise, while linking these features with those that have been tried and proven. It appears obvious that this will primarily only be possible by changing the thinking of the people involved. A modified organisational structure of the Ministry can (and must) 'only' create the basic conditions for a reorientation. By no means can it be the (final) outcome. The reorientation of the Bundeswehr and the Ministry requires a change in thinking. What is needed is a school of thought in which parallel structures are abandoned and joint performance of work on the basis of shared responsibility is enabled and consistently demanded.

The Federal Ministry of Defence provides a new starting point for this, its present organisational structure is essentially as follows:

Figure 1: FMOD Organisational Structure; as of 1 April 2012

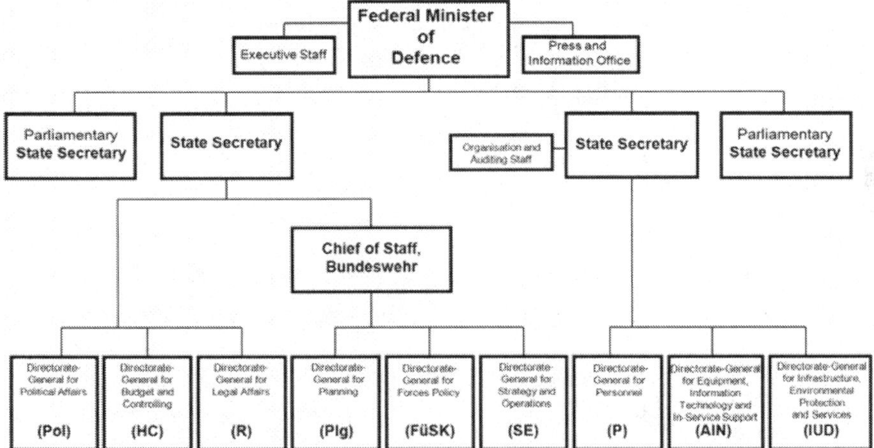

Source: FMOD, authors' diagram

The previous 'Modernisation' Directorate and the service staffs (Army Staff, Air Staff, Naval Staff, Medical Service Staff and Joint Support Service Staff) have been disbanded, as have been the Policy Planning and Central Controlling Staffs. There are now 'only' nine directorates-general below the executive group. The disbandment of the service staffs has led to the complete reassignment of (core) ministerial tasks, thus inevitably putting an end to the 'classic' division of the Ministry into a civilian component (directorates) and a military component (service staffs).

Of course, there are still directors with civilian status and directors with military status today, as in the past. This situation is not intended to change. On the contrary, the structure of the directorates-general now in place was chosen because it allows the option of appointing either a civilian or an officer as a director in the future. There are no longer any 'civilian directorates' and 'military divisions', only directorates-general that are (currently) headed by a civilian or an officer, depending on the status of their director-general. This meticulous use of language is not petty hair-splitting, but reflects the issue that had to be succinctly addressed as part of the reorientation process – the urgently required and fundamental change in the Ministry's organisational structure to finally open the door to full cooperation between military personnel and civil servants/civilian employees for the benefit of the entire Bundeswehr. It will be possible in the future to be flexible with regard to status and to appoint directors in accordance with the respective requirements. Anyone whose reaction to this idea in connection with a specific directorate-general – for example, the Directorate-General for Forces Policy or the Directorate-General for Infrastructure, Environmental Protection and Services – is to say '*never*' or '*nonsense*' – should simply ask themselves: Why not?

The Ministry is neither part of the Armed Forces nor part of the Federal Defence Administration and, simply by the wording of Articles 87a and 87b of the Basic Law, is thus not directly bound by the imperative to keep the Armed Forces and the Federal Defence Administration apart. Accordingly, the Directorate-General for Equipment, Information Technology and In-Service Support or the Directorate-General for Infrastructure, Environmental Protection and Services, elements that assist in the steering of Federal Defence Administration activities by the Ministry, could be headed by an officer of the rank of lieutenant general, as is already the case today with the Directorate-General for Personnel.

Given that the disbandment of the service staffs and the assignment of administrative control over the Armed Forces to the *Generalinspekteur* mean that administrative control over the (single) services is not exercised by a ministerial director, the Directorate-General for Planning, the Directorate-General for Forces Policy and the Directorate-General for Strategy and Operations, which are assigned to the *Generalinspekteur* and currently headed by officers, could now in turn be headed by a civil servant (*Ministerialdirektor*) or a civilian employee. In the main, concerns about this type of staffing arise from nothing more than a '*but we have never had this before*' attitude and are of little value.

This is illustrated by the following example: The Director-General for Forces Policy is a lieutenant general. When he retires, it would be perfectly possible for him, in compliance with labour law regulations, to take up a job as a civilian and be appointed Director-General for Forces Policy. Would the sceptics who claim that a civilian could never head the Directorate-General for Forces Policy 'simply because of his/her lack of military expertise' be right in this instance, too? By no means, as the change of status described in our example cannot be seriously expected to affect the expertise of the person concerned in such a way that what was originally 'military expertise' will be now become 'civilian expertise'. Status has absolutely no bearing on expertise, and never will. You either have it or (unfortunately) you don't.

To guard against the allegation that such an example is merely theoretical and at best 'irrelevant', I would at this point like to just briefly refer to the career of Lieutenant General (Rtd.) Jörg Schönbohm. Jörg Schönbohm is a German Christian Democratic Union (CDU) politician and a retired Bundeswehr lieutenant general. After barely five months in the office of Chief of Staff, Army (27 September 1991 to 18 February 1992), he retired and was appointed Permanent State Secretary for Security Policy, Bundeswehr Planning and Armament. He became Senator of the Interior of Berlin in 1996.

Thus, the new organisational structure that promotes cooperation between the Ministry's civilian and military personnel has laid the foundation for general acceptance of the view that 'expertise determines careers, while status only determines career paths'. Expertise must be acquired by doing and working hard over the course of a career. It may be some time yet before the Ministry's civilian and military personnel are capable of taking on managerial tasks that were hitherto traditionally performed by members of the other status group. The fact is, however, that due to the Ministry's new organisational structure, there are basically no organisational barriers to keep this from happening up to the director-general level. It is up to the younger generation of civilian and military executive personnel to make use of the opportunities arising from this in healthy and fair competition.

The (specialized) tasks that have to be accomplished, which have been roughly outlined below according to the new structure of the Ministry's directorates-general, will generally continue to essentially determine the expertise required:[1]

The Directorate-General for Political Affairs

The Directorate-General for Political Affairs frames and coordinates security and defence policy in the area of responsibility of the Federal Ministry of Defence. It prepares strategic guidelines for ensuring the coherent shaping of this policy. Security and defence policy comprises military and armament policy as well as matters that are of socio-political significance for the Bundeswehr, but the task of shaping it remains the responsibility of the respective directorates. The Director-General for Political Affairs is also the Ministry's Political Director and, in this capacity, advises the executive group on all matters concerning security and defence policy. He deputises for the Ministry at departmental level, at international political meetings and in staff talks.

The strategic guidelines developed by the Directorate-General for Political Affairs serve the *Generalinspekteur* and the directors-general as a basis for determining their primary objectives and the priorities that have to be set to do detailed work on the policies for which they are responsible. The Directorate-

1 The following information basically corresponds to the content of the Guiding Principles for the Reorientation of the Federal Ministry of Defence, which were prepared as part of the project work undertaken at that time (FMOD Organisation project) and in consultation with the Ministerial Directors and approved by the Federal Minister of Defence on 4 October 2011.

General for Political Affairs is divided into two divisions – Pol I 'Security Policy' and Pol II 'Defence and Armament Policy' – and a total of ten branches. There are around 90 posts in the directorate-general's target structure. There has never been an organisational element comparable to this directorate in terms of structure and remit in the history of the Federal Ministry of Defence.

The Directorate-General for Budget and Controlling

The Directorate-General for Budget and Controlling plays a significant part in shaping the budgetary parameters within which plans are prepared for keeping the Bundeswehr running and evolving. The Directorate-General for Budget and Controlling is responsible for ensuring that the procedures for the annual budget (defence budget) are applied properly and it coordinates and steers the activities of the branches responsible for the management of funds in the other directorates-general of the Ministry. Its director-general is the Budget Officer as defined in the Federal Budget Code. He has special responsibility for the preparation of the documents required for financial planning and for the draft budget, for budget execution and for the provision of assistance in matters of financial importance. This directorate-general is not simply a product of the organisational consolidation of the former Budget Directorate and the former Office of the Executive Group Controller, which was essentially a 'mere' advisory element for the executive group.

Rather, its remit now also comprises developing and updating the central management accounting concept, participating in the development of a common, effects-based understanding of management or management models and, above all, exercising functional supervision over the Bundeswehr agencies responsible for this task area. This Directorate-General is divided into two divisions – HC I 'Budgeting Policy; Budget Preparation and Execution' and HC II 'Controlling and Financial Accounting; German SAI Affairs' – and a total of eleven branches. Altogether, there are around 100 posts in its target structure.

The Directorate-General for Legal Affairs

The Directorate-General for Legal Affairs has central responsibility for the legal fields that are directly related to the department's security and defence policy and to the Bundeswehr's specific (operational) tasks resulting from it as well as for those legal fields that are regularly of key significance to the Ministry's executive group because of their political relevance. These include the fields of international law, European law, public and constitutional law, parliamentary law, air law, the law of the sea and space law as well as the legal basis for Bundeswehr operations abroad. They also include human rights law, international contract law, international treaties, stationing agreements, the NATO Status of Forces Agreement and the Supplementary Agreement, criminal law, the law of criminal procedure and military disciplinary law.

In addition, the directorate-general has organisational responsibility for the Administration of Justice, a civilian organisational element. The Director-General for Legal Affairs is the highest legal adviser to the executive group on all ministerial legal matters. The Directorate-General for Legal Affairs is divided into two divisions – R I 'Legal Advice, Legislation, Litigation' and R II 'Administration of Justice, Security' – and has a total of 11 branches. There are also around 100 posts in this directorate-general's target structure.

The Directorate-General for Planning

The Directorate-General for Planning should not be confused with the former Policy Planning Staff. Like the Office of the Executive Group Controller, the Policy Planning Staff was a real staff and thus an advisory element for the executive group which had been established outside the line of management responsibility and which had no authority to make functional decisions or to issue (Bundeswehr) planning directives. In contrast, the new Directorate-General for Planning is a functional directorate-general. It is responsible for producing the conceptual basis for the future development of the Bundeswehr, its capability management and its resources and implementation. Its holistic approach covers all of the civilian and military sectors of the Bundeswehr, making planning an essential part of the development and implementation of an overall Bundeswehr concept.

The Directorate-General for Planning produces the conceptual basis for the Bundeswehr by building on the strategic guidelines developed by the Directorate-General for Political Affairs. It provides key impetus for the further development of the Bundeswehr, taking account both of the ideas put forward by all the major organisational elements and of interministerial and multinational approaches. It must be said that cooperation between the Bundeswehr and industry is a key factor in ensuring that the Bundeswehr can accomplish its tasks reliably and efficiently. Due to the task area for which it is responsible, the Directorate-General for Planning is divided into three divisions – Plg I 'Bundeswehr Future Development', Plg II 'Bundeswehr Capability Management' and Plg III 'Resources and Implementation' – and has a total of 26 branches. There are just over 150 posts in its target structure. The establishment of the Directorate-General for Planning has resulted in the creation of an organisational element of unprecedented importance and size for dealing with Bundeswehr planning, the responsibility for which has specifically been within the remit of the *Generalinspekteur* since the 1970s.

The Directorate-General for Forces Policy

The Director-General for Forces Policy is accountable to the *Generalinspekteur* for the establishment and maintenance of the operational readiness of the entire armed forces. The directorate is responsible for determining the personnel and materiel readiness requirements in the area of responsibility of the *Generalinspekteur* and for exercising ministerial-level control over the armed forces' organisational structures and procedures, up to and including the distribution and allocation of the resources that are available and required for ensuring the operational readiness of the armed forces.

It develops and prioritises the armed forces' requirements in all planning categories with the aim of ensuring their personnel and materiel readiness. To this end, the staff of the Directorate-General for Forces Policy are also tasked with drawing up the requirements that have to be met by the Directorate-General for Personnel, the Directorate-General for Equipment, IT & In-Service Support and the Directorate-General for Infrastructure, Environmental Protection and Services. In addition, they are responsible for assessing the technical aspects of the Medical Service and of the medical elements, in consultation with the highest technical superior in the Bundeswehr Joint Medical Service. The Directorate-General for Forces Policy works on shaping and further developing the concept of leadership development and civic education (Innere Führung) as a leadership strategy which contributes to the establishment of an identity, and implementing the leadership principle of 'mission-type command and control' across all levels. In addition, it has organisational responsibility for the Chaplaincy Service, a civilian organisational element. The Directorate-General for Forces Policy is divided into three divisions – FüSK I, 'Overall Readiness Status of the Armed Forces; Specialized Military Tasks; Military Organisation', FüSK II, 'Personnel Readiness; Leadership Development and Civic Education; Training; Health Care' and FüSK III 'Materiel Readiness, Logistics, Command Support' – and has a total of 18 branches. There are almost 200 posts in the directorate-general's target structure.

The Directorate-General for Strategy and Operations

The Directorate-General for Strategy and Operations assists the *Generalinspekteur* in his duties as

- the military adviser to the Federal Government,
- the highest military representative and representative of the Bundeswehr in the international bodies to which the chiefs of defence of allied or like-minded nations belong,
- the officer responsible for the detailed planning of military policy in accordance with the strategic guidelines issued and the defence policy positions es-

tablished in cooperation with the Directorate-General for Political Affairs, and

- the officer responsible for the planning, preparation, conduct and follow-up of Bundeswehr operations.

The directorate-general is responsible for shaping military policy and for developing and formulating the required military policy basics. This includes matters concerning the representation of German interests on international military bodies and the authority to issue directives and instructions to the German military representatives on the NATO and EU Military Committees.

The Directorate-General for Strategy and Operations assists the *Generalinspekteur* in his task of also working on the preparatory measures needed for the Federal Government to make decisions on the deployment of German armed forces abroad and for the German Bundestag to give its constitutive consent (Directorate-General for Political Affairs). It is responsible for directing Bundeswehr missions at the strategic level. In addition, the directorate develops the strategic directives and instructions issued to the Bundeswehr Joint Operations Command as well as the strategic plans, the operation-related rules of engagement, and the military proposals for decisions on cross-government concepts. The Directorate-General for Strategy and Operations provides the political community and parliament with information on 'Bundeswehr operations', an area that is within the remit of the *Generalinspekteur*.

This directorate's task area covers the early identification of crises, risk analyses and threat assessments, as well as the final assessment of the military intelligence situation at ministerial level, for which the *Generalinspekteur* has responsibility.

The Directorate-General for Strategy and Operations also has three divisions with which to perform these tasks – SE I 'Military Intelligence', SE II 'Military Policy and Operations' and SE III 'Support' –, and a total of 15 branches. There are around 160 posts in its target structure.

The Directorate-General for Personnel

The Director-General for Personnel bears full and chief responsibility for the personnel process throughout the Bundeswehr. This includes human resources management activities such as recruitment, personnel planning and personnel development, but also reserve personnel management, education throughout the Bundeswehr, civilian basic, advanced and follow-on training, personnel-related policy and legal matters, welfare, pay, pensions and benefits and accounting.

The Directorate-General deals with all matters that concern each and every individual employed by the Bundeswehr, and which are thus an important and determining factor for this country's security. It prepares and bears responsibility for the conceptual guidelines required for this.

To ensure that this far-reaching responsibility can be borne effectively and the attendant tasks performed properly, the civilian organisational element 'Personnel', which has to date belonged to the Federal Defence Administration, has been re-established within the Bundeswehr, with the agencies previously responsible for this task area being centralised in organisational terms for the first time. Now that the Federal Office of Languages, the Bundeswehr Universities and the Bundeswehr Education Management Centre have been assigned organisationally to the Federal Office of Bundeswehr Personnel Management, the remit of the Directorate-General goes beyond functional supervision and now for the first time includes responsibility for the organisational structures and procedures that the subordinate agencies need for the personnel process.

On the basis of the strategic guidelines developed by the Directorate-General for Political Affairs and in close coordination with the Directorate-General for Planning, the Directorate-General for Forces Policy and the Directorate-General for Budget and Controlling, the Directorate-General for Personnel is responsible for the Ministry's conceptual guidelines for ensuring the continuous adjustment of the entire body of Bundeswehr personnel so that this need can regularly be met within the career and status groups, in keeping with office, rank and seniority.

The Directorate-General for Personnel also ensures staff involvement in the personnel process through trustful cooperation with those responsible for representing their interests as well as with trade unions and professional associations. The same applies to continuing with the successful process of integrating severely disabled people under the personnel management scheme.

The Directorate-General for Personnel will continue to provide social services, the focus being on operation-related strains borne by Bundeswehr personnel.

The directorate-general is divided into three divisions – P I 'Management; Personnel Marketing; Education and Qualification', P II 'Personnel Development' and P III 'Social Affairs' – and at present still has a total of 22 branches. There are more than 200 posts in the target structure of the Directorate-General for Personnel.

The Directorate-General for Equipment, Information Technology and In-Service Support

The Directorate-General for Equipment, Information Technology and In-Service Support is responsible for the planning, management and supervision of all national and international armament activities with a view to the tasks of the Bundeswehr and the capability profile deriving from them. This also comprises responsibility (or, to use the military term, cognizance) for the operational maturity of all defence materiel, which lies with the Director-General for Equipment, Information Technology and In-Service Support. He is at the same time the National Armaments Director (NAD) and, as such, responsible for the detailed planning of armament policy in accordance with the strategic guidelines (Directorate-General for Political Affairs). He represents Germany's defence materiel and defence industry interests in international bodies. He exercises legal and functional supervision of the tasks performed by the directorate's subordinate agencies for the entire life-cycle management of all products (preparation of technical/economic proposals, project realisation based on agreements on objectives, materiel cognizance for operational maturity and disposal).

The Directorate-General for Equipment, Information Technology and In-Service Support bears full responsibility for the procurement and equipment management process and for IT strategy in the Bundeswehr. It is in charge of elaborating and further developing the relevant rules of procedure. The directorate-general is responsible for drawing up policy on procurement and contracting in the Bundeswehr. This directorate-general encompasses the functions of the IT Director (Chief Information Officer [CIO] or Consultation, Command and Control Principal [C3 Principal]) at national and international level. At national level, the IT Director acts as the departmental CIO and is responsible for representing the defence department's interests at the Chief Information Officers Council, which is presided over by the Federal Ministry of the Interior, for developing and updating an IT strategy for the department that is consistent with the guidelines of the Federal Government and for ensuring ministerial supervision in the areas of IT security, IT architecture, IT standards, IT projects and IT products. In addition, he represents Germany's IT interests in international bodies.

The Directorate-General for Equipment, Information Technology and In-Service Support develops and updates the strategy for procurement (including strategic purchasing).

In consultation with the Directorate-General for Planning, it monitors and harnesses all fields of science and engineering that are of relevance to defence applications and derives prognoses regarding the contributions that certain technologies can make to Bundeswehr capabilities or to filling capability gaps. It harnesses technologies by implementing appropriate defence research and technology (R&T) projects.

The Directorate-General for Equipment, Information Technology and In-Service Support is responsible for management tasks and for providing support to the FMOD in its capacity as a stakeholder in all Federal holdings.

The directorate-general is divided into five divisions:

- AIN I 'Central Tasks of Equipment, Information Technology and In-Service Support',
- AIN II 'Research and Technology; International Affairs',
- AIN III 'Modernisation, Corporate Holdings Affairs',
- AIN IV 'Information Technology; IT Director' and
- AIN V 'Equipment, In-Service Support',

thus taking account of the wide range of tasks in the remit of this directorate-general. These divisions have a total of 21 branches. There are more than 270 posts in the directorate-general's target structure.

The Directorate-General for Infrastructure, Environmental Protection and Services

The Directorate-General for Infrastructure, Environmental Protection and Services prepares and is in charge of the conceptual guidelines for all real estate affairs, being the responsibility for ministerial management in this sector at home and abroad and in the theatres of operation in which the Bundeswehr operates. The directorate-general is responsible for the ministerial management of infrastructure activities, in particular for the construction and operation of facilities, and for all services related to real estate for the armed forces and the Federal Defence Administration.

The executive group uses the Directorate-General for Infrastructure, Environmental Protection and Services to bring overall infrastructure planning into line with planning and budgetary possibilities and to represent the interests of the Bundeswehr as the building contractor and highest technical authority vis-à-vis the other ministries, in particular the Federal Ministry of Transport, Building and Urban Development, the Federal Ministry of Finance, the Institute for Federal Real Estate and the Länder construction authorities.

The directorate-general exercises the public law supervision within its remit for the Bundeswehr and the Allied forces stationed in Germany.The Directorate-General for Infrastructure, Environmental Protection and Services is also responsible for ministerial-level conceptual work on and management of tasks related to travel expenses, separation allowances and the reimbursement of relocation costs under a holistic travel management scheme. This regularly includes representing Bundeswehr interests in the legislative process.

In addition, it has central responsibility for all operational activities related to the running of the Ministry. These include the tasks performed by the Office of Internal Services, the tasks performed by the Information Technology Support Centre and the Staff Message Centre as well as interpretation services.

The Directorate-General for Infrastructure, Environmental Protection and Services is divided into three divisions – IUD I 'Infrastructure', IUD II 'Services, Statutory Protective Tasks' and IUD III 'FMOD Services' – and at present has a total of 17 branches. Because of the diversity of its tasks, also in the domain of Internal Services, which are essential for ensuring that the Ministry runs smoothly, there are nearly 500 posts in the target structure of the Directorate-General for Infrastructure, Environmental Protection and Services.

The organisational processes

The structure and task allocation scheme described above for the first time takes explicit account of the responsibilities and reporting channels of the respective directorates-general and of the working relations between them. The *Generalinspekteur* is clearly integrated, with no parallel structures whatsoever.

All ministerial decision-makers are thus brought together to form a (single) unit capable of planning and taking action, its focus being not only on the responsibilities of the Minister as a member of the Federal Government, as the head of the Ministry and as the Commander-in-Chief of the Armed Forces, but also on the mission and tasks of the Bundeswehr in their entirety. The fundamental changes in the organisational processes and in the ways work is done both at the Ministry and in the Bundeswehr, which have arisen as a result of the new organisational structure, serve to ensure that each responsibility remains within the area in which it is actually needed and is not as a rule be passed or pulled up the line of authority. The fact that parallel structures have been abandoned and a new principle of leadership has been implemented stands out when a comparison is made with the organisational concepts of the past. For example, the 'Organisational Concept for the Streamlining of the Federal Ministry of Defence' of 27 April 1994 expressly provided for the creation of duplicate structures in respect of the service staffs as part of the 'Target Structure 2000'. The concept specified that:

> 'The staffs of the Army, Air Force and Navy will have an identical basic structure, each comprising three divisions covering the following tasks:
> personnel, training and organisation,
> planning, logistics and armament and
> concepts, command and control and operational doctrine.'

Hence, as early as the planning stage for the Ministry's organisational structure under the 'Target Structure 2000' scheme, ministerial management was conceived from the outset as being distinctly separate for each individual service, based on the idea that, in the areas of personnel, organisation, equipment, etc., the Army (still) thinks in Army categories, the Air Force in Air Force categories and the Navy in Navy categories.

To be fair, it must be admitted that there were thoroughly consistent and logical reasons for creating an organisational structure characterised by such redundancies and that this was not at all due to a lack of flexibility in thinking. These reasons included the dual role of the service chiefs of staff, who were both ministerial division chiefs as well as military leaders of their organisational areas, thus also exercising disciplinary authority over the military personnel assigned to them. Hence, the service staffs were not only responsible for ministerial management, but also for exercise of the full administrative control of the Armed Forces. The 'Blankenese Directive' states that 'their (the service chiefs of staff) service staffs are both ministerial directorates and military commands'. This wording was later also largely adopted in the 'Berlin Directive'.

Just as there are similarities between military agencies such as brigades, divisions and operational commands, in the way their command structures are arranged within their organisational structure, the service staffs were also organised in a congruent way.

It is true that as ministerial directors, the service chiefs of staff were subject to the *Generalinspekteur*'s right to exercise executive authority in his capacity as a director-general and as their superior in the special area of responsibility, as laid down in Section 3 of the Ministerial Directive Governing Superior-Subordinate Relations. In terms of administrative control, however, they reported directly to the Federal Minister of Defence. The associated lack of clarity over the subordination of the service chiefs of staff made it difficult for the people responsible for organisation to fully comply with the related official interests and requirements and, at the same time, to avoid duplicate structures.

The need to think, plan and act in joint terms was identified at a relatively early stage (e.g. von Weizsäcker 2000: 48 et seq.). For a long time, however, the service chief of staffs' dual-hatted role and their related responsibilities made it impossible to abandon ministerial duplicate structures and prevented a 'joint approach" from being adopted to the extent that was really commensurate with its importance.

This was compounded by the duplicate structures in the former military staffs (particularly the then Armed Forces Staff) and civilian directorates, which resulted from the fact that even within the Ministry, tasks were regularly viewed in isolation, both by the requesting authorities and by the procurement authorities. This practice that made it necessary for numerous branches to be mirrored organisationally in the staffs and directorates.

The decision to take the service chiefs of staff out of the Ministry in organisational terms, thus putting an end to their dual role and, in this context, also to the isolated view of the requesting authorities and the procurement authorities, has for the first time truly paved the way to abandoning redundant structural models and working relations within the Ministry. The cornerstone decisions taken by the Minister on 18 May 2011 in the scope of the reorientation of the Bundeswehr finally made it possible to break up and ultimately effectively abandon such organisational networks, which seem disorganised when compared with the Ministry's structure today.

After decades in which the Bundeswehr's tasks have been performed separately or in isolation on a single-service basis or as Federal Defence Administration tasks, the way has now been successfully paved for the tasks to be performed on a Bundeswehr basis, by way of the principle of joint task accomplishment. Irrespective of the organisational structure, the ministerial coordination element now regards itself as an integral functional component of a 'Bundeswehr corporation'.

Establishment within the Ministry's organisational structure of the specialized fields of 'Policy' and 'Planning' as core tasks in the directorate-general structure, in particular, has marked a fundamental change in the Ministry's organisational processes and procedures. Due to the establishment of (political) objectives and specifications / priorities for planning, all of the directorates-general will be involved in the processes, via an integrated approach. It has become impossible for directorates-general to 'distance themselves' from one another by acting in isolation or exclusively in their own interests. There are no longer any redundant structures that would enable other decision-makers to be bypassed.

Processes will no longer proceed solely in a 'vertical direction' from the directorates-general to the respective subordinate elements. Objectives will be specified within the Ministry, but they will have been verified for legitimacy, affordability and feasibility as a matter of course beforehand. Resources will then be planned and the establishment of capabilities scheduled. If capability gaps are identified, solutions will be analysed and again verified for legitimacy, affordability and feasibility; an assessment must also be made of their predictability and, if necessary, the target system must be adapted.

This cycle, which is free of redundancies, ensures that the processes run 'horizontally' across the Ministry's directorate structure, without taking responsibility away from the subordinate agencies. As a result, entities' responsibilities are not reduced, and evasion of responsibility is curtailed.

'Problems must be solved at their source' (de Maizière, 2011). Now they are being solved at their source. They are not being pushed downwards or pushed or pulled upwards. It is not about 'clinging to all the reins', but rather a matter of placing them in responsible hands and still maintaining strategic control. Nor is it about power, distrust or increasing one's power. It is about cooperation, interaction and trust.

In this respect, it need hardly be emphasised that the disbandment of the service staffs as ministerial directorates, their organisational detachment from the Ministry and their establishment as subordinate agencies in no way constitute a 'downgrading' or 'disempowerment' of the service chiefs of staff (see Weiland, 2011; Handelsblatt, 2010). In this case, the term 'subordinate' merely refers to the executive's hierarchical structure, which is headed in each government department by a supreme Federal authority. The word 'subordinate' in no way refers to the standing, importance, responsibility or work done by the respective agencies.

Subordinate agencies will in the future take on far greater responsibilities, or retain their existing remit. These responsibilities will be extensive in nature and will become considerably more important in political terms because the sphere of responsibility of the Bundeswehr's top management is widening and this fact alone is making it necessary to adapt legislation.

Section 50 of the Legal Status of Military Personnel Act states that career officers of the rank of brigadier general and above can be temporarily suspended from active duty at any time. They are thus treated in the same way as so-called political civil servants, who must continuously conform to the fundamental political opinions and objectives of the government in the performance of their official duties (Section 31, Subsection 1, Sentence 1 of the Federal Civil Service Framework Act). Officers holding top-level posts in the Armed Forces thus require and deserve the trust of the Federal Government.

The top-level management of the Federal Defence Administration will in future be organised and held accountable along the same lines. Article 4 of the Act Accompanying the Reform of the Bundeswehr states that Section 54 of the Federal Civil Service Act will be modified so that after the act has entered into force, the Director of the Federal Office of Bundeswehr Personnel Management, the Director of the Federal Office of Bundeswehr Equipment, Information Technology and In-Service Support and the Director of the Federal Office of Bundeswehr Infrastructure, Environmental Protection and Services may be temporarily suspended from active duty at any time by the Federal President in the same way as a political civil servant. The act was passed by the German Bundestag on 14 June 2012 and approved by the German Bundesrat on 6 July 2012. Upon signature of the act by the Federal President and its publication in the Federal Law Gazette, the Armed Forces, the Federal Defence Administration and the Federal Ministry of Defence will at last enter into a real 'symbiosis of responsibility' by establishing a 'Bundeswehr corporation', consisting of three components, all of which are indispensable.

The service chiefs of staff and directors-general will honour their legal, political and actual responsibilities in the political and parliamentary arenas in coordination with the Federal Ministry of Defence.

This will ensure that everyone concerned will clearly assume his or her responsibilities, and that the indisputable constitutional principle that 'the Minister calls the shots' remains inviolable.

Bibliography

de Maizière, Thomas (2011): Speech in Berlin on 18 May 2011.

Handelsblatt (author unnamed) (2010): Zu Guttenberg will Bundeswehr radikal umbauen. In: Handelsblatt, 12 August 2010.

Krauss, Bärbel (2012): Schwerer Fehler. Published in: Stuttgarter Zeitung, 22.03.2012.

Mann, Siegfried (1971): Das Bundesministerium der Verteidigung. Bonn: Boldt.

Molt, Matthias (2007): Von der Wehrmacht zur Bundeswehr. Personelle Kontinuität und Diskontiuität beim Aufbau der deutschen Streitkräfte 1955-1966. Heidelberg: Univ. Diss.

Sachs, Michael (Ed.) (2011): Basic Law – Kommentar. 6th Edition. Munich: Beck.

Schmidt, Helmut (1996): Weggefährten – Erinnerungen und Reflexionen. Berlin: Siedler.

Schmidt-Bleibtreu, Bruno/Hofmann, Hans/Hopfauf, Axel (Eds.) (2010): Basic Law – Kommentar. 12th Edition. Munich: Luchterhand.

Spiegel (author unnamed) (1960): Oberbefehl: Im Widerstreit. In: Der Spiegel, No 45, 41 et seq.

Spiegel (author unnamed) (1978): Fall Wust: Ungeheuerlicher Vorgang. In: Der Spiegel, No. 15, 18 et seq.

Walz, Dieter (Ed.) (2006): Soldatengesetz – Kommentar. Heidelberg: Müller.

von Weizsäcker, Richard (2000): Bericht der Kommission „Gemeinsame Sicherheit und Zukunft der Bundeswehr', 23.05.2000.

Weiland, Severin (2011): Guttenbergs grausiges Erbe. In: Spiegel Online, 08.03.2011.

The military services

Dietmar Klos, Heiner Möllers, Dieter Stockfisch

The Army, Air Force and Navy are the services that form the core of the armed forces that Germany maintains to perform the tasks of the Bundeswehr as part of the country's security and defence policy. They have the capability to perform the tasks assigned to them by taking a variety of measures either on their own or together (joint activities), frequently together with allied armed forces (combined activities) and finally by using their capability to fight on land, in and from the air, and at sea. Other major military and civilian organisational elements, such as the Joint Support Service or the armament organisation of the Bundeswehr, perform mainly support tasks.[1] The Bundeswehr and its services, the Army, the Air Force and the Navy, as well as all other major organisational elements, must be seen as a whole; this is an objective everyone involved is consistently working to achieve. Any action taken on a Bundeswehr and a joint basis is governed by the stringent application of the principle of the 'primacy of politics', i.e. the clear subordination of the military leadership to the government and the specific assignment of missions and responsibilities to the military leadership.

This article gives an introduction to the three services, beginning with the Army. The focus is on the development of the Army, the Air Force and the Navy. The article concludes with an examination of cooperation between the services within the Bundeswehr system – particularly with respect to the implementation of procurement programmes – and with an attempt to foresee how the reorientation of the Bundeswehr will change the position of the Army, Air Force and Navy in relation to the Federal Ministry of Defence (FMOD).

The Army

The build-up phase

As the largest of the services and a complex entity consisting of interdependent 'subsystems', the Army has always played a prominent role within the Bun-

1 For an overview of the institutional structure of the policy area of defence in Germany, see the diagram in Ina Wiesner's introductory article in this volume.

deswehr. At the same time, however, it has always had to make greater contributions and accept cuts in connection with changes in defence policy.

The build-up phase of the new German Army lasted approximately ten years, beginning in November 1955, and covered two Army structures. The aim was to set up twelve divisions for assignment to NATO, which means they were to be fundamentally designated for deployment in accordance with national decisions. The intention was to create a strong conventional force to counterbalance the threat posed in Central Europe by the Warsaw Pact and its leading power, the Soviet Union.

Army Structure 1 was strongly modelled on the US Army, since the United States also supplied most of the major military equipment. Besides new and mainly American influences, proven command and control principles taken from German military traditions, as well as the Wehrmacht, were applied to command and control of the Army. To this day, this includes cooperation between the different branches of the Army and other components of the armed forces in so-called 'combined arms combat' and 'mission-type command and control'. With this form of command and control, the subordinate commander is simply assigned a general mission and the required assets; the decision on how to accomplish it in accordance with the overarching objective is left to him. This is the basis of principles such as the manoeuvrist approach, seizing the initiative or acting in accordance with the intent of the higher commander. These principles have been adopted by other allies, such as the US Army, which has sometimes applied them more consistently than the Army of the Bundeswehr itself. A new concept was the Bundeswehr's principle of leadership development and civic education ('Innere Führung'), according to which soldiers are politically mature 'citizens in uniform'.

Within the Federal Ministry of Defence, the Army was represented as from 1955 by Division V and as from 1957 by the Army Staff, headed by the Chief of Staff, Army. Below the level of the three corps, each of which was made up of four divisions, the Army consisted of battle groups instead of the traditional regiments. The battle group staffs were assigned two or three armoured or infantry battalions as well as support units for exercises and operations.

These six armoured and six infantry divisions had a large number of personnel, totalling up to 28,000 soldiers. The armoured division had three strong tank and infantry battalions, while the infantry division had seven infantry battalions and one tank battalion. In addition, these divisions had a large number of combat support and combat service support troops.

This structure was rearranged for the first time only three years later: The new plan was to establish an airborne and a mountain infantry division to replace two of the very large infantry divisions. Transition to Army Structure 2 began in 1959, and this structure remained in place all the way up until 1970. The reason for the new structure was that the security environment and the threat emanating from the tactical nuclear weapons of the Soviet forces had changed. NATO advocated the idea of a mobile defence capability and rapid counterattacks. It was time to make changes and create smaller divisions with the capability to conduct combined arms combat operations under a nuclear threat. The core of the new structure was composed of brigades which, instead of battle groups as command elements, already included organically subordinate units in peacetime.

The armoured divisions were assigned two armoured and one armoured infantry brigade each, while, vice versa, the new armoured infantry divisions were assigned two armoured infantry and one armoured brigade each. The highly combat-capable brigades comprised three to four tank, armoured infantry and infantry battalions, one artillery and one supply battalion each, as well as a number of brigade units. The division troops remained largely unchanged.

In rocket artillery battalions, the required capability to use tactical nuclear weapons was established with Honest John missiles, while at the corps level, it was achieved with Sergeant rocket launchers and – in early artillery battalions – with guns.

Work began in the late 1950s to improve the Army's range of comparatively light equipment. The armoured forces were equipped with American M 48 battle tanks, and the armoured infantry was issued HS 30 armoured infantry fighting vehicles and M 113 armoured personnel carriers. Additional procurement projects were launched from 1965 onwards. This resulted in a considerable modernisation of the Army and an increase in its fighting strength. Examples are the outstanding German Leopard 1 battle tank, the Marder armoured infantry fighting vehicle – of which upgraded versions are still in service today – and the American Bell UH-1D transport helicopter.

The 12th Armoured Division was assigned to NATO in 1965, as the last of twelve divisions, in a move that essentially completed the build-up of the so-called Field Army. Seven armoured infantry divisions, three armoured divisions as well as the first airborne and the first mountain infantry division were operational. Of the 36 brigades that had been planned, 34 were now established. The Army had grown to a total strength of 305,000 soldiers. Its mission was to mount a defence close to the inner-German border within Germany in support of NATO's defence and to protect the territory of the Federal Republic. To this end, the majority of Army forces were deployed in three corps areas in northern and southern Germany, while the reinforced 6th Armoured Infantry Division was deployed in Schleswig-Holstein, and together they formed the core of NATO's land forces in Central Europe.

The Army also assumed the responsibility for 'territorial defence', performing this task as an interservice function for the Bundeswehr. Work began in 1969 on turning a central agency or command that had existed since 1957 into three territorial commands of the so-called Territorial Army based in Kiel, Mönchengladbach and Heidelberg. Until early 2000, this organisation's task was to support not only NATO defence efforts and Allied forces, but also national civil defence agencies within Germany, and to act as a mediator between these 'general defence' elements. It was also meant to ensure freedom of manoeuvre for NATO forces, particularly in rear areas behind the NATO corps, and to provide follow-on supplies for German forces.

The territorial commands were in charge of military district commands at the Federal state level, military region commands at the region level, and military subregion commands at the administrative district and city level. Numerous units, most of them semiactive or non-active, were available for home defence operations and for providing combat and combat service support.

Continuity in the East-West conflict

The years following the build-up of the Army until the early 1990s were characterised by broad continuity regarding NATO's plans for Central Europe and the German Army's mission and structure. The transition to Army Structure 3 began in 1970, mainly due to the Bundeswehr and the Army being adjusted to NATO's new 'Flexible Response' strategy. Its aim was to enable responses to the nuclear and conventional threats posed by the Soviet Union and the Warsaw Pact that could match any level of aggression, with adequate means and in a manner that was unpredictable for the enemy. For this, a variety of sufficient military assets – conventional, tactical nuclear as well as strategic nuclear (only USA, Great Britain, France) – had to be available, and able to be built up quickly through mobilisation.

As far as the German Army was concerned, this meant that its major units (from brigade to corps) had to be better adjusted to new missions and the terrain (e.g. low mountain ranges), its combat forces further strengthened and its brigades assigned additional conventional high-trajectory weapons to compensate for their not having nuclear weapons. In addition, due to limited funds, which is a frequent cause of restructuring in the Army, the decision was taken to establish specialized divisions/brigades for certain terrains and missions, while applying a system of graduated operational readiness. This approach was named the 'Jägerkonzept' (light infantry concept) and involved an increased number of infantry units. Two armoured infantry divisions were reorganised to form light infantry divisions, while their brigades were transformed into light infantry brigades. These brigades each consisted of three light infantry battalions, one tank destroyer battalion equipped with new full-tracked antitank guns and antitank missile launchers, an armoured artillery battalion, and brigade units. The tank regiments planned as 'compensation' at the corps level were only set up partially, with some airborne brigades being set up instead. In addition, some of the division and corps troops were skeletonised, i.e. rendered semiactive or non-active. An overall reduction in forces and operating costs was achieved. The Army's three corps now altogether had four armoured infantry and armoured divisions, two light infantry divisions as well as the mountain infantry and airborne divisions.

One of the main reasons for the subsequent transition to Army Structure 4 was NATO's dual-track decision in 1979 to modernise its intermediate-range missiles in response to the Soviet Union's lead in this area and to create a bargaining chip in the negotiations on mutual limitation. The Warsaw Pact armies had also cancelled out the qualitative edge NATO's land forces had had in terms of primary weapon systems, a development that once again made their numerical superiority more significant. The first measure taken was to establish the remaining brigades and to use them as a model for testing the new structure. It was now possible to assign the planned 36 brigades of the German Field Army to NATO. At the same time, the Bundeswehr began to develop and procure new weapon systems such as the Milan and Hot antitank guided missiles, the Gepard self-propelled armoured air defence gun system, the Leopard 2 battle tank and the first antitank helicopters. The purpose of these measures, in combination with the creation of more, but smaller combat units, was to gain more freedom of action in the commitment of forces in combat.

The brigades were provided with one additional combined combat battalion. Their tank and armoured infantry companies were divided among the other battalions and reassigned for exercises and operations. The battalion headquarters was kept semiactive. The number of battle tanks and armoured infantry fighting vehicles was reduced from 17 to 13 or 11 in all the companies, while each 4th company of the armoured infantry battalions was issued the M 113. The division troops were partially restructured. The artillery regiment was given an additional artillery reconnaissance battalion and the rocket artillery battalion was equipped with light and medium rocket launchers. An antiaircraft regiment with six Gepard gun batteries, two non-active light infantry battalions and one electronic warfare company were established. The military police companies were moved to the corps level. The corps troops, which were meant to be used to establish points of main effort or to conduct long-range operations, consisted of artillery, antiaircraft, signal, engineer, medical and Army aviation brigades (one of each), two logistics commands and special units such as CBRN defence or long-range reconnaissance troops. Together, they formed a substantial force.

The transition to Army Structure 4 was completed by the end of 1981. The 2nd and 4th Light Infantry Divisions were transformed back into armoured infantry divisions and the 1st and 7th Armoured Infantry Divisions were restructured to form armoured divisions. The twelve divisions of the Field Army now consisted of 38 brigades, of which 17 were armoured brigades, 15 armoured infantry brigades, three airborne brigades, and one a mountain infantry brigade, while two were new home defence brigades, which were also assigned to NATO in 1982. The Territorial Army also increased in size. While it had a peacetime strength of just under 50,000 soldiers, its authorised wartime strength was to be approximately 450,000 soldiers. Twelve home defence brigades were established, two of which were active and four semiactive, in addition to numerous non-active home defence regiments. The main purpose of various engineer regiments was to ensure that bodies of water could be crossed in the rear combat zone. The peacetime strength of the Army was 340,000 soldiers; it had approximately 420 battalions, more than 3,100 Leopard 1 and 2 battle tanks as well as about 2,100 Marder armoured infantry fighting vehicles.

The end of the Cold War and German reunification

While the Army had undergone four restructurings in the past 35 years, the era that began in 1990 was one of regular restructurings that began with a massive reorganisation and six subsequent Army structures. The main reasons for this, besides substantial budget cuts and personnel reductions, were Germany's reunification and the search for a configuration of the Bundeswehr and the Army that was appropriate for the new security situation, and for worldwide deployment.

At the end of the 1980s, there were plans to downsize the Bundeswehr from its long-standing size of 495,000 soldiers to between 420,000 and 400,000 soldiers. This was due to the easing of political tensions (e.g. as a result of Perestroika under Gorbachev, the Soviet president), progress in disarmament negotiations and the low birth rate in certain age groups in Germany. Just a short while later, the socialist regime in the GDR began to disintegrate as a result of the 'Peaceful Revolution' initiated by the people there and the steps that ensued towards Germany's reunification. The so-called 'Two-plus-Four Treaty' specified that the Soviet troops were to withdraw from East Germany by 1994 and that the Bundeswehr was to be reduced to a peacetime strength of 370,000 soldiers. This resulted in a restructuring of the Bundeswehr and the Army and the simultaneous disbandment of the National People's Army of the GDR, with some personnel and materiel being taken over. The Bundeswehr therefore initially shot up in size, to approximately 650,000 soldiers, before being drastically cut down in the following four years. The year 1991 also saw the renewal of NATO's strategy and the establishment of the triad concept 'defence capability, dialogue and cooperation'. At the same time, the decision was taken to implement extensive nuclear disarmament, a move that included the halving of the number of nuclear bombs in Western Europe and the destruction of all nuclear artillery grenades and short-range missiles.

The Army was reduced to 225,000 soldiers by 1994, 40,000 of whom were stationed in two divisions in the new Federal states. The length of compulsory military service, with the Army as the main user of conscripts, was shortened from 15 to 12 months. In Army Structure 5, the Army's command and control organisation was adjusted to match that of the other services by putting the Army Forces Command in charge of most Army troops below the level of the Chief of Staff, Army/Army Staff, and in charge both of 'national territorial tasks' as well as of running operations of the Army and the Bundeswehr as the lead command. The Army Support Command was responsible for logistics, armament, the medical service, and key support tasks. The Army Office remained, as it had been for decades, in charge of both conceptual and central Army tasks, and of organising and conducting training. The commandants of the branch schools became 'directors of the branches' and were responsible for their further development.

In this new structure, the number of commands was reduced and the Field and Territorial Armies were to be merged within the peacetime structure. The reorganisation of the Bundeswehr and the Army began in East Germany, with the Bundeswehr Eastern Command functioning as a temporary staff. The Army alone, for example, had to take charge and dispose of 2,350 battle tanks, 5,800 armoured infantry fighting vehicles, 5,000 artillery and air defence systems and 300,000 tons of munitions from the former National People's Army (BMVg, Army Staff I 5, Oct. 2000, Figure 43).

The next restructuring process was implemented as early as 1993, while the previous round of restructuring was still ongoing. The new structure was referred to as Army Structure 5(N), with the letter 'N' indicating 'Nachbesserung', meaning 'subsequent improvement'. The reasons for this restructuring were cuts in financial resources and personnel – particularly among the senior officers, the establishment of multinational corps headquarters and first steps in the extension of the Bundeswehr's task spectrum to include operations abroad. The territorial commands and military subregional commands were abolished under Army Structure 5. The 1st German-Netherlands Corps and the 2nd German-American Corps were established, while the 4th Corps in Potsdam remained wholly German.

An 'Airmobile Forces Command' with three airborne brigades was established. As the Deployable Operations Staff, it also provided the 'National Commander in Theatre'. Eight merged military district commands/divisions and 24 of the former 48 manoeuvre brigades also remained. Eight brigade headquarters were merged with the military region commands. The 'standard brigade' was established, with two tank battalions and two armoured infantry battalions, elements of which were non-active. The Army retained 261 battalions. The division troops remained more or less unchanged, even though some were merged with military district command level units, some of these in the form of regiments. The nuclear elements of the corps and division artillery were disbanded. The transition to the new Army Structure was completed by 1994. The three major challenges facing the Bundeswehr in the early 1990s – the disbandment of the National People's Army, the build-up of the Army in the new Federal states and the process of adjusting and downsizing it to match the new structure – were thus largely completed.

Worldwide operations

Starting in 1992, certain forces were prepared and kept in a state of availability for operations abroad and crisis response operations. They included two armoured brigades, the mountain infantry brigade and three airborne brigades, as well as supporting arms units from all areas. In 1993, German (Army) forces were deployed to Somalia on their first large operation abroad. In 1994, the need arose for the next round of restructuring. The reasons for this were the alignment of the Bundeswehr with the new operational requirements, the renewed reduction in its peacetime strength to 340,000 soldiers, with the possibility of it being raised to the agreed limit of 370,000, of whom 233,000 were to be Army personnel, and the shortening of the length of military service to ten months. For the first time, conscripts had the option of signing up for 'extended voluntary service' for a period of up to 13 months following their basic military service.

While the missions of protection of German territory, as well as national and Alliance defence, remained fully in effect, the Army had to be more thoroughly geared towards crisis response operations and operations abroad. Approximately 37,000 soldiers were earmarked as rapidly available crisis response forces. There were no basic service conscripts among them. The crisis response forces consisted of three division headquarters, six brigades, a variety of supporting arms units and the German elements of the multinational corps. A set of forces were simultaneously designated as main defence forces. They were skeletonised to a greater or lesser degree and so dependent on augmentation. Besides the aforementioned corps, which also performed administrative control functions in peacetime, the Army contributed troops to the European Corps, the 5th (US/GE) Corps, the Allied Rapid Reaction Corps and the Landjut Corps. The latter was combined with Polish forces in 1999 to form the Multinational Corps Northeast based in Szczecin.

Major changes to this structure summarised under the name 'Neues Heer für Neue Aufgaben' (New Army for New Tasks) were the disbandment of the 6th Division/Military District Command VII, three brigades, 19 military region commands and 37 battalions. A total of 22 brigades were available. This number could be increased to 26 in the event of a crisis. There were four types of brigades, ranging in readiness from fully active to non-active. In the event of mobilisation, the non-active brigades were to be raised to full strength with support from other brigades. Most brigades consisted of three combat battalions, one armoured artillery battalion and brigade units. Crisis response and main defence forces were 'meshed' with the major units. This made it possible to raise a sufficient number of ready troops, although the forces that could actually be deployed first had to be 'assembled'.

The air mechanised brigade with antitank and transport helicopters was one of two innovations in the Army. It was modelled on its American counterpart and served as the Army's 'flying fist' for deep operations. The second innovation was the Special Forces Command (KSK), which was set up to carry out combat and special operations behind enemy lines and during evacuation operations. The division troops remained mostly unchanged, with adjustments primarily taking place in the territorial elements. The antiarmour corps was disbanded. A total of 50 territorial liaison teams were set up at the administrative district level. A Berlin garrison command was established. The transition to this Army Structure was completed by 1997, leaving the Army with around 220 battalions.

Since 1995, the Army has deployed strong contingents to the Balkans on peacekeeping operations. In 1999, during the height of the operations in Bosnia-Herzegovina, Macedonia and Kosovo (e.g. SFOR/EUFOR and KFOR), the Army alone had 9,600 soldiers on deployment there. In the later stages, the number of Army personnel who were consistently deployed reached a level of 4,500.

Beginning in 1999, the new SPD/Green Party coalition government (1998-2005) oversaw the next restructuring programme entitled 'Fundamental Renewal of the Bundeswehr', which was to be completed by 2001. Transition to the 'Army of the Future' was scheduled for completion by 2005. This new set of changes was necessary to further improve the Army's capability to conduct the likely kinds of crisis management operations. The need for it had been realised due to the operations in the Balkans and the requirements of collective defence outside of Central Europe. The new Federal Government had also ordered reductions to be made in personnel and military spending. The objective was to realign the Bundeswehr's organisation and equipment with its mission.

The measures taken to achieve this included the creation of new major military organisational elements and the modification of others. The responsibility for support and territorial tasks, for example, was taken away from the services and assigned on to the Joint Support Service and the Bundeswehr Joint Medical Service on a centralised basis. The Bundeswehr Joint Operations Command was established within the Joint Support Service, one of its tasks being to assume national command and control of operations. Cooperation with the private sector was also intensified, which led to further tasks being 'outsourced'. Predefined types of operations were set out as national requirements that had to be met by the armed forces. The Bundeswehr was to be reduced to a strength of 282,000 personnel by 2006, with the Army being reduced to 134,000 soldiers and the number of civilian employees being cut back to approximately 90,000.

Figure 1: Army Structures (HStru) since Reunification

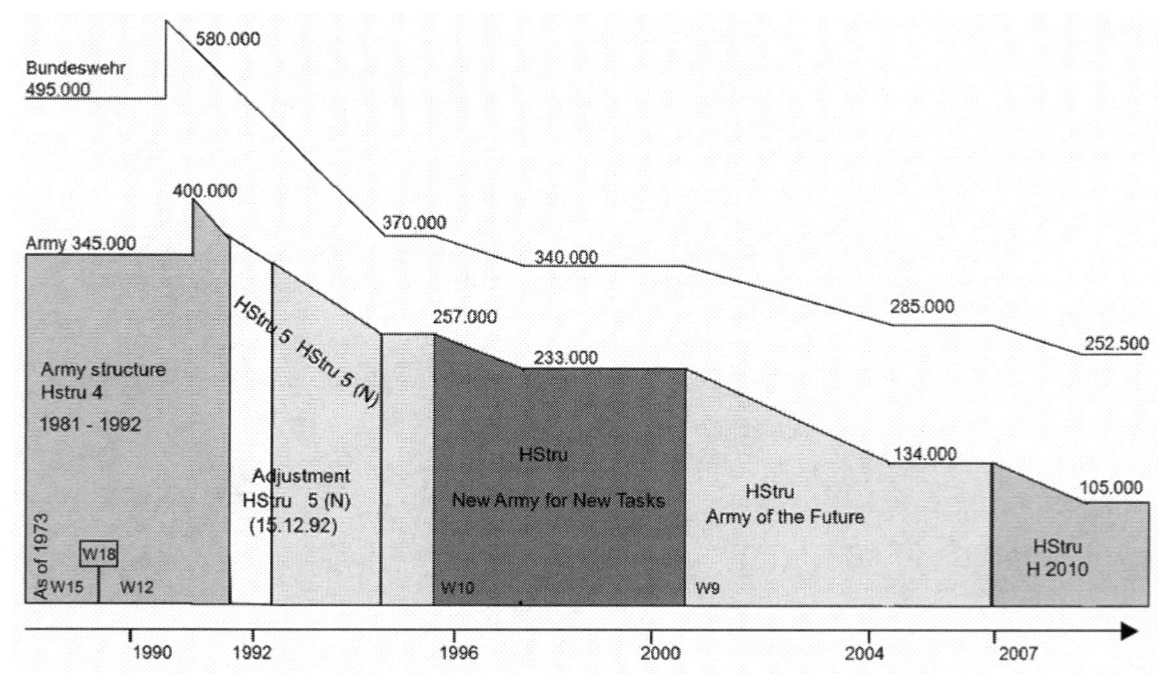

Source: FMOD, Army Staff
Length of military service in months (W18, W15, etc.)

The Army, for instance, had to be capable of providing a reinforced mechanised division with a minimum of two brigades for a 'large-scale operation' in support of a NATO partner. The Army also had to be capable of supporting two 'medium-scale operations' (comparable to the KFOR operation) by sustainably providing 65 per cent of the forces for a brigade equivalent and a large battle group under brigade command. This requirement effectively led to the permanent commitment of ten brigades altogether, for deployment itself as well as for conducting preparations for, and post-operation activities of, follow-on and incoming contingents. Added to that was the requirement for conducting a 'small-scale' rescue, evacuation or protection operation with specialized and rapidly deployable forces. The government maintained its requirement, in the event of protracted national defence operations, for the armed forces to remain capable of building themselves up through mobilisation.

The Army Office and the extensive Army Forces Command remained at the level below the Chief of Staff, Army, and the Army Staff within the FMOD. The Army Forces Command commanded all divisions, all German elements of the multinational corps, and the headquarters of the 2nd Corps. The latter was a national headquarters responsible for planning and conducting operations, including multinational operations. As a result, command and control tasks were no longer carried out by the corps headquarters. The Army Support Command and the 4th Corps were disbanded. The Army retained five mechanised divisions and the new Army Combat Support Command, which, composed of an engineer, an artillery, a CBRN defence and an air defence brigade and two logistic brigades, provided most of the support for the divisions and brigades on a centralised basis. The mechanised divisions each had a reconnaissance battalion, a command support battalion and two strong brigades. Besides three combat battalions, they each commanded an armoured engineer, an armoured artillery and a logistic battalion. The 10th Division was assigned command of an armoured infantry and a mountain infantry brigade as well as the German elements of the French-German Brigade.

The tank battalions consisted of four line companies, while the armoured infantry battalions consisted of four line companies and a mortar company. For reasons of resources, all of the battalions were 'meshed', that is to say, they had different numbers of 'crisis response force' companies that maintained a high level of availability, and 'augmentation force' companies that maintained varying levels of availability. Of the former 1,393 units, a total of 693 remained. 411 of these were crisis response force units and 282 were augmentation force units. The 'Special Operations Division' was newly-established for special, evacuation and protection operations. It consisted of the Special Forces Command and two airborne brigades with two paratrooper battalions and one airborne support battalion each. The Air Mechanised Brigade and the Army Aviation Brigade were assigned to the new 'Airmobile Division'.

In the wake of the terrorist attacks in the United States on 11 September 2001, the Army deployed CBRN and special forces in support of *Operation Enduring Freedom (OEF)* for a number of years. For more than eleven years, it has also been contributing the bulk of forces for the Bundeswehr contingent deployed as part of the *International Security Assistance Force (ISAF)* to establish security and assist reconstruction in Afghanistan, which currently comprises nearly 4,300 soldiers. Besides command and staff personnel, the Army mainly provides combat and combat support forces as the core of the land component in northern Afghanistan. The main effort to improve security in the regions is being undertaken by two task forces and numerous *Operational Mentoring and Liaison Teams (OMLT)* consisting of approximately 30 soldiers working in partnering operations together with Afghan forces. They are supporting the establishment and training of the 209th Afghan National Army Corps at all levels of command. Other smaller operations were to follow in areas such as Africa.

The next restructuring took place before the transition to the 'Structure of the Future' was completed. In 2003, work began to again downsize and restructure the 'New Army', which was later also known as the 'Army 2010', as part of the Bundeswehr's transformation. The adjustments were mainly made on account of the lessons learned from the fight against international terrorism and new operations. However, they were also due to further reductions in resources (funds and personnel). They resulted in the focus being directed even more consistently on the operations that were most likely to be mounted, and on increased centralisation in the Bundeswehr. The main aim of restructuring was to gear the Bundeswehr towards conducting conflict prevention and crisis management operations. The ministerial requirements were such that national defence was to be ensured only through the reconstitution of the armed forces following an extended preparation phase. Further tasks and forces were taken from the services and assigned to the Joint Support Service and the Bundeswehr Joint Medical Service. The transition to the Bundeswehr's new structure, finally featuring a total of 255,000 military and 75,000 civilian personnel, was completed in 2010.

The Army was then allowed to have 105,000 personnel, more than 83,000 of whom would have billets under the new structure and 35,000 were to be conscripts. They ensured that the units could maintain routine duty operations at their home stations. The remaining billets were of no use to the Army because the corresponding personnel were tied up with assignments, longer-term training measures or, in the case of soldiers approaching the end of their terms of service, in-service vocational advancement training. The Bundeswehr divided its forces into three new categories: response forces, stabilisation forces and support forces. These forces were geared to their respective tasks, which also meant that they differed with respect to their personnel, materiel, availability and training. It was hoped that this measure would help save resources.

The response forces were to be provided with modern equipment and would be capable of quickly taking peace-enforcement action against adversaries that were fully military in their structures. The stabilisation forces were intended to be used in protracted military peace stabilisation operations. They were to be able to get the better of adversaries that were partly military in their structures. Task forces were to have the capability to conduct combined arms combat operations. The support forces were to provide support for all operations and ensure the conduct of routine duty operations, the exercise of command and provision of training in Germany.

This Army Structure 2010, which is currently under establishment, provides for 70 per cent of all the forces to be response and stabilisation forces. The capability to fight remains the overarching mission for the Army as a whole. There is operational interplay between the forces in the different categories when they interact in operations. The Bundeswehr's spectrum of tasks requires the Army to have a complex capability profile, ranging from the capability to command not only high-intensity network-enabled operations, stabilisation operations and nation building operations, but also aid and disaster relief operations.

The Army's intent was to support operations by providing ideally complete units whose organisational structure reflected the principle of 'train and organise as you fight'. The top-level organisation remained unchanged. The Army Forces Command was assigned the German elements of multinational corps, five divisions, twelve brigades and 78 battalion-size units. The Army's response forces are made up of the 1st Armoured Division as the *Response Forces Division*, around half of the *Special Operations Division*, the *Airmobile Division* and the French-German Brigade. Two further divisions have administrative control over the four stabilisation force brigades. All of the brigades are viable major units, but are not necessarily the same in terms of structure. All combat battalions have three line companies each and can therefore enable all of the Army's major units to conduct combat operations. The stabilisation force brigades, each with a reconnaissance, an engineer, a command support and a logistic support battalion beside their combat battalions, must be able to flexibly sustain stabilisation operations. The Airmobile Brigade of the Airmobile Division is a new element comprising Army aviation and infantry forces for airmobile operations. The Army Combat Support Command was merged with combat support forces and transformed into a brigade. The Army's restructured reconnaissance units provide an innovative combination of reconnaissance capabilities.

The future Army

Work on the next Bundeswehr reorientation programme began in 2009. The results were approved in 2011 and the structure is to be established by 2015. The main reasons for reorientation were:

- first and foremost, the consolidation of the federal budget, which must be achieved by 2015; this also entails cuts in the defence budget:

- the correction of deficiencies identified in the Bundeswehr's operational capability;
- the future challenges posed by demographic change; and
- therefore once again the attempt to bring the Bundeswehr's tasks, capabilities and financial resources into line.

Agreement has been reached on a new set of basic requirements and modifications for the Bundeswehr. They include a personnel strength of up to 185,000 soldiers, of whom 170,000 are to be regulars and temporary-career volunteers and up to 15,000 are to be military service volunteers (12 to 23 months). The number of civilian personnel is not to exceed 65,000. Universal conscription has been suspended.

The number of directorates at the FMOD is being more or less halved, with their staff being reduced from 3,500 to 2,000. The position of the Chief of Staff, Bundeswehr, as a member of the FMOD executive group and administrative superior of all the military personnel has been strengthened. In addition, the chiefs of staff of the services and the two other major military organisational elements have been abolished as ministerial authorities and moved out of the FMOD structure, becoming commanders of their services and elements with headquarters of their own. The centralisation of basic and operation support tasks within the Bundeswehr is being intensified, while efforts are being stepped up to employ civilian and military personnel together in 'mixed' agencies. All tasks relating to armament and the use of defence materiel will be brought together in a newly-designed armament organisation.

The Federal Minister of Defence issued the new *Defence Policy Guidelines* in 2011. The *Guidelines* state that the operations most likely to be conducted by the Bundeswehr will remain 'conflict prevention and crisis management, to include the fight against international terrorism'. This is what the structures within the armed forces were chiefly geared towards. The national level of ambition was for the Bundeswehr to be able to sustainably deploy 10,000 soldiers in two land and one maritime stabilisation operations at the same time. Additional tasks, such as response operations or national and collective defence operations involving high-intensity combat, also had to be manageable on this basis (principle of a *single set of forces*). Moreover, forces were also to be kept ready for evacuation operations.

The tasks of the land forces therefore remain very varied and complex within a broad spectrum of missions. They can be summed up under the catchwords 'fight, protect, mediate, help'. The capability to fight is the basis upon which the Army proceeds to accomplish its mission. It is plain to see that lessons learned during operations in the past few years have gone into the development of the Army's new structure. The objective was to create balanced and robust structures so as to improve sustainability and cohesion in operations. The structure was accordingly planned via a 'bottom-up' approach in order to improve force cohesion at the tactical level during operations. The 'Systemverbund Heer' (integrated system of Army capabilities), in which all capabilities and forces that can be employed to effectively accomplish missions are combined, is to be maintained. The command structures have been streamlined. The infantry and armoured infantry forces have been strengthened in view of the lessons learned during stabilisation operations.

The Bundeswehr has been permitted to maintain an Army of up to 61,000 soldiers consisting of approximately 55,000 regular soldiers and temporary-career volunteers as well as between over 2,000 and almost 6,000 military service volunteers, depending on the number of applicants. Certain tasks and capabilities have been exchanged between the services to achieve synergy effects. For example, the Army air defence corps and the medium helicopter transport forces, which to date have consisted of two regiments equipped with the medium transport helicopter CH53, are being assigned to the Air Force. All NH 90 transport helicopters, on the other hand, are now assigned to the Army. The Army is also transferring additional capabilities as well as command and control troops (long-haul communication) to the Joint Support Service, along with the CBRN corps and the military music service. On the other hand, Joint Support Service forces such as the explosive ordnance disposal and counter-improvised explosive devices forces will be assigned to the Army's engineer corps.

The national level of ambition requires the Army to provide a total of around 5,000 soldiers for operations. It is meant to be able to sustainably provide two large mixed task forces for two simultaneous operations, in addition to the nucleus of a multinational command element, Army elements of a helicopter task force, as well as evacuation operations and further specific forces and specialists. If national / collective defence operations have to be mounted, a division with three mechanised brigades is to be generated from the active-duty forces and augmentation forces.

The Army has three levels of command. The Headquarters of the German Army with the Chief of Staff, Army, will be composed of elements of the former Army Staff, which has now been moved outside the FMOD, the Army Forces Command and the Army Office. The Headquarters of the German Army will be responsible for all the aspects of administrative control of the Army, the provision of operational Army forces for operations, the provision of Army expertise and support for conduct of operations as well as the provision of the design and shaping of the Army, including its personnel, training and equipment. Below this level, two two-star offices will be responsible for performing the specialized tasks of the former Army Office: the *Army Development Office* and the *Army Training Command*. This office will be in command of the Army's training institutes.

The Army's forces will be grouped in three divisions and eight brigades. The new Rapid Forces Division will include special and specialized forces (Special Forces Command/airborne troops) and all Army aviation troops. The other divisions will command the 'stabilisation forces'. Besides the Special Forces Command, one airborne brigade and the French-German Brigade, six brigades will be the main guarantors of long-term sustainability for stabilisation operations. These brigades will consist of three to four combat battalions, which will retain a similar structure. In addition, five brigades will have one non-active combat battalion each. Every brigade will also have a reconnaissance, an armoured engineer and a logistic support battalion. There will be further combat support forces at the division level. The future Army will consist of five regiments with 44 active battalions and ten non-active battalions that are capable of being augmented.

The FMOD is working to reduce the number of systems already in use and, together with the defence industry, working to reduce the overall number of weapon systems that are to be fielded. For example, the following numbers of main weapon systems have been planned for the Army: 225 Leopard 2A6 battle tanks, 350 Puma armoured infantry fighting vehicles, approx. 200 Boxer multi-role armoured vehicles, 40 TIGER support helicopters and 80 NH 90 helicopters. In addition, a new approach is being adopted towards the way the Army is issued equipment. The units will no longer be issued their full TOE equipment (TOE = Table of Organisation and Equipment). The overall number of systems the Army is issued will now be based primarily on operational requirements, as well as on the requirements for appropriate training in Germany. The forces will be issued 100 per cent of the equipment they need for operational deployment and pre-deployment training, but only around 30 per cent of the equipment they need for other training activities in Germany. The intention behind this is to establish a situation in which the Army has approximately 70 to 80 per cent of the equipment it needs altogether. Moreover, plans are for new equipment to be rolled out in 'half generations' and in two 'five-year stages'.

The new Bundeswehr and Army structures constitute acute change. compared to the previous Army structure, the Army is being even more consistently geared towards its core capabilities and operational capability. It remains to be seen whether the targets that have been set will be achieved, and particularly whether a balance can be struck between mission, capabilities and financial resources.

The Air Force

The Bundeswehr's Air Force has also undergone far-reaching changes in the past ten years or so. Established as a tactical air force within NATO, it was part of the Alliance's integrated air defence in Central Europe. Its tasks have since undergone a fundamental change, not so much due to the fall of the Berlin Wall and reunification of the two German states, but rather due to the pivot brought about by 9/11 and the ensuing fight against international terrorism, including the operation in Afghanistan since 2002. The areas in which air forces of the Federal Republic of Germany are deployed have shifted from Central Europe to Southeastern Europe and the rest of the world. The reorientation of the Air Force and the

Bundeswehr as a whole is being driven by the necessity for rapidly deployable air power and the capability to project military power in other regions of the world. It is worth looking back at the history of the Air Force to understand the constant change that the likely most international of the Bundeswehr's services has undergone.

Planning and establishment

During the planning stage of West Germany's Armed Forces and the establishment of the Bundeswehr as a reaction to the Soviet Union's policy of expansion following World War II and the Korean War, the German Air Force was planned as a tactical air force from the very beginning. Throughout the preparations for the European Defence Community (EDC) between 1950 and 1954, the German Air Force was intended to be a force consisting of 1,400 aircraft that was to be used primarily for air defence purposes. Yet this plan was changed when the Federal Republic of Germany was admitted to NATO. The USA was the dominant power in the Alliance and preferred the German Air Force to be a tactical air force with offensive capabilities. Consequently, on 2 January 1956, the only six-month-old Air Force Training Company in Nörvenich was transformed into an Air Force that would play a central role in NATO's integrated air defence in Europe and would be given a distinct offensive component. The Bundeswehr's first flying combat units were fighter bomber wings that could be equipped with nuclear weapons and remained in service until the end of the Cold War.

Based on the first task forces from all of the three services, but primarily on the training organisation set up during the initial years, the establishment of the Air Force was determined by two factors: the provision of crucial materiel and personnel support by the US Air Force and the integration from the beginning of the Air Force into NATO structures. Most of the equipment the German Air Force initially held were combat aircraft that were no longer needed by the USA and other weapon systems purchased abroad. The German defence industry was still being rebuilt ten years after the war, which meant that it could only provide a very small amount of materiel.

Initial build-up

However, the only units to be established in 1956, the first year of the Air Force, were logistic and training units and the commands coordinating the build-up. This was followed by the activation of Air Transport Wing 61 in Erding as the very first task force in 1957. The restructuring of Weapons School 30 in Büchel to form Fighter Bomber Wing 33 a few days after the activation of Fighter

Bomber Wing 31 in Nörvenich marked the beginning of further Air Force components being assigned to NATO.

The new Air Force units were always set up according to the same process: A skeletonised unit and the required infrastructure were first established at a certain base. The unit was then augmented with personnel from other units, among them units that had often completed their build-up, and surplus materiel from other bases. A problem was posed by the fact that many former military airfields were already occupied by the Allies. Because of this, a number of new airfields and, more importantly, an entirely new infrastructure for the surface-to-air missile forces had to be built – an undertaking that was costly and time-consuming. It was an even greater challenge, however, to recruit and train suitable personnel for the numerous technical posts during the time of the 'economic miracle'. The result was that the Air Force and the other services did not achieve their target force levels straightaway. In the mid-1960s, for example, the Air Force only had 60 per cent of the engineering personnel it required for its flying units, which meant that specialized tasks had to be performed by conscripts without suitable training.

Irrespective of these problems, a modernisation drive began in 1960. The procurement of the single-seater combat aircraft Lockheed F-104G STARFIGHTER, the NIKE Hercules surface-to-air missile and the PERSHING 1 ballistic missile was not only a qualitative improvement, but it also meant an enhancement of the Air Force as a crucial component of NATO's nuclear-capable armed forces in Central Europe. Within the context of the Alliance doctrine of Massive Retaliation (MC 14/2), the Air Force provided means of delivery for nuclear weapons as a contribution towards the nuclear participation scheme, although the warheads always remained in US custody until they were withdrawn. From a politico-military standpoint, this made the Air Force an important part of the Bundeswehr. At the time, the threat of an immediate use of nuclear weapons in the event of an armed conflict, which stood behind the doctrine of Massive Retaliation, served as a kind of military life insurance for Germany. It ensured that the Bundeswehr, which did not possess nuclear weapons itself, had a say in the planning for the use of such weapons and that it was probably even able to influence some decisions. In effect, 'nuclear participation' meant that the fighter bomber pilots knew their nuclear targets by heart and that the NATO SACEUR Strike Plan provided a catalogue of targets that were to be attacked with nuclear weapons in the event of war.

The period of modernisation was inextricably linked with one particular weapon system: with support from the re-emerging aviation industry, which considered this aircraft both a new beginning and an entry into the age of high technology, the Air Force Command was able to push through the purchase of the American F-104 Starfighter as a multirole combat aircraft without subjecting it to thorough testing. The Air Force Chief of Staff at the time, General Josef Kammhuber, saw the Starfighter as exactly the type of multirole combat aircraft that the Air Force needed. Nevertheless, the modifications to the F-104G requested by the German purchasers made it an almost entirely different aircraft than the powerful interceptor that was already in service with the US Air Force. The high demands on the pilots, the shortage of engineers, the inferior infrastructure of the jet units and the lack of preparation within the overall organisation of the Air Force almost inevitably led to the so-called Starfighter crisis in 1965 and 1966.

Although the number of accidents with the Starfighter, when seen in relation to the number of flying hours it clocked up, was average for the time, there were approximately 60 accidents during these two years in which the planes were written off, and almost 40 pilots lost their lives. This increasingly prompted the media and politicians to ask who could put an end to the problems. In 1966, Helmut Schmidt, who was later to become Federal Minister of Defence, criticised the particularly poor organisation within the Federal Ministry of Defence as 'confusion over responsibilities': more than 80 bodies and authorities were working on individual aspects of the Starfighter without there being an overall coordinator. The clear distinction between military leadership (Article 87a of the *Grundgesetz*) and civilian administration was a particularly controversial point for military personnel. On 24 August 1966, at the height of the crisis, the Federal Minister of Defence, Kai-Uwe von Hassel, sacked the Air Force Chief of Staff, Air Marshal Werner Panitzki, who had been unable to push through his reform proposals. Supported by a continuous stream of media coverage, the newly-appointed Chief of Staff, Air Marshal Johannes Steinhoff, was given far-reaching powers as the 'in-service support manager' for the Starfighter. The F-104G system management established was later also applied to other new weapon systems such as the Panavia 200 Tornado and further systems outside the Air Force.

The Air Force began to search for suitable successors to the Starfighter and other weapon systems even before the crisis was over. The testing of vertical take-off aircraft initiated in the early 1960s was discontinued for financial reasons. NATO's doctrine of 'Massive Retaliation' (MC 14/2) was succeeded in 1968 by the doctrine of 'Flexible Response' (MC 14/3). For the Air Force, this change meant additional conventional tasks, especially for the nuclear-capable fighter bomber units using the Starfighter. It was precisely this role as a conventional fighter bomber for which the Starfighter's design was less suitable. Its replacement as a tactical reconnaissance aircraft by the McDonnell Douglas RF-4E Phantom II in 1971 and as a fighter aircraft by the F-4F Phantom II version in 1973 can be seen as evidence that the Air Force had pinned its hopes on the wrong aircraft too early. The Phantom is the only true multirole combat aircraft the Bundeswehr has ever had.

The big change: the structure of the Air Force in 1970

General Steinhoff had already received approval from Defence Minister von Hassel for the long overdue restructuring of the Air Force when he assumed office. The structure he introduced on 1 October 1970 was marked, on the one hand, by functional commands that assumed functional tasks for the entire Air Force. The divisions were structured according to defensive air operations and offensive air operations, as was easy to see from the subordinate units. On the other hand, there were new major commands: the *Air Fleet Command* commanded and controlled the operational Air Force with its divisions and units. The Air Force Office was the headquarters responsible for mission support and training and for common tasks. Under the new Air Force Support Command, the Air Force pooled its logistics operations, including both the maintenance organisations, with their hangars and workshops, and also the depot organisation, whose facilities were spread across Germany. Since that time, Cologne-Wahn, previously Porz-Wahn, has been of eminent importance for the Bundeswehr's Air Force, and this structure remained generally the same until 2012.

There is no overlooking the fact that at that time 'command' at most meant the administrative control that guaranteed operational readiness. Until the end of the East-West conflict, the operational units of the Air Force were assigned to the Allied air fleets, the 2nd and 4th Allied Tactical Air Forces (ATAF). They already had 'operational control' and 'operational command' over the air attack and air defence units assigned to NATO in peacetime. The 'Integrated NATO Air Defence' showed just how closely the Air Force was interlinked with NATO: In West Germany alone, the two multinational ATAFs each possessed two multinational Sector Operation Centres (SOC) as air defence operation centres, to which, in turn, national Control and Reporting Centres (CRC) were assigned. The SOCs used them to command and control the SAM forces and the fighter pilots, who were assigned to them on a regional basis. In the early 1980s, the Air Force provided around 80 per cent of the C2 and communications equipment, 50 per cent of the surface-to-air missiles and 30 per cent of the fighter aircraft for NATO's air defence in central Europe. These figures reinforce the importance of the role that the Air Force played in NATO, as did prominent command assignments of German generals in high NATO commands: From 1981 to1982, Lieutenant General Bruno Loosen was the first German commander of 4ATAF.

Paradigm shift

The changes in the Air Force that resulted from the unexpected reunification of Germany were largely predetermined by two factors: One was that, after gaining full state sovereignty, the Federal Republic of Germany had committed itself to reducing its armed forces to 370,000 personnel – this number was reduced by a further 30,000 personnel in 1993. The weapon system-related figures, which were highlighted when international confidence-building treaties were signed in Europe, meant that the Air Force would experience its first severe loss. Three Alpha Jet wings and two reconnaissance wings were disbanded. After taking over the Air Force/Air Defence Command (AF/AD) of the National People's Army, the first step was to establish a new division in Strausberg-Eggersdorf, later Berlin-Gatow, which initially commanded and controlled all the Air Force units on the territory of the former GDR. As regards the materiel of the former AF/AD, only the MiG-29 Fulcrum fighter aircraft remained in service for a while, with Fighter Wing 73, which had been especially deployed to Laage on account of them – having previously been Fighter Bomber Wing 36 based in Sobernheim. As regards personnel, the Air Force was downsized from a strength of around 110,000 members, including the 15,000 soldiers taken over from the AF/AD, to 34,500 soldiers in Air Force Structure 6, a goal that was to be achieved by 2010 and without including the Air Force personnel in the Joint Support Service.

Right in the middle of the reorganisation process conducted to establish Air Force Structure 4, which came into effect in 1994, fighter bombers and surface-to-air missile forces were deployed during the 1991 Gulf War. At the request of Turkey, NATO also deployed some of its AMF forces to Erhac in Turkey in mid-January 1991 to secure the southern flank, stationing them there for several weeks. While there, 18 Fighter Bomber Wing 43 Alpha Jets from Oldenburg made a contribution that was more political in nature. Their tactical range would not have made them a prime choice for actual use in the war, but this 'show of force' possibly deterred Iraq from extending the war into Turkey.

New scenarios: from the Balkans to Afghanistan

Further Air Force units were sent out on operational deployment as early as 1992 – this time in the Balkans. As part of the United Nations Protection Force, electronic combat and reconnaissance (ECR) Tornados and reconnaissance Tornados were involved in enforcing the UN flight ban over Bosnia and Herzegovina. Transport aviation forces were likewise involved – as they often have been throughout the world –, their mission being to conduct relief flights to the capital, Sarajevo, which was under siege by irregular Serb forces. The deployment of several Tornados in UN missions was a sign that attitudes were changing in Germany: The Federal Republic of Germany was now prepared to participate in peacekeeping or peace enforcement operations out of area as well. The groundbreaking ruling of Germany's Federal Constitutional Court on 12 July 1994 meant that the German Bundestag from then on had to grant its approval for the Bundeswehr to be deployed in armed operations abroad. The parliament is therefore involved in the final stages of decision-making processes on military policy. The remarkable thing about the decision of the Constitutional Court judges was that in addition to the then opposition parties, the SPD and Greens, the FDP parliamentary group also spoke out against the deployment of German soldiers in NATO's AWACS aircraft – an operation that government members of the FDP had voted in favour of. The Constitutional Court made it clear that on account of its membership in NATO and, above all, in the United Nations, the Federal Republic of Germany could participate in the operations approved by these bodies without Germany's constitution having to be amended for this purpose. Nevertheless, the German Bundestag had to approve any deployment of Germany's armed forces in future.

Both in Turkey in 1991 and in the Balkans from 1992, the German Air Force units were deployed under NATO command and in collaboration with the Allies. However, it was never just the number of aircraft provided that was important; their qualitative capabilities mattered more. The Air Force's ECR Tornados offered technical capabilities that NATO did not have, just as the aerial imagery reconnaissance capability of the German RECCE Tornados did. The latter turned out to be a decisive factor for the deployment of RECCE Tornados in Afghanistan. It was just as significant that only NATO, with its structures and operation centres, was in a position to conduct complex, multinational air operations for the United Nations.

In all of the Air Force's operations – whether earthquake relief operations in Agadir/Morocco in 1960 or supply flights over the Hindu Kush in 2012 – Germany's transport aviation forces made an outstanding contribution. True to the motto 'First in – Last out', the transport aviation forces with their C-160 Transall assault aircraft, which today is well advanced in years, bear the brunt of the task of providing logistic support. Any yet there is no overlooking the fact that it was only with the A400M military transport aircraft that the Air Force's transport aviation forces will get their first aircraft that is tailored to the foreign missions that have been conducted since 1991. Until then, the Transall – similar to the remaining weapon systems tailored to the Cold War era – will have to continue to fly.

Outlook

Air Force Structure 4, which came into effect after German reunification, and Structure 5, which had barely been established when it was superseded by Structure 6, cannot obscure the fact that all of the adaptation processes the Air Force has undergone since 1990 have been determined by international treaties on disarmament in Europe or by the dictates of narrowing financial leeway. As a result, the Air Force lost six flying combat units, half of its SAM units and half of its logistics units between 1991 and 2001. Even the outsourcing of common tasks to the Joint Support Service from 2001 had efficiency-optimising motives and – at least for the Air Force – cost-reducing consequences. The reorientation of the Bundeswehr, which has now begun, means that the Air Force, with the motto 'focus on operations', will ultimately have to make longer and more far-reaching contributions to Germany's international commitments with fewer personnel and less materiel. It remains to be seen if the favoured approach of 'breadth before depth' can do justice to the more demanding scenarios. In structural terms, the Air Force aims to meet expectations by dividing its tasks, i.e. by establishing an operational command and a mission support command. This will be accompanied by far-reaching downsizing of all units:

- The surface-to-air missile units will be drastically downsized to form three PATRIOT battalions, this missile also being suitable for ballistic missile defence purposes, and a MANTIS air defence group under a wing headquarters. Training will be conducted entirely in Husum in the future; Fort Bliss will no longer be used as a training base;
- The three future tactical Air Force wings in Neuburg, Nörvenich and Laage, which have around 140 Eurofighters, will perform both air-to-air and air-to ground tasks.
- Around 40 of the remaining 80 Tornados or so in the fighter bomber wing in Büchel will perform the tasks of the traditional fighter bomber with the Taurus standoff missile and the tasks that go with the Bundeswehr's participation in NATO nuclear operations.
- In addition to the performance of imagery reconnaissance tasks with RECCE Tornados and the Heron-1 drone and electronic reconnaissance tasks with the Global Hawk drone, the reconnaissance wing in Jagel will also carry out the tasks of the ECR unit that is to be disbanded, namely Fighter Bomber Wing 32, with 30 ECR Tornados.
- After the fielding of the 40 A400M transporters, only one of the three existing air transport wings will remain a single-type air transport wing in the medium term – the one in Wunstorf –, while a wing with 40 CH-53 helicopters will be based in Holzdorf and Laupheim. The gaps between strategic-operational and tactical air transport will be filled in the course of the 'capability transfer'. The two current transport helicopter regiments of the Army will then be combined into one. In return, the Air Force will dispense completely with the new tactical helicopter, the NH-90, the successor of the Bell UH-1D.
- In addition, there will be the ground combat support regiment, two tactical air command and control groups as well as the Air Force training organisation with its officer and NCO schools. It should be noted, however, that due to the suspension of compulsory military service, only one training battalion in Germersheim now trains recruits and also prepares Air Force personnel at the Air Force operational training centre.

In total, the Air Force now has a strength of fewer than 25,000 soldiers and considerably fewer weapon systems than it used to have. In future, it will have to work even more closely with the Allies and other air forces in future missions in order to conduct effective 'pooling and sharing'. As other air forces are also facing drastic cuts, the NATO partners will have to close ranks. The eminent role of the US Air Force within NATO will thus have to be monitored carefully.

Whether the German Air Force – like the other services of the Bundeswehr – will be sustainable in future missions remains to be seen.

The Navy

As the previous sections have shown, the integration of the Bundeswehr into NATO had a decisive influence on the structures and equipment of both the Army and Air Force in the first decades after it was established. The same applies to the third service – the Navy. After all, on 9 May 1955, the Federal Republic of Germany, as the 15th member of NATO, joined a predominantly maritime defence alliance with the 'North Atlantic' at its core. For the first time in the 20th century, Germany was now on the side of the great Atlantic naval powers, the USA and the United Kingdom.

The build-up of the *Bundesmarine*

On 2 January 1956, the first volunteers joined the new navy, which included almost the entire Federal Sea Border Patrol and the personnel of the Labour Service Unit B (former officers and men of the *Kriegsmarine*, which under American command cleared shipping routes in the North Sea and Baltic Sea of mines left over from the Second World War). The build-up of the *Bundesmarine* had begun. The first units it took charge of were 18 US-owned minesweepers (former minesweepers of the *Kriegsmarine*) and three fast patrol boats from the United Kingdom. It also commissioned 28 Federal Sea Border Patrol units. On 29 May 1956, the 1st Fast Patrol Boat Squadron – with three boats – was activated, the first unit to be so. This was followed on 2 July by the tenders EIDER and TRAVE, former Canadian corvettes, which had originally been acquired by the Federal Ministry of the Interior and converted for use by the Federal Sea Border Patrol.

The mission of the *Bundesmarine* or of Germany's maritime defence contribution to NATO was initially to perform three tasks:

- to defend the Baltic approaches,
- to monitor activities in the Baltic Sea, and
- to protect Germany's sea lines of communication in the southern North Sea and the Baltic Sea.

These tasks were tailor-made for the German Navy since no other navy was so familiar with the characteristics of these narrow and shallow waters, where the weather changes quickly, creating difficult conditions for navigation. The new Navy was initially intended to be equipped exclusively with light maritime forces and was to have a strength of 20,000 personnel.

The *Bundesmarine* assigned its newly-established boat and ship squadrons to NATO from the very beginning. On 1 April 1957, the Navy assigned two minesweeper squadrons to NATO. They were the first units the Bundeswehr assigned to NATO. On 1 January 1958, they were followed by the 1st Fast Patrol Boat Squadron and, on 1 March 1961, by two destroyer squadrons, three fast patrol boat squadrons, four minesweeper squadrons, a landing craft squadron and a naval air wing.

Extension of its mission

The first Chief of Staff, Navy, Vice Admiral Friedrich Ruge (Chief of Staff from 1956 to 1961), recognised that the security of the Atlantic sea lines of communication and of their approaches was a vital issue for Germany and used this as the basis on which to extend the Navy's mission, which resulted from the geographical situation and the integration of the Navy into the Atlantic Alliance. Ruge worked to procure destroyers and frigates, to ensure that the Navy would not be limited to being a mere coastal navy, and to pave the way for it becoming an 'Escort Navy'. By 1958, the Navy had already taken loan of the first of six hard-striking FLETCHER-class destroyers (2,050 tonnes) from the USA. Ruge's findings corresponded with NATO's 'Overall Strategic Concept for the NATO Area' (MC 14/2) and with the doctrine of the 'conventional shield and nuclear sword' forces, which in 1967 was further developed as part of the deterrence strategy (MC 14/3) known as 'Flexible Response'. This meant that the area of responsibility of the *Bundesmarine* now extended far beyond the waters off the coast of Northern Germany. In 1960, a shipbuilding programme was approved for the construction of twelve destroyers, six escort vessels (frigates), 40 fast patrol boats, 12 submarines, 54 minesweepers, 12 landing craft, 2 training ships, 129 accommodation and special-purpose ships and 58 naval aircraft. The 1962 document entitled 'Concept and Build-up of the Navy' set out the main tasks of the Navy, which included protecting the Baltic Sea approaches, monitoring the enemy's sea lines of communication and securing maritime transport. During the Cuban missile crisis in the autumn of 1962, Naval Air Wing 1 was put on stand by, and the 3rd Fast Patrol Boat Squadron was ordered to patrol the middle and eastern parts of the Baltic Sea at battle stations.

Meanwhile, the build-up of the Navy had made swift progress. On 1 October 1963, the Navy had a strength of 32,860 officers and enlisted personnel and, on 1 January 1966, no fewer than 35,000. The first new German ship to be built was the 160-tonne JAGUAR fast patrol boat, which was commissioned in November 1957. The first larger German ship to be built was the frigate KÖLN (2,090 tonnes), which was commissioned on 15 April 1961. Virtually all of the following new ships of the Navy were built at German shipyards, which thus played a major role in the build-up of the Navy. In 1965, the maximum tonnage for the construction of surface units was raised to 6,000 tonnes, having previously been limited to 3,000 tonnes. On 1 October 1963, the naval aviation forces were issued the Starfighter F-104G fighter bomber. By mid-1965 the *Bundesmarine* fleet consisted of around 250 battle ships and auxiliaries as well as 180 combat and training aircraft, which were combined in three naval air wings.

The Navy in the 1970s

The naval exercises that the Warsaw Pact states had been conducting worldwide since 1970 forced the Navy to modify its strategy. The mission was now extended by the task of securing maritime supply routes in the North Sea. The Navy's second concept in 1972 made the integrity of Germany's own territory the top priority. Thought several points were supplemented and amended, it was adopted on 27 January as the third 'Navy Concept'. It provided for ensuring a high level of presence of maritime and naval air forces, the establishment of a rapid operational capability, and the integration of German maritime forces into the standing multinational forces of NATO – the Standing Naval Force Atlantic (Stanavforlant) and from 1973 the Standing Naval Force Channel (Stanavforchan). The two NATO forces demonstrated the Atlantic Alliance's solidarity and confirmed NATO's doctrine of deterrence. This was accompanied by a further build-up of the Navy and a considerable upgrading of its ships, aircraft and weapon systems. For example, three missile destroyers with computer-assisted command and weapons control systems were commissioned in 1970 and the four HAMBURG-class destroyers were equipped with ship/ship-missile systems between 1974 and 1977. Since 1971, the Navy had had 24 hard-striking submarines, and the first ten class-143 missile-armed fast patrol boats were commissioned in 1976/77. With the conversion of ten coastal minesweepers to minehunters and drone vessels for the 'Troika System', the Navy pursued a new and at that time unique path. What is more, this was the time of the development of the Maritime Headquarters (MHQ) C2 and information system, which allowed a real-time response to be mounted to threats from electronically-controlled weapon systems. On 31 December 1978, the Navy had a strength of around 37,000 active-duty personnel and the number of reservists had risen to 151,753, of whom 21,769 were reserve duty personnel (reservists with assigned posts).

The Navy in the 1980s

The high concentration of Warsaw Pact maritime forces on the northern flank of Europe caused NATO to fear that, in the event of war, key geographical positions could be occupied by enemy forces. To allow an adequate response to be mounted to these threats, the national operational restraints that had been imposed on the Navy until then (61° north, on the Dover-Calais line and 18° east, in the Baltic Sea) were suspended in 1981 and NATO's Concept of Maritime Operations was approved. The *Bundesmarine's* mission was now to strengthen the maritime forward defence of NATO's northern flank (in the Baltic Sea, the North Sea and the Norwegian Sea). In order to reduce the enemy's attack potential in the Baltic Sea and to prevent him from using the sea as a staging area, submarines and naval fighter bombers were primarily to be deployed there (Naval Air Wing 1 was equipped with the new Tornado combat aircraft in 1981). In the North Sea and the Norwegian Sea, the focus was on coastal defence and defence against enemy surface action groups. The contribution the *Bundesmarine* made towards this consisted of destroyers, frigates, submarines, supply ships, mine countermeasures vessels, long-range maritime patrol aircraft and naval fighter bombers. The *Bundesmarine* had therefore enabled the stronger navies (USA and UK) of the NATO partners to focus entirely on deterring threats in the Atlantic and out of area. On 31 December 1985, the Navy had a strength of 39,400 personnel.

On 1 September 1986, it issued its fourth 'Navy Concept', in which NATO's strategic guidelines were reaffirmed. In the autumn of 1987, German units formed part of NATO's *Naval On Call Force Mediterranean* (Navocformed) in the Mediterranean. This meant that the Navy was no longer confined to operating on Europe's northern flank but above all demonstrated its political effectiveness on account of its presence in the world's crisis regions. From 12 to 16 October 1989, a naval force of the *Bundesmarine* consisting of the destroyer ROMMEL, the frigate NIEDERSACHSEN and the supply ship COBURG paid the first peacetime call to the Russian (Soviet) port of Leningrad in 77 years.

The German Navy in the 1990s

After German reunification in 1990 and the dissolution of the Warsaw Pact in 1991, the GDR's *Volksmarine* was also dissolved. Most of the *Volksmarine's* ships and boats were sold after being decommissioned and the rest were scrapped. The *Bundesmarine* incorporated 1,385 soldiers into its ranks from the dissolved *Volksmarine*. In 1991, the *Bundesmarine*, the 'Navy of Unity', was renamed the *Deutsche Marine* (German Navy). The German Navy initially assigned itself two chief tasks: It had to remain capable of defending Germany and its allies in the event of an attack and of assisting its allies and partners by contributing to the management of international crises and conflicts at short notice. In the 'planning objectives of the Navy' of 1991, national and collective defence and participation in international crisis management were laid down as the chief tasks. Since then, the task of the Bundeswehr (and thus also of the Navy) has been to participate in international peacekeeping and conflict management operations.

In 1990, NATO once again requested the German Navy's participation in Navocformed (when it later became a NATO standing naval force, it was renamed Stanavformed). The German government provided destroyers, frigates and tankers for this purpose. The *Bundesmarine* had thus taken a further step towards assuming international peacekeeping and conflict management tasks. Following Iraq's invasion of Kuwait in August 1990, the German government decided to dispatch a mine countermeasures force to clear the international sea routes of mines, initially deploying it in the eastern Mediterranean and in 1991 in the Persian Gulf.

In July 1992, the German government decided that German naval units were to participate in the embargo operations against Serbia established by the Western European Union and NATO. In July 1994, the German government passed a resolution stipulating that German naval units would participate in the multinational operation *Sharp Guard* to enforce the embargo against rump Yugoslavia in the Adriatic. German naval forces were deployed there continuously until 1996. In February 1994, a German naval force evacuated the German land component (UNOSOM II) from Mogadishu, Somalia. In March 1999, German naval units were deployed in the Mediterranean and in the Adriatic in support of Allied operations during and after the Kosovo conflict.

Coinciding with the downsizing of the Bundeswehr from approximately 520,000 soldiers to 340,000 by the end of 1994 and parallel to the growth in the number of tasks that the Navy had assumed, financial constraints required the number of naval personnel to be reduced from approximately 39,500 to 27,000 by the year 2000. This target was also achieved by decommissioning boat and ship squadrons.

The German Navy from 2000

The North Atlantic Council classified the terrorist attacks in New York and Washington on 11 September 2001 as an attack under Article 5 of the NATO Treaty and on 2 October 2001 invoked the Article 5 mutual defence clause. For the USA and NATO, the terrorist attacks marked the start of an asymmetric war. A direct consequence of this was that the operational requirements of rapid deployability, optimised interoperability with the Allies and, above all, endurance in distant operating areas were stipulated for the German Navy. The core mission of the German Navy consisted of:

- conducting reconnaissance and maritime surveillance,
- providing strategic sea transport and maintaining security, and
- ensuring security of the operating area from the sea/delivering sea-to-shore fire.

On 16 November 2001, the German Bundestag approved the use of the Bundeswehr in the fight against international terrorism in support of the US-led coalition. In 2002, the German Navy dispatched naval and naval air forces to participate in the multinational anti-terrorism operation 'Enduring Freedom' off the Horn of Africa. A forward logistic base was set up in Djibouti for the Navy's ships and aircraft. NATO's extended concept resulted on 21 May 2003 in the issue of new 'Defence Policy Guidelines' for the Bundeswehr that also provided the Navy with clear guidelines for its participation in international operations involving asymmetric threats. Potential 'asymmetric' threats included the proliferation of weapons of mass destruction, terrorism, extremism, organised crime, piracy and trafficking in drugs and humans. A distinction was made between operations of 'high intensity' (peace enforcement) and of 'medium and low intensity' (peacekeeping).

With boats and ships that were more advanced in terms of quality, but fewer in number than in 2000, the Navy was now meant to be an *expeditionary navy* and to operate worldwide. At the end of 2003, the German Navy was involved in 40 manoeuvres and operations in 116 ports in 39 countries. In the spring of 2006, for example, German maritime forces were deployed in the Indian Ocean and off the Horn of Africa, in the South Atlantic Ocean and off the coast of South Africa, in the western Mediterranean (NATO anti-terrorism operation 'Active Endeavour'), and also in the North Sea and the Norwegian Sea. On 31 December 2003, the Navy had over 90 boats/ships, 69 aircraft and 42 helicopters.

The target structure 'Navy 2005' required the most extensive restructuring (downsizing) of the Navy in its 40-year history. This above all included the dissolution of Naval Air Wings 1 and 2 and the transfer of the TORNADO naval fighter bombers to the Air Force in 2005. The German Navy thus lost one of its strongest capabilities, namely that of conducting naval air operations. On 31 December 2005, the Navy had 24,657 officers and enlisted personnel. Its fleet of boats and ships had shrunk to 75.

In 2006, the German Navy began to provide boats and ships for the UN's multinational maritime operation UNIFIL in the eastern Mediterranean to stop the smuggling of arms into Lebanon across the sea. The German Navy set up a permanent forward logistic base for this operation in the port of Limassol in Cyprus. And since 2008, the German Navy has had frigates and long-range maritime reconnaissance aircraft deployed around the clock in the EU-led counterpiracy mission 'Atalanta' off the Horn of Africa.

Deployable and sustainable anywhere in the world

Since the end of the 1990s, the German Navy has been deployed in crisis and conflict management operations all around the world. Since then, the requirements for the capability profile of boats/ships have changed fundamentally. During the Cold War, the fleet units were designed primarily for military operations in NATO's northern flank area (in the Baltic Sea, the North Sea, and the North Atlantic), that is to say for special operations (minehunting, anti-submarine warfare, surface combat, air defence) in waters close to their home ports, whereas today they have to be versatile and able to operate for long periods of time anywhere in the world. This means covering long distances to get to and return from remote crisis zones, remaining on deployment in areas of operations over four months at a time (two years in future), performing multi roles, covering a broad spectrum of operations (maritime surveillance, reconnaissance, embargo monitoring, evacuation, escort duties, protection of merchant shipping, participation in joint operations) as part of multinational forces operating off enemy shores and facing asymmetric threats. So future requirements are being taken into account when new boats and ships are built, for example the class 125 frigates, which are currently under construction. These ships must meet so-called intensive use standards (sustainability) that ensure that they among other things can remain on deployment in distant operating areas for two years. They are being built according to the mission module requirements so that with the aid of prepared and standardised equipment modules and the appropriate specialists, they can rapidly be made ready to take on specific operational tasks without any major technical adjustments. A high level of automation on the frigates also allows the crews to be confined to a strength of just 120. In the future, a dual-crew concept is to be implemented on the Navy's boats and ships; this means that the units can remain in distant operating areas for long periods of time, while the crews are replaced every four months.

The reorientation of the Navy in 2011

The reorientation of the Bundeswehr that began in 2011, which along with the suspension of compulsory military service is leading to a reduction in personnel strength from approximately 252,000 to approximately 185,000 soldiers and a significant reduction in weapon systems and equipment, also means changes for the German Navy. The German Navy is planned to have a personnel strength of only 13,500 sailors. Only a fleet with far fewer units than in the past can be maintained with this small number of personnel.

The Navy's fleet will in future therefore consist of 55 boats and ships and 40 aircraft and helicopters: 11 frigates, 5 or 6 corvettes and multi-purpose battleships, 6 submarines, 10 mine countermeasures units, 11 naval auxiliaries, 3 fleet service vessels, 2 joint support ships, 8 long-range maritime patrol aircraft, 30 helicopters and 1 naval force protection battalion (special forces).

This relatively small Navy, with a fleet that will nevertheless feature modern surface and subsurface units, has been designed for deployment in protracted global multinational crisis and conflict management operations (UN, NATO, EU) and in the fight against international terrorism. The objective is to counter the threats posed by crises and conflicts and international terrorism where they arise in order to keep them away from Europe and Germany.

Bringing the services' interests to bear

In spite of their special functional characteristics and roles, the services have always been part of a whole, namely the Bundeswehr, as well as NATO and the EU. Even with clear assignment of primary responsibility to the political leadership ('primacy of politics') as a result of the organisational structures of the FMOD, the Bundeswehr's armed forces, i.e. the services, have been an integral part of the Bundeswehr as a whole since 1955. As a result of this and their execution of different missions in pursuit of common objectives, deepened cooperation and mutual appreciation have developed over the decades. A similar situation has also evolved with regard to the armed forces and services of Allied nations. However, this cooperation has required, and continues to require, substantial efforts to be made.

Until now, the services have been incorporated into the FMOD. The chiefs of staff, supported by their 'directorates', or divisions as they are called in the Army, Air and Navy Staffs, have been administrative superiors of the services and at the same time ministerial directors. The chiefs of staff thus have been able to exert an influence on the top political and military leadership and represent the interests of the services directly. This has included, for example, their right to report directly to the minister, the requirement for them to endorse all procedures affecting the services by signing the relevant documents, their membership of the 'Chiefs of Staff Council' chaired by the Chief of Staff of the Bundeswehr as well as the 'Operations Council' and their assignment as the military authorities responsible for the specific materiel of their services.

The responsibility assigned to the Chief of Staff, Bundeswehr, for the overall concept of military defence and later for operations as well has grown ever since the 'Blankenese Directive', a document that also stipulated things such as the responsibilities of the Chief of Staff, Bundeswehr, and the chiefs of staff of the services, was issued in 1970 and above all ever since the follow-up directives were issued in 2005 and 2012. This has further increased the pressure on these bodies to attain a consensus on matters, which they have often done before getting together at meetings. The matters they have had to deal with come from the entire spectrum of topics concerning the armed forces and services, ranging from the implementation of political guidelines and strategies, the specification of details of missions and concept development to involvement in the development of the Bundeswehr concepts, organisational structures, *Innere Führung* (leadership development and civic education), personnel development and management and materiel procurement. It must be pointed out, however, that the main guidelines are political ones, issued by the German government, the Federal Minister of Defence and the German Bundestag or, to be precise, the defence and the budget committee. This applies in particular to the defence budget, the size of the Bundeswehr, major procurement projects and, since the 1990s, to the mandates for Bundeswehr operations.

As the development of the three German services described in the previous sections has shown, NATO and, later, also the EU are other factors that have had (and still have) a significant influence on the structure and capabilities of the Bundeswehr, with planning and operation guidelines that have been drafted jointly beforehand (for example, NATO strategy, Defence Planning Guidance) being taken into account. Mutual influence has regularly arisen from cooperation with NATO and EU partners, and above all with the US armed forces. The USA has always played a particularly influential role on account of its size and significance. Initiatives concerning matters such as army concepts and operational-tactical ideas have often come from the US, even if not all of them have been implemented. On the other hand, ideas from the smaller partners have also come into play, the German Army regularly being one of them. However, the national and multinational framework is such that the individual services have had and still have only limited scope for creating and establishing areas in which they can implement their own ideas.

Although the Army, Air Force and Navy together make up the armed forces of the Bundeswehr, each service has also developed a concept of itself that is defined by its respective roles. As the parameters and foundations that define security policy have continually evolved over time, along with the respective structures, a struggle has often ensued between the services over the limited financial and personnel resources. Over many decades, the formula '7:3:1' applied to the allocation of resources for the Army, Air Force and Navy. This rule of thumb was generally observed with regard to the allocation of personnel and organisational elements, but not with regard to major procurement projects. The Air Force's big projects (combat aircraft) and the Navy's (ships, boats) regularly required substantial shares of the investment funds in the defence budget. The Army thus learned more than the other services how to 'cope with shortages'. One reason for this is that the Army defines itself less by means of specific effect/combat systems it has than more by units and brigades/divisions, which are composed of a system connecting numerous components, such as various organisational elements, arms and services, weapon systems and high staffing levels. It is not easy for anyone, and particularly for those bearing political responsibility, to see this comparably large and almost incomprehensive army as a 'system of systems' and to provide it what it needs.

Since 1 April 2012, the Bundeswehr and the role of the services within the Bundeswehr as a system have changed fundamentally. Having been dispensed with as ministerial authorities and rendered subordinate to the Chief of Staff, Bundeswehr, the chiefs of staff of the services have lost direct influence ('Dresden Directive' of 21.03.2012). Consequently, they are faced with such problems as how to represent their services' interests, how to exert influence to the advantage of their services, how to contribute their 'service expertise', and how to exercise their responsibility for personnel and materiel. The possibility of reporting directly to the Federal Minister or of gaining a hearing in parliament is no longer guaranteed by the organisational structure, but depends on the people concerned, and is thus a matter of uncertainty. There is the danger of a struggle for influence and resources between the services or the major military organisational elements increasing.

The tasks of the Chief of Staff, Bundeswehr, of the military divisions at the FMOD and of the offices that work for them are highly complex and difficult, and they must be performed properly if the services are to be assigned missions and resources in due proportion. At present it seems that the chiefs of staff or representatives of the services will continue to be members of key advisory bodies. Officers from their respective services will also continue to be employed at the FMOD and its offices, but the influence they will be able to exert for their own services will be limited. In comparison with the armed forces of other states, this kind of influence has not been wanted for historical reasons, and experience has shown that the Army at least has only exerted it on a comparably small scale. With the removal of the service staffs from the FMOD, the chiefs of staff can be expected to now have to 'fight their way through the authorities' rather than be able to exert influence directly.

An important example of this is the future participation of the services in procurement projects. The Bundeswehr's armament organisation is being restructured. Under the lead of the 'Equipment, IT and In-Service Support' directorate at the FMOD, the tasks will be performed by a new 'Federal Office of Equipment, IT and In-Service Support' as well as by subordinate agencies for technical and IT tasks. This will mean that the chiefs of staff will lose their so-called 'cognisance for materiel supportability', as this will be administered on a centralised basis in future. Other support tasks, described as 'In-service and Supply Responsibility for the Maintenance of Operational Capability and Readiness', will remain with the services or with major military organisational elements.

The services will submit their materiel requirements to the Chief of Staff, Bundeswehr, via a Bundeswehr planning office and the planning directorate at the FMOD. Approved requirements, some of which may have been amended, will then be forwarded to the 'armament directorate' at the FMOD and its subordinate office. The armament organisation and relevant agencies of the armed forces will cooperate by way of 'integrated project teams'. They will also feature representatives of the services. However, they will no longer have any formal say in the levels/institutions responsible for framing and assessing requirements and ordering them to be met. It is hoped that the expertise of the Army, the Air Force and the Navy, the lessons they have learned from operations and the overarching evaluation of all the aspects of the services by the chiefs of staff can be incorporated into the new central planning and armament structure in a regular and coordinated manner.

Bibliography

Borgert, Heinz-Ludger (1997/98): Die Entstehung und Entwicklung der Marinekonzeption in der Bundesrepublik Deutschland 1950-1964. In: Mars: Jahrbuch für Wehrpolitik und Militärwesen, 3/4, 296-340.

Borgert, Heinz-Ludger (1997/98): Die Entstehung und Entwicklung der Marinekonzeption in der Bundesrepublik Deutschland 1950-1964. In: Mars: Jahrbuch für Wehrpolitik und Militärwesen, 3/4, 296-340.

Borgert, Heinz-Ludger (no year): Die 'Konzeption der Bundesmarine' 1962. In: Marineforum.

Brügner, Gunnar C. (2012): Die neue Struktur des Heeres. In: Europäische Sicherheit & Technik, 61: 2, 36-39.

Clement, Rolf (2011): Die Reform der Bundeswehr. In: Der Mittler-Brief, 26: 4, 1-8.

de Maizière, Dr Thomas (2012): In Verantwortung für Frieden und Sicherheit. Die Neuausrichtung der Bundeswehr gemeinsam gestalten. In: Europäische Sicherheit & Technik, 61: 1, 12-19.

Federal Minister of Defence (2012): Principles for the Top-Level Structure, Chain of Command, and Command and Control Organisation in the Federal Ministry of Defence and the Bundeswehr ('Dresden Directive'). Dresden.

BMVg (1974): White Paper 1974. The Security of the Federal Republic of Germany and the Development of the Federal Armed Forces. Bonn: BMVg.

BMVg (1979): White Paper 1979. The Security of the Federal Republic of Germany and the Development of the Federal Armed Forces. Bonn: BMVg.

BMVg (1983): White Paper 1983. The Security of the Federal Republic of Germany. Bonn: BMVg.

BMVg (1985): White Paper 1985: The Situation and the Development of the Federal Armed Forces. Bonn: BMVg.

BMVg (1990): Military Symbols. Joint Service Regulation (ZDv) 1/11. Bonn, 07.12.1990.

BMVg (1992): Defence Policy Guidelines. Bonn: BMVg.

BMVg (1994): White Paper on the Security of the Federal Republic of Germany and the Situation and Future of the Bundeswehr, commissioned by the Federal Government, ed. Federal Minister of Defence. Bonn: BMVg.

BMVg (2001): Die Bundeswehr der Zukunft – Sachstand der Reformen. Bonn, 01.06.2001. Bonn.

BMVg (2003): Defence Policy Guidelines for the Area of Responsibility of the Federal Minister of Defence. Berlin: BMVg.

BMVg (2004): Outline of the Bundeswehr Concept. Bonn/Berlin: BMVg.

BMVg (2006): White Paper on German Security Policy and the Future of the Bundeswehr. Bonn/Berlin: BMVg.

BMVg (2011): Defence Policy Guidelines. Safeguarding National Interests – Assuming International Responsibility – Shaping Security Together. Berlin: Federal Minister of Defence.

BMVg (2012): Current Status of the Bundeswehr Reorientation. Safeguarding National Interests – Assuming International Responsibility – Shaping Security Together. Berlin.

BMVg Army Staff Branch I 5 (Ed.) (2000): Die Strukturen des Heeres. Bonn.

Freers, Werner (2011): Das neue Einsatzheer – ein Heer für die Einsätze der Zukunft. In: Europäische Sicherheit, 60: 12, 16-22.

Henkel, Manfred/Schulte, Hermann (Eds.) (2005): Entwicklung des Heeres im Wandel der Heerstrukturen. Bonn: Streitkräfteamt.

Klos, Dietmar (2006): Structure of the 'New Army'. In: European Security and Defence, 2-2006, 11-15.

Klos, Dietmar (2011): Die Kampf- und Kampfunterstützungstruppen des Heeres. In: Europäische Sicherheit, 60: 12, 56-61.

Klos, Dietmar (2011): Die Kampf- und Kampfunterstützungstruppen des Heeres. In: Europäische Sicherheit, 60: 9, 53-60.

Klos, Dietmar (2011): Die Kampf- und Kampfunterstützungstruppen des Heeres. In: Europäische Sicherheit, 60: 11, 32-38.

Lonkai, Andreas (1997): Konzeption der Marine und Auftrag im Bündnis. In: Die Marine im Kalten Krieg 1956-1968 / 37. Historisch-Taktische Tagung der Flotte am 08. und 09. Januar 1997, 35-58.

Meier, Ernst-Christoph, Hannemann, Andreas, Meyer zu Felde, Rainer (2012): Wörterbuch zur Sicherheitspolitik. Deutschland in einem veränderten internationalen Umfeld. Hamburg/Berlin/Bonn: E.S. Mittler & Sohn GmbH.

Presse- und Informationsamt der Bundesregierung (Ed.) (1990): Vertrag über die abschließende Regelung in Bezug auf Deutschland. Die Verhandlungen über die Aspekte der Herstellung der deutschen Einheit. Bonn.

Sander-Nagashima, Johannes Berthold (2005): Vor 50 Jahren schlug die Geburtsstunde der Bundesmarine: die Herausforderungen des maritimen Neuanfangs. In: Militärgeschichte, Zeitschrift für historische Bildung, 3, 4-9.

Schraut, Hans-Jürgen (Ed.) (1993): Die Streitkräftestruktur der Bundeswehr 1956-1990. Ebenhausen.

Steinborn, Harmut (2001): Die Fernmeldetruppen des Heeres in der Bundeswehr (1956-1999). In: Antenne, 6: Sonderausgabe 100 Jahre Fernmeldetruppen, 31-35.

Stockfisch, Dieter (adapted) (2009): Der Reibert. Heer. Luftwaffe. Marine Das Handbuch für den deutschen Soldaten. Mittler E.S. + Sohn. Hamburg, 2009.

Walle, Heinrich (2005): 50 Jahre Deutsche Marine: Deutsche Seestreitkräfte im Wandel der Zeit. In: Schiff & Hafen, 57:5, 56-62.

Jointness in the Bundeswehr

Manfred Engelhardt

The rationale behind the establishment of the Joint Support Service

Over the past twenty years, a process has been taking place within the Bundeswehr that has led towards more jointness. This involves the amalgamation of common and therefore duplicate armed forces tasks to a joint major military organisational element. In order to understand this development, one must look back at the Bundeswehr of the 'Bonn Republic'. This phase was characterised by the bipolar conflict between the two power blocs, i.e. NATO and the Warsaw Pact. From the height of the Cold War to the reunification of Germany, the Bundeswehr, with a strength of around 500,000 soldiers, was one of the most modern armed forces within NATO (Epkenhans, 2012: 57). In this bipolar conflict, the territory of the 'old' Federal Republic of Germany, which was limited in depth, was divided into a forward combat zone – lying along the inner-German border and the border with the former state of Czechoslovakia – and a rear combat zone. In the forward combat zone, the sectors of the German and Allied corps were joined together from north to south like a string of beads. The organisation for the defence of the zones required services that could operate as self-sufficiently as possible. The Navy was specialized in securing the North Sea and Baltic Sea approaches, in cooperation with the Allies. The Air Force, together with the NATO partners, would defend the airspace by engaging in aerial combat, and the Army was geared towards conducting sweeping 'combined arms combat' operations from Franconia via the 'Fulda Gap' up to the North German Lowlands.

The services were largely self-sufficient in terms of logistics, communications support and reconnaissance, to name only the most important areas. For example, the divisions and corps of the German Army had access to supplies stockpiled at Field and Territorial Army depots in the division and corps rear areas. Military district and territorial commands were responsible for maintaining freedom of operations and movement control, particularly in the rear combat zone.

Until the fall of the Berlin Wall in 1989, NATO, and with it the Bundeswehr, had spent 45 years preparing exclusively for a possible operation within the framework of the East-West conflict. Since 1989, this scenario of a 'hot war' between the East and West has become increasingly unlikely. Following reunification and the collapse of the Soviet Union in 1991, Germany found itself in a new political role. This was the starting point of the Bundeswehr's most extensive reform, which took place over many years. The operations in Cambodia (1992),

Somalia (1993) and in the Balkans (1995) revealed that the Bundeswehr was not suited to such types of operations. The tactical structures of the services, which were oriented towards 'forward defence', i.e. the need to cover relatively limited operational distances, primarily in a support role, were not suited to ensuring the sustainable support needed for joint operations at a strategic distance of several thousand kilometres. Consequently, the Joint Support Service (JSS) was set up in 2000 as an independent major military organisational element while many of the older outdated structures were dismantled.

In view of the changes in the security landscape, the 'business idea and rationale' underlying the JSS were the pooling of dwindling resources and the amalgamation of duplicate tasks previously performed in the services, accompanied by an increase in cost-effectiveness. Expressed in economic terms, the JSS has become the provider of the 'shared services' of the Army, Air Force, Navy and Joint Medical Service. A similar development had also taken place in the Medical Service. Service-specific Medical Service tasks were transferred to the Joint Medical Service at virtually the same time as the JSS was established.

Oriented towards and designed for operations abroad, the JSS today constitutes the 'strategic link' or 'bridge' between the Federal Republic of Germany and the theatres of operation. It connects Germany's and Europe's personnel and materiel resources with the requirements of the contingents far from home and is also used to convey personnel, materiel, data and services.

As a so-called 'force enabler', it frequently creates the conditions necessary for the deployment of German contingents in the first place. As a 'force provider', the JSS itself assigns a wide range of specialized support personnel to the theatres. By implement the 'reach-back' concept, it is therefore possible to provide extensive support services for the soldiers on deployment from Germany while at the same time reducing the 'footprint' in the theatres.

In addition to the security landscape, this chapter also considers the development towards jointness at the organisational level. Several examples will show how it functions at the operational and tactical levels. Command and control support and the logistic system of the Bundeswehr will be used to explain how jointness has assumed concrete form in routine duty and in operations.

From a defence army to an army geared towards operations abroad

With its newly-regained sovereignty, the young 'Berlin Republic' also had to face new threats to international security, such as failing states, small wars and civil wars as well as terrorism (Chiari, 2012a:15). This did not lead, however, to the independent definition of national objectives for Bundeswehr operations in the sense of a 'National Level of Ambition'. As early as 1992, the Defence Policy Guidelines addressed the subject of the realignment of security policy. According to these guidelines, the Bundeswehr was to 'adhere to the future understanding of security policy and be aligned to the new requirements both in terms of quality and quantity' (BMVg, 1992: para. 37). In an attempt to legitimise the new role of the armed forces, the German government thus endeavoured to further integrate them into existing security architectures such as NATO and to rely more heavily on the EU's new security role (10 Jahre SKB, 2010: 32). The Defence Policy Guidelines of 2003 stipulate 'the multinational integration of the Bundeswehr within the framework of a foreign policy focused on European integration, transatlantic partnership and global responsibility' (BMVg, 2003: 23). This is based on the assumption that the Bundeswehr will conduct armed operations together with allies and partners in a UN, NATO and EU context.

These partners and allies also called on Germany to make a contribution to missions under a NATO or UN mandate that was appropriate to the country's position and economic power. However, the people of Germany were not ready for this and the Bundeswehr was not geared towards it either. The integration of the Bundeswehr in the security architecture of NATO and the EU was another factor that, in addition to operational reality, accelerated its restructuring and increase in jointness.

In 2010, Defence Minister zu Guttenberg described the paradigm shift that had been taking place in the armed forces and society since 1990 as follows: 'This year we will be celebrating 20 years of the Army of Unity. Since 1990, the Bundeswehr has undergone a transformation, unprecedented in its history, from an army for national defence in the shadow of the all-embracing East-West conflict to an army for operations' (zu Guttenberg, 2010a: 1).

The forces driving the development of jointness

In addition to this redefinition of security policy, a further factor necessitating the reform of the armed forces was the shortage of financial resources, which resulted from the nation's priority task of rebuilding the economy of the states in eastern Germany ('Aufbau Ost') in the wake of German reunification and from the financial cost arising from it. This forced the German government at that time to make particularly drastic cuts in the defence budget (BMVg, 1992: para. 37). The concepts for the structures and necessary equipment of the forces were developed at the staffs of the individual services and, at that time, left only limited scope for joint developments. Training and the development of tactics and procedures, for example, had previously been service matters. Arms projects at the time, some of which are being pursued within the Bundeswehr up to today, offered little scope for interoperability. Collaboration between the services only began at the corps level and below that was at best practised by liaison officers.

Its first operations and its involvement in the IFOR and SFOR missions in the Balkans, for example, made it painfully clear to the Bundeswehr that it did not have the necessary structure and equipment for this kind of involvement.

This accelerated considerations on restructuring the Bundeswehr in terms of both the political and the military control of the armed forces. The need for reform was identified in training, force structures, weapons, equipment and also in the operating procedures (10 Jahre SKB, 2010: 25). Considerations about structural reform led to the German government publishing the Cornerstones of the Reorientation of the Bundeswehr on 14 June 2000 and initiated the second large block of reforms for the armed forces after German reunification, which was also accompanied by a further reduction in their staffing levels. Armament cooperation, the reduction of duplicate capabilities, standardisation, the joint performance of tasks, the functional division of labour and role specialisation now determined daily business in the planning divisions of the service staffs at the defence ministry for the coming years.

Jointness developed step by step in the Bundeswehr. It is a process that continues to this day.

In his directive for the further development of the Bundeswehr in 2003, the defence minister at the time, Peter Struck, stated that, among other things, the following changes were needed: 'The capability profile must be examined to determine whether subcapabilities and a reduction in quantity can be dispensed with, the joint approach must be further strengthened and new developments (e.g. network enabled operations) must be adopted.' (Struck, 2003: 3). These factors now formed the central guidelines for the detailed planning of the armed forces and thus for further considerations regarding any continued development of jointness.

The creation of a central service element for the armed forces

The guidelines issued on 14 July 2000 for the reorientation of the armed forces paved the way for the new, extended capability profile and the simultaneous downsizing of the Bundeswehr to a strength to 285,000 soldiers. For the first time in the history of Bundeswehr reforms, joint cost-effective task performance had become a fundamental condition for an effective and efficient reorientation, the result of which the establishment of the JSS in October 2000. The basic idea of this was to permit the efficient performance of common support tasks so as to enable the services and the Central Medical Service to concentrate on their operations-related core capabilities. (Heise, 2001: 26). A common 'service element', known as the Joint Support Service, was created.

This constituted a break with the extensive independence to date of the Army, the Air Force and the Navy. In view of operational reality, expensive duplications and cost pressure led to the realisation that the job of participating in operations can in principle now only be mastered on a joint basis. To the individual soldier on patrol in Afghanistan, for example, it does not matter which service guarantees him survivability and protection. What matters to him is the fact that these capabilities can be provided professionally and sustainably. The reorientation led to a balancing act between specialisation and division of labour and the intent was to resolve this problem by focusing on capabilities. To that end, a capability profile was defined, which even today contains six basic interlinked capability categories:

- Command and control capability
- Intelligence collection and reconnaissance
- Mobility
- Effective engagement
- Support and sustainability
- Survivability and protection (BMVg, 2003: para. 15).

This capability-based approach now allowed the capability itself to be focused on, irrespective of the service or major organisational element that provided it, and avoided it being held by a number of services and thus causing additional expense (10 Jahre SKB, 2010: 41).

For the Bundeswehr, the establishment of the JSS meant breaking new ground at international level as well. The conceptual phase at the defence ministry was now followed by the far more difficult process of implementation, which primarily concerned the integration of the people in the Bundeswehr. The central task areas in the domain of the JSS were: command and control and C2 support, national territorial tasks, military intelligence, logistics, armament and service use, military police, operational information, geoinformation, military music, military support of civil authorities in Germany and CIMIC, binational and multinational cooperation, CBRN defence and protection, infrastructure and stationing, personnel support, training and education, as well as science and research (Heise, 2001: 26).

This led to the establishment of numerous new headquarters and agencies as well as to the assignment of agencies to the newly-established Joint Support Command. The scope of the tasks required the new major organisational element to adopt a command and control organisation based strictly responsibilities, the idea being to achieve this by the creation of new major JSS commands.

Overseeing JSS command and control:
the Joint Support Command and the Armed Forces Office

The JSS's top-level structure is supported by two pillars, an office and a command. During the establishment phase an existing agency, the Armed Forces Office, could be used. A whole variety of specialized tasks, such as initial and further training, PR work, and the further development of the Joint Support Service and also reserve work, were performed under one roof. Since the JSS was established, the challenge for the Armed Forces Office has been to further develop and become a comprehensive support element for the Joint Support Service. In essence, it has been a matter of ensuring that the central official and specialized tasks are performed effectively and cost-efficiently for the entire Bundeswehr (Das SKA, 2010: 187).

When Vice Admiral Heise, the then Chief of Staff of the JSS, inaugurated the Joint Support Command as the JSS's command on 10 April 2001, jointness became tangible below the ministerial level. The newly-created major organisational element grew quickly. A variety of branch colours and uniforms moved into the new shared quarters in Cologne-Wahn. By mid-2002, the headquarters had grown to its full strength and established operational readiness and was thus able to perform tasks and provide capabilities for the armed forces from a single source. With the new personnel in the headquarters of the Joint Support Command, it was not long before a wealth of expertise had been acquired, resulting in an increase in operational capability and a decrease in the use of resources. Of the 1,400 or so military and civilian personnel at the headquarters of the Joint Support Command, the Army provides 58% of the military personnel, the Air Force 33% and the Navy 6%, figures that essentially reflect the proportions of the soldiers in the Bundeswehr (SKUKdo 2011a). The transfer of responsibility to the four Military District Commands (MDC) and to their subordinate units in October 2001 may also be seen as a further important milestone. They are specialized in increasing efficiency and cost-effectiveness in their respective fields. MDC I ('Coast') and MDC IV ('South Germany') command and control all the logistic forces centrally; MDC II and MDC III, for their part, command and control the command support forces. The commander of the Joint Support Command thus also bears responsibility as the National Territorial Commander. The new command experienced its first test with the flooding of the River Elbe and the River Danube in August 2002, when it was called on to assist the subsidiary disaster relief operations. The personnel strength of the command peaked at over 60,000 soldiers and civilians (Das SKUKdo, 2010: 201). The job of taking over the logistics and command and control support tasks of the Army, Air Force and Navy in the new major organisational element was not only an organisational challenge; it was rendered more difficult by the fact that the tasks had to be transferred to newly-aligned joint structures and fitted into a process-oriented arrangement. In other words, in addition to personnel being transferred and materiel being relocated, new structures and workflows had to be designed and implemented in the agencies. This required everyone in the units to be willing and prepared to stop thinking in the service-specific way to which they were accustomed and to support the implementation of the reorganisation measures. The Armed Forces Office and the Joint Support Command therefore had to do groundwork in the divisions responsible for concepts and further development. This process, incidentally, was marked by a high degree of dynamism due to the assumption of responsibility for the JSS contingents deployed on operations abroad. As the JSS's command, it is a 'control centre' and responsible for ensuring the contingents get the support they need all over the world. This makes it the 'Strategic Support and Sustainment Command' of the Bundeswehr.

Jointness in thinking and action

A specific leadership culture evolved in each of the services over the decades. These leadership cultures determined the development of command and control procedures and hierarchical structures within the services, which in turn influenced the spirit among the troops. Joint cooperation was only practised by the upper tactical level at corps headquarters and above. The establishment of the Joint Support Service as an independent major organisational element brought about a clash of views on jointness that even today presents a challenge – also for the coalescence of various leadership cultures. Coinages found only in the Bundeswehr, such as 'uniformed Army personnel', 'uniformed Navy personnel' and 'uniformed Air Force personnel', which are used in the JSS, are simply an expression of how difficult the formation process is. The mission statement of the Joint Support Command from 2005 was intended to include all elements of the heterogeneous command from the operational forces and specialized offices to the headquarters of the Joint Support Command.

Mission statement of Joint Support Command

Who we are:

The command of the Joint Support Service.

The supreme National Territorial Command.

A command with specialized tasks.

Our main tasks are:

With our forces we are a major contributor to intervention and stabilisation operations of the Bundeswehr – acting both in theatre and from Germany.

Military command and control on territorial operations is in our hands.

Our technical competence provides the driving force for the further development of the Bundeswehr in key capability areas.

What we expect:

Our command is characterised by jointness and diversity. We think and act with a sense of joint responsibility and extend the scope for action of everyone involved by applying advanced business administration procedures.

As a central service provider, we are fully geared to meeting the requirements of the forces both in operations and on routine duty. Our first and foremost aim is to provide them support.

We rely on dialogue to harmonise and actively adapt our aims and services.

Over the past ten years, jointness has become even more firmly anchored in the units, training institutes and headquarters of the JSS. The joint logistic system and the Bundeswehr command and control support system are examples of how tangible and successful jointness has become.

Jointness in training and exercises

The establishment of the structures of the JSS also changed the setting for joint training. In the Leadership Development and Civic Education Centre, the Command and Staff College, and the Universities of the Bundeswehr or the Bundeswehr Academy for Information and Communication, the armed forces have training institutes that have always been under centralised command (Das SKA, 2010: 188). Further schools and training centres were set up and assigned to the central training management of the Armed Forces Office. This meant that better use could be made of the resources that had been freed up, and synergies could be exploited due to the adoption of comprehensive, capability-based and common solutions. By drawing on the support of the Army Supply School, the logistic training capacities of the services were pooled in 2006 in the newly-established Bundeswehr Logistics School. Coordinated logistic procedures have since been taught at this new joint school, with account being taken of multinational aspects and the service logistics organisation (SKA, 2006: 64).

With the establishment of the Bundeswehr Command Support School in October 2006, a harmonised new cross-service approach was successfully adopted.

It allows for the increasingly shorter development cycles for IT and multinational standards to be taken into consideration (SKA, 2006: 64).

Germany's involvement in multinational operations and in particular the continuing integration of the Bundeswehr into a European security architecture required the establishment of more joint command and control facilities. Command and control of Bundeswehr operations has been exercised by the JSS from the Bundeswehr Joint Forces Operations Command in Potsdam since July 2001. It was in particular the regular participation of German forces in multinational EU Battle Groups and Germany's readiness to command and control these contingents that led to the establishment of the Response Forces Operations Command in Ulm in 2005. Command and control and planning procedures can only be practised and kept up to requirements at this operational-level headquarters that is both joint and combined by means of joint planned exercises. The series of exercises entitled EUROPEAN ENDEAVOUR, for example, served in 2012 to practise and review the operational command and control of combined ground, air and naval forces. These exercises have also shown, however, that capability gaps exist in network enabled operations and that joint command and control procedures have to be further developed and optimised (KdoOpFüBw, 2010:113).

The JSS has thus also become a key element in the further development of joint command and control procedures.

Providing joint capabilities in operations

The JSS has developed into a central support provider that helps to secure and sustain the Bundeswehr's operations. As a command, the Joint Support Command has forces supporting Bundeswehr operations both in theatres of operation and in Germany, and it provides an average of between 20 and 25% of the personnel in the contingents deployed (Lahl, 2006: 26). The Joint Support Command also provides forces earmarked for quasi-operational commitments for possible NATO Response Force (NRF) and the EU Battle Group operations. It is for operations in particular that the JSS pools joint capabilities to relieve the services. The task of accommodating forces in camps cannot be described as a core capability of the Army, the Air Force or the Navy. It makes sense to have this service provided to each contingent from a single source, by the JSS. The role of the Army consists in providing a deployable unit that has the core capability of 'engaging in combat'. The JSS provides all necessary support for this so that the Army's forces have all of the supplies they need to implement this core capability and are ready to be rapidly mobilized. An example of the joint cooperation practised between the JSS and the Army at the tactical level is the provision of

JSS forces for the Kunduz training and protection battalion's manoeuvre company. In this case, an Electronic Warfare (EW) jammer vehicle is assigned to the unit, which is commanded and controlled by the Army, to give the soldiers protection against IEDs set up in the area by the Taliban. Moreover, the company commander can only communicate with the battalion command at the tactical operations centre (TOC) because the JSS command and control support forces integrated into his company operate a radio link or provide satellite communication (SatCom).

By pooling tasks, the Bundeswehr has been able to ensure the operational capability of the armed forces efficiently and sustainably (Kühn, 2010a: 1). The result of this process is overall systemic jointness. This will now be explained in more detail by looking at the Bundeswehr logistics system and at command and control support.

Development of a joint logistics system

During the Cold War, each service had its own logistics structures. From a joint perspective, common logistics capabilities thus existed in duplicate. With the establishment of the JSS, the logistic forces, assets and procedures, as common logistic support tasks, were combined in the JSS Logistics organisation. This allowed the service logistics organisations to concentrate on the task of providing direct support for their own forces and weapon systems.

This focus on tasks in the armed forces was linked for the first time to the basic idea of a joint common logistics system based on the following formal principles:

- Orientation towards the operational mission in the most likely operational scenarios
- Centralisation of the logistic tasks that can be performed better jointly
- Orientation towards general processes for the provision of services
- Orientation towards the most cost-effective use of assets and resources while continuing to provide effective and assured logistic support
- Intensification of cooperation with third-party service providers

Under this system, logistic services were from now on provided jointly for the armed forces, with support from the service and JSS logistics organisations, the Defence Administration, trade and industry and national and multinational partners. The services contributed their specific subservices and subcapabilities according to defined logistic processes and 'supply chains'. For example, the maintenance forces were taken out of Army units and concentrated in the maintenance battalions of the logistics regiments. Essential services were provided by the Heeresinstandsetzungslogistik GmbH (HIL), based on the model of cooperation with the private sector. The only forces that remained in the Army were those capable of detecting damage and repairing minor defects. Dispensing with their common maintenance forces enabled the Air Force and Navy to concentrate on the weapon-specific systems in their aircraft and ships. The Bundeswehr Logistics System was thus created. With the Logistics/G4 division, the Joint Support Command assumed the responsibility for the central coordination of overriding aspects of logistics within the Bundeswehr and for the specific aspects of the JSS logistics organisation. Today, soldiers in all of the services serve in JSS logistic units and HQs. They contribute their expertise and qualifications to the JSS in order to guarantee service provision for the services.

The JSS logistics organisation as the central element in the Bundeswehr logistics system

Before the JSS logistics organisation could be built up, the old logistics system first had to be changed. For example, the depot organisation of the Field and Territorial Armies was disbanded in the division and corps rear areas. The remaining organisation came under the centralised joint responsibility of the JSS.

The static logistic facilities form the foundation upon which supplies to the armed forces in Germany and on operational deployment are provided from the homeland. They include distribution centres, stores, depots and maintenance centres. Their activities are steered by the Bundeswehr Logistics Centre. The tasks performed include spare part supply management, civilian and commercial transport services, cooperation partner services and the strategic transport of personnel, equipment and supplies to the theatres of operation.

The JSS logistics organisation has mobile logistic forces at its disposal for the provision of services for operations. These forces provide logistics services in the theatres of operation. In the JSS, they have so far consisted of 15 battalions in total, eight of which are logistics battalions with common logistic capabilities and seven specialized units that provide maintenance, transport, supply and special pioneer services. The latter have equipment for building and operating camps to accommodate deployed forces and bulk-fuel installations to store fuels on an operational scale. The battalions are concentrated in a logistics brigade and three logistics regiments. Starting in 2002, these units were taken out of the old structures of the services and became the responsibility of the Military District Commands and thus of the JSS, or they were regrouped. Joint uniformity became the hallmark of these units. The commander of a logistics battalion, for example, wears an Air Force uniform, his deputy an Army uniform and the first sergeant of a maintenance company a Navy uniform.

Bundeswehr command and control support and the Bundeswehr IT system

Until the JSS was established, the individual services were responsible for operating the service and weapon system communication and IT systems. Conceptually and structurally, these systems were designed for Cold War missions and were thus optimised to meet the needs of the services, but they were hardly interoperable. Only the Air Force and the Navy already possessed NATO-interoperable command and control systems, although they were essentially designed to enable the command and control and use of their weapons. The command and control capability of the Air Force and Navy forces was mainly ensured from static operations centres in Germany, while that of the Army was maintained from mobile and deployable operations centres. Whereas the Air Force and the Navy were also technically integrated into NATO command structures, the Army's forces were only under national command.

In the late 1990s, it was no longer possible to finance the many different communication/IT systems, and the systems did not feature the technology needed for the future. The rapid growth of the Internet, increasingly shorter development cycles in the field of information technology and forced cost-cutting led to extensive changes in the IT landscape. The many small and large IT island solutions had to be turned into one standardised, networked Bundeswehr IT System one step at a time, according to central specifications. Structurally, this development was taken into account with the establishment of the JSS and the IT Staff at the FMOD, headed by an IT director. This was followed in 2006 by the founding of a civilian IT company in which with the Federal Government as a partner. This, in turn, resulted in the first pooling of responsibilities for the procurement and operation of information technology and Bundeswehr command and control support. A Bundeswehr task, it today consists of the capabilities of the command and control support forces, assets and facilities of all the major military organisational elements. It is supplemented by commercial IT services.

The JSS bears overall and process-related responsibility for Bundeswehr command and control support, including the use and operation of the Bundeswehr IT System.

Today, the Bundeswehr IT System consists of a large number of interconnected IT components/systems and infrastructure elements that are operated within Germany, at Bundeswehr agencies abroad and in the theatres of operation. Various military and civilian IT service providers provide IT services via the Bundeswehr IT System, not just for the armed forces across the task spectrum, but increasingly for other Federal Government ministries and Allied forces as well, particularly for operations.

In Germany, parts of the Bundeswehr IT System are operated by BWI Informationstechnik GmbH and by military command and control support forces. The command and control support forces of the JSS use their military capacities and capabilities to do work on and for operations. They set up and operate the complex networks and IT systems at field facilities, camps and bases of operations. For this purpose, round-the-clock security must be maintained for the manifold satellite connections with Germany, and all IT in theatres must be managed, monitored and protected from cyber attacks on a cross-system basis. Only they can create the conditions needed for the establishment of an extensive network of military forces and assets in the theatres of operation. But in spite of this, there are considerable deficits in the Bundeswehr in the concept regarding the capability for network-enabled operations and in the provision of equipment to establish and maintain it. With projects to establish network-enabled operations capability, important steps have since been taken towards the development of common and compatible command and control systems, as well as the harmonisation of command and control procedures. The joint command and control information system fielded in the Bundeswehr has so far failed to meet the requirements of the network-enabled operations environment in such a way as highly complex combined operations demand. In particular, ensuring interoperability between the command and control information systems of the services and of our partner nations will require considerable technical and financial expenditure over the coming years.

Command and control support in operations – ISAF

In joint and combined operations such as ISAF, command and control support is a core element that connects all the forces and assets of the Bundeswehr by means of an information and communications network. This enables operations to be conducted (by performing an 'enabler function'). Command and control support is an integral part of operations planning at every level. Its capabilities and services are provided reliably around the clock.

For ISAF, the Bundeswehr has contributed the German command and control support element to the Afghan Mission Network (AMN). This involves command and control support services being planned, provided and managed jointly by the JSS across a spectrum ranging from virtually static to mobile, and not just at national level, but also in a multinational context. This allows the German forces on deployment access to information and IT services of NATO, ISAF and the participating nations. In return, the Bundeswehr provides information and IT services for the headquarters and nations in the AMN.

Command and control support forces are forward elements in German Army patrols and operations. It therefore does not matter at all which service they belong to. Jointness has above all become a tangible reality among the command and control support forces.

Reorientation of the Joint Support Service

The debate about enshrining the so-called debt brake in the German constitution forced the Federal Government in 2010 to introduce further measures to consolidate the budget. Moreover, unsustainable operational structures also made further reforms necessary. In his much-noted keynote speech at the Bundeswehr Command and Staff College on 26 May 2010, Defence Minister zu Guttenberg introduced the third major reform of the Bundeswehr's armed forces since 1990 and justified it with the words: 'With the present structures and some procedures, my data clearly indicate that in the long term we will find it difficult to sustain the efficiency of our Bundeswehr' (zu Guttenberg, 2010b: 7).

In spite of the extensive reform efforts of the past twenty years, it remains clear that the number of forces necessary for operations can only be provided for a limited amount of time. Decision-making processes and procedures are still too bureaucratic and require further streamlining (BMVg, 2012: 1).

In the course of the structural planning for the reorientation of the Bundeswehr, a potential for optimisation has been identified that allows a paradigm shift to be made from a structure-based to a capability-based organisation (Chief of Staff, JSS, 2012: 7). This will result in the removal of the last remaining structures from the Cold War era. In future, forces, control elements, expertise and capabilities accessible in Germany, as well as training and further development, will be consolidated in the capability coordination commands and task area centres under unified technical administrative responsibility (BMVg, 2012: 11). The JSS will thus be recognised even more as the central major military organisational element responsible for the cost-efficient, process-oriented and effective provision of services for operations and during routine duty.

The demand made by the Federal Minister of Defence, Thomas de Maizière, for as much responsibility to be exercised at the lowest level possible has not been implemented with this degree of clarity in any other major military organisational element. The JSS will in future provide a differentiated and graded capability profile for Bundeswehr operations. This means, on the one hand, making available a broad spectrum of capabilities with the largest possible number of courses of action for military and political leaders, but, on the other, restricting the sustainable provision of military services and thus the necessity of resorting to third-party services for operations. It will not be possible to benefit from the full spectrum of military support services in all operational options without drawing on tried and tested third-party support. In peacetime and during routine duty, this is already now the main tool for implementing the 'comprehensive approach', by increasingly connecting capabilities, services and platforms increasingly with civilian and commercial cooperation solutions. Because it is always goal and process-oriented, it is also a powerful driving force for the reorientation of the Bundeswehr. In future, this focus on capability will be achieved by adopting capability-based command structures. The centralised approach to command and control support will continue to be pursued consistently in the newly-established 'Bundeswehr Command and Control Support Command'. With a total of approx. 6,000 soldiers, the command area will be smaller than the sum of forces in today's structure. However, the six command support battalions, the Bundeswehr IT System's operating centre and the Bundeswehr Command Support School will be directly subordinate to the new command, and will serve as the central elements for joint command and control support in the Bundeswehr. The result of this will be that management, operation, further development and training for command and control support in the Bundeswehr will be combined jointly in one command. Consequently, the IT services can be provided for operations and exercises via the Bundeswehr IT System by the command as a 'central provider'.

In the field of logistics, all future logistics tasks of the Joint Support Service and military motor vehicle affairs will be handled at the Bundeswehr Logistics Command. This includes the technical and administrative control of the JSS mobile logistic forces, the Bundeswehr Logistics Centre with the newly-subordinated static logistic facilities and the Bundeswehr Logistics School with the newly-assigned driver training facilities. The new logistics command area will have a strength of approx. 14,700 military and civilian personnel in the target structure.

Since its establishment in 2001, this major organisational element has proven it can provide a wide range of services. The JSS draws its particular strength from a constant exchange of personnel with the other services, the pooling of multiple competences acquired in the individual services and the network connecting them. The joint services of the JSS are now indispensable both during routine duty and in operations. The JSS also serves as a model for the armed forces of Allied partners that are considering integrating steps of the Bundeswehr reform into their own plans.

In the units and agencies, the JSS is already 'living' jointness in its daily activities. This is not expressed by 'uniformity', but by the 'colourfulness' of the uniform colours right down to company level. Navy blue, Air Force blue and

Army grey can naturally be seen side by side at all levels of command. Around 70% of members of the JSS are from the Army, 22% from the Air Force and 8% from the Navy.

In spite of all the progress that has been achieved, it will be even more important for the Bundeswehr to continue to develop joint thinking and action so as to embrace the entire Bundeswehr. The increased mix of civilian and military positions in future will further strengthen the basis of trust between soldiers and civilian personnel and thus enhance thinking in terms of the Bundeswehr as a whole. Meanwhile, large numbers of Defence Administration personnel have participated in operations and have consequently been able to acquire experience that is important for the Bundeswehr's operational capability. Soldiers and civilian personnel are thus helping to establish the vital preconditions for the further development of the Bundeswehr in the entire task spectrum.

Joint training, such as the National General/Admiral Staff Officer Course, which has been held at the Bundeswehr Command and Staff College since 2004, has already produced a new generation of officers who have experienced jointness at an early stage in their career. This is something we must build on in the years to come.

Bibliography

10 Jahre Streitkräftebasis (SKB) – Motor und Produkt der Transformation (2010). In: Kühn (2010): 19-59.

BMVg (1992): Verteidigungspolitische Richtlinien für den Geschäftsbereich des Bundesministers der Verteidigung. Bonn. 26.11.1992.

BMVg (2003): Verteidigungspolitische Richtlinien für den Geschäftsbereich des Bundesministers der Verteidigung. Berlin. 21.05.2003.

BMVg (2012): Leitlinien zur Neuausrichtung der Bundeswehr. Berlin.

Chiari, Bernhard (2012a): Krieg als Reise? Neueste Militärgeschichte seit 1990 am Beispiel des militärischen und sicherheitspolitischen Wandels in Deutschland. In: Chiari (2012): 13-40.

Chiari, Bernhard (Ed.) (2012): Auftrag Auslandseinsatz. Neueste Militärgeschichte an der Schnittstelle von Geschichtswissenschaft, Politik, Öffentlichkeit und Streitkräften. Militärgeschichtliches Forschungsamt, vol 1. Freiburg i.Br.: Rombach Verlag.

Epkenhans, Michael (2012): Das Ende der Geschichte? Der Wandel deutscher Politik und Gesellschaft im Hinblick auf die Anwendung militärischer Gewalt. In: Chiari (2012): 55-62.

Heise, Bernd (2001): Die Streitkräftebasis. In: Wehrtechnik (wt) II/2001: 26-32.

Inspekteur der Streitkräftebasis (InspSKB) (2012): Weisung zur Weiterentwicklung und Realisierung der Streitkräftebasis (WWRealSKB). Bonn.

Kommando Operative Führung Eingreifkräfte (KdoOpFüBw) (2010). In: Kühn (2010): 109-115.

Kühn, Wolfram (2010a): Die neue Einsatzrealität. In: FKH Infobrief. 2/2010: 1.

Kühn, Wolfram (Ed.) (2010): Chronik 10 Jahre Streitkräftebasis. Berlin.

Lahl, Kersten (2006): Streitkräfteunterstützungskommando – Geleitwort des Befehlshabers SKUKdo. In: Wehrtechnischer Report 9/2006: 26.

Streitkräfteamt (SKA) – Das Amt der Streitkräftebasis (2010). In: Kühn (2010): 187-193.

Streitkräfteamt (SKA) (2006): Streitkräftegemeinsame Ausbildung. In: Wehrtechnischer Report 9/2006: 61-64.

Streitkräfteunterstützungskommando (SKUKdo) (2010): Führungskommando der Streitkräftebasis. In: Kühn (2010): 195-201.

Streitkräfteunterstützungskommando (SKUKdo) (2011a): 3.3 Die Organisation des Streitkräfteunterstützungskommandos. In: SKUKdo (2011): Ziff. 3.3.

Streitkräfteunterstützungskommando (SKUKdo) (Ed.) (2011): Chronik des Streitkräfteunterstützungskommandos. Köln.

Struck, Peter (2003): BMVg – Weisung für die Weiterentwicklung der Bundeswehr. Berlin, 01.10.2003.

zu Guttenberg, Karl-Theodor (2010a): Den Wandel gestalten. In: Europäische Sicherheit. 59/2010: 1.

zu Guttenberg, Karl-Theodor (2010b): Grundsatzrede an der Führungsakademie der Bundeswehr. Hamburg. 26.05.2010.

The Bundeswehr reserve

Armin Müller

In the early hours of 19 May 2007, a bomb blast struck the market square in Kunduz in northern Afghanistan, taking three victims, members of the regional reconstruction team of the Bundeswehr. The three soldiers killed were reservists on so-called special foreign assignment in Afghanistan. Reservists on foreign deployment are no rarity at all. At that time, there was one reservist for every twelve active-duty Bundeswehr soldiers in Afghanistan. The reserve soldiers performed a wide range of functions there. They served as regional cultural advisors or construction engineers, as legal advisors or as common soldiers or – and this was the case with the three soldiers who were killed – as members of the field defence administration. To this day, reservists support the Bundeswehr during virtually all of its missions abroad, and the reserve also seems to be taking up a firm position in the Bundeswehr as an expeditionary army. This does not go without saying, because the original idea of having reserves evolved from the need to provide large contingents of troops to defend German territory on very short notice. In principle, former regular soldiers should be kept available for service in the armed forces. Appropriate structures regarding the equipment as well as the initial and follow-on training for reservists were established to maintain the defence capability of the country. During the Cold War the task of ensuring national and Alliance defence also made it necessary for the armed forces of the Federal Republic of Germany to establish a reserve system.

Yet, like the Bundeswehr as a whole, the reserve system repeatedly underwent extreme changes. It was adapted to new concepts and strategies. However, this often took a long time, and reservists were mostly referred to as 'late-comers' (Langer, 1998: 127). Still, for many years, the reserve stood beside universal conscription as an important link between the military and society. Reservists act as multipliers within an extremely wide range of professions and walks of life, establish transparency through their alternating between the civilian and military worlds and also often adopt a critical view towards the armed forces from the outside. Like universal conscription, they are attributed the capability to foster or even to safeguard the embedding of armed forces within the constitutional democracy (Müller, 2012: 175-186). The purpose of this essay is to show how the Bundeswehr reserve has developed and what changes it has had to undergo. It aims to cast a light on the problems associated with these changes and to examine the question of whether the reserve can deliver what is demanded of it.[1]

The reserve during the Cold War (until 1988)

During the first few years following re-armament, reservists did not figure in the defence planning of the Federal Republic of Germany. During the establishment of the Bundeswehr, priority was placed on the units assigned to NATO. In addition, under Army Structure 1, the peacetime and wartime strengths of the peacetime forces were identical. It was not until late 1956, when it became clear that the ambitious personnel plans of the initial phase could not be implemented, that the gaps were filled with so-called wartime billets which only had to be manned in the event of war. Due to the scarcity of resources, however, the respective planning was mostly based on the 'pure hope that requirements could be met', and this 'remained predominant with respect to the handling of reserve matters for many years' (Langer, 1998: 127). The first reservists were assigned fixed billets in their former units in 1958 and were even deployed as substitutes or instructors under the individual reserve duty training scheme.

Army Structure 2 in 1959 brought about the reorganisation of units into brigades as fast-moving and mobile units. Those were also meant to be able to operate on a nuclear battlefield. Each brigade was assigned an alert battalion whose members were ideally reservists who lived within a radius of 50 kilometres from the brigade's station. But it was the building of the Berlin Wall in 1961 that led to the establishment of viable reserve structures. For example, the German cabinet ruled in September 1961 that all conscripts had to complete three months of reserve duty training following their term of regular military service. As a consequence, all units assigned to NATO were brought up to their wartime strength. This measure, however, made reserve duty trainees a firm feature of the army even after it had been completed and when compulsory military service was extended to 18 months in August 1962. More attention was focused on mobilisation and territorial defence tasks, i.e. the contingents not assigned to NATO (Langer, 1998: 138). The requirement for reserves for non-active units, so-called equipment-holding units, and for the basic organisation doubled by 1964 to almost 200,000 men, while the requirement for reserves in NATO-assigned units grew by 60,000 to over 230,000 men. This caused considerable logistic difficulties, which were only very slowly addressed.

1 This essay is an updated and extended version of the essay entitled 'Kämpfer, Spezialist, Lückenbüßer' (Müller, 2012).

Army Structure 3 of 1969 brought about another distinct augmentation of the reserve structure (Rink, 2005: 145). For example, plans were meanwhile based on the assumption that reserves would constitute a share of 60 per cent of the wartime strength. This share was 45 per cent for NATO-assigned units and 85 per cent for territorial defence. For the year of 1977, the Army had billets for 580,000 reservists. Furthermore, the range of tasks was extended. In 1976, for instance, large-scale civil-military cooperation exercises involving the armed forces and organisations such as the police, the Technisches Hilfswerk (German Federal Agency for Technical Relief – THW), the Red Cross and the fire departments took place for the first time. A great number of reservists were involved in these exercises, and the Bundeswehr reserve became a constant factor in the defence planning of the Federal Republic.

But not just the Federal Republic of Germany established a reserve system during the Cold War; there also were reservists in the German Democratic Republic (GDR). Even before the founding of the National People's Army, the Barracked People's Police staged courses for party members, through which they attained a reserve rank. And, contrary to the Bundeswehr, the National People's Army was designed from the outset as a mobilisation army (Wenzke, 1998: 340-347). From the beginning, retired soldiers continued to be registered as reservists and students could become reserve officers, especially in technical fields. By January 1961, the East German National People's Army had 228,000 registered reservists. From the introduction of universal conscription in 1961 until the mid-sixties, a level of 563,500 reservists was achieved. Using the NCO schools and training centres, it was possible within an extremely short period of time to mount mobilisation divisions that were to be operational after a lead time of just ten days. To ensure this, most reservists were assigned to units close to their home towns, as was the case with the alert battalions in the west. In addition, professional qualifications were of high priority for these assignments. By the end of the sixties, the national defence system had infused all walks of life (Wenzke, 1998: 342). In addition, mobilisation plans for the party organs of the mobilisation units were already drawn up during peacetime. By the end of the eighties, the reserve potential of the National People's Army amounted to 2.5 million trained reservists, one million of whom were under the age of 35.

The Bundeswehr reserve had experienced a considerable increase in importance during the last few years of the Cold War. If half a million reservists were considered sufficient to ensure the defence of the Federal Republic under Army Structure 3, the figure skyrocketed during the final stages of the Cold War. According to the 1985 White Paper, more than 880,000 reservists were meant to ensure the capability of the Bundeswehr to augment to more than 1.3 million soldiers in the year 1988. During the nineties, the number of reservists would have exceeded a million. The reason for this was the belief that the onset of nuclear disarmament would increase the importance of the conventional domination of the Warsaw Pact. The resulting threat was meant to be countered with increased mobilisation capacities (Brugmann, 1998: 93-104). In a state of defence, two out of three soldiers deployed would have been members of the Bundeswehr reserve.

The downsizing of the mobilisation army (1988 – 1994)

The mobilisation army never reached such a size. The radical changes in the East European countries, the fall of the Berlin Wall and German reunification created a new situation for German defence. Suddenly, the Bundeswehr itself, and with it the freshly integrated elements of the GDR's National People's Army, became a subject of disarmament negotiations. The Two-Plus-Four Treaty of 12 September 1990 set the upper limit for the personnel strength at 370,000 soldiers. The concomitant lowering of the wartime strength to less than 700,000 soldiers affected the reserve directly. But even from the point of view of domestic politics, the reserve system at that time was no longer justifiable. Before reunification, the high number of reservists could only be reached by making soldiers undertake to undergo reserve duty training after their discharge from active military service. Even several years after the end of their terms of service, former conscripts had to remain available for reserve training exercises that extended over several days to maintain their proficiency and mobilisation capability. After the disappearance of the threat from the East, however, it became less and less possible to expect the individual citizen to observe this obligation and to perform military service to this extent. The public demanded a peace dividend.

In a first step, the reserve was downsized by about half a million billets in the wake of the general troop reductions in Europe. At the same time, however, new security challenges for Germany and for the Bundeswehr emerged in the wake of the Second Gulf War, the disintegration of Somalia and the civil war in former Yugoslavia. The focus was no longer on home defence, but on stabilisation operations in more distant crisis areas. The new Army structure, which was first labelled 'Army Structure 5 (N)' and then 'New Army for New Tasks', led to the division of the troops into crisis reaction forces and main defence forces (Rink, 1998: 149). One idea behind this was to create a combat force that could be employed together with Allied forces in combat operations such as the Second Gulf War after just a short lead time. The other was for classic national and collective defence operations to be conducted by the main defence forces, which were dependent on an appropriate augmentation capability.

The 1994 White Paper had this to say on the subject:

> Owing to the fact that the main defence forces are heavily dependent upon mobilisation, reservists are needed for virtually all assignments, including the command of units and formations and, to a higher degree than in the past, the operation of primary weapon systems.

The latter aspect in particular changed the demands on the reserve system. As early as late 1991, the Federal Ministry of Defence noted that

> (…) most of the brigades assigned to NATO will be augmented according to the principle of division. This means that one out of two modern weapon systems will be operated by a reservist. (…) Thus, the weight and credibility of Germany's contribution to NATO will be determined by the technical capabilities and skills of these reservists.

The White Paper was followed on 2 September 1994 by the new 'Reserve Concept'. This document was driven by the wish to maintain the national and collective defence capability which had been considerably affected by the downsizing of the Bundeswehr. Reservists were included in the augmentation plans for the main defence forces rather than for crisis reaction. This approach was severely criticized from the outset, since reserves had also already found their way into the Bundeswehr's missions abroad. Soldiers of the reserve were deployed in missions such as UNTAC in Cambodia or UNOSOM II in Somalia. The 'Beledweyne Reservists Group', for example, was founded in September 1993 by 30 reservists deployed with the German Support Unit in Somalia. While in its official declarations the Bundeswehr was maintaining its former high personnel levels for national defence by using reservists in a classic cold war manner, a new era of missions abroad had long since begun for the reserve.

Focus on operations (1994 – 2003)

The strategic assumptions on which the 'Army Structure 5 (N)' had been based turned out to be unrealistic. Instead of the high intensity combat operations that were expected after the Second Gulf War, the missions that had actually been mounted were rather at the lower end of the escalation spectrum. Lengthy peacekeeping operations in crisis areas and civil war zones became the new challenges. The Bundeswehr adjusted itself to them, and also the legal foundations of out-of-area operations were specified in a ruling by the Federal Constitutional Court in 1994.

The first big deployment was in the Balkans after the civil war in Bosnia and Herzegovina ended in 1995 with the Dayton Agreement. Yet, neither the main defence forces nor the crisis reaction forces were properly structured for the tasks arising from this. As a consequence, specially-tailored task forces had to be formed on an ad-hoc basis. This indirectly placed a heavy strain both on the main defence and the crisis reaction forces as they constantly had to provide personnel for the missions (Frank, 2005: 22).

The set-up of the KFOR mission in Kosovo in 1999 in the aftermath of NATO's air war against the Federal Republic of Yugoslavia worsened the situation regarding the involvement of reservists. Another theatre of operations of the Bundeswehr, posing new political, humanitarian and cultural challenges, once again demanded that reserve specialists be deployed with KFOR. But reserve work in Germany was undergoing change as well. As a result of the new Army structure, the majority of the 335,000 reservists were assigned billets in non-active units. The classic replacement and home defence battalions were hardly looked after by the active units. Even thought they had affiliations with them the non-active units were hardly looked after because the active units were under severe pressure to modernise (Dieter, 2005: 40-42). The formerly common tool of reserve duty training exercises, the so-called live exercises, for which complete units were called up together for a limited period of time, was slowly dying out. This development was also caused by a decrease in resonance on the part of reservists. Thus, in September 1998, the Vice Chief of Staff of the Army – the general in charge of reserve work – reported to the Chief of Staff of the Army that absenteeism was rising slowly but surely in the Army and that it had reached an average of 40 to 50 per cent for live exercises. Individual reserve training with active units became the rule, that is to say, individual reservists were called up to deputize, for example, for active-duty soldiers on deployment abroad.

The new operations abroad posed challenges which had hitherto played no more than a subordinate role for the armed forces. For example, the operation in the former civil war zone of Bosnia and Herzegovina involved assuming a humanitarian role in this ravaged country and engaging in its reconstruction. This was the great moment for many reservists because active soldiers were usually not prepared for, say, rebuilding destroyed civilian housing. Under the umbrella term of civil-military cooperation (CIMIC), many reservists with corresponding civilian professional qualifications were deployed to the theatre. Even though the Reserve Concept of 1994 only marginally provided for the employment of specialists abroad, this became a rule for the theatres of operation thus unintentionally creating a new type of reservist. The classical image of the former soldier who partakes in a national defence exercise for a few days per year was no longer wanted. The new reservist had to be available for a longer time period, and had to have those qualifications that active personnel did not have to a sufficient degree, if at all. The unemployed civil engineer became the synonym for the reservist on deployment. But also professionals with a background in the humanities were sought after: In every new theatre, the Bundeswehr needed translators or experts in history and culture who they could not train on their own. Yet besides the filling of open spots for experts reservists in general seemed to offer an uncomplicated way of manning the contingents that were bound for deployment abroad.

It was CIMIC in particular which strongly shaped the German public's impression of operations abroad. For years, it was the image of 'drilling of wells' instead of close combat that was the German public had of its soldiers deployed to Afghanistan. The desire to just carry out 'good' operations abroad and to keep the Bundeswehr out of combat actions superimposed the perception of the real ISAF mission. In 2009 at the latest, and following the public debate after the bombing of two hijacked tank trucks causing the death of more than 100 civilians – the blurred public conception about the nature of the ISAF mission finally came to an end. Twenty years after the fall of the Berlin Wall, the German public was hit hard by the reality of combat operations.

While the Bundeswehr was permanently committed out of area with their operations, a fact that was also reflected clearly by the 'Army of the Future' structure which came into effect in 2001, the reserves remained in Germany, with a level of proficiency and equipment that dated back to the late 1980s. The attacks of 11 September 2001 were followed by larger and larger Bundeswehr contingents being deployed in support of ISAF in Afghanistan. The focus of the armed forces was inevitably directed on worldwide deployments, spanning a wide spectrum of missions and operations. As a consequence, the Defence Policy Guidelines issued in 2003 state the following: 'At present, and in the foreseeable future, there is no conventional threat to the German territory'. The reservist as a defender of the homeland seemed unwanted for good.

And now homeland defence again? (2003 – 2011)

The reserve concept of 2003 stated:

> The potential provided by reservists is to be consistently exploited in order to complement the capabilities of the active forces. This way they also relieve the regular forces of some mission stress.' It goes on to read: 'Particular importance is accorded to reservists with specialized knowledge and skills for special peacetime operations abroad …

Some reservists were happy about this increased acknowledgement of their role in operations. This new concept, however, entailed extensive changes for the remaining reserves. Almost all of the non-active units, that is to say, those units which consisted mostly of reservists and which had hitherto been the key point of reference for the training and careers of reservists, were largely disbanded. This meant a reduction of the reserve down to 90,000 billets, about a tenth of its size at the end of the Cold War. This step gave rise to some doubts among Bundeswehr leaders.

General Kirchbach (ret.), for example, the former *Generalinspekteur*, or Chief of Defence, said (2003: 8-11) that

> ... action must definitely be taken to avoid units being disbanded for the sake of short-term savings effects that will later perhaps be urgently needed and can then only be re-established with great effort and with uncertain prospects of success.

At first, however, the focus was not on this. In their practical work, reservists had to compensate another deficit of the shrinking Bundeswehr, that of maintaining a presence throughout the country. For example, under the Bundeswehr Concept of 2004, the remaining 25 military regional commands – which had up to then been manned with active-duty personnel and had to function as a bridge between the Bundeswehr and the civilian agencies in the event of an emergency – were downsized to 11 *Land* commands. The 50 active government district liaison groups, which had just been established shortly before to compensate for earlier reductions and which served as liaison elements to the government districts, were disbanded and their tasks were transferred to reservists (von Krause, 2005: 101-102). They were meant to liaise with government agencies and other organisations and to coordinate Bundeswehr support activities in the event of a natural disaster or a grave accident.

With respect to operational deployment, the Bundeswehr was conversely striving to cover classic fields in which reserves had been employed together with competent personnel, especially in view of the increasing intensity of the Afghanistan mission. In 2003, the field of civic-military cooperation was transferred to today's CIMIC Centre, which had specifically been established for this purpose. In 2007, the Psychological Operations Centre became the new home for the subjects of host nation orientation and cross-cultural competence, which were then combined under the name of 'Cross-Cultural Operational Advice'. The tasks of the 'cultural adviser' were performed not only by reservists, but also increasingly by civilian specialists who were taken on by the Bundeswehr (despite quite considerable administrative difficulties) as temporary-career volunteers, as civilian employees or as contingent personnel. They received military training before being sent out on operational deployment.

Still, the numbers of reservists in operations abroad appeared to remain high. The personnel of the field defence administration enhanced this impression, which did not quite reflect reality. When they are on operational deployment, they wear uniforms and hence have reservist status, but they are actually civilian employees and thus are Bundeswehr personnel. Almost half of reservists on operational deployment abroad belong to this group.

The current reserve concept once again places more focus on home defence. In February 2012, this new 'Reserve Concept' was presented in the wake of the recent restructuring of the Bundeswehr. In addition to strengthening the structures of military-civil cooperation at home, it provides for the establishment of new non-active units to take over guard and support assignments. The category of deployable reserve personnel is no longer to be found in the document. Instead, there is more emphasis on the importance of the reserve for integrating the military into democratic society. Whereas in 1988 the most one could read with regard to this category of personnel was something about 'public relations' for the Bundeswehr, the situation in 2011 is this:

> Reservists are 'citizens in uniform' and identify themselves with the ideal of the soldier as a 'citizen in uniform'. They act in accordance with the principles of leadership development and civic education and endorse the tradition of the Bundeswehr as an 'armed force in a democracy'. (…) Against the background of the suspension of compulsory military service, reservists are gaining more and more importance as convincing, authentic mediators. The Bundeswehr is becoming increasingly dependent on reservists who commit themselves to taking on this role throughout the country regardless of whether they have an assignment or not.

The question is whether this is already the next capability gap which the Bundeswehr wants to fill with its reserves.

Outlook

The Bundeswehr reserve has undergone just as much drastic change in the history of the Bundeswehr, and particularly after the end of the Cold War, as the armed forces themselves. However, it is possible to name consistent characteristics that describe how the Bundeswehr has treated its reservists:

One is that the reserve concepts all appear to be primarily reactive. For instance, it has been a case of far more changes that had already been implemented being laid down in them than future-oriented concepts being elaborated. By the time the concepts were published, they often had been overtaken by new developments.

Another was that the focus of planning and deployment, especially recently, was on retaining capabilities which the Bundeswehr later decided to do away with due to the constant reforms: the capability to mobilise large units, the capability to maintain a presence throughout the country, and the capability to defend the homeland serve as convincing examples of this. Despite a steady decrease in personnel, the reserve has had to shoulder more and more duties from which the Bundeswehr itself has backed away. Further analysis will be needed to find out how far this has been expedient and successful.

A third one is that the reservists have been a welcome asset for filling capability and personnel gaps, especially when the Bundeswehr was on the way to becoming an expeditionary force. The fact that the life and deployment reality of each individual had changed drastically since the end of the Cold War, that demands on reservists today are completely different, and that this has also created a completely different type of reserve, has only been included in the concepts to a limited extent. The public also seems to believe that the much-quoted, although non-judgmental, lack of interest in the armed forces seems to particularly apply to the reserve despite the drastic changes that have taken place. For instance, the social prestige of an assignment in the reserves remains limited, even though each reservist has a civilian life outside the armed forces and is part of this society. In the end, it will be exactly this way of looking at each individual person, his capabilities as well as the perceptions of society as a whole of him and its reservations about him which can say a lot about the path the Bundeswehr has taken to become an army geared towards operations.

A fourth one is that the reserve has effectively disintegrated into a multiple-class society, creating a personnel body comprising an extremely wide range of profiles. A limited number of well-trained and frequently even highly specialized professional reservists have found their place within the active structures, which have been undergoing fundamental change themselves. With great personal commitment and often on their own initiative, they have done a professional job in routine duty and on operational deployment. They have done so in a cumbersome system that has often shown itself to be capable of communicating directly with individual reservists and still less so of developing long-term training and career plans for its 'external' specialists. In Germany, there is still no legal and material basis for making this group of people a binding and financially attractive offer for serving in the Bundeswehr for a certain length of time – modelled, for instance, on the United States National Guard. From the point of view of the active forces, this has substantially hampered the drafting of reservists because, in practice, they have often not been available when needed. Furthermore, a considerable proportion of reservists has failed to keep up with developments as the Bundeswehr has become an army focused on operations. Independent sectors such as voluntary reserve work today contribute towards embedding the Bundeswehr in society, but are sometimes too far away from everyday business and the professional development of the volunteer army. The same applies to the ever-changing structures of the civil-military cooperation sector, which still has to prove its efficiency.

In the end, the Bundeswehr is still looking for a solid reserve concept that could bridge the gap between the different needs of the armed forces, on the one hand, and the underlying structural, material and social conditions, on the other hand.

Bibliography

Bremm, Klaus-Jürgen/Mack, Hans-Hubertus/Rink, Martin (Eds.) (2005): 50 Jahre Bundeswehr 1955 bis 2005. Freiburg i.Br./Berlin: Rombach Verlag.

Brugmann, Gerhard (Ed.) (1998): Die Reservisten in der Bundeswehr. Ihre Geschichte bis 1990. Hamburg/Berlin/Bonn: Mittler Verlag.

Brugmann, Gerhard (1998a): Reservisten in Planung und Einsatz. In: Brugmann (1998): 93-122.

Chiari, Bernhard (Ed.) (2012): Auftrag Auslandseinsatz. Neueste Militärgeschichte an der Schnittstelle von Geschichtswissenschaft, Politik, Öffentlichkeit und Streitkräften. Freiburg i. Br./Berlin/Vienna: Rombach Verlag.

Dieter, Hans Heinrich (2005): Neue Reserve-Rolle und Aufgaben in der Transformation. In: Frank (2005): 37-54.

Frank, Hans (Ed.) (2005): Reserve im Umbruch. Von der Landesverteidigung zur Krisenbewältigung. Hamburg/ Berlin/Bonn: Mittler Verlag.

Frank, Hans (2005a): Von der innerdeutschen Grenze zum Hindukusch. In: Frank (2005): 17-28.

von Kirchbach, Hans-Peter (2003): Neuland in Sicht. In: LOYAL. Das deutsche Wehrmagazin, 10/2003, 8-11.

von Krause, Ulf (2005): Vom „KTV“ zum SKUKdo. In: Frank (2005): 91-112.

Langer, Wilhelm (1998): Die Reservisten des Heeres. In: Brugmann (1998): 123-206.

Müller, Armin (2012): Kämpfer, Spezialist, Lückenbüßer? Die Reserve der Bundeswehr auf dem Weg in die Einssatzarmee. In: Chiari (2012): 175-186.

Rink, Martin (2005): Das Heer der Bundeswehr im Wandel: Von Himmerod zum „Heer der Zukunft“ 1950-2005. In: Bremm/Mack/Rink (2005): 137-154.

Wenzke, Rüdiger (1998): Die Reservisten der NVA. In: Brugmann (1998): 337-354.

The Federal Defence Administration

Dieter Heuer

The materiel requirements of the armed forces have always been high. Most people may think of defence goods, but a soldier's basic needs such as food, clothing and housing also have to be satisfied, not to forget his or her payment. While, in the early days of the industrial revolution, such goods (and services) were still relatively simple, of manageable sizes and able to be used for quite a long time, the present-day armies require an unfathomable range of defence materiel. The items of supply required range from weapon systems and equipment that only the armed forces need to services such as research assignments, studies and maintenance work to commercial articles or consumer goods that are purchased off the shelf, so to speak. This is why there always was and still is more to military affairs than just strategy and tactics and the establishment and training of forces. They necessarily also comprise the provision of support from within, the procurement of goods and services from trade and industry, and meeting personnel and materiel requirements. Therefore, this chapter covers the organisations of those financial, economic, technical and administrative aspects of the Bundeswehr.

The development of the Defence Administration within the Bundeswehr

The Bundeswehr concept – the armed forces and their administration

Following the decision to rearm the Federal Republic of Germany, Theodor Blank was appointed Federal Minister of Defence on 7 June 1955, and the 'Blank Office' became the Federal Ministry of Defence. The mission of the armed forces was defined as national and collective defence. This had a profound influence on the entire defence organisation, including the defence administration.

The concept of the defence administration had to take into account the fact that national defence does not only include military tasks in the narrower sense, but, logically, also administrative functions. While the Bundeswehr Concept required the purely military tasks to be carried out in accordance with the principle of obedience to orders so as to boost military clout, the administrative functions had to be discharged by specially-trained civilian personnel in accordance with general administrative principles. Accordingly, the command and administrative tasks were distributed and defined so precisely that it was possible to draw a distinct line between the specific military functions and general administrative activities. The basic requirement was for the soldier to devote himself fully to his core military tasks and for the administrative functions to be discharged by duly qualified specialists. Although the civilian defence organisation was easily distinguishable from the armed forces, it was also linked so closely to them that if taken away, the armed forces would not be able to sustain themselves or function properly (Minutes of the 92nd session of the 2nd German Bundestag: 5218).

The personnel of the defence administration were thus assigned civilian status. Administrative tasks that were directly connected with specific units and agencies of the armed forces had to be performed by civilian administrative personnel assigned to those units and agencies for that purpose. At the intermediate and lower levels, equivalent civilian defence administration authorities and agencies were established beside the military territorial headquarters and now assigned responsibility for all the services (Reinfried/Walitschek, 1978: 32 et seq.).

A defence administration that was independent of the armed forces was not at all unprecedented. As early as 1655, the Great Elector had two administrative lawyers set up the *Generalkriegskommissariat*, or General War Commissariat, to which he then granted independent status and which functioned as an independent authority alongside the General Field Marshal.

The integration of the Armed Forces and the Federal Defence Administration into the Basic Law (*Grundgesetz*)

The establishment of the armed forces and the tasks and structure of the Federal Defence Administration were covered in the Articles 87 a and 87 b, which were added to the *Grundgesetz*, or Basic Law, the constitution of the Federal Republic of Germany of 23 May 1949 under the Act to Amend the *Grundgesetz* of 19 March 1956.

The term Federal Defence Administration was chosen because the term military administration was already being used by the victorious powers of World War II to denote the administration established in Germany after 1945. Having initially used the term defence administration, the Ministry of Defence disassociated itself from it since, with respect to armed conflicts, it denoted the state's responsibilities not only in the field of defence, but also in the fields of labour, the economy, transport, finance and administration – all of which had to be managed not only by all of the Federal ministries, but also by the *Land* and local governments.

This is also why the Federal Defence Administration was designed as a mainly internal administration that provided the goods and services required by way of fiscal transactions, i.e. private law transactions (Maunz/Dürig, paragraph (4a) of Article 87 b). Any laws that empower the Federal Defence Administration to interfere with the rights of third parties also require the consent of the *Bundesrat* (fourth sentence of paragraph (1) of Article 87 b of the *Grundgesetz*). This requirement does not apply to laws regarding personnel matters.

Article 87 b of the *Grundgesetz* also gives expression to the fundamental organisational separation of the Federal Defence Administration from the armed forces. A key difference is the principle of obedience to orders. Orders are a command and control tool whose use is confined to the military. Only a military superior – not a civil servant or a civilian employee – may issue or be issued orders. Orders and directives are both based on the principle of hierarchy. For reasons of necessary cohesion and military clout, however, an order constitutes a special kind of official instruction; it is a directive in intensified form. The legal implications of orders and directives differ both as regards what the people to whom they are issued are obliged to do and what consequences they face if they fail to observe them. The soldier must obey orders as a matter of principle, to the best of his ability, fully, conscientiously and promptly. Reviewing the binding character of orders and the right of remonstrance in accordance with Section 63 of the Federal Civil Service Act run counter to military service law. An order, however, that violates human dignity or that is not given for service-related purposes does not have to be obeyed. An order must not be obeyed if a crime or an offence would be committed (Section 11, Legal Status of Military Personnel Act). Disobedience and refusal to obey orders result in criminal sanctions under the Military Penal Code. To ensure the readiness and striking power of the armed forces, the intent of the commander must be implemented simply and quickly. Orders cannot be issued in the same way for administrative procedures to be implemented and, anyway, the general goal of administration is not to use force to get an organised unit of people to work together, but rather to implement individual measures and decisions (Reinfried/Walitschek, 1978: 47).

Still topical today, the main reasons the German legislator demanded the organisational separation of the armed forces and the Federal Defence Administration were:

- to ensure that administrative tasks are performed by specially-trained civilian administration specialists;
- to ensure that the 'general constitutional principles of administration' are also applied in the Bundeswehr;
- to relieve the armed forces of performing any administrative tasks, and
- to ensure that Federal Defence Administration personnel have civilian status only and hence to avoid their having any mixed form of legal status, as was

the case for civil servants in the Wehrmacht. (Minutes of the 92nd session of the 2nd German *Bundestag*: 5218 and 5219).

Tasks of the Federal Defence Administration

The Federal Defence Administration is responsible for providing the armed forces with all personnel and materiel resources they require to accomplish their military mission. The Federal Defence Administration is therefore solely responsible for performing non-military tasks. To honour this responsibility, it works in a wide range of areas that are governed by public and civilian law, making it 'the most versatile administration' in Germany. (Voigt/Seybold, 2004: 142; Johanny, 2005: 201).

Meeting personnel requirements

One of the Bundeswehr's most important administrative tasks is personnel management, i.e. the recruitment of regular military personnel, temporary-career volunteers, civil servants, and civilian employees. It involves dealing with matters concerning the establishment and termination of employment contracts, promotions and evaluation reports, transfers and secondments, the granting of leave and even disciplinary punishment of any breaches of duty.

The recruitment organisation (Reinfried/Steinebach, 1983: 65) was for a long time responsible for providing the armed forces with conscripts and, thus, for ensuring that the Bundeswehr had enough personnel to sustain its operational readiness. During the Cold War era in particular, the recruitment organisation was of prime importance for security and defence in Germany. Its main tasks include the registration and preparticipation examination of people liable to military service and calling them up in accordance with their fitness and availability, especially for basic military service and exercises. Since universal conscription, i.e. compulsory basic military service, was suspended on 1 July 2011 in response to the changes in the defence and security environment, the significance of the recruitment organisation has dwindled. However, it still retains the task of calling up conscripts with no prior service experience for voluntary basic military service and reservists for reserve duty training.

An area that is closely related to personnel management is that of pay and allowances, i.e. the determination and disbursement of pay and allowances to Bundeswehr personnel, including family separation allowances, relocation expenses or allowances for medical care, nursing care and birth care.

Civil service benefits and pensions or military service benefits are paid to civil servants, judges and soldiers who retire from active service or duty because they have reached the applicable retirement age, or for certain other reasons. Besides retirement pay for regular soldiers, the military service benefits are mainly transition allowances and severance benefits for temporary-career soldiers.

Vocational advancement is another important aspect in the area of benefits and pensions and adds to the attractiveness of serving in the Bundeswehr. Under the vocational advancement scheme, temporary-career soldiers who are due to leave the forces are offered suitable initial and advanced vocational training to facilitate their reintegration into civilian working life after they have completed their military service.

Social welfare services cannot go unmentioned, as they are meant to take account of the particular strains soldiers come under due, for example, to having to work irregular hours, to be frequently away from home or to contend with difficult conditions when on operational deployment. One of the ways in which social welfare is implemented is by doing social casework involving the provision of both counselling and care to personnel in distress or affected by illness, injury and death, and by providing support in housing, vacation and recreational matters.

Satisfying materiel requirements

The Federal Defence Administration is responsible for providing and operating an adequate and efficient infrastructure for the entire Bundeswehr and for keeping it in working order. This infrastructure includes not only all fixed installations on the territory of the Federal Republic of Germany that the Bundeswehr and other NATO armed forces use for accommodating, training and rendering services to their troops, but also specific military facilities such as airfields, missile sites, depots, pipelines or communications facilities.

The decentralised procurement of goods also falls within the Federal Defence Administration's remit. This in particular comprises the fields of food and clothing, for which contracts are awarded on the basis of public invitations to tender, with special consideration being given to small and medium-sized or regional companies.

As no use has been made of the empowerment specified in the third sentence of paragraph (1) of Article 87 b of the *Grundgesetz*,[1] the Bundeswehr has no au-

1 'Responsibilities connected with pensions for injured persons or with construction work may be assigned to the Federal Defence Administration only by a Federal law requiring the consent of the *Bundesrat*.'

thority of its own to construct installations or facilities. Bundeswehr construction projects are implemented by the construction authorities of the *Länder* on the basis of administrative agreements concluded with the *Länder* and against reimbursement. Infrastructure requirements are met on the basis of relevant norms of the Federal Government and the *Länder*. These include in particular the Federal Building Code, the Acquisition of Land for Military Purposes Act, the Act on the Restriction of the Use of Land for Military Defence, the Aviation Act, regional planning legislation, environmental protection legislation, water management legislation, soil protection legislation and the Federal Budget Code and the *Länder* building codes.

Facility management encompasses the management and maintenance of all real estate and buildings of the Bundeswehr. This particularly includes the provision of utilities and disposal services, the operation and maintenance of technical installations, the cleaning and guarding of buildings and facilities and grounds maintenance. Facility management in the Bundeswehr is essentially subject to the same regulations as civilian facility management. These regulations are merely supplemented by special public sector requirements such as public contracting or budget law.

The grounds maintenance organisation is responsible for looking after all Bundeswehr premises. This particularly includes green area management, road construction at training areas, maintenance of sports facilities, the cleaning of roads and snow clearing and gritting. Grounds maintenance work is done to meet military purposes and, whenever possible, in compliance with user requirements, with particular attention being given to ecological and economic aspects.

All tasks of the Bundeswehr are meant to be carried out with as little strain as possible on people and the environment and account is meant to be taken of the principle of sustainability. Hardly any other government organisation in Germany is affected by environmental legislation as comprehensively as the Bundeswehr. The primary aim is to ensure that water, air and soil are handled in a sustainable manner. The issues range from waste avoidance and waste processing to emissions reduction and the avoidance of soil compacting. Another matter is that of establishing regulations to ensure that the countryside on Bundeswehr property and, during exercises, on open ground is treated with care. Other tasks include noise protection, recycling and waste management, which include the special aspects of the phasing-out and disposal of equipment, and handling of hazardous goods and materials. The so-called protective tasks include fire prevention. In contrast to the responsibilities of the *Länder*, the Bundeswehr has its own fire brigades. In certain areas, e.g. at airfields and ammunition depots, these fire brigades are responsible for active fire prevention. Fire prevention is the responsibility of the Federal Defence Administration at all Bundeswehr premises.

In the field of public supervision, enforcement and monitoring, the special supervisory responsibilities in the area of technical environmental protection and occupational safety assigned to the Federal Minister of Defence by the legislative authorities deserve special mention. The Occupational Safety and Health Act of 1996 and the Agreement to Amend the Supplementary Agreement to the NATO Status of Forces Agreement of 29 March 1998 extended these supervisory responsibilities to visiting forces. The tasks in this area are performed as part of the public supervisory function of the Federal Defence Administration.

Other tasks

Like any institution, the Bundeswehr participates in general legal dealings as well. Special mention should be made of the fact that it concludes and executes civil law contracts in the fields of labour law, sales law, law on contracting for work and services, tenancy law and the law governing loans, as well as the settlement of non-contractual claims for damages. The latter include the examination of any liability issues in connection with its own personnel and third parties for a breach of duty by a member of the Bundeswehr and, vice versa, the assertion of government claims for damage to Federal Government property or injury to Bundeswehr personnel to whom the government has undertaken to provide services, for example, to pay compensation for service-related disabilities or to provide free health care. In both cases, the processing of traffic accidents involving Bundeswehr vehicles is of particular importance, especially as the Bundeswehr is the self-insurer of its vehicles.

In view of the Bundeswehr's integration in international collective defence structures, there was a substantial need for foreign language expertise right from the start. Only English and French are accepted as working languages within NATO; German is not (Reinfried/Steinebach, 1983: 171). Moreover, in the course of transformation of the Bundeswehr from a purely defensive army to an army focused on operations, foreign languages such as Arabic, Pashtun, Dari, Farsi or Kiswahili are gaining importance. In addition to all kinds of contracts, agreements and legal norms, a host of technical regulations, instructions, and operating and maintenance manuals for the weapons and other technical equipment provided by the USA or other NATO partners have to be translated. Interpreter services are also needed for international negotiations and for operations abroad, to ensure that the Bundeswehr can communicate with its local staff, the authorities in the countries in which it is deployed, and civilian partners with whom it concludes contracts. Finally, adequate basic and follow-on language training must be provided so as to give the Bundeswehr's military and civilian personnel involved in operations enough language skills to communicate in everyday life.

Tasks of the Federal Defence Administration in operations abroad

When the Federal Republic of Germany attained full sovereignty in the wake of reunification on 3 October 1990, its allies expected it to make a due contribution to international security, notably by participating in the implementation of peacekeeping measures. Since the Federal Constitutional Court eliminated any constitutional concerns about this in the so-called AWACS decision of 12 July 1994, the Bundeswehr has been involved since 1994 in operations abroad conducted by collective security systems such as the United Nations, NATO or the EU.

Operations abroad naturally require most of the services that are the responsibility of the Federal Defence Administration to be provided locally. As a rule, the *Länder* do not come into consideration as actors in this case, as they do not normally maintain administrative structures of their own in the theatres of operations. By the way, in addition to its traditional tasks, the defence administration has to perform mission-specific tasks in the theatre of operations, since these either do not arise at home or are performed by other agencies (for example, in Germany construction projects are handled by government building authorities). Other tasks are modified due to the particular circumstances in each region.

With respect to personnel, great importance is attached to the employment of local staff, who then work as builders, kitchen staff, cleaners and guards. Interpreters play a key role, because it is only through them that contacts can be established with the local staff in the countries of deployment, so this makes them indispensable for a number of tasks (Federal Ministry of Defence (BMVg), 2010: 28). As the Bundeswehr's personnel management and pay affairs agency, the Federal Defence Administration is responsible for all tasks associated with the employment of local staff, ranging from the conclusion of bilingual employment contracts and the production of detailed job descriptions to taking labour law action in the event of breaches of duty (Dreist, 2004: 290; Johanny, 2005: 212). The employment of local staff also helps to strengthen the local labour market. The regions are often devastated by war or civil war and jobs with the Bundeswehr are in many cases the only kind of work available (Dreist, 2004: 290).

In the field of real estate affairs in connection with operations abroad, the Federal Defence Administration is responsible not only for satisfying requirements and contracting, but also for actually doing construction work, because the *Länder* building authorities, which are really responsible for this in Germany, do not have offices in the theatres of operations. Often, however, third parties are brought in as prime contractors, for example, the Deutsche Gesellschaft für Internationale Zusammenarbeit (GIZ) or the NATO Maintenance and Supply Agency (NAMSA). Facility management is handled by the field office of defence administration with both its own assets as well as private contractors and local employees. Consideration often has to be taken not only of extreme climatic conditions, but also of local standards, which are often hard to bring into line with German standards (BMVg, 2010: 27). During operations abroad, some facility management tasks are performed by the forces themselves if no camps are set up on a permanent basis (Dreist, 2004: 290).

Procurement, e.g. in the fields of food and clothing, is characterised by the coexistence of two complementary procurement channels. While high-value goods and commodities are usually procured on a centralised basis via homeland logistic base facilities – if only to ensure adequate competition between potential providers – items of daily need such as fresh food, consumables or spare parts for commercial equipment are mainly procured on a decentralised basis from providers in the countries of deployment (BMVg, 2010: 15; Dreist, 2004: 292 et seq.), if they can thereby be delivered quickly without any loss in quality. In the field of procurement, use can also be made of support services offered by other armed forces, the host country (Host Nation Support) or civilian firms. Soldiers serving in international headquarters or in small contingents have their meals in local military dining facilities, whereas the smaller contingents in Djibouti und Mombasa have their meals at the hotels at which they are put up (Dreist, 2004: 288).

Multinational accounting is another responsibility of the civilian defence administration during operations abroad, i.e. accounting of services rendered by the Bundeswehr to, or received from, other troop-contributing nations, multinational organisations or civilian users (Dreist, 2004: 291).

How the Federal Defence Administration is organised

On 24 October 1955, that is to say, three weeks before the swearing-in of the first Bundeswehr volunteers, the Federal Ministry of Defence in Bonn established the 'Andernach administrative office'. This new administrative agency and its civilian staff were given the task of doing the administrative work necessary to enable the establishment of the military agencies. This was, so to speak, the date of establishment of the Federal Defence Administration (Johanny, 2005: 199; Greyer-Wieninger, 2006: 229; Blasius, 2006: 221).

Development since 1955

Although the so-called 'Blank Office' established by Federal Chancellor Adenauer started working on defence issues as early as in December 1950 and was renamed the 'Federal Ministry of Defence' (FMOD) on 7 June 1955, the tasks of the Federal Defence Administration outlined above did not have to be performed until the armed forces were established, i.e. when the first 101 volunteers were sworn in at Ermekeil Barracks in Bonn on 12 November 1955.

These tasks were initially performed solely by the Ministry itself; throughout the country, however, the Ministry was, of course, represented by branch offices, of which Andernach was the oldest and most well-known. In late 1956, the civilian Federal Defence Administration had a staff of approximately 15,000 employees (Greyer-Wieninger, 2006: 229). After Article 87 b had been incorporated into the *Grundgesetz* on 19 March 1956, providing for the defence administration to have an organisational substructure of its own, the branch offices were turned into independent agencies on 26 September 1957 (Hahnenfeld, 1975: 21 et seq.). As a large share of the administrative tasks had to be performed within as close proximity to the forces as possible, which were spread all over the Federal Republic of Germany, the idea right from the start was to maintain a marked local deconcentration ('deployment').

Military District Administrative Offices I to VI, based in Kiel, Hanover, Düsseldorf, Wiesbaden, Stuttgart and Munich respectively, constituted the intermediate level of the defence administration (Hahnenfeld, 1981: 4). As for the recruitment organisation, so-called regional recruitment offices and later thirty military regional offices were added to the district recruitment offices, which were integrated into the military district administrative offices as divisions. In 1968, the military regional offices were turned into branch offices of the military district administrative offices (Reinhart, 1996: 103; see also Federal Law Gazette *BGBl.* I-56: 654). At the local level, the defence administration was comprised of 106 selection and induction offices and 197 garrison administrative offices, but by just 1981, only 96 selection and induction offices and 184 garrison administrative offices were left. Each military district also had a pay office, a clothing office and a subsistence office. Other agencies of which mention should be made are the Federal schools of defence administration in Mannheim (1956), Huntlosen (1963), Mölln (1972) and Oberammergau (1974) as well as the Federal Republic of Germany Offices of Defence Administration Abroad, which were established in 1958.

Finally, a variety of higher Federal authorities were established to perform so-called common Bundeswehr tasks on a centralised basis, aside from the relatively short-lived Federal Recruitment Office (1956) (Reinhart, 1996: 103; see also Federal Law Gazette BGBl. I-56: 654), these included the Federal Academy of Defence Administration and Technology in Mannheim (1961), the Bundeswehr Office of Defence Administration in Bonn (1962) and the Federal Office of Languages in Hürth (1969). By 1989, the number of people working in the defence administration had increased to 180,000 (Greyer-Wieninger, 2006: 229; Hahnenfeld, 1981: 5).

Expanding the Federal Defence Administration to the new *Länder* after the reunification of Germany posed a particular challenge. In the former German Democratic Republic (GDR), the defence administration had been fully integrated into the 'armed organs'. The fact that the Federal Defence Administration began in 1990 to 'detotalise' the structures there strongly contributed to German unity (Johanny, 2005: 200). To manage the 90,000 soldiers taken over from the National People's Army of the former GDR, the Bundeswehr had to create an entirely new military district, its agencies including Military District Administrative Office VII in Strausberg, 26 selection and induction offices and 19 garrison administrative offices (Schrömbgens, 2006: 254). Finally, in 1994, Federal School of Defence Administration II moved from Siegen to Berlin-Grünau. Most of the personnel from the former GDR military defence administration were taken over and employed in the establishment of the Bundeswehr defence administration in the new *Länder*, the reassignment resulting in the total number of defence administration employees rising to 230,000 for a short while (Greyer-Wieninger, 2006: 229). 3,000 of the new employees had to be given notice due to their having worked for the GDR state security service (Stasi) (Schrömbgens, 2006: 254; Military District Administrative Office East, 2010: 8).

Particular importance was attached to establishing a new infrastructure, renovating the facilities inherited from the National People's Army and cleaning up contaminated sites on the real estate taken over by the Bundeswehr (Schrömbgens, 2006: 255; Military District Administrative Office East, 2010: 23).

The Section for Special Tasks Arising from Unification, a unique element of Military District Administrative Office VII, is responsible for transferring pension entitlements acquired by members of the former National People's Army to the pension systems of the Federal Republic of Germany (Schrömbgens, 2006: 257; Military District Administrative Office East, 2010: 31).

Soon after the fall of the Iron Curtain, however, it became apparent that in view of the changed defence and security environment, there was a need for a reduction in the size of the armed forces and, accordingly, for downsizing and concentrating the defence administration. As early as in 1991, the Federal Defence Administration Office integrated the Bundeswehr Data Processing Office and has since been known as the Federal Office of Defence Administration. Since 1994, a substantial number of selection and induction offices and garrison administrative offices have been closed. The latter were renamed Bundeswehr Service Centres on 1 January 2007 after the Accounting, Pay and Quartermaster Sections, which hitherto had been elements of the military structure, had been integrated into them (Martini, 2007: 77 et seq.). Moreover, the branch offices of the military district administrative offices that were left over after the successive reduction were closed. In 1997, the pay, subsistence and clothing offices were integrated into the respective military district administrative offices.

The Bundeswehr reform launched by a cabinet decision of 14 June 2000 constituted an enormous step. On 1 January 2002, the number of military district administrative offices was cut from seven to four, and the remaining three were turned into branch offices (Baron von der Ropp, 2006: 253).

In the course of the 'transformation process' that began in 2004, the defence organisation also geared itself more and more towards mission-related tasks by pooling central tasks to suit mission requirements. It streamlined the organisation of the military district administrative offices and their branch offices and reduced the number of selection and induction offices even further from 81 to 52 and that of Bundeswehr service centres from 80 to 52 (Federal Ministry of Defence (BMVg), 2004: 5 et seq.; Greyer-Wieninger, 2005: 171 et seq.); Federal School of Defence Administration III in Mölln was closed in 2007. By 2010, the number of civilian employees had to be cut from its peak of 230,000 to 75,000 (Greyer-Wieninger, 2006: 231).

In addition to the permanent reduction in civilian personnel, increased cooperation with private enterprises is another current trend within the defence administration. The Framework Contract on Innovation, Investment and Economic Efficiency in the Bundeswehr concluded on 15 December 1999 constituted an initial milestone on the road to cooperation with private enterprises. It provided the foundation for a strategic partnership between the Bundeswehr and trade and industry aimed at using trade and industry's capacity for innovation, boosting the Bundeswehr's capacity for investment and improving the economic efficiency of its operational routines and procurement procedures. The focus was on reforming the development and procurement procedures by streamlining them, cutting the length of time it takes to procure items, applying customary market terms and using civilian financing and payment modalities while increasing the responsibility borne by the enterprises (BMVg, 2009: 6 et seq.).

To gain basic knowledge about the most economical way to provide the required services, agreement was reached to initially conduct fourteen pilot projects to test the new form of cooperation with private enterprises (BMVg, 1999: 8). Projects were conducted in the domains of materiel management, computer centre management, the creation of communication and data networks, vehicle fleet management, and the reorganisation of facility management. While some of the pilot projects were carried out throughout the country, others were initially confined to specific military districts or even specific units or agencies.

In addition, a framework agreement on the promotion of cooperation in the field of vocational qualification and employment was also concluded with commercial enterprises on 8 July 1999. Finally, the first public-private partnership project companies were established in 2000.[2]

The present structure

In Germany

Until the new structure is established as part of the reorientation of the Bundeswehr, the intermediate level of the territorial defence organisation, which is directly subordinate to the Ministry, is represented by four military district administrative offices named after the four main directions: Military District Administrative Office, North, in Hanover; Military District Administrative Office, West, in Düsseldorf; Military District Administrative Office, South, in Stuttgart; and Military District Administrative Office, East, in Strausberg. They have branch offices in Kiel, Wiesbaden and Munich. These branch offices are characterised by a higher concentration of functions than resources. They perform most of the required administrative tasks in their respective military districts. In addition to handling organisational issues, the Central Affairs divisions are responsible for civilian personnel management matters, including basic and advanced training and medico-social, medical officer and fiduciary physician affairs. Another division, Recruitment, Social and Legal Affairs, in particular deals with satisfying requirements under the Compulsory Military Service Act, which includes handling medical and psychological service matters, social and welfare issues, the settlement of non-contractual legal matters, occupational safety and health and technical environmental protection. The Infrastructure, Environment and Economic Affairs division is responsible for central infrastructure matters, construction project management, economics and procurement (e.g. food). Finally, the Personnel Accounting division is responsible for all payment affairs concerning military and civilian personnel. Moreover, Military District Administrative Office, West, and Military District Administrative Office, South, are also responsible for handling matters associated with the pay and benefits of these groups of personnel, a task that is classified a common Bundeswehr task. Exercising legal and functional supervision over the selection and induction offices and the Bundeswehr service centres is another responsibility of the military district administrative offices.

2 See also the article by Gregor Richter in this volume.

Whenever specialized, common and control tasks of the territorial defence administration have to be centrally coordinated, this is done by the Federal Office of Defence Administration in Bonn, which is a higher Federal authority. One of this office's primary responsibilities is that of acting as the base for the Territorial Defence Administration Operations Centre, which is responsible for planning, preparing, controlling and performing civilian mission-related tasks during Bundeswehr operations abroad. Another is that of phasing in IT systems and dealing with international contract matters. And, finally, it is responsible for the legal and technical supervision of the Bundeswehr agencies abroad and in part also of the military district administrative offices (Federal Office of Defence Administration, 2009: 4 et seq.; see also Großkraumbach, 2006: 232). The Federal Academy of Defence Administration and Technology in Mannheim is another higher Federal authority, and its responsibilities include the provision of technical service career training and a great variety of further training. Lastly, there is the Federal Office of Languages in Hürth.

At the local authority level, there are currently 53 Bundeswehr service centres throughout Germany, performing a variety of tasks in the fields of budgeting and accounting, personnel and payment affairs of certain groups of employees, social welfare, procurement of food and clothing, facility management and environmental protection. To ensure that these tasks are performed as locally as possible, the Bundeswehr service centres have also established branch offices called 'garrison service points'. Recruitment matters are still currently handled at the local level by 52 selection and induction offices, which are responsible for the registration, pre-induction examination and assignment of individuals performing military service. In addition, there are seven so-called pre-induction examination centres, which, in turn, are assigned to the selection and induction offices.

The provision of initial and further training for clerical class civil servants or equivalent employees of the defence administration is in particular a matter for the remaining Federal schools of defence administration in Berlin-Grünau and Oberammergau and – especially in the field of engineering – the school in Mannheim. The Bundeswehr subsistence office in Oldenburg is an exception, as it is responsible for the whole of the Federal Republic of Germany even though it is just a local authority. It is responsible both for providing supplies for mess facilities and for managing the procurement, storage and distribution of food for operations, crisis and emergency situations. This includes providing 300,000 so-called individual field rations per year.

Finally, the provision of support for German military and civilian personnel stationed in NATO partner countries is the responsibility of Germany's seven Offices of Defence Administration Abroad, which are based in Mons, Kerkrade, Illkirch-Graffenstaden, Harefield, Decimomannu, Stettin and Reston, Virginia. In addition to the tasks that have to be performed by a Bundeswehr service centre, they deal with customs issues, translator and interpreter services, and housing-related services.

In theatres of operations

In view of the special conditions and needs in theatres of operation, the defence administration has developed a parallel structure for dealing with operations abroad: The tasks that it has to perform during operations abroad are managed and coordinated by the Territorial Defence Administration Operations Support Coordination Centre of the Federal Office of Defence Administration in Bonn. It is the central point of contact for the armed forces for all mission-relevant tasks (BMVg, 2010: 19). Field offices of defence administration have been set up in the theatres of operation, e.g. in Mazar-e Sharif (Afghanistan), Prizren (Kosovo) or Dobrinja (Bosnia and Herzegovina). The function and task spectrum of these field offices can be compared at the national level with those of the Bundeswehr service centres. Like these centres, they also operate 'garrison service points' so as to provide their services locally. The field office in Mazar-e Sharif, for example, has set up garrison service points in Kabul, Kunduz, Faizabad and Termez (Uzbekistan) (BMVg, 2010: 24). In addition to these agencies, specialized agencies like the 'food transshipment points' have been set up in the theatres of operation in Kosovo and Afghanistan (BMVg, 2010: 29).

At present, some 200 to 270 defence administration staff are deployed at any one time in operations abroad. Before they take up their duties, they undergo general military training during which they learn the most important elements of basic military training such as how to conduct themselves as soldiers, what rights and duties soldiers have, how to handle and use small arms and how to administer self aid and buddy aid. To ensure sufficient personnel resources, so-called operational posts have been established, the incumbents of which are primarily earmarked for deployment, their routine duties in Germany being only of secondary importance (BMVg, 2010: 34).

At present, the vast majority of defence administration personnel participating in operations abroad have a military status (Greyer-Wieninger, 2006: 230), and as such they are called up for reserve duty training – which generally lasts four months.

Involvement of the private sector

After the tasks of the defence administration had been performed for decades by government authorities, the changes in the defence and security environment and the associated transformation in the task spectrum of the Bundeswehr revealed a need for reforms. After the fall of the Iron Curtain in 1989, for example, the national defence system that had evolved during the Cold War era became less and less important for the Federal Republic of Germany, as it was now solely 'surrounded by friends'. On the other hand, new tasks evolved for the Bundeswehr, notably ones associated with operations abroad. With an eye to the frequently lamented underfunding of the Bundeswehr (Hans-Peter von Kirchbach in the foreword of BMVg, 1999: 5), it was acknowledged that that the defence administration's antiquated structures would render it increasingly unable to provide sustainable support to armed forces in operations (Biederbick, 2005b: 169).

Thoughts on how to alleviate this situation were based on the assumption that commercial services could be provided more efficiently by the private than by the public sector (Biederbick, 2005b: 170; Hummel/Schwarz, 2006: 237). Private-sector business structures were believed to permit quicker decision-making and were therefore considered more effective for providing support than the interlocked administrative structures of the traditional defence administration with its lengthy coordination processes. Furthermore, specialized private partners were, it was believed, often able to provide more of the expertise that was needed for the increasingly complex tasks of the defence administration than the defence administration itself (Hummel/Schwarz, 2006: 239). So ways were sought of using both the technical know-how and financial assets of private actors for defence administration tasks (Wieland, 2003: 3; Lecheler, 1994: 556).

There are basically three ways of involving the private sector in the performance of public administration tasks: One is for the administration to draw on the experience of private-sector businesses to optimise its internal procedures. Another is for the tasks to be performed by private enterprises that come under corporate law. And the third and most radical option is for all the tasks to be performed in their entirety by private businesses, i.e. through outsourcing (Biederbick, 2005b: 170; Greyer-Wieninger, 2009: 4; Greyer-Wieninger, 2006: 230). Since the last option would have to be considered a case of material privatization, it would not be compatible with Article 87 b of the *Grundgesetz*, and so the only option remaining for the Federal Government, besides the optimisation of internal procedures, was to establish joint enterprises with private sector companies, whereby it would exercise the management and control functions.

The involvement of the private sector in the performance of defence administration tasks started on 17 May 2000 with the establishment of the Development, Procurement and Management Group (g.e.b.b.), which, as a parent holding company, initially controlled the activities of a number of project companies that are to different extents government owned (Wieland, 2003: 2; Gramm, 2003b: 14; Biederbick, 2005a: 1). Established in 2002, the Bundeswehr-Fuhrpark-Service GmbH, in which the Federal Government has a shareholding of 75.1 per cent, is responsible for the centralised procurement of commercial vehicles. By contrast, the procurement, storage and disposal of the stocks of clothing and the management of the required 'service stations' (formerly clothing stores) were the responsibility of the Lion Hellmann Bundeswehr Bekleidungsgesellschaft (LH Bw), which was also established in 2002 and in which the Federal Government has a 25.1 per cent minority holding (Wieland, 2003: 3; Hartenstein, 2004: 147). By introducing the commercial supply chain management system, the company succeeded in the very first year in reducing the procurement costs by 21 per cent (Biederbick, 2005a: 2) and lowering the number of missing parts to just over one per cent (Greyer-Wieninger, 2009: 3). This number has been reduced even further since then.

The transformation process is being accompanied for the Federal Ministry of Defence by the specialized directorates and service staffs and last, but not least, by the new Modernisation Directorate, which was established on 15 May 2006 (Hummel/Schwarz, 2006: 236 et seq.). Besides the management of the share holdings in the g.e.b.b. and its subsidiaries, this directorate is mainly responsible for the development of IT technology, notably by way of the Herkules project.

The Federal Defence Administration in the 2011/2012 reform process

The reorientation of the Bundeswehr was driven by its inadequate orientation towards the current and future security environments, the inadequate provision of funds and the demographic development in the Federal Republic of Germany. The idea behind it is to remove structural deficiencies, notably the fact that too few forces are available for operational deployment, the low level of sustainability, and cumbersome decision-making processes and procedures. The aim of the reorientation is to produce a Bundeswehr the tasks and capabilities of which are tailored to the security requirements, with a structure that can stand up to the demographic development and that is underpinned by sustainable funding.

When Federal Minister of Defence Dr Thomas de Maizière presented the cornerstones of the reorientation of the Bundeswehr on 18 May 2011, he outlined the basic structures of the future Bundeswehr and explained how the reorientation was to be implemented. Together with the Defence Policy Guidelines of 27 May 2011, the security policy fundamentals, these cornerstones define the parameters for the future structure and orientation of the Bundeswehr. They are derived from the analyses and findings of the Commission on the Structure of the Bundeswehr (October 2010), of the *Generalinspekteur*, of the directors at the Federal Ministry of Defence, as well as from the decisions taken by the Federal Government on the suspension of conscription on 1 July 2011 and the downsizing of the Bundeswehr (2011).

The structural reorientation: concentration and responsibility

The new basic structures of the Bundeswehr are based on a prioritized capability profile. The armed forces have the structures they need to accomplish the core mission of the Bundeswehr. They are supported by the overall system modelled in integrated processes and the services of the civilian organisational and resource elements. The Bundeswehr is organised in accordance with the principle of congruity between technical expertise and organisational responsibility. This yields clear-cut, process-oriented structures.

The future structures of the Federal Defence Administration are characterised by a paradigm shift. The administration, which hitherto had agencies throughout the country and provided its services for the forces locally, as a single service provider, is being replaced by a 'sector model' (BMVg, 2011a: 6 et seq.), modelled on the private sector. Its tasks will be performed by the specialized authorities responsible for a specific 'resource element'. The way in which its tasks have been distributed is being revised to take account of this sector-oriented approach. Even the distinction that has hitherto been made between the Territorial Defence Administration and the armament organisation will be removed. By the time the reform activities are concluded, only 55,000 posts will be left for the performance of all tasks assigned to civilian personnel in the Bundeswehr.

The Federal Ministry of Defence

The Federal Ministry of Defence is the central command and control instrument of the Federal Minister of Defence in his capacity as commander in chief of the armed forces and head of the Federal Defence Administration. The reorientation of the Federal Ministry of Defence and its organisation aims to optimise the discharge of ministerial functions as a whole, concentrate more on core ministerial and strategic tasks, and delegate operational-level matters to the subordinate agencies of the Bundeswehr.

The 'Dresden Directive' issued by the Federal Minister of Defence on 21 March 2012 lays down the new management and command and control philosophy and structures, the principles governing the top-level organisational structure, the management and command relationships and the management and command and control organisation, both at the FMOD and in the Bundeswehr. This directive supersedes the 'Blankenese Directive' of 21 March 1970 and the 'Berlin Directive' of 21 January 2005. It ensures that the guiding principles of the reorientation, such as the joint performance of tasks, the pooling of responsibilities, the reduction of interfaces and the concentration of expertise and responsibility, are applied throughout the Bundeswehr.

Combining technical and organisational responsibility in one source will lead to the restructuring of the defence administration and to a reassignment of tasks. The responsibilities for satisfying the armed forces' requirements will be pooled in the Federal Defence Administration and reflected in terms of structure in the three resource elements 'personnel', 'infrastructure, environmental protection and services' and 'equipment, information technology and in-service support'. These elements will completely absorb the current organisational elements of the Territorial Defence Administration and the armament organisation. The Administration of Justice Services and the Chaplain Service will remain in their current structures.

Figure 1: The tasks of the Territorial Defence Administration

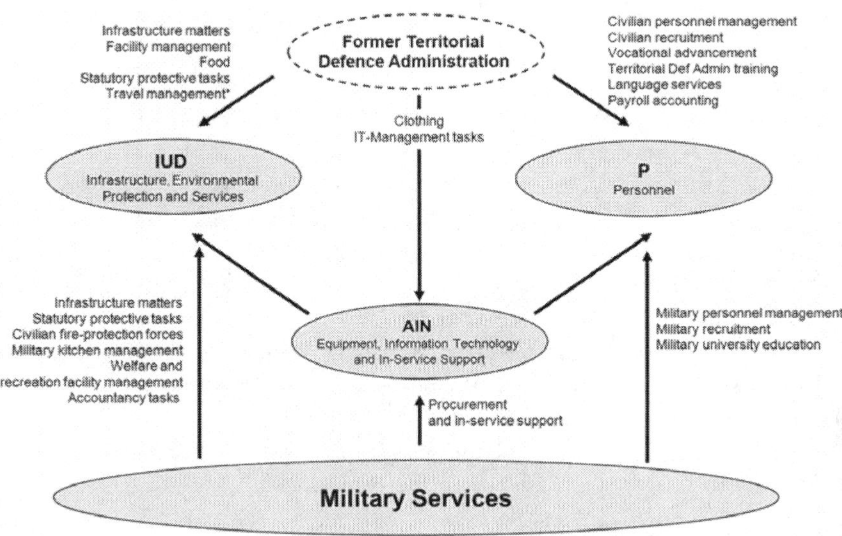

Source: FMOD, Directorate-General for Infrastructure, Environmental Protection and Services

The Directorates-General for Personnel, for Equipment, Information Technology and In-Service Support and for Infrastructure, Environmental Protection and Services are the elements of the Federal Ministry of Defence that manage resources. The previous principle of single services that involved, in particular, the pooling of services rendered by the military district administrative offices and control of on-site support of armed forces will be abandoned in favour of process-orientation. In other words, the individual technically responsible for a task will also decide how and where the task is performed and which resources will be used.

The Infrastructure, Environmental Protection and Services element

The Directorate-General for Infrastructure, Environmental Protection and Services will continue to be the major organisational element that performs the tasks previously discharged by the Territorial Defence Administration, although its responsibilities will change significantly. The element will have some 21,400 posts in total, 20,580 for civilian staff and 830 for military personnel. The Bundeswehr service centres will have a total of 15,900 civilian posts.

Tasks

The Directorate-General for Infrastructure, Environmental Protection and Services will deal with the task areas of infrastructure; statutory protective tasks; food, welfare and recreation facility management; and other services. Technical and organisational expertise will be pooled wherever possible. And, wherever permissible and justifiable, tasks are to be performed in mixed civilian-military structures. The idea behind this is to simplify coordination, strengthen technical responsibilities, eliminate interfaces and streamline and expedite processes. Infrastructure tasks concerning all infrastructure projects at home, abroad and in the theatres of operation in which Bundeswehr forces are deployed will be performed in a single Bundeswehr infrastructure organisation.

The protection of people and the environment is a national responsibility which is assigned great importance in the Bundeswehr. The Bundeswehr must comply fully with all legal and political specifications, especially those regarding environmental protection and occupational safety and health, nature conservation and water protection, ecological aspects, supervision under public law and fire protection.

The Directorate-General for Infrastructure, Environmental Protection and Services will also bear the technical responsibility for fire protection and the Bundeswehr's civilian fire brigade. This will include ensuring that all the fire brigade personnel receive the same training, further developing fire protection and making decisions on fire fighting equipment.

The services include in particular food, welfare and recreation facility management, travel management and guarding Bundeswehr facilities. Overall responsibility for the provision of food in the Bundeswehr and for management of all mess facilities that are run for Bundeswehr units and agencies engaged in routine activities and in operations – except for the galleys on board Navy vessels – lies with the Directorate-General for Infrastructure, Environmental Protection and Services. As a result, Bundeswehr personnel are offered food from a single source that, in addition to military dining facilities and canteens, includes welfare and recreation facilities such as officers', NCO and junior ranks' clubs.

The merging of all 80 or so agencies responsible for dealing with duty travel matters into one Centre of Expertise for Travel Management will not only help increase efficiency, but also enhance services provided for Bundeswehr personnel on temporary duty travel.

The services element is also responsible for performing a wide range of tasks in support of the armed forces during everyday activities at home and abroad. This includes handling legal matters and claims, regulating administrative procedures, operating facilities, procuring materiel, and managing both services provided to the Bundeswehr and the Bundeswehr's disposal services.

Organisation

The Directorate-General for Infrastructure, Environmental Protection and Services at the Federal Ministry of Defence exercises administrative and functional control over the entire organisational element. It is responsible for technical development and organisation matters. The new organisation is notably characterised by more efficient structures – two levels of organisation instead of the previous three – and a centralisation of tasks. Technical and organisational expertise will be combined wherever feasible.

With regard to the agencies below the ministry level, the Federal Office of Bundeswehr Infrastructure, Environmental Protection and Services is going to be established as a higher Federal authority in Bonn. This office will be responsible for performing all the management and implementation tasks in the fields of infrastructure, statutory protective tasks, services, legal affairs, financial and controlling affairs. It will also draw up regulations for statutory protective tasks that will be applicable throughout the Bundeswehr and take account of any ministerial specifications. These regulations will then be implemented by the service headquarters and the offices of the major organisational elements in their respective areas of responsibility.

In connection with the seven regional centres of expertise for construction management, the Federal Office will work closely with the *Länder* and the Federal Government construction authorities to ensure that comprehensive infrastructure services are provided to the Bundeswehr throughout Germany, abroad and in the theatres of operations. The seven centres of expertise for construction management will be established at the locations of the military district administrative offices and their branch offices that are going to be closed down.

Figure 2: Structure of the Directorate-General for Infrastructure, Environmental Protection and Services

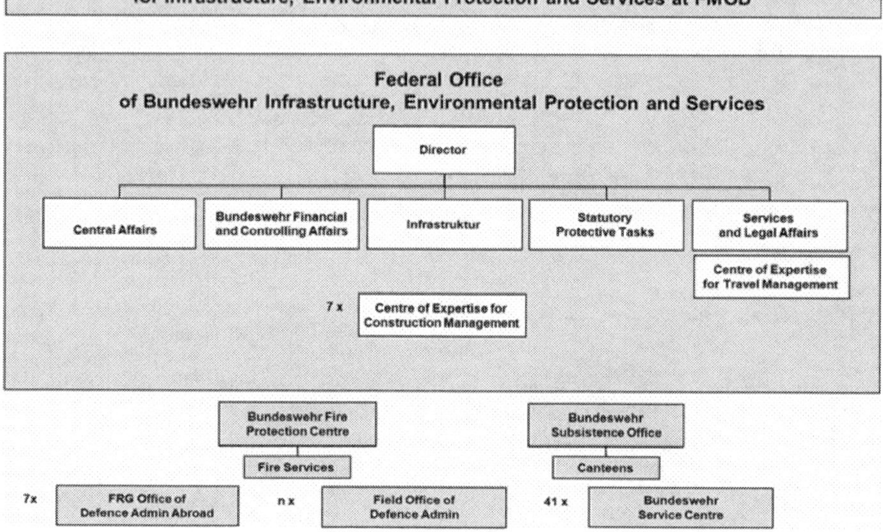

Source: FMOD, Directorate-General for Infrastructure, Environmental Protection and Services

The Bundeswehr fire protection centre in Sonthofen, a new agency, will take over all the operational level technical responsibilities, notably management, the development of technical specifications and the training and use of civilian Bundeswehr firefighting personnel.

The Bundeswehr subsistence office in Oldenburg will be responsible for operational-level management of both the static messing facilities run for Bundeswehr units and agencies engaged in routine activities and the welfare and recreations facilities, including standard and further training of civilian catering staff and military catering specialists through limited-duration employment. The subsistence office will be responsible for awarding all food service contracts, that is to say, the procurement of food, equipment, housekeeping material and personnel services for Bundeswehr units and agencies engaged in routine activities and in operations.

The present 80 or so duty travel agencies of the Bundeswehr are to be merged into a centre of expertise for travel management that will be part of the Federal Office of Bundeswehr Infrastructure, Environmental Protection and Services. At the local level, a total of 41 Bundeswehr service centres will provide their services for the armed forces in the individual specialized sectors. The service centres will form the backbone of the major organisational element Infrastructure, Environmental Protection and Services and ensure that the service sector is right where it is needed by forces on a daily basis. Seven offices of defence administration support the armed forces in a number of other countries in Europe, the United States and Canada.

The personnel element

The suspension of conscription and the demographic development necessitate the establishment of a new recruitment organisation. Furthermore, all personnel management work is being transferred to a single personnel office. This will enable the Bundeswehr's military and civilian personnel to be better interlinked. The education courses and facilities the Bundeswehr has to offer will be managed at a single education management centre to generate synergy effects. The aim of the new personnel management system is to ensure that the Bundeswehr has a body of personnel that is of the appropriate age and fits the structure. To this end, young women and men must continue to see the Bundeswehr as an attractive employer. The chance to attain qualifications and undergo advanced training, as well as career opportunities and adequate pay, are important incentives for serving in the Bundeswehr. It has been decided that there will be up to 185,000 military personnel and 55,000 civilian personnel in the future personnel structure of the Bundeswehr. Reorientation in personnel management will require structural changes to be made in all military careers. The challenges arising from demographic developments will be met by reducing the number of new personnel required each year from the present figure of 20,000 to around 14,000.

The resource element Personnel will be established as the personnel process is optimised. It will then reflect the entire task area of personnel services and the associated parameters, handling matters on a process basis and with as few interfaces as possible, making full use of personnel and content-related synergies. The military and civilian personnel management systems will be interlinked for this purpose. Each personnel management task will be performed only once, in a continuous line that starts at the directorate level at the ministry and ends at the local level.

By concentrating on five agencies that report directly to the Directorate-General for Personnel (the Federal Office of Bundeswehr Personnel Management, the Federal Office of Languages, the Bundeswehr University, Hamburg, the Bundeswehr University, Munich, and the Bundeswehr Education Management Centre), the technical and organisational responsibility for the entire personnel process will be centralised. The target strength of the major organisational element Personnel is 7,400 civilian and 2,150 military posts. The new Personnel element will perform the previous tasks of both the personnel induction offices and the recruitment organisation. The result will be a single new nationwide, customer-oriented and competitive recruitment organisation for the entire Bundeswehr in which both civilian and military personnel will work. The Bundeswehr Vocational Advancement Service will be part of this recruitment organisation.

To make sure that potential job applicants receive comprehensive information and are counselled about all the civilian and military job profiles that exist in the Bundeswehr as close to their homes as possible, a total of 110 permanently-staffed Bundeswehr career information offices will be set up throughout Germany. There are also plans for up to 200 mobile information offices to be created. Furthermore, 16 Bundeswehr career centres will be established to provide comprehensive information and counselling on the Bundeswehr as an employer for political and public authorities, the business sector, the Federal Employment Agency and other Bundeswehr agencies. Applicants for employment in the Bundeswehr will in future undergo aptitude testing in one of eight of these career centres, which will be located all over Germany.

The Federal Office of Bundeswehr Personnel Management is another key component of the Personnel element. This new office is going to be established by merging the existing military personnel offices and the civilian personnel management offices which have hitherto been collocated with the twelve higher and intermediate authorities. It will be responsible for specific aspects of personnel management (military personnel and civil servants up to and including pay grade A 16, civilian employees from pay grade 9), for the centralised coordination of recruitment activities and the pooling of pivotal specialized and management tasks.

The Bundeswehr's two universities will be detached from the Joint Support Service and incorporated into the major organisational element Personnel. Their tasks and structures will remain unchanged. They will be developed as a top-level segment of education, recruitment and retention and may even be opened to civilian students.

The responsibilities for school education and vocational training will also be centralised in the new Personnel element. For the first time, there will be a uniform concept for the implementation of educational and training measures for civilian occupations, action will be taken to push ahead with the certification of specific military qualifications, and the technical control of this process will be centralised below the ministry level – in a new Bundeswehr Education Management Centre. This centre will play a key role in the new education and qualification landscape in the Bundeswehr. In terms of organisation, it will link the Federal Academy of Defence Administration and Technology to the three Federal schools of defence administration. It will manage the ten Bundeswehr schools of general vocational education and the seven Bundeswehr schools abroad. Finally, the centre will perform general administrative tasks for the Federal Defence Administration Department of the Federal College of Public Administration.

The reorganisation also serves the purpose of meeting the content-related and organisational requirements for the recognition and certification of skills and qualifications that have been acquired during basic, advanced and follow-on training. This will improve the chances of Bundeswehr personnel to change careers within the institution and of temporary-career volunteers to be reintegrated both into the civilian labour market and into other areas within the Bundeswehr.

The Federal Office of Languages will also be incorporated into the major organisational element Personnel and will report directly to the Federal Ministry of Defence. Its primary responsibility will remain that of providing career, post-related and predeployment language training for military and civilian Bundeswehr personnel and – being a higher Federal authority – language training as part of interministerial language instruction given at supreme Federal authorities.

The Federal Office of Bundeswehr Personnel Management will be based in Cologne, while some of its work will be done in Düsseldorf, Siegburg and St. Augustin. It will be assisted in the performance of its personnel management tasks around the country by service centres in Hanover, Strausberg and Stuttgart.

The Equipment, Information Technology and In-Service Support element

The major organisational element Equipment, Information Technology and In-Service Support bears responsibility for national and international armament activities. Clear-cut responsibilities involving definite decision-making authority and fewer interfaces are assigned on the basis of a new efficient and uniform system of equipment and in-service support management. This allows undivided responsibility to be assigned for defence materiel throughout the various life cycles.

Taking over in-service support tasks from the Army Office, the Naval Office, the Bundeswehr Medical Office, the Bundeswehr Logistics Office and the German Air Force Weapon Systems Command is a decisive part of the restructuring of the armament organisation. Another important component is the merger of armament and information technology. The Federal Office of Defence Technology and Procurement and the Federal Office of the Bundeswehr for Information

Management and Information Technology and their agencies bring their entire task spectrum to bear in the new organisation. Merging the offices and integrating the in-service support elements into a new organisation will help eliminate efficiency gaps and improve communication and coordination processes. The Equipment, Information Technology and In-Service Support element will also perform tasks previously assigned to the Territorial Defence Administration. The tasks relating to the fields of clothing, the use of information technology and the procurement of transport services will be transferred to it. The Equipment, Information Technology and In-Service Support element will combine the task areas of research and technology and development and procurement of Bundeswehr equipment, including information technology and in-service support management. This major organisational element's basic functions will be to procure the goods and services needed to ensure the Bundeswehr's operational capability and to exercise single-manager responsibility for materiel readiness.

The future major resource element will be comprised of a new higher Federal authority with a portfolio of its own that will report directly to the Directorate-General for Equipment, Information Technology and In-Service Support at the Federal Ministry of Defence. The new Federal Office of Bundeswehr Equipment, Information Technology and In-Service Support and its agencies will have some 9,450 posts. The structure of the new office will ensure that project management and in-service support management are interlinked. It will have single-manager responsibility for the Bundeswehr's materiel readiness. So-called integrated project teams will in future form the link between the forces, which will use the materiel, and the defence administration.

The Federal Office of Bundeswehr Equipment, Information Technology and In-Service Support will be assisted by eight technical centres and research institutes and the Bundeswehr Information Technology Centre. Moreover, the Naval Arsenal will provide maintenance and repair services for the Navy. A liaison office in the United States will represent the defence technology and defence industry interests of the Bundeswehr vis-à-vis Germany's partners in the US and Canada.

The Administration of Justice element

Strictly speaking, neither the Administration of Justice element nor the Chaplain element, which is described farther below, is part of the Federal Defence Administration. However, since both belong to the major civilian organisational elements (see also introductory article by Ina Wiesner in this volume), they are briefly addressed at this point.

Even after the Bundeswehr has completed its reorientation, the Administration of Justice element will be responsible for providing legal advice to military superiors, especially on issues relating to military, criminal and operational law, and for giving lessons in law in the armed forces. The safeguarding of human dignity and basic rights and the adherence of the armed forces to the rule of law are both key to the image that Bundeswehr military personnel have of themselves, and permanent tasks. Focusing the Bundeswehr increasingly on operations will require its personnel to be well-trained and to be given comprehensive and qualified advice on legal issues relating to the use of military force. Providing its personnel appropriate training and instruction so that they know the law and know what to do in a given situation is an important criterion for ensuring the operational readiness of the Bundeswehr.

The personnel in the Administration of Justice element provide advice, give lessons and take decisions on legal affairs. In this way, they impart legal knowledge, improve legal awareness and help maintain military discipline, which itself is based on law. All in all, the Administration of Justice element has about 200 legal advisers and legal instructors, disciplinary attorneys and judges at Bundeswehr disciplinary and complaints courts. The demands on the legal personnel in the Administration of Justice element are high. In addition to specific knowledge in the fields of military law and military constitutional law and the relevant areas of international law, they must have the ability to make both de facto and ethical judgments on issues concerning all aspects of the use of armed forces.

The increasing focus of the armed forces on operations also requires the legal personnel in the Administration of Justice element to maintain a constantly high level of operational readiness. Besides intellectual competence and foreign language skills, they must maintain a high level of physical fitness. The organisational structure of the Administration of Justice element, its procedures and the matters it deals with are all being optimised to meet operation-related requirements. The Administration of Justice element has offices at more than fifty locations in Germany and abroad. The Bundeswehr Disciplinary and Complaints Courts, South and North have chambers at six locations nationwide.

The Chaplain element

The Chaplain Service remains an independent major organisational element and a joint matter for the state and the church. It rests on a partnership that preserves the autonomy of the two institutions. The Chaplain Service is the church for military personnel. Considering the great diversity of opinions and values, military personnel need to be clear about what they want to do with their own lives and about the fundamentals of taking responsible action. This becomes all the more necessary as the number of operations carried out in support of international crisis prevention and crisis management increases.

For military personnel, military chaplains are both advisers on ethical issues and reliable companions during operations. Together with military psychologists, the Bundeswehr Social Service and the family support organisation, they are an integral part of Bundeswehr's social networks. Besides providing religious support, they greatly contribute in this function to the morale and welfare support available to military personnel and their families. The Chaplain Service is basically geared towards the structure and deployment requirements of the armed forces. Below the ministry, it is organised in three tiers. At the top, there are the two higher Federal authorities, the Office of the Protestant Church for the Bundeswehr and the Catholic Military Episcopal Office in Berlin. Then there are nine military deaneries. And these deaneries in turn supervise a total of 185 military parish offices and six agencies abroad.

Outlook

Establishing the Federal Defence Administration as an independent second pillar alongside the armed forces was a bold step that pointed the way ahead and is unrivalled to this day. There were no models on which to build and shape this system. The Federal Defence Administration is now well over fifty years old, and it can definitely be said that the practice of distributing tasks between the armed forces and the Federal Defence Administration as laid down in the *Grundgesetz* has been a complete success both at home and abroad, and particularly during operations abroad.

Following Germany's reunification, the Bundeswehr was downsized drastically in accordance with the changed security and defence requirements. Several structural reforms entailed the reduction of the number of posts for civilian personnel to 75,000 by 2010. The target figure of the ongoing reform is 55,000 civilian posts. The new basic structures of the Bundeswehr are derived from a prioritized capability profile. The new basic structures of the Bundeswehr are derived from a prioritized capability profile. The armed forces will have structures that enable them to accomplish the core mission of the Bundeswehr. Even so, they will be dependent on an overall system that is composed of integrated processes, as well as on the services of the civilian organisational and resource elements. The Bundeswehr is being realigned according to the principle of congruity between technical expertise and organisational responsibility. The result will be clear-cut, process-based structures.

Within the bounds of the mission it is assigned under the *Grundgesetz*, the Federal Defence Administration had a decisive influence on enabling the Bundeswehr to function during the Cold War era, during the process of German reunification and during the assumption operation-related tasks. The civilian Federal Defence Administration can look back on an impressive record, and the job it has done so far is highly recognized by its military partners. As for the future, the civilian and military personnel in the new major organisational elements will continue to perform their jobs for the armed forces in their accustomed professional manner, even after the new structures have been established. The only difference will be that they will do so in a way that serves the entire Bundeswehr, with fewer interfaces and thus with even more efficiency. As in past decades, the diversity of their tasks and the daily challenges they face at home, abroad and during operations abroad will be both an incentive and a source of motivation for the experts of the Federal Defence Administration.

Bibliography

Baron von der Ropp/Götz-Friedrich (2006): Die Wehrverwaltung im Süden – Aufbau, Konsolidierung, Neuausrichtung. In: Die Bundeswehrverwaltung, 2006: 252 et seq.

BAWV, Bundesamt für Wehrverwaltung (2009): Das Bundesamt für Wehrverwaltung – Im Zeichen des Merkur am Puls der Zeit. Bonn.

Beutel, Joachim (1970): Die verfassungswidrige Truppenverwaltung – Eine Entgegnung. In: Die Bundeswehrverwaltung, 1970: 251 et seq.

Biederbick, Klaus-Günther (2005a): Die ökonomische Modernisierung der Bundeswehr. In: Die Bundeswehrverwaltung, 2005: 1 et seq.

Biederbick, Klaus-Günther (2005b): Transformation, Modernisierung, Privatisierung: Über den Weg zur Wehrverwaltung der Zukunft. In: Die Bundeswehrverwaltung, 2005: 169 et seq.

Blasius, Rainer (2006): Ziviler Geist gegen grasende Generäle. In: Frankfurter Allgemeine Zeitung, 29.03.2006: 10 et seq.; quoted from: Die Bundeswehrverwaltung, 2006: 221 et seq.

Blümel, Willi (1990): Verwaltungszuständigkeit. In: Isensee, Kirchhoff (Ed.) (1990), Band IV: § 101.

Boehm-Tettelbach, Wolfgang (2009): Wehrpflicht- und Soldatenrecht. Munich: Beck-Texte im dtv.

Bremm, Klaus-Jürgen/Mack, Hans-Hubertus/Rink, Martin (Eds.) (2005): Entschieden für den Frieden: 50 Jahre Bundeswehr 1955 bis 2005. Freiburg: Rombach Verlag.

BMVg (1999): Bundeswehr und Wirtschaft – Eine strategische Partnerschaft auf dem Weg in den modernen Staat. Bonn.

BMVg (2004): Die Stationierung der Bundeswehr in Deutschland. Bonn.

BMVg (2010): Wehrverwaltung im Einsatz – Ein Überblick. Bonn.

BMVg (2011a): Die Stationierung der Bundeswehr in Deutschland – October 2011. Bonn.

BMVg (2011b): Bundeswehr im Einsatz. Bonn

Bundesrechnungshof (2011): Jahresbericht 2011. Bonn.

Clausewitz, Carl Philipp Gottlieb von (1832): Vom Kriege. Berlin: Ferdinand Dümmler.

Clement, Rolf/Joris, Paul Elmar (2005): 50 Jahre Bundeswehr. 1955 – 2005. Hamburg/Berlin/Bonn: Verlag E.S. Mittler & Sohn.

Dehnert, Hans (1970): Grundgesetz und Truppenverwaltung – Eine Entgegnung. In: Die Bundeswehrverwaltung, 1970: 244 et seq.

Dreist, Peter (2004): Wehrverwaltung im Auslandseinsatz – die Aufgabenwahrnehmung. In: Unterrichtsblätter – Die Bundeswehrverwaltung, 2004: 281 et seq.

Expertenkommission zur Frage der Gefährdung durch Strahlung in früheren Radareinrichtungen der Bundeswehr und der NVA (2003): Bericht. Bonn.

Fabian, Otto (1973): Die Zusammenarbeit mit der Bundeswehrverwaltung aus der Sicht der Streitkräfte. In: Die Bundeswehrverwaltung, 1973: 145 et seq.

Fischer, Hans Werner (1999): Die Territoriale Wehrverwaltung hat sich auch im Auslandseinsatz bewährt. In: Die Bundeswehrverwaltung, 1999: 145 et seq.

Gramm, Christof (2003a): Privatisierung bei der Bundeswehr. In: Deutsche Verwaltungsblätter, 2003: 1366 et seq.

Gramm, Christof (2003b): Bundeswehr und Privatisierung in der Praxis. In: Neue Zeitschrift für Wehrrecht, 2003: 13 et seq.

Greyer-Wieninger, Alice (2009): Die Modernisierung der Territorialen Wehrverwaltung. In: Die Bundeswehrverwaltung, 2009: 2 et seq.

Greyer-Wieninger, Alice (2006): 50 Jahres Bundeswehrverwaltung – Standortbestimmung und künftiger Kurs. In: Die Bundeswehrverwaltung, 2006: 229 et seq.

Greyer-Wieninger, Alice (2005): Die Transformation der Territorialen Wehrverwaltung. In: Die Bundeswehrverwaltung, 2005: 171 et seq.

Großkraumbach, Rainer-Georg (2006): Wo Bundeswehr drauf steht, steckt auch Wehrverwaltung drin. In: Die Bundeswehrverwaltung, 2006: 231 et seq.

Hahnenfeld, Günter (1975): Bundeswehrverwaltung gestern und heute. In: Die Bundeswehrverwaltung, 1975: 18 et seq.

Hahnenfeld, Günter (1981): 25 Jahre Bundeswehrverwaltung. In: Die Bundeswehrverwaltung, 1981: 1 et seq.

Hartenstein, Frank-Helmut (2004): Die Wehrverwaltung im Veränderungsprozess der Bundeswehr. In: Die Bundeswehrverwaltung, 2004: 145 et seq.

Hummel, Alfred/Schwarz, Günter (2006): Transformation und Modernisierung. In: Die Bundeswehrverwaltung, 2006: 236 et seq.

Ipsen, Knut (Ed.) (1999): Wehrrecht und Friedenssicherung. Festschrift für Klaus Dau zum 65. Geburtstag. Neuwied: Luchterhand Fachverlag.

Isensee, Josef/Kirchhof, Paul (1990): Handbuch des Staatsrechts der Bundesrepublik Deutschland. Heidelberg: C. F. Müller Verlag.

Jarass, Hans/Pieroth, Bodo (2010): Grundgesetz für die Bundesrepublik Deutschland. Munich: C. H. Beck Verlag.

Johanny, Karl (2005): Ein Teil der Bundeswehr wie die Streitkräfte – 50 Jahre Bundeswehrverwaltung. In: Bremm et al. (Ed.) (2005): 199 et seq.

Lecheler, Helmut (1994): Privatisierung von Verwaltungsaufgaben. In: Bayerische Verwaltungsblätter, 1994: 555 et seq.

Lorse, Jürgen (2004): Das Verhältnis zwischen Streitkräften und Bundeswehrverwaltung im System des Grundgesetzes. In: Neue Zeitschrift für Wehrrecht, 2004: 177 et seq.

Mann, Siegfried (1971): Das Bundesministerium der Verteidigung. Bonn: Boldt Verlag.

Martini, Bernd-Rüdiger (2007): Die neuen Bundeswehr-Dienstleistungszentren in der Territorialen Wehrverwaltung. In: Die Bundeswehrverwaltung, 2007: 77 et seq.

Maunz, Theodor/Dürig, Günter/Herzog, Roman (1985): Grundgesetz Kommentar. Munich: C. H. Beck Verlag.

Oulik, Helmut (1971): Probleme der Truppenverwaltungsbeamten – Eine kritische Betrachtung. In: Die Bundeswehrverwaltung, 1971: 169 et seq.

Reinfried, Hubert (1958): Die Bundeswehrverwaltung. In: Die Öffentliche Verwaltung, 1958: 144 et seq.

Reinfried, Hubert/Steinebach, Nikolaus (1983): Die Bundeswehrverwaltung. Heidelberg, Hamburg: R.v.Decker's Verlag, G. Schenk.

Reinfried, Hubert/Walitschek, Hubert F. (1978): Die Bundeswehr. Eine Gesamtdarstellung. Band 9. Streitkräfte und Bundeswehrverwaltung. Regensburg: Walhalla u. Praetoria Verlag.

Reinhart, Rainer (1996): Die Bundeswehrverwaltung – Die vierzigjährige Geschichte einer fast unbekannten Schönen. In: Die Bundeswehrverwaltung, 1996: 100 et seq.

Sachs, Michael (2008): Kommentar zum Grundgesetz. Munich: C. H. Beck Verlag

Schmidt, Heinrich (1970): Grundgesetz und Truppenverwaltung – Eine ergänzende Ausführung. In: Die Bundeswehrverwaltung, 1970: 252 et seq.

Schmidt-Radefeldt, Roman (2006): Streitkräfte und Bundeswehrverwaltung im Auslandseinsatz. In: Die Bundeswehrverwaltung, 2006: 169 et seq.

Schmidt-Radefeldt, Roman (2007): Die Bundeswehrverwaltung im bewaffneten Konflikt. In: Die Bundeswehrverwaltung, 2007: 73 et seq.

Schrömbgens, Heinrich Michael (2006): Aufbau Ost in der Wehrverwaltung. In: Die Bundeswehrverwaltung, 2006: 254 et seq.

Sodan, Helge (2009): Grundgesetz – Beck'sche Kompaktkommentare. Munich: C. H. Beck Verlag.

Steinlechner, Wolfgang (1970): Grundgesetz und Truppenverwaltung. In: Die Bundeswehrverwaltung, 1970, 169 et seq.

Strauß, Franz-Josef (1961): Aufgaben und Stellung der Bundeswehrverwaltung. In: Die Bundeswehrverwaltung, 1961, 193 et seq.

Voigt, Rüdiger/Seybold, Martin (2003): Streitkräfte und Wehrverwaltung. Eine verfassungsrechtliche Analyse des Verhältnisses von Art. 87 a zu Art. 87 b GG. Baden-Baden: Nomos Verlagsgesellschaft.

Voigt, Rüdiger/Seybold, Martin (2004): Verfassungsrechtliche Rahmenbedingungen für den Einsatz von Soldaten im Bereich der Bundeswehrverwaltung. In: Neue Zeitschrift für Wehrrecht, 2004: 141 et seq.

Walz, Dieter (1997): Auslandseinsätze deutsche Streitkräfte und Art. 87b Grundgesetz. In: Neue Zeitschrift für Wehrrecht, 1997: 89 et seq.

Walz, Dieter (1999): Die verfassungsrechtlichen Grundlagen der Bundeswehrverwaltung – Abschied von der Zwei-Säulen-Theorie? In: Ipsen (Ed.) (1999): 301 et seq.

Wehrbeauftragter des Deutschen Bundestags (2011): Jahresbericht 2011. BT-Drucksache 17: 8400.

Wehrbereichsverwaltung Ost (2010): 20 Jahre Wehrbereichsverwaltung Ost. Strausberg.

Wieland, Joachim (2003): Verfassungsrechtliche Rahmenbedingungen für Privatisierungen im Bereich der Bundeswehrverwaltung. In: Neue Zeitschrift für Wehrrecht, 2003: 1 et seq.

Witte, Franz-Werner (1963): Truppe und Verwaltung. Band 3. Die rechtliche Stellung der Bundeswehrverwaltung. Hamburg-Berlin: R. v. Decker's Verlag, G. Schenck.

Witte, Franz-Werner (1964): Der materielle und formelle Begriff der Wehrverwaltung. In: Deutsche Verwaltungsblätter,1964: 60 et seq.

Wolff, Heinrich Amadeus (Ed.) (2011): Die Zuständigkeit der Bundeswehrverwaltung für das Personalwesen der Bundeswehr. Vorgaben des Art. 87 b Abs. 1 GG für eine Strukturreform der Bundeswehr. Bonn: Verband der Beamten der Bundeswehr e. V.

Part III

The political economy of German defence

Theoretical determinants and practical design of the federal budget as exemplified by Departmental Budget 14

Stefan Bayer

Many Bundeswehr members feel that they have to fulfil an ever-growing number of tasks with dwindling financial resources. This impression has been confirmed by both military and civilian personnel of different generations – so it is not really something new. Also in private enterprises, this phenomenon can be observed more and more frequently – economically speaking, it is the requirement to increase efficiency. This focus on efficiency in the Bundeswehr reflects the zeitgeist of an increasingly globalised society, too. However, there is a difference between the Bundeswehr and private enterprises with respect to the measurability of output: Private enterprises make profits or are punished for wrong decisions by the market; they produce losses and, as a final consequence, are put out of business.[1] These laws of the market do not apply within the Bundeswehr – irrespective of specific services in individual areas of responsibility, the Bundeswehr's task is to effectively protect the nation from external risks. Frequently, it is not a central focus whether, or to what extent, this happens efficiently. Nevertheless, § 7 of the Federal Budget Code *(Bundeshaushaltsordnung; BHO)*, which is referred to as the precept of economic efficiency, applies to the Bundeswehr as well: 'The principles of economic efficiency and economy must be observed in preparing and implementing the budget plan.' This means that the Bundeswehr, too, must meet a standard of efficiency in the services it has to provide (for introductory considerations on the possibility of conducting a monetary evaluation of different Bundeswehr services from a national economic point of view, see Bayer, 2009a).

Mission accomplishment[2] in the Bundeswehr very much depends on the financial resources made available by the legislator. In general, tasking an actor only makes sense if the budget required for the respective purpose is provided, too. However, a cardinal problem consists in actually quantifying the resources 'appropriate' for mission accomplishment.

1 Unless, that is, governments decide that these companies are of particular value to the national economy, e.g. system-relevant institutions.

2 For the Bundeswehr's current security interests and objectives as well as Bundeswehr missions and tasks derived from them, see the Defense Policy Guidelines of 2011, BMVg (2011a), chapters III and V. However, for reasons of space, these aspects shall not be dealt with in greater detail in this essay.

The aspects mentioned – and of course many more – must be considered in the budget process. Thus, the implementation of the Federal Government's financial policy aims requires careful planning of the financial means needed to achieve them. For this purpose, planned revenue and planned expenditure are presented separately in public budgets. Planning approaches are legitimised by parliament in the Federal Republic of Germany. In addition, the government's financial behaviour can be controlled by the public. In order to fulfil these planning and supervisory functions, the federation (but also the federal states and the municipalities) sets up financial plans, some of which are passed as laws by the legislative institutions (parliaments and municipal councils). Categories of public financial plans are: short-term budget plans (annual or two-year budgets), medium-term financial plans, and long-term plans for public infrastructure projects (traffic, education). However, we will not be able to examine the long-term plans in more detail in this essay for lack of space.

In the following, we want to deal with the budget process – which is of major importance also to Bundeswehr mission accomplishment – in more detail, through a presentation and analysis. We intend to do this in two parts:[3] first, the key fundamentals of the German budget system shall be presented, while already referring to the defence budget in individual cases. Second, the focus will be on Departmental Budget 14, the defence budget, which will be analysed from different perspectives. A conclusion will round off the two parts and attempt to provide an outlook. It is not possible to make a comparison of different nations' defence budgets in this paper because the constitutional prerequisites for their creation vary considerably from country to country.[4] One last preliminary remark: This essay is based on information that stems exclusively from publicly-accessible sources, which are referenced in the bibliography.

3 Reference shall be made here to a 2009 essay of similar content by the author that analyses the conflict between the funds provided and the Bundeswehr's mission situation; see Bayer, 2009b.

4 An example to be mentioned here is the federal structure of the Federal Republic of Germany, as opposed to the rather centralist form of the government of France. In France, expenditure for schools, etc. is recorded in the equivalent to the federal budget, whereas in the Federal Republic of Germany, this mainly falls under the responsibility of the federal states. The interested reader may refer to the NATO website (http://www.nato.int/cps/en/natolive/topics_49198.htm?, last accessed 07.06.2012), where comparisons of defence expenditure are based on the figures of the gross domestic product, which are considerably more informative in this respect.

1. The federal budget

This chapter serves to present and explain the fundamentals of budget development and implementation in the Federal Republic of Germany. In addition to the short-term budget plan (1.1), part 1.2 also deals with medium-term financial planning (the Federal Financial Plan).

1.1 The short-term budget plan

The short-term budget plan, which is passed as the Budget Act by the legislature, provides a binding foundation for the implementation of financial measures taken by a territorial authority within a specified period of time.[5] It has to be set up every year (in some federal states every second year). It contains all revenues and expenditures, i.e. it comprises the overall financial activity of a local authority in a planning period, including what is referred to as 'commitment appropriations' (administrations are authorised to incur financial commitments for future years). The statements on the short-term budget plan provide the basis for the analysis and discussion of the respective Departmental Budget 14, the defence budget of the current period.

1.1.1 Functions

The budget plan fulfils the economic planning function and is an instrument of democratic control. Planning prerequisites are: to identify objectives and tasks, to realise these tasks in a cost-effective manner and to allocate these tasks to the individual government and administration levels. The planning function consists of ensuring that these requirements are met. The government's duty to prepare a budget plan obliges it and the administration to make rational plans. The planning function comprises the following subfunctions:

- *political programme function:* The budget plan must express the government's action programme in terms of monetary value. However, it also gives the legislator and the public the possibility to obtain information about the financial actions planned by the executive in order to enable them to exercise their control function. This underpins the fact that the right to appropriate funds is the key right of parliament.

5 In the following, see also Cansier/Bayer, 2003: 49-69, where specific individual statements are analysed and explained in much more detail.

- *function of economic efficiency:* Tasks must be accomplished in a way that takes into account cost effectiveness and avoids waste (BHO, § 7).
- *organisational function:* The responsibilities to be assumed shall be allocated to the different government and administration levels in a sensible way. Budget estimates provide a financial basis for task accomplishment by the administration.
- *procurement function:* The budget plan must ensure that expenditures are covered by sufficient revenue. Ex-post budget deficits or budget surpluses must be avoided (referred to as the 'principle of connexity').
- *overall economic function:* The budget plan must guarantee that the state manages its finances in line with overall economic development.

The fact that the budget plan is passed as a law ensures ex-ante control by the legislature and offers the public the possibility of obtaining information about the way the government and the administration manage finances. Parliament's right to appropriate funds is one of the traditional basic pillars of democracy. Once the budget plan has become a law, budget estimates become binding for the implementation of measures by the administration. Budget law provides an ex-post basis for courts of auditors and the legislature to review whether authorised estimates were adhered to by the individual departments. In order to ensure that the various functions are fulfilled, budget law contains special provisions, which are referred to as budget principles.

1.1.2 Key budget principles

Principle of anteriority: The budget must be laid down by law before the start of the budget period to which it applies (Art. 110 (2), first sentence of the Grundgesetz (Basic Law); § 1 BHO). Anteriority is a requirement of objective-oriented behaviour. This principle is often violated. In such cases, 'emergency rules' (Art. 111 of the Grundgesetz) apply: If the budget is not laid down in time, the government is entitled to spend funds in the amount necessary to sustain state administration functions and to meet existing obligations until parliament passes budget legislation (which is referred to as temporary budgeting). In such a situation, the government cannot pursue real financial policy and is therefore in effect gridlocked.

Principle of unity: All estimated revenues and expenditures of a territorial entity shall be included in a single budget plan (prohibition of subsidiary budgets). This is intended to guarantee financial transparency, which is both a prerequisite for rational financial behaviour in general and an essential requirement enabling third parties to exercise effective control over the administration. Exceptions are permitted for special trusts and for federal enterprises (Art. 110(1) of the Grundgesetz).

Principle of completeness: Estimates of all expected revenues and all expenditures that will probably have to be incurred must be included in the budget (Art. 110 (1) of the Grundgesetz). No revenues or expenditures may intentionally be left out of the budget estimate. It is therefore prohibited to account for revenues and expenditures outside budget plans (ban on illicit accounts). In addition, an account of all revenues received and expenditures made must be submitted upon completion of the fiscal year (Art. 114 of the Grundgesetz). Accordingly, the principle of completeness serves to ensure comprehensive planning and control; in this respect, the principle of completeness corresponds to the principle of unity.

Gross principle: All revenues and expenditures must be submitted and accounted for separately and in full (§ 12 (1), page 1 of the Budgetary Principles Act; Haushaltsgrundsätzegesetz – HGrG). In balancing accounts, care must be taken to avoid covering up individual transactions. This transparency requirement is decisive for facilitating the control function. In the Federal Republic of Germany, the gross principle is implemented by listing revenues and expenditures separately in each departmental budget.

Principle of specialty: This principle supports the control function of parliament (§ 27 (1), sentence 1 of the Budgetary Principles Act as well as § 45 (1), page 1 of the Federal Budget Code). It has a quantitative, a qualitative and a time-related aspect. Its aim is to ensure reliable implementation of the budget plan.

The partial principle of quantitative specialty means that expenditures must only be made in the amount provided for in the budget plan. Unscheduled expenditures (which are not provided for in the budget plan) and excessive expenditures (outlays beyond the estimated amounts) are prohibited. But exceptions exist even for this principle: If situations arise (e.g. disasters) in which adhering to the budget neither makes sense nor is feasible, the following rules apply:

Deviations are allowed within certain limits (for all or some categories of expenditure). In case of 'unforeseen and unavoidable necessity', the Federal Minister of Finance may authorise expenditures in excess of budgetary appropriations and for purposes not contemplated by the budget, which, however, must subsequently be approved by parliament (Art. 112 of the *Grundgesetz*). If the need arises for major unforeseeable increases in expenditure, a supplementary budget must be set up, to which the same principles apply as to the normal budget, especially the principle of anteriority.

According to the principle of *qualitative specialty*, the funds contained in the budget plan must only be used for the indicated purpose. It shall not be possible for the administration to shift appropriations to different task areas. This principle aims to ensure that the budget structure originally intended by the legislator is actually implemented. The inflexibility of this rule leads to drawbacks. Rigidly laid down budget items do not allow for flexibility. In case of unexpected changes, it must be possible to adapt budget implementation. Exceptions may therefore be made for budget items for which one-way virement and reciprocal virement is stipulated by law or expressly noted in the budget plan. In accordance with § 15 (3) of the Budgetary Principles Act and §20 (2) of the Federal Budget Code, an administrative or objective connection must exist between expenditure budget items in the event of virement. In the defence budget, reciprocal virement has already been realised in some cases; however, what is generally missing is flexibilisation oriented towards tasks and across departmental boundaries, which formally represents a move away from the principle of qualitative specialty. As far as the comprehensive approach is concerned, the Federal Republic of Germany still lacks a budgetary foundation that is tailored to this objective.

According to the principle of *time-bound budgeting*, funds must be used within the period for which they have been authorised. Unused funds (referred to as 'budget remnants') lapse at the end of a budget period (§ 27 (1), sentence 1 of the Budgetary Principles Act as well as § 45 (1) of the Federal Budget Code). In this context, the following exceptions apply: Unused credit authorisations remain valid. Certain budget items may additionally bear transfer notes (§ 19 of the Federal Budget Code). This particularly applies to investments. In this case, unused funds may be used in the next period. This rule makes sense for economic reasons. Time-bound budgeting, however, sometimes leads to inefficiencies, often referred to as 'December fever' in German. Since appropriations lapse at the end of a budget period, there is the temptation to spend unused funds shortly before the closure of accounts. Whether or not the respective expenditures are in line with § 7 of the Federal Budget Code (principle of economic efficiency) needs to be verified in each individual case. For some time, economists have proposed instruments to encourage economic efficiency that may to some extent mitigate the 'December fever' phenomenon (e.g. putting a share of the funds saved at the disposal of the individual who bears cost responsibility, for the purpose of funding morale-boosting measures for subordinate personnel).

The principle of time-bound budgeting is deliberately ignored by introducing what is referred to as 'commitment appropriations' (§§ 16 and 38 of the Federal Budget Code). They constitute an exception in the form of a quantified commitment at the expense of special budget items in subsequent years. Commitment appropriations are to facilitate long-term investments which cannot be procured completely within a single budget period. Among other things, they are of considerable importance in the defence budget for the procurement of major items of military equipment – without commitment appropriations, this would almost be impossible because of the long duration of the procurement process. In the federal budget for 2012, commitment appropriations for Departmental Budget 14 are provided in the order of around 8.9 bn euros for the fiscal years from 2013 onwards – the major part of this sum is to be spent and accounted for as future expenditure in the years 2013 to 2015. Thus, the sum of commitment appropriations in the year 2012 exceeds expenditures foreseen for defence investments (see chapter 2 of this essay). Commitment appropriations must be identified separately in the expenditure estimates of the budget plan in order to ensure continuous control over the scope of prior commitments of future fiscal years. As a rule, commitment appropriations lead to zero or only minor expenditures in the current year, but they may limit the long-term financial scope of a budget. This also limits the political leeway of the future parliament authorising the budget.

Principle of overall coverage: All revenues serve as covering funds for all expenditures. This makes it possible to orient task accomplishment towards the interests of society. This principle implies a prohibition on earmarked revenues (§ 7, sentence 1 of the Budgetary Principles Act, as well as § 8, sentence 1 of the Federal Budget Code), which would lead to an arbitrary and thus inefficient structure of public spending.

Principle of budget transparency: This principle includes the postulate to ensure transparency of the budget plan (see §§ 10, 11 and 12 of the Budgetary Principles Act or §§ 13, 14 and 17 of the Federal Budget Code). In particular, its structure must clearly show the origin and amount of estimated revenues, the purposes for which expenditures are expected and the reasons for the specified amount, as well as the scope allocated to certain government expenditures. This postulate requires a suitable budget system (structure based on the ministerial and functional principles). The principle of budget transparency is essential in facilitating the control function.

Principle of budget accuracy: This principle includes the requirement to exactly estimate probable revenues and expenditures, as well as a prohibition on concealing or feigning amounts and facts (fulfilment of the control function). Future revenues and expenditures depend on numerous uncertain factors such as the development of the real social product, the price level, wage development, foreign trade, etc. Therefore, it is inevitable that deviations between planned and actual parameters will occur. It must also be avoided that the uncertainties mentioned will induce anyone to intentionally make wrong estimates ('fake budgets'). For example, revenues may be overestimated for strategic reasons in order to increase expenditures during election periods ('campaign gifts').

Principle of publicity: This principle requires the budget plan to be published (in the Federal Gazette, after it has been passed as a law) and budget debates in parliament to be public. Exceptions apply to funds earmarked as 'secret', which means that the respective resources may only be reviewed by the President of the Court of Auditors.

Principle of indebtedness ('limits of borrowing'): The *Grundgesetz* stipulates what is referred to as 'limits of borrowing' for net new borrowing (Art. 115 sentence 2 of the *Grundgesetz*): 'This principle shall be satisfied when revenue obtained by the borrowing of funds does not exceed 0.35 per cent in relation to the nominal gross domestic product.' Exceptions to this rule are addressed in the same sentence. The political debates about the modification of the old indebtedness rule in Art. 115, sentence 2 of the *Grundgesetz*, which laid down that borrowing had to be in line with investment by the Federal Republic, cannot be analysed here for lack of space.

Looked at individually and in combination, the individual principles serve to achieve the functions of public budgets in the Federal Republic of Germany mentioned under 1.1.1. Of course, they all also apply to the defence budget and explain general conditions for dealing with public funds.

1.1.3 The budgetary cycle (life cycle of a budget plan)

The periodic process, which begins with budget preparation and ends with the granting of a 'budget discharge' to the government by the legislator is referred to as the 'budgetary cycle'. It is carried out in four phases. Here, we will concentrate on the provisions that apply to the federal budget.

a) Preparation of a draft budget

Before a draft budget in a narrower sense is prepared, important financial policy decisions are taken on a regular basis. For example, the Federal Government initially submitted its projection of the medium-term economic development in October of the year before last (i.e. in the year 2010 for fiscal year 2012). Subsequently, a medium-term tax revenue assessment was then made by the *Arbeitskreis Steuerschätzung* (a working group on tax revenue estimates) in November of the previous year in order to determine the key parameters of government revenue for the medium term (roughly five years). At the beginning of the actual planning year, the Federal Government submitted the annual economic report of the Federal Government in response to the report by the German Council of Economic Advisors in January of the same year (in this case: 2011).

Actual budget initiative rests with the Federal Government and with the Federal Minister of Finance (§§ 28 and 29 of the Federal Budget Code). Accordingly, more detailed planning of the federal budget for fiscal year 2012 began in mid-March 2011 at the latest. At the suggestion of the Federal Ministry of Finance, benchmarks are adopted which ensure adherence to the constitutional debt brake and provide a binding basis for further budget preparation in the departmental budgets. This is followed by the usual procedure of budget preparation within the government, with the departments applying for budget funds, which is completed by the cabinet's decision on the federal budget and the financial plan. Further details will not be dealt with here; on this subject, see e.g. Cansier/Bayer, 2003: 58 et seq. and BMF, 2011c.

Finally, the draft overall budget is forwarded to the cabinet. Consultations focus on those issues where the departments and the Ministry of Finance have failed to reach an agreement. In this context, the Federal Minister of Finance has a particularly strong position, which manifests itself especially in the fact that, in accordance with § 26 para. 2 of the Federal Government's rules of procedure, he can prevent decisions in matters of 'financial importance', provided he is supported by the Federal Chancellor. Cabinet decisions require the majority of the entire cabinet, including the Federal Chancellor, if the Federal Minister of Finance does not agree.

b) Parliamentary debates and passing as a law

As a draft law of the Federal Government, the draft prepared by the cabinet is forwarded to the legislative bodies for consultation and decision-making, as a rule in August before the start of the respective fiscal year. Further steps largely correspond to the normal legislative procedure with the participation of the *Bundestag* and the *Bundesrat* (see also Cansier/Bayer, 2003: 60-61). Upon completion of the procedure, the Federal Budget Act is signed by the Federal President and countersigned both by the Federal Chancellor and the Federal Minister of Finance. Subsequently, it is promulgated in the Federal Law Gazette and thus enters into force.

c) Execution of the budget

The Federal Budget Act allocates funds for certain purposes to the individual departments. They are obliged to adhere to these allocations. The departments receive a certified copy of their respective departmental plan. The ministers and the respective heads of department distribute the allocated funds to the subordinate authorities. At the same time, the cashiers receive directives – referred to as 'allotments' – instructing them to make the respective funds available. For the disbursement of funds, certain principles must be observed (§§ 34-69 of the Federal Budget Code): Expenditure estimates are maximum amounts that may, but need not, be spent.

The following principles must be observed:

- The administration shall ensure economic efficiency and economy in using the funds;
- Cost-benefit analyses shall be carried out for certain projects in order to verify efficiency (§ 6, para. 2 of the Budgetary Principles Act and § 7, para. 2 of the Federal Budget Code);
- Revenues shall be ascertained in a timely and complete fashion;
- Revenues and expenditures shall be accounted for through the obligation of bookkeeping, documentation and billing. Ex-post budget accounts must be prepared.

d) Budgetary control

The budget plan and/or the Federal Budget Act can only fulfil their functions if their binding character is maintained. This is the chief purpose of budget control. It is mainly carried out by independent audit institutions (e.g. by the *Bundesrechnungshof*, Germany's Supreme Audit Institution (SAI), as well as by the audit offices of the federal states). Like law courts, the audit institutions are not bound by instructions. Their members enjoy complete judicial independence. The aim of the audit institution is to ensure the proper conduct and economic efficiency of the administration's budgetary and economic administration. It forwards the result of its examination to the constitutional bodies (*Bundestag*, *Bundesrat* and the Federal Government). The audit institution report makes it possible to exercise political control. Based on this report, parliament decides whether to grant a 'discharge' to the government. The discharge completes the budget cycle. However, several years may pass from the preparation of the draft budget to the discharge. Therefore, discharge and/or disapproval have no political consequences in most cases. If clear budgetary overspending and uneconomic behaviour occurred and the government has changed in the meantime, the responsible individuals can no longer be held to account.

1.1.4 Drawbacks of the short-term budget plan

Focus on the short term: Planning for a period of one year makes it almost impossible to be guided by medium and long-term aspects. It does not force the government or the legislator to consider long-term consequences of decisions. They may decide on action involving only little expenditure in the current year but resulting in high financial burdens in future years. Short-term planning promotes the general human tendency to neglect long-term follow-on costs. In addition, a short-term focus does not exert much pressure to carefully establish intertemporal priorities in expenditures because the focus is on imminent issues and not on longer-term or long-term requirements.

Input orientation of budget planning: Planning refers to expenditures and not to tasks. Deliberations focus on spending rather than on tasks.

The principle of bottom-up planning, which was altered in fiscal year 2011, after having been standard practice for many years: With this approach, the aims of government bureaucracy were a major priority. As a rule, superordinate aims of the government were not sufficiently considered in bottom-up planning. At the same time, the excessive power of the executive in the budget planning process resulted in limited influence by parliament, a fact that was politically questionable. Therefore, a top-down planning approach has been in place since fiscal year 2011. It stipulates that *'important budget benchmarks are to be laid down by the Federal Cabinet in advance, which thus serve as the basis for the procedure of departmental budget preparation within the government'* (BMF 2011b: 1). The effects of this change cannot yet be assessed.[6]

Success control: There is no systematic success control, i.e. a result-oriented evaluation of the financial programmes with appropriate feedback and consequences for future spending policy – successful programmes should be continued or even intensified, and less successful ones stopped or modified.

1.2. Financial planning: medium-term financial planning

The medium-term financial plan supplements the short-term budget. It extends the planning horizon to the medium term. It is a non-statutory compilation of all expected expenditures of a public body and the revenues foreseen to cover these expenses, taking into account interrelations with the respective economic development. It is established by the Ministry of Finance and submitted to parliament for information purposes. Expenditure estimates for future years are meant to reflect the intended medium-term programme of work of the government (political programme function), also with respect to its levels and structure. In this sense, this financial plan lays down a future spending framework for the different departmental budgets, i.e. including the scope of expenditure for the defence budg-

6 It should be mentioned here that the procedural change will probably yield centralisation benefits, although at the expense of in-depth knowledge at upper administrative echelons, which means that decentralisation advantages are given up. Depending on the intensity of the two effects, efficiency will either improve in the following fiscal years, as is hoped, or the exact opposite will occur (for further ideas on this, see also Cansier/Bayer, 2003: 241-258).

et. In this respect, it also sets out the medium-term framework for defence policy, which falls under the responsibility of Departmental Budget 14.

Medium-term financial planning formally comprises a period of five years. The current financial plan of the federation concerns the years 2011-2015.[7] This financial plan was submitted together with the 2011 draft federal budget. The first 'planning year' is the fiscal year when the financial plan is passed (§ 50, para. 2 of the Budgetary Principles Act), i.e. in this case 2011. Therefore, the values for this year mainly represent actual values and not planning variables. The second planning year is identical with the budget period of the short-term budget plan. This means that for the year 2012, the financial plan contains the same parameters as the federal budget. Real additional planning is available only for the subsequent three years.

This is referred to as 'rolling planning'. The Growth and Stability Act prescribes annual adaptation and continuation of the financial plan. Rolling planning ensures that the planning period remains constant at all times and does not decrease as the lifetime of the plan proceeds – as is the case with one-time planning.

With the extension of the temporal planning horizon, the following aims are pursued:

- more efficient harmonisation of present and future interests,
- improved intertemporal harmonisation of expenditures and revenues. Undesired budget deficits (and budget surpluses) are to be avoided (financial normative function),
- more effective design of economic and growth policy. Since the Federal Government is encouraged to make longer-term plans, it has to think about long-term economic development, and
- more efficient intertemporal coordination of expenditures by the federation, the federal states and municipalities. Expenditure levels and structures are to be better harmonised between territorial entities.

Future tax revenues and government expenditure will depend on future economic development. Therefore, assumptions must be made about prospective economic parameters. The most important macroeconomic variables are the real growth rate of the gross domestic product (or the gross national product), the rate of inflation, the unemployment rate and the foreign trade balance (net exports). In

7 The Federal Republic's new financial plan for 2012-2016 was submitted to the cabinet as a draft in late March 2012. It lays down the benchmarks for growth-promoting consolidation within the specified period; however, this financial plan had not been passed by parliament at the time this article was printed. Therefore, this paper deals with the currently valid financial plan.

medium-term financial planning, a *target projection* is made. The Government establishes benchmarks for intended real growth, the foreign trade balance, the tolerated inflation rate and the unemployment rate for the individual years, which are used to estimate actual revenues and expenditures.

In planning government expenditure and government revenue, there is the problem of the interdependence of fiscal parameters and macroeconomic variables. On the one hand, public revenues and expenditures are a result of the overall economic development. On the other hand, they also influence it. Thus, target benchmarks must not be established exogenously. They are not independent of government revenues and expenditures. Practical financial planning operates on the method of 'successive approximation': The variables of the system are estimated separately – provided they are not directly controlled by the decision-maker.

Overall, the most important advantages and drawbacks of medium-term financial planning are: It is useful because intertemporally more efficient financial policy decisions are promoted and the harmonisation between revenues and expenditures is improved. It helps to avoid undesired deficits due to financial policy measures involving long-term follow-on costs. The enforced long-term perspective raises the government's awareness of the importance of public investment for long-term economic growth, which in turn promotes an improved growth policy through steady and appropriate investment planning. On the other hand, medium-term financial planning for a considerable part only represents a continuation of the estimates of short-term budget planning. The evaluation of medium-term financial planning is indifferent with respect to the binding character of planning: There is no legal right that the fund allocations laid down in the medium-term financial plan will in fact be available in the relevant budget period. Fluctuations in the economic situation or unforeseen events therefore very often lead to adaptations of medium-term planning with in some cases considerable consequences (e.g. for the new acquisition of major items of military equipment for the Bundeswehr).

1.3 Conclusion

The federation, the federal states and the municipalities are obliged to establish a budget plan. This short-term budget plan fulfils social planning and control functions. Their obligation to prepare a budget plan forces the government and the administration to rationally plan revenues and expenditures for the welfare of the population. The fact that the budget plan is passed as a law ensures ex-ante control by the legislature and gives the public the possibility to obtain information about financial policy. Budget law provides an ex-post basis for audit institutions and the legislature to review whether authorised expenditures have been complied with. Budget planning requirements are specified by budget principles. These principles chiefly serve as instruments of democratic control. Medium-term financial planning extends the time perspective of budget planning by three years. This makes it possible to improve planning with respect to the budget's long-term effects and implications. This planning, however, should urgently be orientated towards overall economic aims in order to permanently ensure an efficient use of funds.

2. *The defence budget – Departmental Budget 14*

Our detailed preliminary considerations, which are of key importance for understanding the background of, among other things, Departmental Budget 14, are based on Art. 87a (1) of the *Grundgesetz*: 'The Federation shall establish Armed Forces for purposes of defence. Their numerical strength and general organisational structure must be shown in the budget.' This is an expression of the primacy of politics: When, in passing the federal budget of a certain calendar year, the German *Bundestag* decides to provide more or less funds to the Bundeswehr, this directly affects the financial viability of the Bundeswehr's defence policy. In order to fulfil the missions and tasks assigned by politics, financial resources are required. These are provided in Departmental Budget 14. If these funds are reduced while the spectrum of missions and tasks remains the same – as is usually the case – the Bundeswehr is called upon to increase its efficiency. As a matter of principle, it is the responsibility of the defence experts within the purview of the Federal Ministry of Defence to decide on the employment of financial resources for mission accomplishment.[8]

Let us first take a glance at Departmental Budget 14 for budget year 2012. Overall, the Minister of Defence has 31.87 bn euros at his disposal, which are roughly split into four parts: operating expenditure (2012: 57.3 per cent of the overall budget, i.e. 18.26 bn euros), defence investment expenditure (2012: 23.1 per cent, i.e. 7.36 bn euros), pensions and benefits expenditure for retired servicemen and women, as well as retired civilian personnel (2012: 14.7 per cent, i.e. 4.69 bn euros), and expenditure for operator solutions (2012: 4.9 per cent, i.e. 1.56 bn euros). The bulk of operating expenditure is made up of personnel costs, amounting to almost a third of the total expenditure of Depart-

8 This reflects the ministerial principle (departmental principle) of German budgetary policy. However, in reality, this principle is not always complied with; note e.g. the debates about closing garrisons in structurally-challenged areas, which are often based on regional political considerations rather than on defence policy as a whole.

mental Budget 14. This de facto also includes pensions and benefits that since budget year 2006 have been estimated as decentralised budgets in the respective departmental budgets; these of course are not available for active defence measures and should be subtracted from the defence budget for long-term comparisons. In addition to personnel costs, operating expenditure includes expenses for maintenance (2012: 8.1 per cent, i.e. 2.59 bn euros) and other operating expenses (2012: 17 per cent, i.e. 5.41 bn euros). Defence investment expenditure (which, from an economic point of view, does not represent investment) falls into four categories: research, development and testing (2012: 2.9 per cent, i.e. 0.92 bn euros), military procurement (2012: 17.2 per cent, i.e. 5.48 bn euros), military installations (2012: 2.6 per cent, i.e. 0.83 euros) and other investment (2012: 0.5 per cent, i.e. 0.14 bn euros). We will come back to these items when taking a closer look at how the defence budget's structure has developed since the establishment of the Bundeswehr in 1955/56.

Before conducting a time-related analysis of the defence budget in budget year 2012, a long-term analysis will be made to examine the importance of the defence budget in the respective budget years, as depicted in figure 1.

Figure 1: Development of the defence budget over time

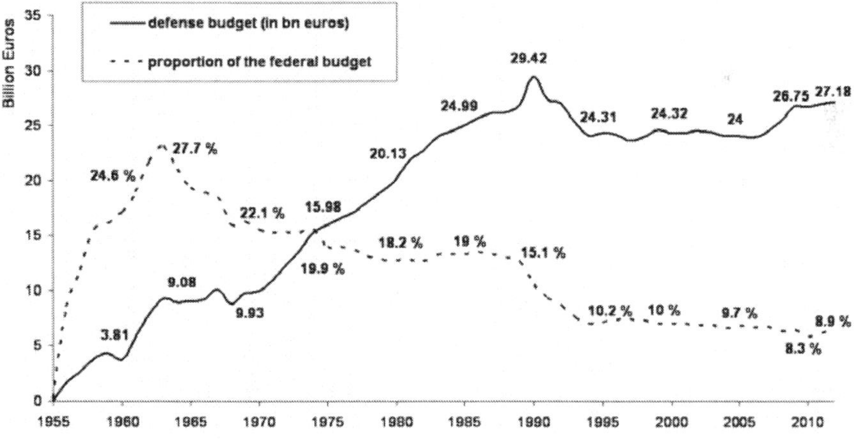

Source: Federal budgets, several years, our own computations

When looking at the relative proportion of defence expenditure compared to overall federal expenditure (dashed line in figure 1), it becomes obvious that the defence budget has a clear tendency to decrease. In absolute figures, the funds allocated since the early 1990s have remained roughly stable (solid line in figure 1); however, the figures represented are non-inflation-adjusted absolute numbers: The real volume of Departmental Budget 14 has steadily decreased since that time (or, more precisely: what can be bought with Departmental Budget 14 in the year 2012 e.g. is considerably less than what could be procured in 1991).

A conclusion can be drawn from the political programme function of budget plans: The political significance of Departmental Budget 14 has been decreasing continuously in relation to the federation's overall expenditure for the past 20 years. The political weight attributed to other government expenditures (and thus also other government tasks, mainly expenditures for the social sector) is much greater than that of the defence budget (see also Figure 2).[9]

Figure 1 depicts the development of defence expenditure without expenditures for pensions, which have been included in Departmental Budget 14 since 2006. If these were integrated into the above graph of expenditure, expenses that could be spent as part of Departmental Budget 14 would increase by the amount of 4.0 bn euros (2006) and up to 4.69 bn euros (2012). This in turn would suggest to the reader that Departmental Budget 14 increased by much more than 10 per cent in 2006. This argument has occasionally also been used in the political environment, especially when talking about cost savings. The integration of pensions and benefits expenditure was meant to better implement the principles of budget transparency and budget accuracy: Departmental Budget 33, which existed until 2006 and into which all expenditure for pensions and benefits of the federation was entered, was dissolved. Now (from 2006) all expenditures for pensions and benefits of all ministries are entered into the respective departmental budgets. Critics, however, regard this measure as rather the exact opposite of more budget transparency: All prognoses expect pension expenditure to rise, mainly due to demographic developments (more pensioners, who in addition claim pensions for a longer period of time as a result of increased average life expectancy) – in Departmental Budget 14 by more than 17 per cent since 2006. An explicit Departmental Budget 33 would have made this rise clearly visible at first glance,

9 It is often claimed that, since reunification, the Federal Republic of Germany has been able to reap a 'peace dividend' because its security environment has improved considerably. However, our argumentation should take into account that this assumption need not hold true today, at least since the terrorist attack on the World Trade Center in 2001 – this, however, is not reflected in Departmental Budget 14 in the form of a relative increase of its proportion in relation to the federation's overall expenditures. It may be politically opportune to sell the relative cuts in Departmental Plan 14 under the heading of 'peace dividend' in order to make it easier to communicate and to justify the need to shift funds away from Departmental Plan 14.

too. We think that, with the current procedure, this can be hidden even better in order to avoid having to deal with this block of expenditure, which is expected to rise over the next 25 years and may fuel financial controversy in all budget negotiations. Furthermore, the observant reader will certainly ask himself how budget accuracy and transparency are actually and specifically dealt with in other areas of the departmental budget. There is a multitude of examples that the expenditures included in Departmental Budget 14 do not or do not only serve the aims of defence policy, and that the Bundeswehr is also meant to promote overall economic aims. This is not critical per se, but it may become a risk for the strategic orientation of the Bundeswehr if the two interrelated objectives were to conflict and one aim could only be achieved at the expense of the other. This might be the case regarding issues of regional policy and/or the Bundeswehr's policy concerning garrisons (requirements of defence policy versus support of structurally-weak areas), industrial policy (same conflict, e.g. support of major European companies versus procurement of systems already well established on the market) etc. In all these cases and in others, a modification of existing budget principles would be conceivable in the Federal Republic of Germany, also based on the argument of budget accuracy.

Accordingly, to maintain real buying power in Departmental Budget 14, both inflationary compensation and slightly higher allocations would be required due to the predicted permanent rise in expenditure for pensions and benefits. Furthermore, the new foreign policy dimension of defence policy of this millennium, which focuses on 'armed forces geared towards operations abroad', results in additional expenditure. From the Bundeswehr's point of view, this should be carefully considered in establishing and discussing future budgets in order to be able to successfully accomplish all politically-assigned missions, also on a permanent basis (see principle of connexity).

Is the reduction of its relative proportion a special characteristic of Departmental Budget 14? To answer this question, let us have a look at the development of the five most important categories of federal expenditure (see Figure 2).

Figure 2: Comparison of important expenditure categories in the federal budget

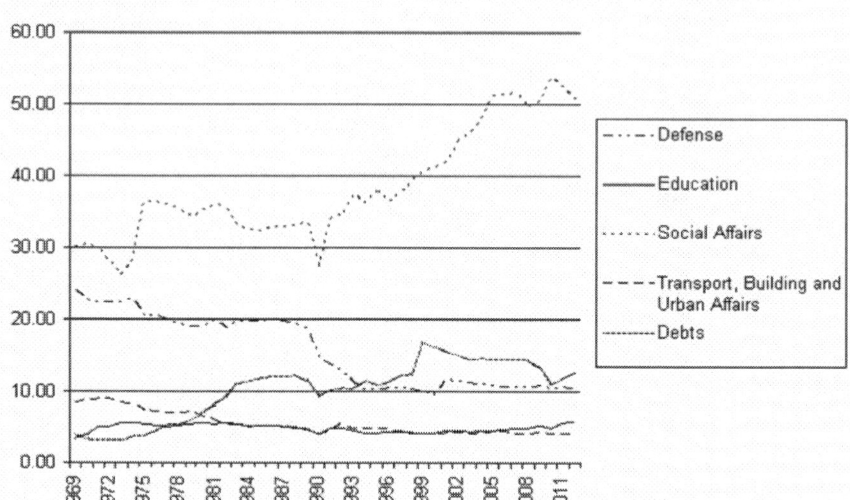

Source: Federal budgets, several years, our own computations. To enable comparison, figure 2 takes into account all funds allocated to the respective departmental budgets (including expenditure for pensions and benefits).

Figure 2 is a representation of the relative percentage of overall federal expenditure in the budget years since 1969 that depicts the political programme function of the respective federal budgets over a relatively long period of time. One finds that besides Departmental Budget 14 only Departmental Budget 12 (Transport, Building and Urban Affairs) has been reduced in a similar way over time. As shown in figure 2, the federal budget is dominated by expenditures for social affairs (represented by the dotted line); a little over 50 per cent of the federation's overall expenses fall into this category. Their major part is made up by the Federal grant towards the statutory pension insurance scheme, which increased considerably especially in the 1990s.[10] The solid line for the proportion of education spending by the federation remains relatively constant at around 5 per cent – in

10 This is not least due to the tax increases that made this possible at the time: Both the coalition of Christian Democrats and Liberals (who increased the standard VAT rate from 15 to 16 percent as from 1 April 1998) and the subsequent coalition of Social Democrats and the Green Party (who introduced the 'eco-tax' as from 1 April 1999) considered these measures to be a way – although alien to the system – of stabilizing the statutory, pay-as-you-go pension insurance system. On the aspect of system adequacy, see Bayer (2008).

this context, however, it must be remarked that the major part of these expenditures is accrued at federal state level. Only in exceptional cases does the federation participate in these tasks, e.g. in the case of mixed financing when building new universities or improving existing structures. The development of the dashed/dotted curve depicting the proportion of Departmental Budget 14 need not be explained in any more detail. Expenditures of Departmental Budget 12 (Transport, Building and Urban Affairs), which are represented by a dashed line, were reduced by about 50 per cent, i.e. a little less than the amounts allocated to the defence budget – reasons for this are mainly the relative reduction in repair work on degradation caused by wear and tear (failure to reinvest) in the federation's structural and civil engineering sector (see the debates about potholes now occurring on the formerly exemplary German interstate highways after the past few winters).

A very interesting development is depicted by the hatched curve, which represents the proportionate amount of interest paid by the federation. In the meantime, the federation's debt has increased from 254 bn euros (1989) to around 1,100 bn euros (2012) – about 350 bn euros of which have accrued in the years since 2001 alone. Nevertheless, the proportion of the federation's overall expenditure made up by interest payments has decreased since 2001. In other words, the average decrease in interest rates per period carried more weight than additional net borrowings by the federation, which caused relative spending on interest per period to decline.[11]

Finally, we would like to return to the issue of the structure of Departmental Budget 14. In addition to the current defence budget 2012, figure 3 below illustrates the structural development of the defence budget since the establishment of the Bundeswehr in 1955, split into the categories 'operating expenditure', 'defence investment expenditure' and 'operator solutions'. For reasons of comparison, it was drawn without considering pensions and benefits expenditure – this would overemphasize personnel costs in the recent past. The figure shows the respective expenditure categories in each budget year, as a percentage of overall defence expenditure. These percentage shares are subsequently joined to form one line for each category.

11 However, the Federal Minister of Finance has very little influence on this – the currently historic low of refinancing costs in the Federal Republic of Germany is mainly caused by the euro zone crisis, which ought to result in a further reduction of relative interest spending in the medium term. In the medium term, though, there is a risk of increasing interest rates and thus of increased relative interest spending, which may reduce the federation's active financial leeway in the future. If, then, the assumption proves right that both Departmental Budget 14 and Departmental Budget 12 will continue to lose political significance, the consequences for future defence budgets are not difficult to imagine.

Figure 3: The structure of the defence budget over time
(proportion of the annual defence budget accounted for by various expenditure categories)

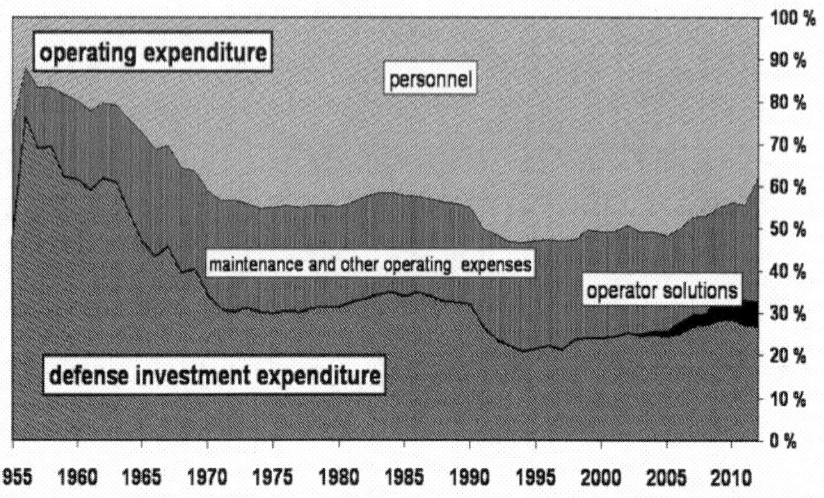

Source: Federal budgets, several years, our own computations.

In this context, it is interesting to observe that, from 1955 to 2012, a clear shift took place away from defence investment expenditure to personnel costs. Only in budget year 2012 did a relatively pronounced decrease occur in the latter, i.e. by about 5 percentage points. Although objectives have always remained the same in many Bundeswehr Plans since 2005, the target value of 30 per cent for defence investment expenditure has not been achieved so far, despite additional efforts to promote this through the introduction of operator solutions since 2003.

A few supplementary remarks must be made with respect to personnel costs: In comparison to 1989, military personnel strength had been reduced by almost half by the year 2012; for civilian posts, a decline by about 40 per cent can be identified. Nevertheless, personnel costs have risen by roughly 10 per cent compared to 1989 in both categories, which cannot be explained exclusively by the inflation that has occurred since then. Rather, a shift in the payment structure can be observed when looking at the personnel lists enclosed with every budget plan: Taking military personnel as an example, the percentage of personnel reaching the respective higher and final ranks within their rank categories has increased. This may be necessary both in order to render the service in the armed forces more attractive and to meet international requirements. From a budgetary point of view, though, it explains the rise in personnel costs (another reason is the fact that relatively low-cost personnel categories such as conscripts and extended service volunteers have been abolished and the respective personnel have left or are leaving the military in large numbers). Observant readers who would like to verify my considerations are referred to the personnel lists of Departmental Budget 14, which, in the interest of public information, are accessible to all those interested.

Between 1955 and 2010, maintenance and other operating expenses always amounted to roughly between 21 and 24 per cent of the funds of Departmental Budget 14. This, however, has clearly changed from budget year 2012 onwards. In the year 2012, this percentage share makes up almost 30 per cent of the entire expenditure of Departmental Budget 14 – this can be seen in the widening of the vertically hatched area at the right edge of figure 3. The reason for this is rent payments by the Bundeswehr to the Institute for Federal Real Estate (*Bundesanstalt für Immobilienaufgaben*; *BImA*) for the installations it uses. They are accounted for under the item 'other operating expenses'. Next year, i.e. 2013, is the deadline when the operation of all facilities belonging to Military District Administrative Office, West, will be transferred to the Institute for Federal Real Estate. Consequently, a further rise of this expenditure item is to be expected. Although the Federal Minister of Finance has promised to compensate for these Bundeswehr expenditures, there is an obvious resulting effect: Personnel costs dropped by about 5 percentage points in budget year 2012. This was not realised through the release of personnel (which is hardly possible in the case of military personnel and civil servants) but by transferring personnel costs for civilian personnel, which are still above the target value of the 'old' Personnel Structure Model 2010, to Departmental Budget 60 (Financial Administration and Common Services; budget item 461 72-981, augmentation of personnel expenditures of Budgetary Group 4 for civilian surplus personnel within the area of responsibility of the Federal Ministry of Defence.). The funds appropriated for this amount to 1 bn euros. It remains up to the reader to judge to what extent the budget principles of budget accuracy and budget transparency are still implemented in this case. However, from a functional and pragmatic perspective, the following key question arises: What will happen if personnel costs for civilian personnel cannot be reduced significantly in the medium term? As a logical consequence, another reorientation ('version 2.0') would have to be considered, which would include another intensive review of both personnel and materiel, with the possible outcome of a need for further reductions. This takes us back to the introductory remark about the true primacy of politics in Bundeswehr mission accomplishment, which is based on Art. 87a of the *Grundgesetz*. How far this spiral effect can go remains to be seen, but this issue urgently requires a detailed analysis within the area of responsibility of the Federal Ministry of Defence and, if required, this matter should be communicated politically and brought to the public's attention.

For the future financial means of the Bundeswehr, the federation's Financial Plan 2011 projects the following development: In the draft federal budget 2012, expenditures amounting to around 31.7 bn euros are estimated for the departmental budget of the Federal Ministry of Defence; in the Financial Plan up to 2015, expenditure estimates are as follows: about 31.4 bn euros for the year 2013, about 30.9 bn euros for the year 2014 and for the year 2015, about 30.4 bn euros. As a result, the level of expenditures determined by financial policy decreases – as planned – by approximately 1.3 bn euros for the following three years, accompanied by a rise in expenditures for pensions and benefits. Thus, Departmental Budget 14 is de facto reduced more than indicated in the Financial Plan. The percentage of the federation's overall expenses made up by Departmental Budget 14 will also drop because shrinking defence spending will occur in an environment where the federation will raise its expenditure by around 3 per cent between 2012 and 2015.

Nevertheless, these figures represent the basis for the Bundeswehr Plan that is to be established by the Federal Ministry of Defence. However, it must be pointed out once again that the federation's medium-term Financial Plan does not give the Bundeswehr a legal entitlement to actually be allocated the financial means outlined in the years specified. Especially in the current climate of the euro zone crisis, with severe public debt in several European countries, it is impossible to foresee to what extent guarantees can be given or further 'bailouts' may become necessary, which in turn will have real repercussions on the design of individual budget plans.

3. Conclusion and outlook

Analyses of the defence budget clearly show that, in the future, the primacy of politics as laid down in Art. 87a of the *Grundgesetz* will be felt even more intensely by the Bundeswehr. While its real financial resources are dwindling, the Bundeswehr is confronted with a complex and comprehensive spectrum of missions and tasks and must already bear a heavy burden in connection with operations. Accomplishing these tasks sustainably will remain a permanent challenge. From an economic point of view, the traditional answer to such problems is to increase both efficiency and effectiveness. In my opinion, a systematic and comprehensive assessment of these factors within the Bundeswehr's reform and/or reorientation process is still lacking. The focus should be on asking, and above all, finding, answers to the key question of what role the Bundeswehr should in fact assume as part of a comprehensive approach, and how this may make it possible to use public funds more efficiently and effectively. If an effective interdepartmental comprehensive approach is to be achieved, we should also reflect on the question of whether the German budget system, which has been described and analysed here through various examples, makes such an approach possible at all, de jure and de facto. In my view, comprehensive changes in the budget system are required in order to effectively put into practice functioning interdepartmental cooperation.

I think that (in a budget system that may already have been modified) one possible approach to increase the funds allocated to Departmental Budget 14 would be the attempt to introduce another factor into the discussion about Departmental Budget 14, which exclusively focuses on expenditure: the return yielded. For this purpose, the services the Bundeswehr generates – mainly peace, liberty and security for the population of the Federal Republic of Germany – would have to be assessed in monetary form. A few starting points already exist in the assessment of the environment as a public good (especially in the evaluation of climate change). An analogous application to the output side of the Bundeswehr would be conceivable in order to enrich the debate about the efficient use of scare public resources by adding the aspect of economic efficiency.

Bibliography

Bayer, Stefan/Zimmermann, Klaus W. (Eds.) (2008): Die Ordnung von Reformen und die Reform von Ordnungen: Facetten politischer Ökonomie. Marburg: Metropolis.

Bayer, Stefan (2008): Zur Renaissance des Konzepts der Eigenverantwortung im Sozialversicherungssystem der Bundesrepublik Deutschland. In: Bayer/Zimmermann (Eds.) (2008): 301-345.

Bayer, Stefan (2009a): Nutzen und Kosten von Auslandseinsätzen – eine ökonomische Perspektive. In: Jaberg et al. (Ed.) (2009): 235-255.

Bayer, Stefan (2009b): Die Mittelausstattung der Bundeswehr – Der Einzelplan 14 im Spannungsfeld zwischen Auftragslage und (finanzieller) Realität. In: Gießmann/Wagner (Eds.) (2008): 224-234.

Bundesministerium der Finanzen (BMF; Federal Ministry of Finance): Bundeshaushalt und Finanzplan des Bundes, different years (http://www.bundesfinanzministerium.de, last accessed 08.06.2012).

Bundesministerium der Finanzen (BMF) (2011a): Finanzbericht 2012. Die volkswirtschaftlichen Grundlagen und die wichtigsten finanzwirtschaftlichen Probleme des Bundeshaushaltsplanes für das Haushaltsjahr 2012. Berlin: Bundesanzeiger (published annually).

Bundesministerium der Finanzen (BMF) (2011b): Eckwertebeschluss zum Regierungsentwurf des Bundeshaushalts 2012 und zum Finanzplan 2011 bis 2015, Berlin (http://www.bundesfinanzministerium.de, last accessed 08.06.2012).

Bundesministerium der Finanzen (BMF) (2011c): Die Aufstellung des Bundeshaushalts, last accessed 08.06.2012.

Bundesministerium der Verteidigung (BMVg; Federal Ministry of Defence) (2011a): Verteidigungspolitische Richtlinien. Nationale Interessen wahren – Internationale Verantwortung übernehmen – Sicherheit gemeinsam gestalten. Berlin.

Bundesministerium der Verteidigung (BMVg) (2011b): Der Verteidigungshaushalt 2012, Source: Bundesministerium der Verteidigung, www.bmvg.de last accessed 08.06.2012.

Cansier, Dieter and Bayer, Stefan (2003): Einführung in die Finanzwissenschaft. Grundfunktionen des Fiskus. Munich and Vienna: Oldenbourg.

Gießmann, Hans J./Wagner, Armin (Eds.) (2008): Armee im Einsatz. Grundlagen, Strategien und Ergebnisse einer Beteiligung der Bundeswehr. Baden-Baden: Nomos.

Jaberg, Sabine/Biehl, Heiko/Mohrmann, Günter/Tomforde, Maren (Eds.) (2009): Auslandseinsätze der Bundeswehr. Sozialwissenschaftliche Analysen, Diagnosen und Perspektiven. Berlin: Duncker & Humblot.

Neumark, Fritz in cooperation with Andel, Norbert and Haller, Heinz (Eds.) (1977): Handbuch der Finanzwissenschaft, 3. completely revised edition, volume I. Tübingen: J. C. B. Mohr (Paul Siebeck).

Senf, Paul (1977): 2. Kurzfristige Haushaltsplanung. In: Neumark (Ed.) (1977): 371-425.

Wille, Eberhard (1977): 3. Mittel- und langfristige Finanzplanung. In: Neumark (Ed.) (1977): 427-474.

The armament acquisition process – nature, development, challenges

Helmuth Heumann

> Who, after all, would include in the *real 'conduct of war'* the whole litany of subsistence and administration, which, although invariably linked to the employment of troops, is so distinctly different! – Clausewitz 1832 (2010): 84, original italics)

The big bang – Article 87b of the Grundgesetz

In the opening quotation, Carl von Clausewitz states that the development of standing armies over the centuries increasingly brought with it the need for specialists to take on defined tasks in the administrative and material-technical fields. A glance at the German encyclopaedia *Meyers Großes Konversationslexikon* of 1909 reveals that these specialists were generally referred to as military civil servants. They were members of the armed forces and held a military rank, but were legally civil servants. In the Wehrmacht, they were also members of a service. The *Ingenieurkorps* (engineer corps) of the Luftwaffe, for example, had names of its own such as the *Fliegeringenieur (Leutnant)* (flight engineer – second lieutenant).

Rainer Blasius referred to the military historian Hartmut Schustereit (2000) who pointed out a severe weak spot of the so-called *Intendantur-System* (only partially comparable with the commissariat systems in other countries) for the administration of the *Wehrmacht* when he wrote that, as a result of a dual command relationship, the civil servant in the Wehrmacht also had a military superior besides his administrative superior – however, without being integrated fully into the military hierarchy because he had no authority to issue orders to soldiers. He could normally not be issued orders himself with respect to performance of his administrative tasks. Certain military superiors found a way of circumventing this by moving a matter from the administrative side to the military side and then declaring it a command issue. Subsequently, the civil servant of the *Wehrmacht* had to obey because of his dual, sometimes mixed command relationship (Blasius, 2006:10). It is just as difficult to determine whether this construction also had a negative effect on the *Ingenieurkorps* of the *Wehrmacht* and its achievements on the basis of the literature available as it is to say whether former members of the *Ingenieurskorps* were involved in developing ideas on how to reorganise the (German) Federal Defence Administration and hence the armament organisation. The fact is that military engineering led to a wide range of ground-breaking inventions and developments in research, industry, government agencies and the Wehrmacht, although they were often first used in operations by the victorious powers.

It was because of these negative experiences – which were probably the result of the *Intendantur* solution for the administrative sector – that MPs from several parliamentary groups of the *Bundestag* insisted on a re-organisation when the Bundeswehr was established in 1955.

During its session on 10 June 1955, the *Bundesrat* unanimously expressed the expectation that soldiers would only be employed in military units, and that the administration would be entrusted to civil agencies (Blasius, 2006:10). In the Bundestag, Theodor Blank, the new minister of defence, made the following announcement on 27 June 1955:

> Whereas, in the interest of the striking power of the armed forces, purely military tasks will be carried out according to the order principle, administrative tasks shall be handled by specially-trained civilian personnel according to general administrative principles. Therefore, it will be necessary to establish for the armed forces a specific Federal Government defence administration designed as a strictly civilian administration. Its personnel will have civilian status. There shall be no more hybrid forms of the legal status, as in the case of the civil servants of the former Wehrmacht.

Since it was deemed necessary to have a law for this, the Bundesrat approved an amendment to Germany's constitution, the Grundgesetz, or Basic Law, which was published as Article 87b in the Federal Law Gazette on 19 March 1956. It reads:

> (1) The Federal Defence Administration shall be conducted as a federal administrative authority with its own administrative substructure. It shall have jurisdiction for personnel matters and direct responsibility for satisfaction of the procurement needs of the Armed Forces (…).

This created a novelty in German military history that is also something special as compared to the military administrations of the allies and, in this sense, can thus be called the 'Big Bang'. However, one should not fail to note that there were people in the research sectors of other countries who thought that the solution found did not seem desirable with respect to the effects it could have on Germany's armament policy (Geyer, 1984).

Many years later, Federal Minister of Defence Peter Struck (2002-2006) called the Federal Defence Administration the 'twin sister of the armed forces' (Blasius, 2006:10). The form of the strict division between the military armed forces and the civilian administration was significantly influenced by Ernst Wirmer. He was in charge of administration and budgeting at the Blank Office and later *Abteilungsleiter* (director) of administration at the Federal Ministry of Defence (FMOD). Generally considered the father of the so-called two-pillar concept, he demanded that the defence administration serve the armed forces 'without being a servant in the sense of being subjugated' (Blasius, 2006:10).

The armament acquisition organisation was also part of the new civilian defence administration. Its function was to work on a centralised basis to meet the requirements of all the services, to establish a structure of its own in accordance with general administrative rules and to apply the procedures with 'civic courage of conviction' (Ernst Wirmer quoted in Blasius, 2006:10).

The main challenge for the armament acquisition organisation in carrying out its tasks was to define a large number of interfaces with the so-called client, i.e., the armed forces, and to establish the procedural and organisational structures needed to achieve an optimum armament acquisition process.

As this chapter will reveal, very different attempts have been made in the history of the Bundeswehr to address this issue. From today's point of view, the general criticism is that, despite many attempts, all efforts to establish fundamental legislation that clearly delineates the competences of the armed forces and the defence administration have failed (Blasius 2006).

This delineation of competences between the armed forces and the civilian defence administration, which is considered insufficient by some players, led and continues to lead to conflicts between 'grazing generals' and 'attempts to achieve dominance for prestige purposes' within the Federal Defence Administration in the case of each of the many reforms of the Bundeswehr (Ernst Wirmer quoted in Blasius, 2006:10).

This problem, which is difficult for the military to grasp, has been reflected for years in an ironic saying according to which the enemy is replaced by the defence administration in peacetime.

The definition of the armament acquisition process

Process is the name given to intended action by interactive means and activities which turn inputs into results. According to Brigadier General Raimund Max Rothenberger, armament can thus be defined as follows (quoted in Anspach/ Walitschek, 1986: 26, highlighted in the original):

> In the field of security policy, the term *'armament'* has two meanings: (1) the term stands for the '*weaponry'* or equipment of the armed forces, (2) armament in a functional sense is used to denote 'all the coordinated measures which concern the *provision* and the *preparation for use* of the material equipment of the armed forces, including the means, facilities and procedures serving this purpose'.

Rothenberger further explains that the armament acquisition process combines personnel and materiel elements, i.e., it incorporates all the measures associated with project planning and the development and procurement of defence materiel. Accordingly, armament is a 'permanent process' during which the Army, Air Force and Navy act as military users – the 'clients' in lingo. Thus, the armament acquisition organisation of the defence administration acts as the provider (contracting authority), and the industry as the fulfiller (contractor). The client, the provider and the fulfiller have to cooperate closely.

According to Rothenberger, this process was particularly characterised by the initiative of the client, the creative efforts of the provider and the coordination and planning measures of the overall management effort.

Moreover, he said that armament acquisition in the Federal Republic of Germany had to comply with a number of security policy factors. Rothenberger cites the geostrategic situation, the economic conditions of the country, the status and development of scientific research and the state of technological progress. Added to that are the threat posed by a potential adversary, Alliance commitments as well as the state of materiel and manning in Germany's own armed forces.

So armament acquisition was 'a comprehensive command task which requires – in close association with other command tasks – a firm command and control organisation for the purposes of planning, steering and monitoring' (Anspach/ Walitschek, 1986: 26).

In the cooperative sense of Articles 87a and b of the *Grundgesetz*, Rothenberger believed that the armament acquisition domain of the Bundeswehr comprised not only the armament directorate at the FMOD and the subordinate Federal Office of Defence Technology and Procurement, but also the service staffs at the FMOD, as well as the subordinate agencies of the services. Although some decades have elapsed since then, the definition of the armament acquisition process (called armament in a functional sense by Rothenberger) is still largely accurate.

Nowadays the armament acquisition process includes requirements, research and development, engineering testing, operational testing, evaluation, review, acquisition approval, procurement, deployment, logistics. In this context force levels, training requirements, RAM (reliability, availability, maintainability) and life cycle costs must all be taken into consideration.

Evolution of the armament acquisition process in the Bundeswehr

The improvisation and consolidation phase

During the first ten years of its existence, the new armament acquisition organisation only had one goal – to satisfy the rapidly growing requirements of the armed forces as fast as possible (Kollmer, 2005). The armament acquisition process resembled a 'knee-jerk procedure' (Roeske, 1995). The Directorate V/ Koblenz Branch of the Blank Office (the predecessor of the FMOD) was the 'germ' of what would later become a technical agency responsible for procurement both for the Bundeswehr and for the Allied forces stationed in Germany (Wirtgen, 2005).

On 7 June 1955, the establishment of the FMOD was decreed and, on 31 May 1957, the later Federal Office of Defence Technology and Procurement (*Bundesamt für Wehrtechnik und Beschaffung – BWB*), initially a higher authority with technical and economic functions, was created. The *BWB* was responsible for the centralised procurement of defence materiel, for quality assurance and control with respect to supplies and services, for preparing manufacturing, particularly for drafting technical specifications, as well as for the establishment of test centres and naval arsenals for ship maintenance.

In this same period, the political decision was made to employ the Anglo-American model, i.e. not to found companies under national direction, as, for example, had been done in France. Later on, the Prime Contractor (PC) principle was established, as a way of giving armament projects a system-related orientation.

Since the German defence industry was still being built up, the requirements in the first few years were mostly satisfied by purchasing the defence materiel from Allied nations. German corporations were initially contracted to do maintenance work and provide support. Licensed production helped in acquiring the know-how that was needed for project development and cooperation. Those involved in armament work at the time reminisce about how administrative paths and procurement periods would never again be so short, with only minor administrative obstacles. The service offices took great advantage of this leeway.

Nevertheless, the deficiencies inherent in the system must not be ignored. There was no planning and coordination within the armament acquisition process other than that conducted by the services. It was simply a case of procuring materiel that was available at a given moment. The result was a jumble of weapon systems and items of equipment. At first, the logistic problems were less important because it was assumed that the materiel would only be in use for a short time. The work involved was made easier by the fact that the defence budget was a considerable share of the federal budget, reaching levels that would never again be attained.

In 1965, the FMOD for the first time issued an armament acquisition process structure which regulated the workflows and responsibilities for planning, implementation (drafting of military requirements and development of directives), materiel deployment and the establishment of logistic supportability.

The respective order gave precedence to clear delineation of responsibilities over the ‘dialogue principle’ that would be cultivated later on. Under the new armament acquisition process structure, the *BWB* was responsible, for instance, for all of the work that had to be done from the moment a development directive or a military requirement was received until the items of equipment were delivered.

On the road to system management – EBMat

On 5 June 1970, a commission was established on the orders of Federal Minister of Defence Helmut Schmidt to develop proposals for new procedures and structures for the armament acquisition organisation.

In its report (BMVg, 1970), the commission listed a number of deficiencies:

- the Ministry was bogged down by micromanagement; as a result, the implementation level did not hold sufficient responsibility and often evaded complying with directives;
- there were deficiencies in planning in all areas;
- the procedures for weapon systems and projects were too bureaucratic and rigidly bound to the responsibilities of the organisational structure;
- there was a lack of effective management, which led to underestimation of the decisive role played by the client;
- within the Ministry, a non-helpful distinction was made between technological and economic aspects;
- the management structures at the FMOD and the *BWB* were strictly monocratic and thus inadequate.

Figure 1: EBMat

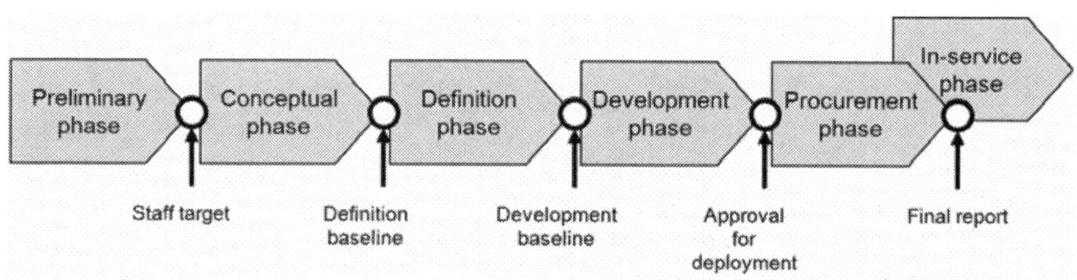

Source: Author's diagram

Due to each armament project being embedded in the overall armed forces system (personnel, logistics), the commission recommended that the system manager should have a master plan drawn up and implemented, starting at the beginning of the concept phase. It also recommended that the system manager should be under the command of the chief of staff of the service involved. After a preliminary phase, each armament project should be implemented in a number of phases, which were later laid down in the EBMat (*Durchführungsbestimmungen zu den Rahmenbestimmungen für die Entwicklung und Beschaffung von Wehrmaterial* – Implementation Regulations concerning the Framework Regulations for the Development and Procurement of Defence Materiel) (BMVg 1973).

This process was derived from industry practice. After each phase, the targets and results had to be recorded in phase documents and presented to management for approval. The matrix organisation and dialogue principle were among the essential innovations. In line with similar industry procedures, personnel resources were pooled in specific specialized organisational units that could be accessed by the management-oriented organisational units within each project's management.

The dialogue principle was meant to ensure that all parties involved in the process had a say during all phases of the defence materiel development cycle. The advantage of this was that all relevant aspects were permanently taken into account during the armament acquisition process. It had the disadvantage, however, of requiring a great deal of coordination and of long and drawn-out procedures for decision-making when differences of opinion arose in the management teams.

The advantages of better utilisation of specialized personnel, their continued development due to the acquisition of knowledge from several projects and standardized solutions were counteracted by a large amount of coordination and the additional need to prioritize. The recommendations of the commission led to the '*Rahmenerlass zur Neuordnung des Rüstungsbereichs*' (Basic Directive on the Reorganisation of the Armament Organisation) (BMVg, 1971) and finally to the implementation regulations of 1973 referred to earlier. These implementation regulations quickly became the 'Bible' of project management. They defined almost every project stage, but they also allowed leeway for checking 'which steps must be omitted completely, interchanged or repeated in order to attain optimum results' (BMVg, 1973).

In the preliminary phase, the equipment gaps were identified by joint study groups headed by the planning divisions of the service staffs. The representative of the Directorate General of Armament was a permanent member, and it was agreed with the functional divisions that he would be responsible for tabling possible technical solutions, estimating the costs involved and issuing statements on their financial feasibility.

The output of each study group's work was a *staff target*, which, following approval by the FMOD Executive Group, became the basis for subsequent management tasks. Depending on the complexity involved, a distinction was made between systems and projects. Equipment – especially the procurement of COTS equipment items – was the responsibility of the service offices and of the *BWB*.

The system management started its work at the beginning of the conceptual phase. It consisted of a military system manager from one of the armament divisions of the services, a military system officer from the respective service office, a civilian project director from the Directorate General of Armament at the FMOD as well as a civilian project manager from *BWB*. To solve problems, the system manager and the project director drew on the know-how of the specialized divisions of the FMOD and the service offices in their working group.

In the conceptual phase, the concept for achieving the staff target was prepared with the involvement of possible prime contractors from industry and used to formulate the *Definition Baseline* phase document.

Upon approval of the *Definition Baseline*, the project manager from *BWB* and the system officer from the service office took charge of implementing the definition phase, which served the aim of specifying the concept in sufficient detail to minimise budget and timeline risks for realisation of the overall project.

The result of this second step was the *Development Baseline,* which was the binding foundation for the development phase. The completion of the development contract by industry was followed by trials, often with integrated service tests. Other steps were the attainment of the qualification for production, the engineering clearance and the determination of the design status, the declaration of its suitability for military use as well as the final processing by the military elements.

The *Approval for Deployment* gave clearance for its procurement and initiated logistic supportability. Upon completion of procurement, a *Final Report* documenting the lessons learned and the deficiencies identified for the benefit of future projects had to be produced.

The endeavour to achieve more economic efficiency – CPM

In search of a possibility to bring unbridled planning in line with the dwindling Bundeswehr budget, a directive was issued in 1987 for reassigning armament tasks via a step-by-step approach. The phases were designed to allow a check to be conducted during each one to establish whether the cost-benefit ratio was acceptable for providing operational defence materiel that met the absolute minimum requirements. The result was the Procedural Regulation on Procurement in the Bundeswehr (Customer Product Management – CPM), which became effective on 14 July 2000 and has been modified several times since.

By applying CPM, the Bundeswehr relies much more on the innovation potential of trade and industry, utilises their expertise and strengthens the autonomy of the enterprises doing the work by inserting functional elements in the statements of work and having managerial accounting done by a government agency.

The very naming of the procedural regulations emphasizes the core targets of CPM: professional management is intended to work on a customer-driven basis to provide economic and operational products and services in due time for bridging gaps in the capabilities of the armed forces as quickly as possible.

Unlike the former guidelines of the Bundeswehr, CPM does not constitute a 'recipe book' describing each work step, but is more aimed at achieving results. For the achievement of goals, it provides a framework within which the responsible players can meet project-related requirements. This flexibility makes it possible to modify work steps, to embark on new paths if necessary, and to react to unforeseen developments. Consequently, it becomes possible to meet even immediate operational requirements (IOR) in a timely and adequate manner by adhering to the rules and principles of CPM.

Procurements will be carried out as projects and will be divided into several phases. The projects will be particularly influenced by the complexity of the required functionalities as well as by budget and time-related prerequisites. The process will be guided by just a small number of markers (mandatory interim results), two milestones (phase completions) and the point at which the product is handed over to the user (commencement of in-service use) (Flume, 2009: 62)

Under CPM, requirements will be established and satisfied in the following phases (BMVg, 2001).

Figure 2: CPM 2001

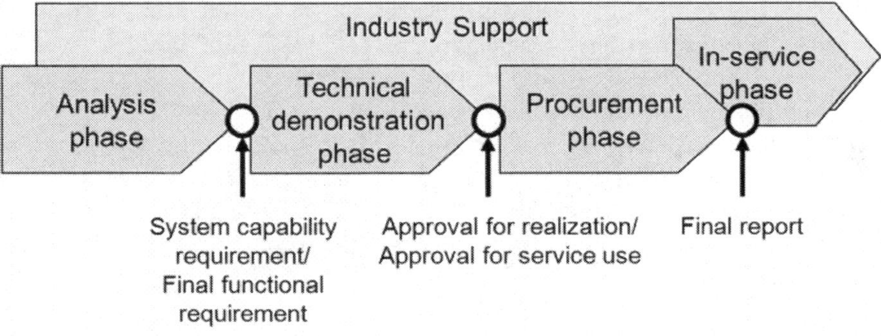

Source: Author's diagram

During the analysis phase, the *Integrated Capability Analysis Working Groups (Integrierte Arbeitsgruppen Fähigkeitsanalyse – IAGFA)* define the capability gaps by preparing the *System Capability Requirement* step decision under the supervision of the *Generalinspekteur* (Inspector General) of the Bundeswehr- the highest-ranking German soldier. These working groups are manned by the services concerned, the armament acquisition organisation and other organisational elements.

The path that is to be followed is laid down in one (or more) *Final Functional Requirement(s).* The *Generainspekteur* is responsible for the establishment of requirements. In the technical demonstration and procurement phases, a project manager from *BWB* is in charge of implementing the final requirement within the set budget and timeframe.

The Approval for Realisation provides the justification needed to authorise the payment of funds required for procurement. The objective of the procurement phase is to procure products that are already available (possibly with adaptations). New products are to be manufactured on the basis of the selection decisions.

To ensure that his product passes the acceptance test, the contractor must prove that it complies with the contract specifications and thereby meets the functional requirements. The government side must conduct an operational suitability test and ensure that the product is operational by the time it is handed over to the user.

If the operational suitability test is passed, the *Approval for Service Use* step decision is taken. This is the basis for the product to be handed over to the user, who appoints an in-service support manager. The Final Report completes the work of the project manager.

Reform of the armament acquisition organisation – the equipment and in-service support process

In support of the reorientation of the Federal Ministry of Defence, Federal Minister Thomas de Maizière decided to close down the Modernisation Directorate at the FMOD and to transfer the former Directorate General of Armament to the new Equipment, Information Technology and In-Service Support Directorate (*Abteilung Ausrüstung, Informationstechnik und Nutzung – AIN*). This directorate has the following responsibilities:

- central tasks
- research and technology, as well as international affairs
- modernisation and government participation issues
- information technology and IT director
- equipment and in-service support

To ensure consistency, the BWB was merged again with the Federal Office of the Bundeswehr for Information Management and Information Technology (*Bundesamt für Informationsmanagement und Informationstechnik der Bundeswehr – IT-AmtBw*) and additionally assigned the in-service support tasks that up to now were carried out by the service offices. The name of the new office is the Federal Office of Bundeswehr Equipment, Information Technology and In-Service Support (*Bundesamt für Ausrüstung, Informationstechnik und Nutzung der Bundeswehr – BAAINBw*).

The author believes that this will correct the wrong decisions taken back in 2002, when the Federal Office of the Bundeswehr for Information Management and Information Technology was separated from the BWB. The Federal Office of the Bundeswehr for Information Management and Information Technology was assigned the task of phasing IT procedures and systems into the Bundeswehr. However, the separate procurement of IT technology and other defence materiel was not, and is not, in line with the times. Military IT is an inseparable, and sometimes even dominating, part of modern weapon systems, and therefore having a separate decision-making was often counterproductive.

Modernisations will only succeed if they are mainly initiated and supported by the operational organisational elements. Staff elements responsible for modernisation – like those planned for the Equipment, Information Technology and In-Service Support Directorate – can act as providers of ideas provider under the roof of the directorate and implement their own cooperation projects.

The *Abteilungsleiter* (Director) of AIN, Mr Detlef Selhausen, is the head of the 'equipment, IT and in-service support' project at the FMOD, and he has announced that responsibilities will be clearly delineated and interfaces reduced. Furthermore, staffing procedures will be dispensed with as far as possible. What is meant by staffing is the involvement of the offices which are affected by a project. They review not only its contents, but also its formal correctness. The result is that either opposing concepts are presented or the project concerned is approved. Staffing procedures can be very time-consuming and dilute results because of the involvement of so many offices.

According to Detlef Selhausen, the staffing procedures will be replaced in future by the introduction of *checks and balances* for the equipment and in-service support process (BMVg, 2011). The organisational procedures, with their responsibilities, objectives, activities and working steps, are described in the document entitled 'Procedural regulations for the establishment and satisfaction of requirements and in-service support in the Bundeswehr' (*Verfahrensbestimmungen für die Bedarfsermittlung, Bedarfsdeckung und Nutzung in der Bundeswehr*) (FMOD framework directive 2012). It states that the aim will be to 'establish requirements on a capability basis, to satisfy requirements in a timely and economically efficient manner by providing operational products and services, and to ensure their efficient use'. It goes on to state:

> The overriding objective is to combine quality, efficiency and flexibility with clear-cut responsibilities, unequivocal decision-making powers and fewer interfaces so as to provide the best possible support, especially to the armed forces. The principles of economic efficiency shape the entire procedure. Working with international partners is the aim.

The responsibilities are laid out as follows:

> As part of his overall accountability for the future development of the Bundeswehr, the *Generalinspekteur* will be responsible for the operational capability and readiness of the armed forces, as well as for their employment. He shall direct the measures necessary for this within the integrated planning process. To take on this responsibility, he will be supported at the ministry by the Directorate for Planning, the Directorate for Forces Policy and the Directorate for Strategy and Operations.
>
> The Director of the Equipment, Information Technology and In-Service Support Directorate (AIN) will be responsible for all aspects of products and services, from the development of materiel solutions and their implementation and in-service management to their disposal. All technical 'system know-how' (including Life Cycle Cost – LCC) that has been acquired throughout the life cycle will be managed by the subordinate Federal Office of Bundeswehr Equipment, Information Technology and In-Service Support. Together with feedback from operations, the lessons learned in this way will be integrated effectively into the development of new products and the further development and adaptation of products already in service.
>
> The President of the Federal Office of Bundeswehr Equipment, Information Technology and In-Service Support (BAAINBw) shall act as the single manager for the operational readiness of all products. His responsibilities will include the implementation of all product-related management activities that ensure the safe and correct use of a product.
>
> In compliance with their 'operating and support responsibility for maintaining the operational capability and readiness' of their services, *Inspekteure* (chiefs of staff) of the services, or the heads of the major civilian organisational elements, will be responsible for the materiel element of operational readiness and the sustainability of the units and agencies in their areas.

Another new aspect is the establishment of integrated project teams, which include representatives from trade and industry. They will attend to items of materiel throughout their life cycles and will operate under the direction of the managers responsible for each of the phases. The life cycle has been divided into the analysis phase, the implementation phase and the in-service phase.

Figure 3: The equipment and in-service support process

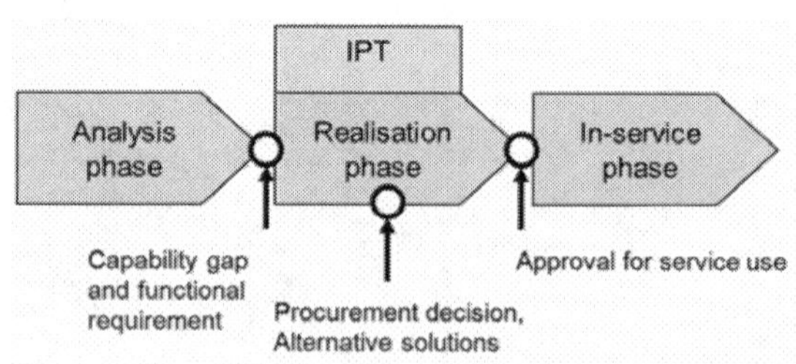

Source: Author's diagram

Previous regulations for satisfying the so-called immediate operational requirement (IOR), i.e., the requirement directly connected to the operational deployments of the Bundeswehr, will be taken into consideration as an integral part of the equipment and in-service support process.

In the analysis phase, capability gaps identified by any of the major organisational elements must be converted into a functional requirement, possible solutions must be shown and one solution must be selected. The *Generalinspekteur* directs the necessary measures, supported by the FMOD Planning Directorate as well as by the subordinate Bundeswehr Planning Office, which will be responsible for identifying planning gaps. Unlike previous armament processes, during which the services acted directly as clients, the Bundeswehr Planning Office will now be the only client for the Federal Office of Bundeswehr Equipment, Information Technology and In-Service Support. The *capability gap and functional requirement* phase document must be approved by the *Generalinspekteur*. Then, the Equipment, Information Technology and In-Service Support Directorate at the FMOD will take over responsibility and task the Federal Office of Bundeswehr Equipment, Information Technology and In-Service Support through the project manager to prepare materiel solution proposals. After consulting with the head of the Equipment, Information Technology and In-Service Support Directorate, the *Generalinspekteur* will select the solution, and it will be recorded in the *alternative solution selection decision*. For tier 1 projects (there are four tiers altogether) valued at above 25m euros, the Equipment, Information Technology and In-Service Support Directorate at the FMOD will conclude a target agreement for realisation and in-service support with the Federal Office of Bundeswehr Equipment, Information Technology and In-Service Support. The idea is to speed up the process by excluding interventions from outside the ITP. Through their integrated accounting activities, the contractors, i.e. trade and industry, must prove their compliance with the contractual and legal provisions, and that they are ensuring the technical safety of the products. The future user will also conduct an operational suitability test, a measure that lies within the overall responsibility of the project manager. This process step will be concluded with the issue of the *Approval for Service Use*. The implementation phase ends with the delivery of the last item. In the in-service phase, the *materiel cognisance for operational readiness* is vested in the Federal Office of Bundeswehr Equipment, Information Technology and In-Service. The commanders/chiefs of staff of the services will bear *operating and support responsibility for maintaining the operational capability and readiness.*

Comparison with previous armament acquisition processes

Looking at process reform from a historical perspective, changes are often triggered by deficiencies that are blown out of proportion, and solutions are most often chosen based on embellished criteria. This holds true for armament acquisition processes.

Figure 4: Armament acquisition processes of the Bundeswehr

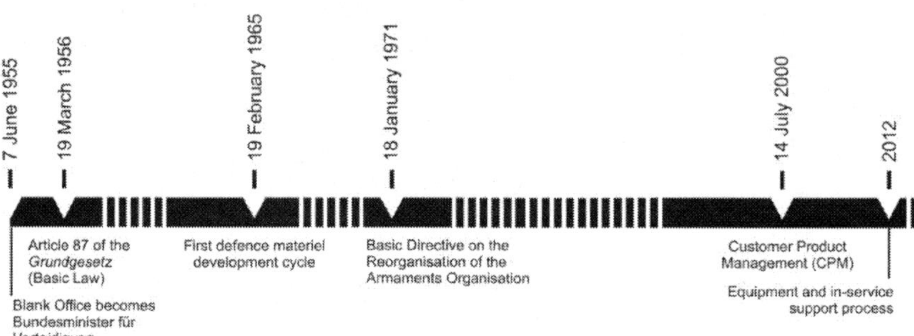

Source: Author's diagram

The regulations of 1965 had clear, one-sided responsibilities; the lead responsibility rested mostly with *BWB*. With EBMat and the dialogue principle, the armed forces were able to strongly influence all of the phases; the CPM again tended towards clear responsibilities which will be even further strengthened in the new equipment and in-service support process.

In the past, it was possible to note in some cases that shifting limited process responsibility to the civilian armament acquisition organisation caused some sectors in the armed forces to retain their capacities and set up mirror organisations.

All armament acquisition processes of the Bundeswehr rest upon the many generally valid legal foundations and administrative regulations which would also be binding for a purely military armament acquisition organisation. Potential contractors need signposts to lead them through the jungle (see Anspach/ Walitschek, 1986).

But process changes are also initiated when practicable solutions are 'perfected' over time in such a way that they lead to incrustations and calcifications. New organisational forms (e.g., agencies) are then seen as the way out, amid hope that administrative perfection will take some time to regain the upper hand.

In hindsight, one can say that although this armament acquisition process was the most complex one, the EBMat of 1973 and the dialogue principle have largely proven valuable since they complied with the German disposition of consensus-building through negotiation. If the main players worked to achieve a target

– which was true in most cases – the decision-making paths were short, but could otherwise barely be kept under control. The EBMat also was a relatively flexible tool and permitted improvements such as the *value analysis* or *commercial approach*. Moreover, its implementing instructions provided a helpful golden thread for less experienced civilian, military and industrial project managers. During the Cold War era, it was ideal for generally meeting military requirements while trying to limit costs and putting realisation last.

Armament acquisition processes are also influenced by international management trends (such as *smart acquisition* and *controlling*). Ever-increasing budget pressure also plays a role. Thus, CPM 2000 concentrated on economic aspects, commercial solutions and participations. The benefit of controlling within the armament acquisition process has remained limited to the provision of standardized information to the management and has been unable to fulfil hopes for *top-down pushbutton management* since it is mostly based on the assessment of the measurable factors. The benefit that controlling has for industry cannot be transferred to government since no administrative has sole control of resources. Furthermore, a word like 'requirements controlling' triggered associations in the military with 'control' by civilians, which did not go down well. A dialogue between the armed forces and the defence engineers was and has proven to be the more workable solution in the long run.

The new 'equipment and in-service support process' is right because it reduces the number of phases, decreases the interfaces and drastically shortens the time it takes to complete projects by replacing the staffing procedure. Up to now, considerable delays and additional costs have been incurred due to the long lag times between the phases and the approval of follow-on contracts.

The success of the new defence materiel development cycle will decisively depend on whether all organisational elements assign top-level personnel to the integrated project teams only, without co-employing them in any mirror organisation. Additional challenges will certainly be the new interfaces that exist during the in-service phase between implementation, materiel cognisance for operational readiness (*BAAINBw*) and operating and supply support responsibility for maintaining the operational capability and readiness, which is a task of the chiefs of staff of the services.

Remarkably, no previous German armament acquisition processes (and those of Germany's partners as well) – with the exception of the 'immediate operational requirement' – has put in place procedures for existential threats. Israel is a good example in this respect. The process steps are quite comparable, but the way Israel handles them is different because of the permanent existential threat the country faces. On the one hand, it can make decisions at short notice and think and act in ways that maximise quick success instead of minimising the risk of projects being terminated. On the other hand, it also has a far-sighted defence research strategy which concentrates resources on acquiring means to attain new operational capabilities and advantages (e.g., unmanned systems, artificial intelligence, a high level of protection) and which partly dispenses with the resource-sapping development of its own capabilities.

Variables influencing the armament acquisition process

The parliamentary audit and the German SAI (*Bundesrechnungshof*)

Since the role of parliament in the political field of defence is covered comprehensively elsewhere, mention shall only be made here of a particularity for armament acquisition projects: In 1981, parliament created another auditing instrument. Since then, the Federal Minister of Defence has had to submit to the German *Bundestag* all agreements or contracts entailing commitments worth more than 50 million German Deutschmarks (BMVg, 1985).

The German SAI is another auditing instrument, the role of which H.-G. Bode (Reinfried/Walitschek, 1978: 39) remarked upon as follows:

> Besides parliament, the German SAI, under Article 88 of the Federal Budget Code (*Bundeshaushaltsordnung – BHO*), also deals with armament activities, doing so from the point of view of their cost effectiveness, by issuing detailed audit comments and, in its capacity as the 'commissioner for economic efficiency in the federal administration', by issuing advisory opinions.
>
> The effectiveness of the auditing and advisory activities of the German SAI is partly being reduced because the agencies affected deny that it has the technical competence required and/or because the conclusions drawn by the administration side sometimes do not seem to justify the amount of work necessary for the audit. However, this is not a specific problem of the military – also with respect to the fact that comments issued by the German SAI always risk being used as ammunition in party political disputes and thus being neutralised. Even so, the auditing and advisory activities of the German SAI have initiated a number of improvements in the armament sector, as well.

The role of technology

Technology plays a decisive role in equipment and armament. Even Clausewitz commented on the role of technology for military equipment by saying that 'fighting has determined the nature of the weapons and equipment employed. These in turn influence combat; thus an interaction exists between the two' (Clausewitz (1832 (2010)).

Historically speaking, a number of roles can be defined for technology such as, firstly, its role as an operational 'joker', secondly, as a classic provider, thirdly, as a means for limiting risk, fourthly, as a link between defence technology and commercial use and, fifthly, as a global steering element. These various roles of technology are briefly examined here.

No revolutions in military technology – from the fighter aircraft all the way to nuclear weapons – have come about because a military requirement was formulated and a technical solution was sought to meet it, but rather because farsighted conceptual thinkers have realised how new technologies could be applied.

Revolutionary technologies are not, in principal, predictable. They emerge from individual path-breaking ideas or from broad fundamental research that allows leeway for creativity. Fundamental research in the field of military technology must be conducted in a permanent dialogue with military planners who are able to transform visions into new concepts and drive the development of the armed forces. When new technologies have reached a certain degree of development, they need to be tested for operational use. The fact must be accepted that, unlike the evolutionary armament strategy of satisfying a requirement, success must not be pre-programmed.

Against this background, the United States, following the Sputnik shock of the 1950s, established the Defense Advanced Research Project Agency (DARPA) with the following simple codex: Only such programmes that promise a high operational benefit ('quantum leap'), or that entail a high success risk (traditional development programmes remain in the armed forces) and yield verifiably significant operational (not technological!) advantages may be pursued.

Unlike development programmes which aim to be 100 per cent successful, the yardstick for the success rate of DARPA was set at 75 per cent. If it is exceeded, the agency gets a negative rating – because it has been too conservative in setting its goals. Thus, a relatively high risk of failure is accepted to allow operational quantum leaps.

DARPA, a small elite agency, has often overcome resistance from the US armed forces to achieve such technological breakthroughs as stealth technology or unmanned aerial vehicles – as well as the Internet, without which life today would be unimaginable.

The second role of technology – that of a provider – has been described in the previous chapters in different forms. A precondition for this solution to be successful is that extrapolations, i.e., forecasting threats and the capabilities needed to confront them, must remain possible up until a weapon system is fielded and throughout its entire life cycle.

Technology is also a means for limiting risk. In general, the impression that armament acquisition processes are barely controllable is becoming a generally accepted view. This is due to the ever-growing complexity of weapons, to the high share of administrative 'lag time' needed for internal and external decision-making, to subsequent changes in the objectives as well as to the lack of efficiency in international programme processing and the adjustment of programmes to match the availability of budget funds.

As a consequence, there is a risk of immature technologies being selected for development. Therefore, it is necessary to not only conduct simulations, but to demonstrate the operational benefit of critical technologies beforehand.

Technology also constitutes a link between defence technology and commercial use. For thousands of years, military technology has been the driving force of technological change. If a commercial product benefits from what was originally military research, it is called a *spin-off*. In the meantime, commercial technology has taken on a life of its own and has gained a lead over military research in many fields.

The necessity to cut costs in the defence sector is increasingly leading to the application of commercial technologies when it comes to procuring defence materiel (*spin-on*). Nowadays, the classic transfer of technology between the military and civilian worlds, also called reactive technology transfer, is taking place in both directions (*spin-off* and *spin-on*).

An approach that will be viable in the future, called proactive technology transfer, is the combined development of key technologies. It provides for basic technologies to be supported jointly by the armament acquisition sector and civilian ministries. Work to further develop them into specific solutions is then done in the respective areas of interest.

Finally, technology is also a global steering element. The Federal Republic of Germany has never adopted a self-sufficient approach regarding armament. Instead, it has always strived for complementarity and partnership in the development and procurement of defence materiel. For economic reasons, the idea has been for national and international partners to establish so-called *centres of competence* – especially within the industrial sector. It increasingly looks as if the present, requirement-based programmes will only be able to retain the necessary industrial core competence in a few areas. The consequence of this is that the European defence industry has been and still is shrinking and consolidating.

There is broad agreement that exporting, cooperation/team-building, the retention of industrial core competence with experienced key personnel as well as increased prototyping, i.e., the development, building and testing of technology carriers with the potential to bring about a quantum leap (technology and operational benefit), will help achieve the aim of preserving the core defence engineering capabilities.

Defence research and industry

Thomas de Maizière, the German minister of defence, has underlined the importance of defence technology for the reorientation of the Bundeswehr, saying (de Maizière 2011):

> The clear aim of the Federal Government is to provide our soldiers with the best equipment they need to accomplish their missions. To achieve this, we need a powerful and innovative defence industry. Having defence capabilities of our own is a prerequisite for participating in the shaping of the European integration process. Only nations with a powerful defence industry have the appropriate weight to influence decisions made by the Alliance.

Whereas partner nations also conduct defence research at universities, in Germany this work is mainly done within the industry, at the civilian Bundeswehr technical centres and at the FMOD-funded institutes that have teamed up to form the Fraunhofer-Verbund Verteidigungs- und Sicherheitsforschung (Fraunhofer Group for Defence and Security). In addition to the civilian research results, the following goals have been set (Muller/Geyer, 2006):

> Provision of the scientific and technological know-how required to make intelligent and economic decisions on armament; presentation of new technological solutions and recognition of the relevance of new technologies for military capabilities; preparation of generic new (sub) system concepts; elaboration of input to a European research and technology base as well as to cooperation; and assistance in the maintenance of a defence engineering competence in Germany.

In parallel to the downsizing of the armed forces, the defence industry, which had provided top-of-the-line products for the Bundeswehr and its allies over decades, needed to drastically reduce its capacities. It had to accept unequal competitive conditions, such as subsidies for state-owned enterprises, differences in export support or violations of EU laws through offset claims. This is another reason why globally-operating German companies are increasingly withdrawing from the field of defence technology – a trend which persists today.

In 2007, the FMOD concluded an agreement with the Defence Economics Committee of the BDI (Federation of German Industry) on indispensable national core defence capabilities.

International cooperation

The Bundeswehr is responsible at the national level for providing the armed forces with the equipment and supplies they need, but, as an integral part of international alliance systems, it also engages in a wide variety of international cooperation to develop a large number of weapon systems.

The German *Bundestag*, the FMOD, the Federal Foreign Office and the Federal Ministry of Economics and Technology are the leading players with respect to the initiation of cooperation projects. Observing the large variety of the relations between states, the armed forces and armament acquisition organisations explore the possibilities for cooperation and submit planned projects to one of the bodies of the alliances.

Since its founding in 1949, NATO, the transatlantic cornerstone of security policy, has developed a broad and deeply staggered system for armament cooperation. From the beginning, the three core targets have been rationalisation, standardisation and interoperability.

After the annual summit meetings of the heads of state and government comes the North Atlantic Council (NAC) as the highest body authorised to also take unanimous decisions on general armament questions. The Conference of National Armaments Directors, (CNAD) with its supporting bodies turns the requests submitted by the armed forces of interested NATO members and of countries participating in the Partnership for Peace programme into concrete programmes.

For this purpose, appropriate organisations and agencies have been and continue to be established. The fields in which they operate are:

- development, procurement and in-service use
- logistics
- standardisation
- civil emergency planning
- air surveillance and defence
- airborne early warning
- communication and information
- electronic warfare
- meteorology
- military oceanography
- research and technology
- (follow-on) training

They are assisted in their work by accredited *centres of excellence*. This structure ensures that both project-related and general functions are performed.

The actual agencies responsible for development, procurement and in-service use (such as the NATO EF 2000 and TORNADO Production and Logistics Management Agency, NETMA, the NATO Helicopter Design and Development and Logistics Management Agency, NAHEMA) have charters of their own and are monitored by the steering committees of the participating nations.

These agencies have a variety of organisational models. For example, there are relatively large organisations with specialized departments of their own, but there are also small agencies with a core team that concentrates on management tasks and relies on the technical competence of the participating nations. Here, the organisational matrix, although managed at the international level, to a large extent reaches down to the national level.

Steering committee decisions must be made on the basis of consensus, which often is very time-consuming and does not always lead to the best possible solution from an operational, technical or economic point of view. Deviations from the standard product result in national solutions which, in turn, conflicts with the overall aim of standardisation.

The major advantage of an agency solution lies in the short reporting and decision-making channels, since all resources are in the hands of one organisation and the industrial partner is normally closely involved. General difficulties arising from the different armament acquisition processes applied by the participating nations can often be resolved through tailored solutions. In the case of one major project, it was possible to convince all countries involved to agree to accept the civil code of the host nation as the contractual basis, which saved a considerable amount of time.

In the face of growing budget pressure, NATO is currently trying to implement a reform with the intention of streamlining the existing 14 agencies into three programmatic themes- procurement, support, and communications and information.

By pooling the areas of finance, accounting, general procurement, personnel management and general information technology into one new *NATO Procurement Agency,* more synergy, greater transparency and less overhead cost are expected. If adopted, this centralist approach will mean that the present agencies will no longer have direct access to all resources that have up to now been needed for programme management.

For decades, there have been attempts to strengthen the European defence structure. Overlapping memberships in NATO and the European Union (EU) make this difficult. For example, there are some nations that are only members of NATO, others are only members of the EU, whilst many belong to both.

Yet, besides cooperation within the framework of the transatlantic Alliance, possibilities have also emerged for purely European armament cooperation. Some of the numerous bodies dealing with European armament cooperation have changed their names, members and aims over the decades.

A substantial step was achieved in 1996 with the establishment of the Organisation for Joint Armament Cooperation (*Organisation Conjointe de Coopération en Matière d'Armement,* OCCAR), even though it only became a legal entity in 2001. Some nations are members of OCCAR, while others participate in programmes without being members. OCCAR has its head office in Bonn and the programme bureaus are located where the general contractors are based.

OCCAR's objective is to promote greater competition by awarding contracts on the basis of performance instead of on financial involvement. The idea is to achieve this by lessening the obligation to assign a nation a share of the work that is equivalent to the share of the cost it bears (often called 'offset'). Instead, compensation is intended to be provided across all programmes and over several years. This is a difficult endeavour, since the partners in each single programme are not the same.

A next step was the founding of the European Defence Agency (EDA) in 2004. The EDA is the central forum for European defence cooperation. Its aims to include the creation of a European defence market, the harmonisation of national procurement guidelines and the pooling of defence research activities.

Despite all the praiseworthy activities undertaken, it is indispensable 'to deal with the inner, mental mechanisms which in the end decide whether cooperation is possible or not and whether it is economically justifiable or reasonable' (Defourneaux, 1977).

The French armaments director Jean-Laurens Delpech made an attempt at a German-French symposium back in 1976 to express the difficulties of international cooperation in formulas (Sextus Iulius Frontinus Iuvenis 2010: 90 et seq.).

He postulated that if the number of programme participants was n, the cost of a programme had to be multiplied by $\sqrt[2]{n}$, the time needed to implement it would be $\sqrt[3]{n}$ and that an increase of n^3 had to be expected due to the difficulties in connection with export. In 1977, Ingénieur Général de l'Armament Marc Defourneaux – with Gallic precision and irony – formulated the pitfalls of international cooperation and put them into formulas. He did so by using the Delpech approach as the basis and considered the operational, industrial, psychological and political aspects that had to be taken into consideration for cooperation and that were often concealed behind the noble proclamations issued to outside observers. Anyone involved in the planning, realisation, supervision and evaluation of a cooperation programme should be familiar with and aware of his postulations (Defourneaux (1977) quoted in Sextus Iulius Frontinus Iuvenis, (2010: 99-130)).

Personnel development

The acquisition of intercultural competence is of central importance for people working in the armament acquisition sector due to the international character of defence cooperation considered in the previous section, – after all, almost all major weapon systems that the Bundeswehr acquires are produced through international cooperation. An appreciation of the way in which the partners get things done, of their 'national cultures', decides whether a project is a success or a failure. A typical view is expressed by these words of someone involved, who after a less successful project sarcastically said: 'Now I understand why we waged war with our partner for 100 years.'

The problem of how to best deal with different views, mentalities and procedures has led to a number of theoretical studies, but has also motivated the people involved in the various projects to make pragmatic arrangements. It is therefore imperative to familiarise potential staff of international organisations and projects with the theoretical fundamentals as well as to pass on the experience acquired and to establish personal networks.

Intercultural competence, however, is not the only challenge in armament acquisition, as exemplified by a quotation of D. Wellerhoff (1997:103) in which he criticizes the failure to produce a professional synopsis of the specialized fields in view of the ever-increasing specialisation of the civil executive personnel and in which he complains about a lack of 'generalists':

> It is not normally possible for us in Germany to acquire this important qualification at university. This is probably because Germany does not have a distinct culture of academic follow-on education for a second or third stage of a career. It is good and right that future higher-level executives first earn their stripes in their specialized field. After passing the second state examination, a German upper-level civil servant has, like people in many other professions, completed his education. Like his counterpart in industry, he does not have time for any further learning, e.g., for taking a course at a university, nor his company have the money. He is indispensable. (...) Advantage is rarely ever taken of the two-month core courses at the Federal Academy for Security Studies, which offer real general training for top-level assignments.

In 1996, the 'Personnel Development Concept for the Higher Intermediate-Level and the Higher-Level Services in the Bundeswehr' was established by the FMOD to remedy lacking qualifications (FMOD, 1996). It consolidated the instruments of personnel planning and personnel management in order to achieve targeted assignment planning and to man executive positions. There were problems, however, in implementing it. For example, too little consideration was given in the engineering sector to the fact that an engineer must have the same rights as a manager, have the opportunity for promotion and have the possibility of later changing over to higher management levels. The excessively short periods for which junior engineers are assigned posts and during which they have a chance to develop their own capabilities have proven to be particularly problematic. They are often not long enough for the agencies to get a *return on investment* and for the employees to qualify for promotion. In addition, they have a demotivating effect on top performers, who are forced to discover that *job hopping* is more highly regarded than doing an outstanding job during a long posting.

Future executive personnel not only receive lifelong special follow-on training in the respective courses at the Federal Academy of Defence Administration and

Technology, but are also offered chances to attain methodological, social and personal skills.

It is important that follow-on training take place in coordination with the armed forces, which already account for 30 per cent of the students in courses at the Federal Academy of Defence Administration and Technology.

Figure 5: The principle of complimentary competences

Top management level
State Secretary for Armaments
Management level III (B 5 - B 9)
Management level II (A 16 - B 4)
Management level I (A 12/13 - A 15)
Security policy aspects
Administration / Legal Affairs
Methodology / Social Affairs / "Personality"
Technology
Business Management
Entry into employment
Professional base

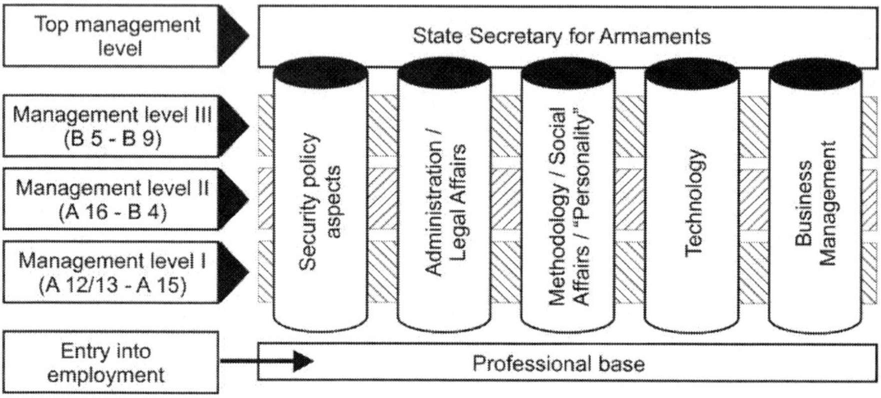

Source: Author's diagram

Lower capital investment in defence has also influenced personnel development within the armament organisation. While at the beginning of the author's term of service the teams at the agencies and in industry could draw on experience acquired from several programmes before being assigned a major project, this is often no longer the case today due to the lack of new projects. The resulting deficiency in experience may have negative consequences. This could be remedied in part by Management in Prototyping and by the Concept of Complimentary Competences (Heumann, 2006). This concept is based on the assumption that staff members can perform complex and changing tasks effectively and efficiently if they can develop their skills holistically and if they link the necessary capabilities. This will enable them to become modern-day 'generalists'.

Has armament reached a dead end?

The equilateral triangle composed of achievement, time and costs is out of balance. For decades, observers have noticed that, through tremendous effort, performance objectives can for the most part be met, and costs kept within acceptable limits. Prioritization of these parameters, however, has drastically affected timetables.

Although this is not comforting, it is helpful to see that major civilian projects – like the building of operas, express trains, airports or commercial aircraft – are facing the same problems. Rail passengers are not interested in whether the manufacturer has to pay contractual penalties to the operator. They must bear with delays and overheated compartments. Troops on operational deployment are even less interested in the reasons for deficiencies and delays; they want and need equipment that is superior, functional, and provides protection.

Therefore, it is necessary to look for the reasons for this systematic failure and to quickly remedy the situation. The aerospace industry was proud of having developed a tool in the sixties which went on to also enable other branches of industry to manage complex systems. The tool is known as *Systems Engineering.* The basic idea is simple: A complex system is split up into manageable elements with controllable functions and interfaces. These elements are then developed and tested and gradually integrated down to the system level. A vast number of – both technical and contractual – attempts have been made to get the complexity of systems under control. All of these have led to some improvements, but they have missed the target of breaking the trend. In the end, satisfactory results could often only be achieved by using customers as guinea pigs – however, this is not acceptable with fighting troops. Already in 1982, Norman R. Augustine wrote down in his sarcastic 'Augustine's Laws' what he believed to be the snares of armament acquisition management. The problems and challenges remain unchanged to this day.

The initiative launched by the journal *Aviation Week & Space Technology* (AW&ST) to put Systems Engineering to the test at a congress and to draw attention to new approaches is very interesting (Warwick/Norris, 2010). The root of the problem is that new systems are becoming not just more *complex* but also increasingly *complicated.* While Systems Engineering works successfully in splitting up complex systems, the tool fails with complicated systems because they are not separable into parts by definition. Unintended and unexpected interactions take place between the system elements, some of which are not detected until the systems are in service and are often the result of the explosive growth in software.

Thus, the specifications and simulation models not only have to describe and test the interfaces, but also allow predictions to be made on the positive and negative effects the elements have on each other and on the overall system.

With the 'Key Figures for Immeasurable Quantities', Peter F. Drucker (2008: 294) has pointed out a special problem which also plays decisive role in the management of armament acquisition processes:

> A big problem in management is the balance between what is measurable and what is not measurable. (...) They are anything but 'immaterial' – they are indeed very 'material'. (...) Measurements which do not also explicitly list the presumed assumptions about the non-measurable statements are therefore misleading.

Ways out of the dead end

Ways out of the dead end can only be found by adopting a holistic approach. While it is true that Systems Engineering adds value in terms of concept and design, this is less the case with regard to testing, production and in-service use. Therefore, all life cycle phases of systems, and all influencing factors, must be more closely examined.

The trend towards completely outsourcing subsystem responsibilities should be questioned. Technical problems and the resulting delays are often disastrous. The hoped-for economic advantages may well become disadvantages, as the example of the latest commercial aircraft is showing – not to mention possible damage to the company's reputation.

When the holistic approach is applied to armament acquisition in the Bundeswehr, a whole number of aspects, which are listed further below, should be taken into consideration. Each aspect by itself would justify a paragraph or even a subchapter of its own. Yet, they are only listed here as key points since the focus of this examination has been on presenting and analysing the armament acquisition process. However, in view of the challenges faced by the armament acquisition process in Germany that are presented in this chapter, it seemed fitting to not simply conclude with a summary, but with one or two suggestions on how the armament acquisition process can be developed and made more effective.
Consideration could therefore be given to these suggestions when future reforms are envisaged.

Everyone involved, at every level, should apply the principles of Auftragstaktik. Auftragstaktik is a special type of mission command developed by Prussian officers after the defeat by Napoleon. It replaced the strict act under order system. Field Marshal Carl Bernhard Graf von Moltke formulated in 1869 the essentials of Auftragstaktik, quoted by Stephen Bungay (2011) as follows:

> The higher the level of command, the shorter and more general the orders should be. The next level down should add whatever further specification it feels is necessary.
>
> It is vital that subordinates fully understand the purpose of an order so that they can continue trying to achieve it should the circumstances demand that they act differently than they were originally ordered to do.

> The rule to follow is that an order should contain all, but also only, what subordinates cannot determine for themselves, with a view to achieving a particular aim.
>
> Overall direction should be communicated in a cascade. Each level is guided by the intention of the one above, which whenever possible was articulated in a face-to-face briefing as well as in writing.
>
> Having been briefed about what to achieve and why, the lower level specifies what it intends to do and repeats the results back up the chain in what has become known as a 'backbrief'.
>
> Understanding an order means grasping what is essential and taking measures that put this key aspect before anything else.

Bungay considers von Moltke to be a master of modern management. Auftragstaktik has resulted in modern military mission command styles. Trade and industry apply these principles in the form of management by objectives.)

- There should be consistent application of the principle of *lean administration requires lean legislation.*
- The bureaucratic obstacles should be removed by establishing clear procedural and organisational structures.
- Programme managers should have more leeway in decision-making.
- The principle of management by objectives should be adopted and micromanagement should be dispensed with.
- A reversal must be made to the creeping process of giving priority to political affinity over professional competence in the assignment of management positions.
- Questions should be asked to determine why there are lengthy and cost-pushing interruptions in phases due to the submission of contracts worth over 25 million euros to the German *Bundestag.*
- There should be an open discussion of new concepts among the experts.
- Arrangements should be made to cover existential threats.
- A national armament strategy should be developed, approved and implemented.
- There should be a national reorganisation of the procedural and organisational structures, but not until *after* their consultations have been held with the most important armament acquisition partners, since the areas in international projects in which there is friction are mostly determined by procedural differences.
- Reforms should be planned and implemented as a control loop.
- New tools such as concept development and experimentation (CD&E) should be used.
- Regulations should be drawn up in such a way as to maximise quick success and not, as before, to minimise the risk of projects being terminated.

- The decision-making methodology should be graded and adjusted to the complexity of the project (e.g., preparation of phase documents and negotiation of complex contracts at closed meetings).
- Long-term perspectives should be developed and there should be observance of the phenomenon that efficiency (i.e., do the thing right) may first decrease in the case of measures intended to boost effectiveness (i.e., do the right thing); action should be taken to create phases of consolidation during which the new measures can be understood, implemented and allowed to take effect.
- A closer and regulated link should be established between the armed forces, the armament acquisition organisation, industry and science, similar to that in the partner countries (e.g., project teams)
- The concept development capabilities should be expanded in order to remain capable of dialoguing with armament acquisition partners, and especially the USA.
- A DARPA-like capability with a strong national component should be created at European level.
- The competitiveness of the defence industry should be strengthened, particularly by means of technology demonstrators and equal opportunity in the field of exports.
- There should be cooperation with industry only when economic advantages can be gained from this, not for ideological reasons.
- There should be targeted investments in the early phases of the armament acquisition process in order to minimise risks and reduce life cycle costs.
- Technical and management training should be improved, with personnel from the procurement offices, armed forces and industry undergoing some training together so that they get the chance to acquire some joint experience through simulation, technology programmes and prototyping.
- Personnel should undergo specific preparation for international assignments so that they can defend national interests.

The recommended measures will only be successful, however, if each sector can build on the competence of its own personnel and entrust them with the design and realisation of new structures. Even if these suggestions appear too ambitious, one has to concede that, in a fair evaluation, the German armament acquisition community-soldiers, government officials, industry and science – has been internationally competitive for decades and, applying extremely different procedures, has provided the forces equipment for which they have often been envied.

Yet, despite this joint and truly cooperative way of going about things, a sentence attributed to Colonel General Guderian is still valid today:

> All of the technicians lie. However, you can only tell that they do after one to two years have passed, when their ideas cannot be realised. The tacticians lie as well. But you only realise this after a war has been lost, and then it is too late.

Bibliography

Anspach, Joachim/Walitschek, Hubert F. (1986): Die Bundeswehr als Auftraggeber. Koblenz: Bernard & Graefe Verlag.

Augustine, Norman R. (1982): Augustine's Laws, New York, American Institute of Aeronautics and Astronautics, Inc.

Blasius, Rainer (2006): Ziviler Geist gegen grasende Generale. In: FAZ, 29.03.2006: 10.

BMVg (1970): Bericht zur Neuordnung des Rüstungsbereichs, vorgelegt von der durch Ministerweisung vom 5. Juni 1970 eingesetzten Organisationskommission.

BMVg (1971): Rahmenerlass zur Neuordnung des Rüstungsbereichs des BMVg, Der Bundesminister der Verteidigung, 28.01.1971.

BMVg (1973): Durchführungsbestimmungen zu den Rahmenbestimmungen für die Entwicklung und Beschaffung von Wehrmaterial, BMVg-Org 1 – Az 72-01-02 of 06.03.1973.

BMVg (1985): Zur Lage und Entwicklung der Bundeswehr (White Paper 1985). Bundesministerium der Verteidigung. Bonn (1985).

BMVg (1996): Personalentwicklungskonzeption für Beamtinnen und Beamte des gehobenen und höheren Dienstes der Bundeswehr, BMVg-P I 1 –Az 17-01-01, 30.01.1996.

BMVg (2001): Customer Product Management (CPM 2001), as of 12..07.2000.

BMVg (2011): Interview, Abteilungsleiter Rüstung Detlef Selhausen, Bonn/Berlin: BMVg, www.BMVg.de/portal. 26.08.2011 (accessed 19.03.2012).

BMVg (2012): Verfahrensbestimmungen für die Bedarfsermittlung, Bedarfsdeckung und Nutzung in der Bundeswehr (ressortinterne Rahmenweisung).

Bremm, Klaus-Jürgen; Mack, Hans-Hubertus; Rink, Martin Rink (Eds.) (2005): 50 Jahre Bundeswehr. Freiburg i.Br.: Rombach Verlag.

Bungay, Stephen (2001): Moltke –Master of Modern Management. In: The European Financial Review, 05.04. 2011.

Clausewitz, Carl von (1832-34): Vom Kriege. Kindle Edition: Fair Price Classics, 29.03.2010.

de Maizière, Thomas (2011): Speech on the occasion of the 8th Handelsblatt Conference in Berlin on 25.10.2011.

Deutscher Bundestag (2010): Grundgesetz der Bundesrepublik Deutschland vom 8.5.1949 as amended on 21.07.2010 (BGBl I: 944).

Drucker, Peter F. (2008) Daily Drucker. Heidelberg: Springer Verlag.

Flume, Wofgang (Ed.) (2009): Die Ausrüstung der Bundeswehr 2009. Sankt Augustin: CPM Communication Presse Marketing GmbH.

Geyer, Michael (1984): Deutsche Rüstungspolitik1860 – 1980. Frankfurt: edition suhrkamp.

Heumann, Helmuth (2006): Die strategische Ausrichtung der Bundesakademie für Wehrverwaltung und Wehrtechnik. In: Bundeswehrverwaltung, Jubiläumsausgabe 2006, Köln: Carl Heymanns Verlag.

Hubatschek, Gerhard (Ed.) (1995): 40 Jahre Ausrüstung der Streitkräfte. Bonn: Report Verlag.

Hubatschek, Gerhard (Ed.) (2005): 50 Jahre Wehrtechnik und Ausrüstung. Bonn: Report Verlag.

Kollmer, Dieter H.(2005): Die materielle Ausrüstung der Bundeswehr von den Anfängen bis heute. In: Bremm, Klaus-Jürgen; Mack, Hans-Hubertus; Rink, Martin Rink (Eds.), 50 Jahre Bundeswehr. Freiburg i.Br.: Rombach Verlag, 215-230.

Meyers Großes Konversationslexikon, 6th edition, 1905-1909

Müller, H.; Geyer, T.: (2006) Institute forschen für Sicherheit und Verteidigung; Fraunhoferverbund Verteidigungs- und Sicherheitsforschung, Freiburg.

Reinfried, Hubert/Walitschek, Hubert F. (1978): Die Bundeswehr – eine Gesamtdarstellung, Band 10, Rüstung in der Bundesrepublik Deutschland. Regensburg: Walhalla u. Praetoria Verlag.

Roeske, Hans-Rüdiger (1995): Rüstungsführung im Wandel der Zeiten. In: Hubatschek (1995): 19-32.

Schustereit, Hartmut (2000): Deutsche Militärverwaltung im Umbruch. Berlin: Oderbaum Verlag.

Sextus Iulius Frontinus Iuvenis (2010): STRATEGEMATA oder Von den Listen wider die Rüstung Germaniens. Münster: edition octopus, Verlag Monsenstein und Vannerdat.

von Moltke, Carl Bernhard (1925): Ausgewählte Werke, Erster Band. Berlin: Reimar Hobbing Verlag; S.160-166

Warwick, Graham; Norris, Guy (2010): Is it time to revamp systems engineering? In: Aviation Week & Space Technology, 01.11.2010.

Wellershoff, Dieter (1997): Führen Wollen – Können – Verantworten. Bonn: Bouvier-Verlag.

Wirtgen, Rolf (2005): Aspekte aus der Geschichte des Rüstungsbereichs In: Hubatschek (2005): 20-47.

Modernisation in the Bundeswehr – privatisation and public-private partnerships (PPP)

Gregor Richter

Definitions: modernisation, privatisation, public-private partnerships (PPP)

While the terms used to describe reforms in the Bundeswehr have changed from time to time during the past few years – in 2011, for example, the word 'transformation' gave way to 'reorientation' (*Neuausrichtung*) –, the concept of 'modernisation' has established a firm foothold as the term used to describe the economic aspects of reform. For example, Brigadier General Günter Schwarz, head of the Centre of Expertise for Modernisation (*Kompetenzzentrum Modernisierung*), formerly the control centre for privatisation projects at the Federal Ministry of Defence (FMoD), put it this way as early as 2003: "When we talk about modernisation, we are referring exclusively to the modernisation of the support sector with a view to achieving greater cost-effectiveness." (wt 2004) Since the term 'modernisation' tends to generate positive associations (sending the desired political signal) and because of the specific reference to a clearly-outlined field of reforms, it has survived to this day (2012).

The objective of modernisation projects is to sustainably increase efficiency in the provision of services in the Bundeswehr's support and service sector. To achieve this, examinations are conducted on the basis of so-called efficiency analyses (*Wirtschaftlichkeitsuntersuchungen*, see Steuer, 2012) into how a functional requirement of the armed forces to accomplish their mission can be met more cost-effectively, i.e. with fewer budgetary funds. At the same time, examinations are explicitly carried out to determine whether the private sector can provide an economically favourable alternative. Basically speaking, efficiency analyses involve comparing options (in-house models, outsourcing models) and assessing these in monetary terms. Subsequently, a decision may be taken to order a package of services from a private-sector provider. In practice, however, staffing, regulations and military policy are usually also considered in addition to mere economic and cost-effectiveness factors, and these arguments occasionally override the results of efficiency analyses.

From the point of view of public administration, there are three basic types of privatisation (see Portugall, 2007: 144). The following does not include asset privatisation, where only government-owned property (land, infrastructure, facilities, etc.) is sold to private sector parties.[1] In the case of a material or real privatisation, a service previously provided by government staff and with government resources is transferred to a private sector provider. The government transfers responsibility for guaranteeing, financing and executing the service (see: Bogumil/Jann, 2005: 55). This kind of privatisation has not taken place so far in the defence department and is unlikely to in the future, since due to provisions contained in Germany's Basic Law, in particular Article 87a and b, and also due to the character of national defence as a public good, the transfer of guarantee and financing responsibility is either politically undesirable or cannot be implemented on account of the possibility of market failure. In the case of a formal privatisation, a government service is provided by an organisation under private law (usually in the form of a limited liability company), in which the shares remain 100 per cent publicly-owned. In this case, one therefore tends to speak of a 'false' privatisation. This kind of privatisation is rarely found in the Bundeswehr. The usual option for the defence department is that of a functional privatisation, which involves transferring the responsibility for execution, i.e. the job of providing a service that was formerly provided by the government is taken over by a private company, but the government ultimately retains its obligation as the guarantor and is responsible for the financing. Functional privatisations in the defence department are typically designed as public-private partnerships (PPP) in which the Federal Government holds shares.

PPPs are formed for the following reasons: By drawing on the private partner's management know-how and his technical and project expertise, the government hopes to increase effectiveness and efficiency in the provision of a service. If the focus is on this aspect, it is known as a 'management-oriented PPP' (Budäus, 2003: 224). A PPP also allows private capital to be activated for the provision of government services – at a time when public funds are in short supply, this is probably the main reason why PPPs are formed. In the case of 'finance-oriented PPPs' (ibid., 225) the private partner provides his own financial resources and cooperation generally extends across several stages of the value-added process. It is precisely this aspect that constitutes the PPP, as the "practical possibility [...] of making financial means available at the 'right' points in time during the contract period in order to minimise the overall costs" (Beckers/Klatt, 2009: 29) is often the main economic advantage of a PPP solution for the public sector. This at least partially gets around the problem of budgetary restrictions (keyword: year-to-year budgeting). Responsibility for financing, however, remains with the government, which as a rule has to provide the PPP company

1 In connection with the closure of military stations and real estate as a result of the previous Bundeswehr reforms, there have been many cases of assets being privatised over the past few years. Most of the revenue resulting from this goes to the Federal Ministry of Finance (FMOF). Today the Institute for Federal Real Estate (*Bundesanstalt für Immobilienaufgaben*) in Bonn is responsible for the utilisation of government real estate. It is under the technical and legal supervision of the FMOF.

with service payments. On the other hand, a PPP often enables the private partner to expand his business activities into a government area to which the market or the private sector previously had no access. Ideally, a PPP should take account of the interests of both parties; it is only efficient when synergy effects arise and a so-called win-win situation is created.

> In the language of the FMoD, the terms cooperation and PPP will always be used when services that have hitherto been provided or could be performed by the government are carried out in future together with the private sector in the form of cooperation that is long-term, contractual and regulated in part by corporate law (Rieks/Keller, 2009: 127).

This definition of terms concurs with the general concept of PPPs within the field of administrative sciences. PPPs can thus relate to areas of activity that were previously the responsibility of the government, but they can also from the outset be considered an option if a new set of requirements arises, as was the case with the operation of messing and service facilities at Bundeswehr garrisons in the mid-1990s.

The current situation: privatisation projects in the service sector of the Bundeswehr

The 'Framework Contract on Innovation, Investment and Cost Efficiency in the Bundeswehr' (1999), which has now been in existence for twelve years, was the starting point for stepping up cooperation between the Bundeswehr and the private sector on the basis of the PPP model. Numerous companies have signed this contract and a number of cooperation projects have been initiated. The contract formulated the following objectives, which are still valid today:

- Use was to be made of the ability of German industry to innovate and – derived from this – to increase the Bundeswehr's investment possibilities.
- The power of innovation of both trade and industry and the armed forces was to be strengthened and stabilised.
- The cost-effectiveness of the operation and procurement processes of the public contractor and companies was to be improved.
- Resources were to be used more effectively so as to create new scope for investment.

A vital role in the provision of private-sector know-how for the Bundeswehr and in the initiation of PPPs in the Bundeswehr's service sector is played by the Gesellschaft für Entwicklung, Beschaffung und Betrieb mbH (g.e.b.b.). It commenced its business activities in 2000 and can be described as an in-house company, allowing the government to continue providing government services, but now within the corporate form of private law. As the sole partner holding 100 per cent of the shares is the FMoD, it is a formal privatisation. The following PPP projects implemented in the Bundeswehr's service sector deserve closer examination, due to their personnel and financial scope.

In June 2002, BwFuhrparkService GmbH (BwFPS) was founded. The major shareholder, with 75.1 per cent, is the Federal Republic of Germany; the Deutsche Bahn AG holds 24.9 per cent of the shares. The BwFPS's job is to operate the Bundeswehr's non-military mobility requirements more economically. The idea was to maintain a smaller but modernised fleet of vehicles, and to make more efficient use of it. With 24 mobility centres across Germany, around 120 service stations and four support centres, the BwFPS says that its 26-thousand vehicle fleet can be used by the Bundeswehr any time any place. As of August 2012 the company has 400 employees as well as around 1,200 civilian drivers provided by the Bundeswehr.

In August 2002, LH Bundeswehr Bekleidungsgesellschaft mbH (LHBw) opened for business. The Federal Republic of Germany holds 25.1 per cent of the shares; the two cooperating companies LION APPAREL Deutschland GmbH and Hellman Worldwide Logistics GmbH & Co. KG. hold 74.9 per cent of the shares. With 2,500 employees and approximately 150 facilities, the LHBw has been commissioned to reorganise the Bundeswehr's entire clothing management in the private sector, particularly in the areas of purchasing, logistics, development and service.

In 2005, Heeresinstandsetzungslogistik GmbH (HIL) commenced its business activities. It is a private enterprise combining an industrial partner determined by competition – the HIL Industrie-Holding GmbH – and the Federal Government, which has a substantial minority interest. The HIL relieves the Bundeswehr of materiel maintenance work during routine duty, supports training and exercises and is geared towards the armed forces' focus on operations. As of August 2012 the HIL has a workforce of approximately 1,963, of which 1,679 employees and civil servants are personnel provided by the Bundeswehr.

Founded in 2006, BWI Informationstechnik GmbH (BWI) is a service alliance which has the strategic objective of modernising the Bundeswehr's entire commercially available, non-military IT and telecommunications infrastructure. The BWI's business model is based on the following shareholder structure: As soon as the main contract was signed, the Federal Government, Siemens Business Service GmbH & Co. OHG (SBS) and IBM Deutschland GmbH (IBM) set up a joint enterprise with the legal form of a limited liability company. The Federal Government holds 49.9 per cent of the shares of BWI, SBS 50.05 per cent and IBM 0.05 per cent. The industrial partners contributed their shares of the joint stock in cash, while the Federal Government made contributions in kind by providing its already existing information and communications technology. As of today (August 2012) the BWI and its service companies employ 2,900 staff of which about a half are employed by the Bundeswehr and the other half are Siemens and IBM employees. The modernisation of the Bundeswehr's civilian IT infrastructure, a project that rightly deserves its name 'HERKULES', has a total volume of over 7.1 billion euros, making it the largest procurement project in Europe implemented within the framework of a PPP.

In addition to these four Bundeswehr partnerships, local projects have also been launched, for example the 'Fürst Wrede Barracks' PPP structural engineering project in Munich, in which the private partner has taken over responsibility for planning at a barracks, doing construction work there, providing financial resources for it and operating it (see Link, 2010). PPP projects in catering, on the other hand, have so far not been very successful (Portugall, 2007: 151); the private sector service enterprise involved in the partnership terminated its contract prematurely. In addition to this, PPP projects in the defence department feature the following structural, economic and legal peculiarities:

PPPs in the Bundeswehr cover service sectors and support services. Until now they have not been found in core military areas such as the preparation, conduct and follow-up of operations or in the field of arms development and procurement.

PPPs in the Bundeswehr are designed to ensure that standardised services can be provided to civilian and military agencies across the country, i.e. the service contracts are not negotiated or awarded individually at regional or local level. The BwFPS, for instance, is responsible for meeting the mobility requirements of all the Bundeswehr's agencies via its current 400 or so stations in Germany. Likewise, at all stations in Germany, the BWI is uniformly modernising the information and communications technology with largely standardised equipment. PPPs in the Bundeswehr are usually formed with large supraregional and sometimes international partners from industry and the service sector that have the necessary financial resources as well as management, branch and project expertise. Medium-sized companies are at best considered as subcontractors and local service providers commissioned by PPP companies.

PPPs in the Bundeswehr have a project and service organisation that covers a large part of the country and that takes account of different needs on several hierarchical levels. For them it is particularly true "[...] that both an ad hoc and a continuous need for coordination between the partners are becoming essential features of the value-added process that characterises a PPP" (Budäus, 2006: 15). For planning and controlling purposes, a dual organisation is often created by the Bundeswehr and the PPP companies.

PPPs in the Bundeswehr predominantly employ personnel for whom the Bundeswehr is still the actual employer and over whom the holding companies 'only' have the authority to issue technical directives. The percentage of the total workforce of PPP companies and of their subsidiaries provided by the Bundeswehr is 75 per cent in the case of the BWFPS, 85 per cent in the case of the HIL, and 50 per cent in the case of the BWI (author's calculations based on the figures above). As far as the companies' workforces are concerned, the personnel who work in the operational area are mostly members of the Bundeswehr; management positions are primarily staffed by former personnel from the companies of the private partners or by external staff.

Empirical surveys conducted among members of the Bundeswehr reveal that soldiers, civil servants and employees tend to be critical of privatisations and PPPs (Krampe, 2011: 127 et seq.). The common arguments in favour of and against PPPs in the Bundeswehr are summarised in Table 1.

Table 1: Common arguments in favour of and against PPPs in the Bundeswehr's service sector

In favour	Against
A PPP enables capital injections and private financing to be used to relieve the federal budget in the short term (defence budget) in the case of projects requiring large investments.	A PPP conceals government debt, as the provision of services has to be financed one way or another by the federal budget in the long term.
A PPP enables an expansion of know-how for the Bundeswehr and the integration of management, project and technical expertise from the private sector.	PPPs produce capability losses in areas of work that were previously covered by the Bundeswehr's civilian and/or military personnel. The result is a higher dependency on external (human) resources.
A PPP allows military personnel to be relieved of support tasks, which in turn allows the focus to be placed on core military capabilities, and this is advantageous for an 'army geared towards operations abroad'.	A PPP causes higher costs for bureaucracy and coordination between the core military areas and the privatised secondary service sectors; an undesirable consequence of this is that military specialists lose experience.
A PPP allows the transparent and effective economic control of holding companies by agreements on objectives, incentive systems, contract management and participation controlling.	A PPP means losses of direct (ministerial) influence and control over previously subordinate areas (losses of technical and legal supervision under public law).
Private sector management and business alignment of PPP companies yield efficiency advantages for the Federal Government.	The profit motive of private partners in connection with diverging interests between public and private partners outweighs any possible efficiency advantages.

Assessment: An increase in the efficiency of mission accomplishment via PPPs?

Legislation and regulations stipulate unequivocally the cases in which a government service in general and also a military requirement in particular may be provided or met by a private company or via the instrument of a PPP: "(1) The principles of cost-effectiveness and economy must be observed during the drafting and implementation of the budget. These principles include the obligation to examine the extent to which government tasks and economic activities serving public purposes can be performed by means of outsourcing and denationalisation or privatisation. (2) Appropriate efficiency analyses must be conducted for all cash flow measures. [...] in suitable cases, private bidders must be granted an opportunity to show whether and to what extent they can perform government tasks or economic activities serving public purposes just as well or better (expression of interest procedure)" (Federal Budget Code *BHO – Bundeshaushaltsordnung,* section 7(1) and (2)).

The passages cited here emphasise two points: On the one hand, the Federal Government has the option of privatising a task if no specific legal provisions exist. On the other, it is not obliged to privatise or use the instrument of the PPP, even if the results of an efficiency analysis favour cooperative models. Efficiency analyses are no substitute for, and do not replace, (political) decisions; all PPP solutions of the Bundeswehr are ultimately nothing more than options. But they are desirable if increases in the cost-efficiency of task accomplishment can be expected.

There is a severe dispute within and outside the Bundeswehr over whether and to what extent the objective of increased cost-efficiency has really been attained with the PPP projects implemented to date, those involving service clothing, the civilian vehicle fleet, army maintenance and the recent modernisation of the Bundeswehr's IT. Reliable efficiency analyses and independent evaluation studies are not usually (publicly) available for PPP projects in the defence sector – a circumstance that is sadly true of other areas in the government sector as well and that may be partly responsible for the fact that so far no extensive empirical assessments of the economic value of PPPs from the point of view of the public sector have been carried out. The reasons for the difficulty of drawing "conclusions about the overall cost-efficiency of the PPP approach" (Beckers/Klatt, 2009: 334) range from the inadequate quality of data on costs, expenditure, quantities etc., to questions concerning the methods of conducting efficiency analyses (net present value method, cost-benefit analysis) and to sometimes questionable studies whose authors "have direct or indirect interests in the implementation of PPP projects" (ibid.).

The "new institutionalism" school of thought in economics and sociology can be quite useful for understanding modernisation in the Bundeswehr (see Richter/Portugall, 2008: 153 et seq.). The focus is increasingly on a neoinstitutionalist approach to the sociology of organizations (see Powell/Di Maggio, 1991).[2] Neo-

2 For the analysis potential of new institutional economics, in particular regarding transaction cost economics, see Williamson (1985); for the fundamentals of PPPs outside the defence department, see Mühlenkamp (2006).

institutionalism distances itself from the idea that internal optimisation processes trigger organisational change, but argues that external legitimacy pressure compels organisations to assume institutional elements from the environment. The central thesis of neoinstitutionalism is this: The emergence and stability of certain operational procedures and instruments (i.e. institutional elements) in organisations, whether private companies or the public administration, can increasingly be traced back to social influences and accepted notions of the effect of operational procedures and instruments on efficiency, rather than to their actual efficiency-increasing effect. Neoinstitutionalist approaches reveal that rules, operational procedures and instruments deemed to be rational in the environment are not adopted by organisations in the first instance because they can be used to optimise internal control processes and workflows in real economic terms, but because adopting these rules increases the legitimacy of the organisations in the social environment. If therefore – to apply this idea to modernisation in the Bundeswehr – the instrument of the PPP is used in the defence sector, its main function is perhaps that of meeting the institutional environment's expectations. In response to politicians and the public, the Bundeswehr can refer to the fact that it satisfies the requirements of a modern administration, as, with the institutional integration of private sector management competence and technical expertise as well as solidarity with industry, it is making every effort to more efficiently structure the provision of services and military procurement, and thus to save the tax-payer money.

The instruments and concepts of New Public Management (NPM), which also include privatisation concepts and PPPs, have been regarded in recent years as legitimate procedures and instruments for modernising administration at the national level as well (see Richter/Elbe, 2012: 267). In other words, the procedures and instruments have the status of 'rational myths' (Meyer/Rowan, 1983 [1977]), and their effectiveness depends on a divided belief in them, so that they cannot and need not be subjected to an objective examination. According to neoinstitutionalism, therefore, the increased use of PPPs in the Bundeswehr is founded less on the actual evidence of their cost-effectiveness – which, as shown above, has either not yet been produced or cannot (should not?) be produced – but on the assumption that business-like thinking in PPP companies, as well as modern private-sector management and accounting techniques, are superior to classic administrative practices in terms of efficiency and effectiveness.

As for the Bundeswehr PPPs to date, it can be claimed to a certain extent that the PPP approach was only adopted as a 'ritual' and that perhaps in spite of their real effect on efficiency, the projects implemented are designed in a way that is far removed from any private-sector business processes and market mechanisms. In the case of the modernised vehicle fleet, for instance, demand and supply monopolies diametrically oppose each other (Bundeswehr and BwFPS) and incentive mechanisms for promoting competition fail to take effect. In the case of the g.e.b.b., a 100-per cent subsidiary of the Bundeswehr provides advisory services exclusively for its own partner, the Bundeswehr, which is a member of its supervisory board – this does not allow for 'third-party transactions' with other federal ministries or the private sector. In the case of the BWI, BwFPS and the HIL, well over 50 per cent of the employees are members of the Bundeswehr with their corresponding professional biographies in the public sector and their corresponding backgrounds in administration. It is at least questionable whether and to what extent Bundeswehr PPPs can still satisfy general notions of privatisation at all.

Outlook: Expansion of privatisation?

The restructuring of the FMoD, as part of the current reorientation of the Bundeswehr, had also ensured that from April 2012 the technical tasks of modernisation, which had previously been split and performed by several civilian directorates and military staffs, can be integrated and performed in a single ministerial division. Above all, the merger of the function of a holding company and the respective controlling/accounting was overdue. Can one conclude from this reorientation of ministerial technical responsibilities that there will also be a privatisation policy renaissance in the Bundeswehr?

The last relatively extensive PPP project to be initiated concerned the IT modernisation programme and the founding of the BWI in 2006. Since then, no such extensive privatisation efforts have been observed. There are probably at least three reasons for this:

The 'low-hanging fruit' was already picked when the management of the vehicle fleet, clothing and IT was privatised. More extensive privatisations in the welfare and messing sectors, where potential for rationalisation could still be expected, have not yet been actively pursued by the agencies technically responsible for this. This is mostly due to the impossibility of employing the Bundeswehr's catering personnel in other areas.

PPP projects that have already been implemented have so far been unable to prove convincingly that they have led to any real cuts in the federal budget; instead, the criticism of the defence ministry's privatisation practice – for example, by the German SAI (*Bundesrechnungshof*) – is never-ending.[3]

3 Take the following example: Contrary to the vehicle fleet PPP's original objective of making the organisation processes more efficient by means of the transfer of knowledge and experience from the private sector and by the contribution of private-sector IT and project expertise, virtually the opposite seems to have occurred: namely, there has been an increase in interfaces and the persistence of bureaucratic procedures or patterns of administrative culture. The German SAI estimates that the administrative costs incurred by the Bundeswehr in connection with dual organisation of the availability of vehicles are 100 million euros per annum (Griephan-Briefe 28/11, of 11.07.2011: 4).

A major driving force behind modernisation projects– true to the spirit of sociological neoinstitutionalism – was the privatisation-friendly climate in the decade after 2000 and the spilling over of the NPM approach into the Bundeswehr. A Europe-wide, if not worldwide, counter-movement and the ebbing of the neoliberal wave of privatisation also dampened the euphoria for PPP projects in the Bundeswehr.

Nevertheless, there are still those who expect to see an expansion in privatisation activities in the Bundeswehr: 'Until now, modernisation projects that focused on service and administration tasks primarily comprised the fields of logistics, training, real estate affairs and administrative services. Within the future modernisation scheme, an integral approach will have to be pursued that also includes military support and core tasks in these analyses.' (Rieks, 2012: 175). In the end, however, more modest expectations of future cooperation between the Bundeswehr, industry and the private sector are more realistic. In the coming years, the priorities will be to consolidate projects implemented to date, strengthen the trusting cooperation between the partners in PPP projects[4] and evaluate the lessons learned by the partners in previous projects for the benefit of future projects.

Bibliography

Beckers, Thorsten/Klatt, Jan Peter (2009): Eine institutionenökonomische Analyse der Kosteneffizienz des PPP-Ansatzes. In: Zeitschrift für öffentliche und gemeinwirtschaftliche Unternehmen. Vol. 32, Issue 4, 2009: 325-338.

Bogumil, Jörg/Jann, Werner (2005): Verwaltung und Verwaltungswissenschaft in Deutschland. Einführung in die Verwaltungswissenschaft. Wiesbaden: VS Verlag.

Budäus, Dietrich (2003): Neue Kooperationsformen zur Erfüllung öffentlicher Aufgaben. Charakterisierung, Funktionsweise und Systematisierung von Public Private Partnership. In: Harms/Reichard (Eds.): 213–233.

Budäus, Dietrich (2006): Public Private Partnership – Kooperationsbedarfe, Grundkategorien und Entwicklungsperspektiven. In: ibid. (Eds.), 11-28.

Budäus, Dietrich (Ed.) (2006): Kooperationsformen zwischen Staat und Markt. Theoretische Grundlagen und praktische Ausprägungen von Public Private Partnership. Baden-Baden: Nomos.

Harms, Jens/Reichard, Christoph (Eds.) (2003): Die Ökonomisierung des öffentlichen Sektors: Instrumente und Trends. Baden-Baden: Nomos.

Helmig, Jan/Schörnig, Niklas (Eds.) (2008): Die Transformation der Streitkräfte im 21. Jahrhundert. Militärische und politische Dimensionen der aktuellen ‚Revolution in Military Affairs'. Frankfurt/ New York: Campus.

4 For details on the HERKULES project, see Portugall/Richter (2010).

Krampe, Thomas (2011): Privatisierung im Meinungsbild von Bundeswehrbediensteten. In: Die Bundeswehrverwaltung – Fachzeitschrift für Administration, Vol. 55, Issue 6, 2011: 127-132.

Leonhard, Nina/Werkner, Ines-Jacqueline (Eds.) (2012): Militärsoziologie – Eine Einführung, 2nd updated and extended edition, Wiesbaden. VS-Verlag.

Link, Stefanie (2010): Erstes Hochbauprojekt der Bundeswehr im Rahmen einer Öffentlich-Privaten Partnerschaft. In: Die Bundeswehrverwaltung – Fachzeitschrift für Administration, Vol. 54, Issue 5, 2010: 102-103.

Meyer, John W./Rowan, Brian (1983 [1977]): Institutional Organizations: Formal Structure as Myth and Ceremony. In: Meyer/Scott (Eds.): 21-44.

Meyer, John W./Scott, Richard W. (Eds.) (1983): Organizational Environments. Ritual and Rationality. Newbury Park: Sage.

Mühlenkamp, Holger (2006): Public Private Partnership aus Sicht der Transaktionskostenökonomik und der Neuen Politischen Ökonomie. In: Budäus (Eds.): 29-48.

Portugall, Gerd (2007): Die Bundeswehr und das Privatisierungsmodell der ‚Öffentlich-Privaten-Partnerschaft (ÖPP)'. In: Richter (Ed.): 141-158.

Portugall, Gerd/Richter, Gregor (2010): Project HERKULES: a living partnership? IT modernization of the German armed forces by PPP. In: Performance, Vol. 3, Issue 2: 22-27.

Powell, Walter W./DiMaggio, Paul J. (Eds.) (1991): The New Institutionalism in Organizational Analysis. Chicago: University Press.

Richter, Gregor (Ed.) (2007): Die ökonomische Modernisierung der Bundeswehr. Sachstand, Konzeptionen und Perspektiven. Wiesbaden: VS-Verlag.

Richter, Gregor (Ed.) (2012): Neuausrichtung der Bundeswehr. Beiträge zur professionellen Führung und Steuerung. Wiesbaden: Springer VS.

Richter, Gregor/Elbe Martin (2012): Militär und Verwaltung. In: Leonhard/Werkner (Eds.): 264-283.

Richter, Gregor/Portugall, Gerd (2008): Ökonomische Modernisierung von Streitkräften – Anmerkungen aus Sicht des ‚Neuen Institutionalismus'. In: Helmig/Schörnig (Eds.): 147-164.

Rieks, Ansgar (2012): Modernisierung in der Bundeswehr – Formen, Felder, Ausblick. In: Richter, (Ed.): 167-181.

Rieks, Ansgar/Keller, Hans-Dieter (2009): Modernisierung in der Bundeswehr. Wirtschaftliche Gestaltung einer Großorganisation. In: Die Bundeswehrverwaltung – Fachzeitschrift für Administration, Volume 53, Issue 6, 2009: 126-129.

Steuer, Arne (2012): Rechtliche und haushalterische Rahmenbedingungen für wirtschaftliches Handeln in der Bundeswehr. In: Richter (Ed.): 49-63.

Williamson, Oliver E. (1985): The Economic Institutions of Capitalism. Firms, Markets, Relational Contracting. New York/London: Free Press.

wt (2004): wt-Gespräch mit dem Leiter Kompetenzzentrum Modernisierung. In: wt, Zeitschrift für Wehrtechnik u. Verteidigungswirtschaft II, 2004, 84-86.

Part IV

Current debates in German defence

Public opinion, the Bundeswehr and public affairs

Jörg Jacobs

The Bundeswehr sees itself as an army in a democratic state, with a place at the centre rather than on the fringes of society. As such, it needs to gain support for the objectives of legitimised operations. At the same time, members of the Bundeswehr keep expressing a concern that the armed forces deployed on operations do not get enough support by the public and that they encounter reservations, scepticism and doubt in parts of society.

It therefore suits some worldviews that public opinion is often dismissed as unstable, unstructured and unfit for influencing political decision-making. Results of U.S. empirical research on attitudes conducted in the 1950s and 1960s suggested precisely that and led to the Almond-Lippman Consensus in attitude research. According to this mainstream view public opinion displays these very characteristics and is thus an unstable basis for a predictable foreign policy (see Holsti, 2004). George F. Kennan, the father of the containment policy, compared public opinion in the 1950s with a huge dinosaur in which impulses had to travel a long distance to get from the end of its tail to a small brain. However, once this animal perceives a threat, it reacts in an utterly uncontrollable and unforeseeable manner, ceasing to distinguish between friend and foe and destroying everything within its reach (see Nincic, 1992: 35).

The Vietnam War and the public reaction to it also initiated a change of thinking in the social sciences (see Kinder, 1983). Analysing results of research conducted on attitudes to security policy issues from the 1950s to the 1980s in the US, Robert Page and Benjamin Shapiro in 1992 developed the thesis of the Rational Public: They claimed that public opinion is a rational reaction to available information. This does not mean that people have an extensive knowledge about foreign and security policy matters. The opposite is true. A low degree of knowledge about this subject is accepted as an empirical fact. And it is this low level of knowledge in particular that leads to the conclusion that attitudes must derive from other mechanisms (Hurwitz/Peffley, 1987). As 'cognitive misers' (Conover/Feldman, 1984), or misers with cognitive (knowledge) resources, people seek out heuristic tools that allow them to cope with the limits of the brain's ability to process information in a complex environment. They may adopt positions that are held by recognised figures or parties or classify and rate issues according to values (see Kinder, 1983; Sniderman, 1993). Hurwitz und Peffley (1987) showed that attitude structures, that is to say, attitudes about policy positions derived from values and general orientations can always be found when a political issue has not yet received much attention and when people have only a low level of knowledge about it. With a minimum of effort, attitudes towards new political issues are derived from existing opinions and are thus 'rationalised' without any or little knowledge of the facts.

The Bundeswehr and the German public

Basic research on attitudes to foreign and security policy issues (see Rattinger/Holst, 1998; Jacobs, 1995) has only been conducted sporadically in Germany, but it seems to confirm the above mentioned findings for the U.S. One of the recent studies conducted by the Bundeswehr Institute of Social Sciences, for example, has shown that a majority of respondents admits to knowing little about Bundeswehr operations (see Fiebig, 2011). It is easy to name reasons for this lack of knowledge. On the one hand, the Bundeswehr operates in parts of the world that are physically and ideally far removed from the everyday lives of people in Germany. This is why people do not experience any direct threat that has to be countered. Furthermore, the consequences of the transformation of the Bundeswehr into a force ready to be employed out of area are unclear and somewhat eerie to many because until 1990, the imperative in Germany was to exercise military restraint. Then the motto was 'Be capable to fight so you won't have to fight'. This political guideline became scientifically systematised in the idea of the federation being a 'civilian power', which implied that it was in the country's interest to pursue only 'civilian' foreign and security policy (Maull, 2007). Finally, the political actors have difficulty explaining to people the imponderabilities and the rationale of (combat) operations abroad and the danger to life and limb that Bundeswehr personnel face during operational deployment. They also find it hard to explain why an achievement of civilisation – i.e. peaceful conflict resolution – should be given up in favour of military intervention. This problem is also due to an acceleration of rituals and processes of political communication on account of the digital revolution in the media, which leaves hardly any room for well-founded and detailed explanations.

One such example for the latter is the failure of the attempt to put the suspected atrocities of the war in Afghanistan into perspective by portraying the employment of the Bundeswehr as a 'technical emergency service with guns' (Naumann, 2008). The stark contrast between available information on deaths and injuries and the official portrayal of the situation resulted in a decline in public support for the deployment of the Bundeswehr in Afghanistan and nurtured doubts about the true situation on the ground. It may be possible to cover up political facts for a certain length of time, but the public will in the end uncover inconsistencies and then react even more vehemently.[1]

One look into the general idea the public has of missions out of area, however, helps to see the political logic of the arguments used for the portrayal of the mission in Afghanistan, with which the reality of events has caught up. There is agreement among the public that the task of the Bundeswehr is to defend Germany, and qualified majorities also speak out in favour of supporting the defence of NATO territory (see Figure 1). The public is also in favour of United Nations peacekeeping missions, which already received great support in 1991 and which more than three quarters of respondents have supported since 1999. There is contention, however, over combat missions, which in the following figure are shown with an indicator relating to support for 'peace-enforcement operations'. The indicator in Figure 1 does not measure the support for a specific operation, but the general attitude of the public towards combat missions. It shows that around half of the respondents are in favour of the Bundeswehr conducting combat missions, while the other half is opposed to it – even if the missions have a mandate given by the United Nations. It is notable that the respondents' answers to this question in particular have changed over the years: From 1991 to 2001, there was a continuous rise in the approval for combat missions. It is worth looking back at the high-profile military conflicts of the 1990s: The civil war and the disintegration of state order in Somalia, the genocide in Rwanda, the disintegration of Yugoslavia, the genocide in Srebrenica, the threat of civil war in Kosovo and in particular NATO's military intervention in Kosovo, which is considered a success – all of these events intensified the impression that international conflicts could be resolved by military action. Since 2001, however, other events have been likewise reflected in the public approval for combat missions, e.g. the situation in Iraq, which even today is still far from being a mission accomplished, despite the high-profile declaration issued by former US President George W. Bush that combat operations against the Iraqi armed forces were over. The influence of this conflict on the public emphatically shows the boundless effect of media coverage. Although no German soldiers were involved in the conflict, it was seen as an 'action of the West', which Germany considers itself to be a part of. The drop in the approval rate for combat operations in 2001 as well as the fluctuations in the period from 2001 to 2011 can be interpreted as a rational public reaction to the attitude and actions of the US administration and the international situation.

1 Abraham Lincoln put it in a nutshell: 'You can fool some of the people all of the time, and all of the people some of the time, but you can not fool all of the people all of the time.' Particular account is taken of this realisation in public affairs conducted by the government, the integral elements of which are truthfulness, credibility, transparency and reliability.

This suggests that the people are well aware that the US has the lead role in NATO.

Figure 1: Approval for types of Bundeswehr operations between 1991 and 2011 in per cent (percentages have been rounded)

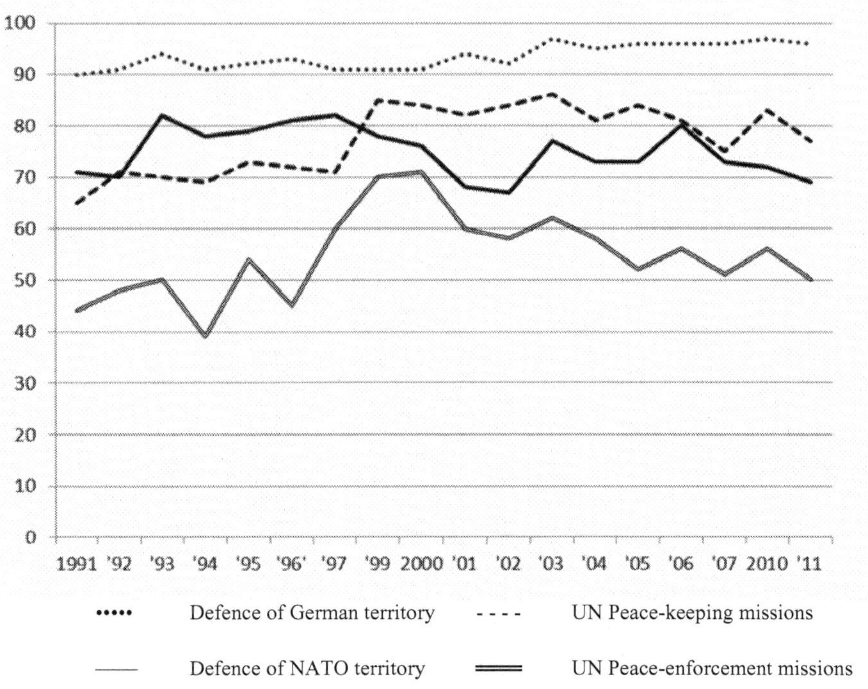

Sources: Data compiled on the basis of the following studies:
The Security Situation in 1990-2007, BACES 2009,
WDD 2011

Another important factor which has caused the decline in approval for combat operations is surely the Bundeswehr mission in Afghanistan. By 2009 the Federal Government seemed increasingly untrustworthy because it portrayed the mission in a way that did not reflect the public perception through media accounts of the conflict. Ever since the Bundeswehr suffered its first casualties, if not before, the mission in Afghanistan has been perceived by the public as an act of war. Even so, the Federal Government for a long time stuck to the wording of the United Nations mandate, which described the Afghanistan mission as a stabilisation mission, avoiding the use of the terms 'war' or 'soldiers killed in action'.

This position was not corrected publicly until a new minister of defence took office in 2009. Following an attack near Kunduz in 2010, in which three German soldiers were killed and eight were injured, both the former Federal Minister of Defence, Karl-Theodor zu Guttenberg (2009-2011), and Federal Chancellor Angela Merkel spoke of war – even though the operational situation of ISAF in northern Afghanistan was still qualified as an 'armed conflict under international law' (Federal Foreign Minister Guido Westerwelle in the German Bundestag on 10 February 2010).

It is this very chronology of reactions to events in Afghanistan that shows the particular adaptability and strength of a democracy. A democratic regime is able to counter and correct undesirable developments, whereas other political systems are hardly able to admit mistakes without endangering their sheer existence. Secondly, the analysis of these attitudes and the publicly displayed political positions clearly shows the primacy of politics, which applies to the German Armed Forces and the way they present themselves to the public. Thirdly, the Afghanistan mission particularly highlights how significant public legitimacy of political actions is as an effective element of checks and balances in a democracy.

In addition to approval for the tasks of the Bundeswehr and thus also for the functional dimension of the armed forces, surveys are regularly conducted on the public's general approval for the armed forces as a political and social institution in Germany. On the whole, the Bundeswehr is highly trusted as an institution by the public. Since 1999, at least 80% of the respondents have stated every year that they approve of the Bundeswehr. At the same time, the proportion of respondents who disapprove of the Bundeswehr fell below 20% in 2002 and even reached a record low of seven per cent in 2011 (see figure 2).

In a study conducted by the Bundeswehr Institute of Social Sciences in 2010, a significantly higher number of respondents stated that they trusted the Bundeswehr as an institution, compared to the Federal Government, the German Bundestag or the media. The Bundeswehr ranks third behind the Federal President and the Federal Constitutional Court in the support it has among the respondents. The training the Bundeswehr provides, its equipment and its reputation are also generally held in high regard by the public. No matter how surprising these results may seem at first glance, this phenomenon is in fact well known in political cultural research. Political institutions that are obviously involved in the 'dirty' business of day-to-day politics are significantly less trusted by the public than institutions that deal with fundamental matters and are therefore considered less political (see Pickel/Walz, 1998).

Figure 2: General disapproval of the Bundeswehr in per cent
(figures have been rounded)

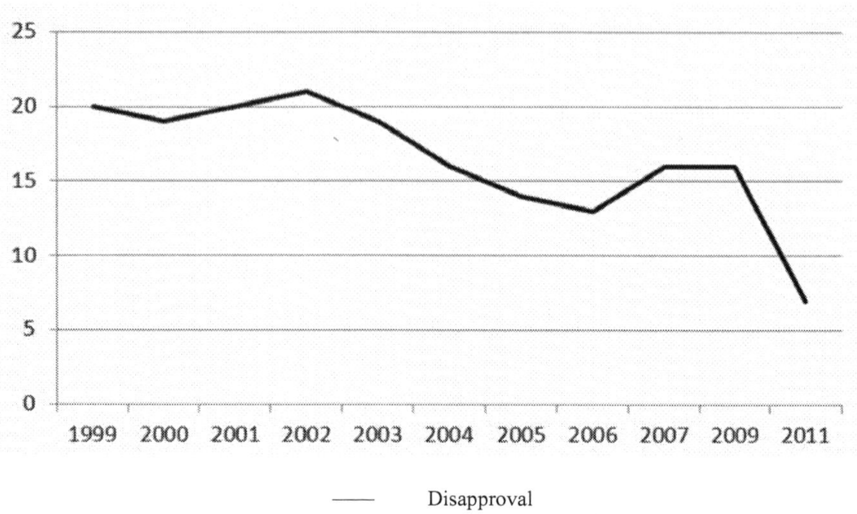

Sources: Data compiled on the basis of the following studies:
The Security Situation in 1990-2007, BACES 2009, WDD 2011-2007, BACES 2009, WDD 2011

The conclusion that can be drawn from this data is that the Bundeswehr is at present firmly embedded as an institution in the midst of our society. Whether this will remain the case in the future is an open question, considering that the Federal Government assigned new tasks to the Bundeswehr in its 2006 White Paper, including that of securing international trade routes and Germany's economic interests, and that the public believes that international interventions after 1990 have at best brought mixed results.

Bundeswehr and public affairs

After describing the attitude of the German public towards the Bundeswehr and its tasks, I now turn to the Bundeswehr's position on public affairs. It must initially be mentioned again that the Bundeswehr is an institution that reports to the Federal Ministry of Defence – and hence to the Federal Government. So the Bundeswehr has two motives for actively shaping its public affairs activities that are not always congruent. On the one hand, there is the short-term interest the Federal Government has in explaining its security and defence policy to the

German public and in explaining decisions. The aim of publishing information is ultimately to gain public support for current events and missions. On the other hand, there is the question of the legitimacy of the Bundeswehr as an institution. The Bundeswehr as an institution recognises the primacy of politics is under the control of the German Bundestag and sees itself as a democratic army in a democratic state. Members of the Bundeswehr are granted the privilege of being 'citizens in uniform', which influences the image the Bundeswehr has of itself. For this reason, public affairs activities serve to reassure society. They help to ensure that actions taken by the Bundeswehr not only are legal, but also enjoy a high degree of legitimacy.

One aim the Bundeswehr pursues is to provide information on the intentions and projects of the Federal Ministry of Defence as well as on the Bundeswehr's mission, tasks and operations. This is an element of the Federal Government's public affairs of the German armed forces and includes processing and analysing all aspects of security and defence policy and the Bundeswehr's missions and tasks, making them topics of public debate.[2] This debate is meant to promote trust in Germany's security and defence policy. The activities aim to stress to the public that the Bundeswehr upholds the basic principles of the free democratic order on the foundation of Germany's Basic Law, or *Grundgesetz*, as stated in Articles 87a and b of the Grundgesetz (The Federation shall establish Armed Forces for purposes of defence), Article 24 (… the Federation may enter into a system of mutual collective security), Article 26 (… a war of aggression … shall be unconstitutional) and Article 115a (state of defence). Public affairs activities not only serve to communicate the security and defence policy to the public, but are also intended to have an effect on the Bundeswehr itself, to contribute to the development of a corporate identity and to promote the image that members of the Bundeswehr have of themselves. The digital campaign 'We. Serve. Germany.' has given this intention a face since 2011 (www.wirdienendeutschland.de). The self-image is shown and communicated to the public in a tangible manner that is through portraits of motivated civilian and military Bundeswehr personnel. Instruments of digital public relations are used, tested and further developed, with a high degree of visualisation, short video statements and invitations to the public to engage in an online dialogue.

The introduction of virtual interaction and the harnessing of structural changes in the media environment lend new significance to the ability to listen. Up to now, media coverage could be assessed by evaluating a relatively static number

2 Public affairs activities by the government are based on a decision by the Federal Constitutional Court. In essence, the state's aim is to inform the public in such a manner as to allow people to form their own opinions on political issues (*see Federal Constitutional Court, 20: 56 [100]).*

of press releases compiled by a limited number of actors. Direct interaction with the public was confined to personal contacts or to recording telephone enquiries that were made and electronic or classic letters that were received. Personnel involved in public relations hence had time to ask the competent authorities for a reply and, after such a check, to convey this information back to the enquiring individual. Enquiries were sorted according to the numbers in which they were received and the subjects they addressed and were then included in the assessment of the information situation. There was no particular need to listen in order to give quick feedback. The development of the digital world significantly changed this situation. The monitoring of posts published in the digital world is rightly also referred to as social listening. The public affairs challenge is that the number of actors is increasing and that, in theory, an infinite number of 'citizen journalists' can contribute directly to the formation of opinions. A new challenge is the capability to distinguish volatile opinions, voices, moods, trends and basic positions in this multilogue and recognising which debates in the digital world have an effect on the real world. Secondly, the Internet is a fast-moving medium in which the numbers and types of sources can (still) change relatively quickly. For example, interest groups can form in social networks as a result of events and establish themselves as opinion leaders. The opposite can also happen, with established and recognised sources quickly losing significance because framework conditions or driving forces change or a source loses its credibility and integrity. To conduct targeted communication campaigns that is abreast of developments, it will therefore become increasingly important to ascertain published and public opinion by evaluating media coverage and opinion polls. Building on the assessment of the situation, the purpose of future research will be to develop communication strategies and plans for action that are in line with the directives issued by the Press and Information Office of the FMOD.

Structurally, public affairs are currently divided into media relations, public relations, security policy communication, publishing and troop information. The ultimate aim is to get through to people in Germany. Media relation is done to communicate specifically with the national and international public via journalists. Note that commanding officers and agency heads are responsible for ensuring this communication in their areas of competence and responsibility. Due to how the Bundeswehr conducts public affairs, it is possible to respond to events on a regional basis, for example, by drawing attention to fund-raising events in support of the German War Graves Commission in a specific region in the local papers.

Public relations activities target both the public and a select group of multipliers, and the methods used include distributing brochures, paying calls to units to provide them with information, or participating in trade fairs. Public relations activities are fundamentally only conducted in Germany and, in addition to the projects done by the Bundeswehr, the aim is to specifically portray the tasks, capabilities and assets of the services and major organisational elements of the Bundeswehr. Public relation is also promoted through political education seminars, the employment of 100 full-time youth officers[3] and meetings, seminars and events devoted to security policy topics.

Security and defence policy communication aims to establish a critical dialogue with the interested public. The explicit intention is to note suggestions, interests and attitudes of the public and to integrate these into the decision-making process. This communication also includes the provision of basic material, audio-visual and technical auxiliaries, as well as specialized literature.

Media relations are aimed at promoting a basic consensus on security policy in public communication by cooperating with media companies (e.g. in film projects). The Bundeswehr employs personnel to produce a monthly journal and a weekly paper, and to engage in online-communication (www.bmvg.de and www.bundeswehr.de). Troop information activities are primarily intended for the military personnel in the Bundeswehr, but they are also part of general information activities. While the Generalinspekteur in his capacity as Chief of Staff bears overall responsibility for troop information as corporate communication, the Press and Information Office of the FMOD is responsible for exercising control and functional supervision.

The Press and Information Office coordinates all of the FMOD's public affairs activities. The armed forces and the Federal Defence Administration employ full-time and part-time personnel to conduct public affairs, depending on the tasks that need to be performed. In order to ensure that adequate personnel can be provided, appropriate training is conducted on a centralized basis under the functional supervision of the Press and Information Office.[4] In the services and (civilian) major organisational elements, the press and information centres (PIC) are responsible for planning, controlling and conducting public affairs for the respective subordinate agencies. These PICs, which are under the direct technical control of the commander of the service or head of the agency to which they belong, give advice to their commander or agency head and are points of

3 The main task of the youth officers is to convey a basic understanding of security and defence policy, describe the mission and tasks of the Bundeswehr and provide a forum for discussion. In addition to the political experimental game POLIS, youth officers use lectures in school classes (by invitation) as a tool to enter into a dialogue on security and defence policy. Their tasks explicitly do not include recruitment or promotion for the Bundeswehr.

4 The Bundeswehr Academy for Information and Communication is the central training facility for personnel involved in public affairs and regularly conducts courses for public affairs officers and youth officers. It is at the same time a conference centre for the Bundeswehr and conducts seminars for so-called public multipliers such as teachers.

contact for the FMOD's Press and Information Office. The Joint Support Service, which is the military major organisational element in charge of performing the so-called common tasks of the Army, Air Force and Navy (for example, military police tasks), coordinates the Bundeswehr's national public affairs via its territorial commands for the Bundeswehr as a whole. In addition to the regional support they get from territorial commands, Bundeswehr entities with a strong public profile (e.g. Bundeswehr universities, Bundeswehr hospitals) design and conduct their own activities.

Conclusion and outlook

The philosophy of the soldier as a 'citizen in uniform' is as deeply embedded in the image that the armed forces have of themselves, as in the minds of the public. Despite public criticism of misconduct on the part of some members of the Bundeswehr, its current standing is a good basis for providing information on the politically-required changes to the Bundeswehr's mission and tasks in changed security and defence environment.

During times of change, the fact that the public tends to want to see non-military solutions for international conflicts is not necessarily a bad mechanism to control political actions. The public is certainly expected to legitimize military operations. Being palpable without being visible gives the armed forces credit and (critical) recognition from within the society. A Federal Government instrument whose job is to help resolve crises and conflicts could hardly attain a better position in an open society, and definitely not when, according to media system logic, it is bad news that makes the headlines. The challenge the Bundeswehr's public affairs activities is facing lies in the fact that the consequences of its politically desired transformation into a force ready to deploy out of area have not yet been fully realized by the society. Today, participation in international missions is a routine aspect of the military profession. Discussions on ethical questions concerning the military's use of unmanned aerial vehicles or new kinds of warfare in cyberspace are only now starting to reach broader parts of society. In the foreseeable future, public affairs activities will be shaped by the way the end of ISAF is evaluated, and if peace can be established in Afghanistan after the guns fall silent. With its public affairs policy, the Bundeswehr can react to the challenges posed by current developments beyond the short-term emotional response, since it can build on a solid foundation when it comes to explaining security and defence policy decisions made by the Federal Government and communicating the mission and tasks assigned to the Bundeswehr.

Bibliography

Conover, Pamela J./Feldman, Stanley (1984): How People Organize the Political World: A Schematic Model. In: American Journal of Political Science Vol. 28: 95-126.

Fiebig, Rüdiger (2011): Kenntnisse über die Auslandseinsätze der Bundeswehr. In: Thomas Bulmahn; Rüdiger Fiebig; Carolin Hilpert (Eds.): Sicherheits- und verteidigungspolitisches Meinungsklima in der Bundesrepublik. Forschungsbericht Nr. 94, Sozialwissenschaftliches Institut der Bundeswehr. Strausberg.

Holsti, Ole R. (2004): Public Opinion and American Foreign Policy. Revised edition. Ann Arbor: University of Michigan.

Hurwitz, Jon/Peffley, Mark (1987): How Are Foreign Policy Attitudes Structured? A Hierarchical Model. In: American Political Science Review, 81(4): 1999-1120.

Jacobs, Jörg (1995): Einstellungen zu out-of-area-Einsätzen der Bundeswehr und ihre zeitliche Stabilität. Unveröffentlichte Diplomarbeit, Universität Bamberg, Bamberg.

Kennan, George F. (1985): American Diplomacy. University of Chicago Press: Chicago. Kinder, Donald R. (1983): Diversity and Complexity in American Public Opinion. In: A.W. Finifter (Eds.): Political Science: The State of the Discipline. Washington: 389-425.

Maull, Hanns W. (2007): Deutschland als Zivilmacht. In: Siegmar Schmidt; Gunther Hellmann; Reinhard Wolf : Handbuch zur deutschen Außenpolitik. Wiesbaden: VS Verlag.

Naumann, Klaus (2008): Ein bisschen Verdummung der Wahlbürger. Interview on Deutschlandfunk, 02.02.2008.

Nincic, Miroslav (1992): Democracy and Foreign Policy – The Fallacy of Political Realism. New York: Columbia University Press.

Page, Benjamin I/Shapiro, Robert Y. (1992): The Rational Public: Fifty Years of Trends in Americans' Policy Preferences. Chicago: Chicago University Press.

Pickel, Gert/Walz, Dieter (1998): Demokratie- oder Politikverdrossenheit? Die Entwicklung des politischen Institutionenvertrauens und der politischen Unterstützung in der Bundesrepublik Deutschland seit 1989. In: Susanne Pickel; Gert Pickl; Dieter Walz (Eds.). Politische Einheit – kultureller Zwiespalt? Frankfurt a.M.: Peter Lang: 59-80.

Rattinger, Hans/Holst, Christian (1998): Strukturen und Determinanten außen- und sicherheitspolitischer Einstellungen in der Bundesrepublik. Abschlussbericht des DFG-Projektes. In: www.uni-bamberg.de/~ba6po5/forschung/publications/textband.pdf (accessed 14.09.2012).

Sniderman, Paul M. (1993): The New Look in Public Opinion Research. In: Ada W. Finifter (Ed.): Political Science: The State of the Discipline II, Washington: American Political Science Association: 219-245.

Between rejection of war and intervention fatigue – the armed forces, the state and society in Germany

Gerhard Kümmel

Civil-military relations and the political and democratic control of the armed forces is a recurrent theme that repeatedly features on the agenda of a 'political society' (Greven, 2009) – and rightfully so.[1] This issue's popularity is, however, subject to some fluctuation. During the phase of decolonialisation following World War II, for instance, the focus was on armed forces that no longer accepted political control and instead assumed political power themselves by doing what is widely feared, i.e. staging coups against governments (see Finer, 1962; Luttwak, 1979). Armed forces were then also examined in the context of 'defective democracies' (see e.g. Merkel, 2006) and their role in different 'waves of democratisation' (see e.g. Huntington, 1991; Diamond/Plattner, 1996; Krämer/Kuhn, 2006) as well as in connection with transformation processes after the collapse of the Soviet Union and the dissolution of its sphere of influence (see e.g. Gow, 1992; Bebler, 1997; Danopoulos/Zirker, 1998; Kuhlmann/Callaghan, 2000; Cottey/Edmunds/Forster, 2002; Lambert, 2009).

This led to an increased focus on a number of countries in other parts of the world where democratic control of the armed forces was still, or had again become, a problem (Croissant/Kühn, 2011). This included Western societies that were considered to be stable democracies. Particularly in the United States, this led to 'a recent, but brief, interlude of American self-doubt about the effectiveness of civil control in the United States' (Bland, 1999: 7). A research project focusing on the 'civil-military gap' headed by Peter Feaver and Richard Kohn (2001) concluded that this gap had increased to an alarming size in some areas.

Civil-military relations, i.e. the relationship between the armed forces, society and politics, are frequently a topic of political and public debate in Germany, too. In this context, it is worth noting the current discussion about the appropriate treatment of (foreign deployment) veterans in German society and the suggestion put forward by the current Federal Minister of Defence, Thomas de Maizière, to establish a veterans day. One should also note the continued and vehement complaints by Bundeswehr soldiers about the lack of support for soldiers and their deployments within German society and German politics (see e.g. Seliger, 2013).

The following article first develops the theoretical and conceptual foundations regarding the relationship between politics, society and the armed forces and

1 This article reflects the personal opinion of the author.

then outlines civil-military relations in Germany since the end of World War II. It proposes that the beginning and the end of this period can be described by rejection of war and intervention fatigue, respectively. For the sake of completeness, it should be added that the end point, which will also serve as the designation for this period, is by no means final but is instead still taking shape.

Theoretical considerations

In order to understand the relationship between the armed forces, the state and society from a theoretical and conceptual perspective, this article uses a system theory approach such as the one presented by Martin Edmonds (1990: esp. 113 et seq.). It initially defines the armed forces as a subsystem of the overall system of *society*. It is important to emphasise this because it means that the military is part of society without being identical to it. This military subsystem follows a specific system logic and differs from its system environment and other subsystems, which are in turn governed by other codes. It is indeed necessary 'for the armed forces to remain apart from society with distinctive organizational structure and culture or ethos in order to do its job' (Dandeker, 2000: 29). The French military sociologist Bernard Boëne describes this as 'military uniqueness' and turns his attention to the important question of how 'unique the military really is – and ought to be' (Boëne, 1990: 3). The answer he provides to his own question is nuanced and differentiated (Boëne, 1990: 58):

> If anything, it [his text, G.K.] has shown the subject of military distinctiveness to be a most complex issue. The answer varies according to whether the comparison runs in terms of social structure, recruitment, skill requirements, culture, lifestyles, degree of social and political integration into the parent society, legal status or any other trait.

In the end he affirms the existence of 'military uniqueness' because

> [t]here are (...) a few permanent, universal traits, related to the sacred character of war for any society, once it has embarked on such a course – obedience, loyalty, unlimited liability for service, a stronger degree of coercive institutional authority – as well as its violent nature (transgression of civilian taboos). (ibid.)

His British colleague Christopher Dandeker (1999: 85) agrees:

> The military is unique in the nature and extent of the demands it places upon its personnel. They are obliged to train to kill and to sacrifice self, to participate in a military community where one works, lives and socialises with other service personnel and, when, necessary, to respond to a 24-hour commitment with the risk of separation from family at short-notice.

In view of the special code of the military subsystem, it is not surprising that there is a difference in comparison to other subsystems, and in comparison to society as a system environment. One strand of the debate even focuses exclusively on this aspect. As early as the 19th century, sociologists such as Auguste Comte and Herbert Spencer pursued the idea of the fundamental incompatibility of armed forces with industrialised societies and assumed that an acceptance of this incompatibility would eventually become established not only in people's minds but also in everyday socio-political practice (see Wachtler, 1983). In the 1980s the German sociologist Wolfgang Vogt (1986a) followed up on this idea and reworded and radicalised it for the nuclear age. In an idealised construct, he described the incompatibility of civilian logic and military logic.

His assumption of incompatibility is thus primarily based on the development of nuclear weapons, while the reasoning of Comte and Spencer was primarily based on economic aspects and industrialisation theory. What all three authors have in common, however, is the inherent teleology of their thinking. Neither the incompatibility theorem – derived using different methods – nor the teleological style is, however, shared in this instance (see also von Bredow, 2000: chapter 5). Expressed in Vogtian terms, humanity will, as a result of persistent insecurity, continue to depend on military logic, as a prerequisite for civilian logic, for the foreseeable future. In addition, the juxtaposition of the military on the one hand and civilian society on the other as the long-standing *ex ante* version of the often cited picture of the military as a state within the state is hardly realistic from an empirical point of view, because there are various overlaps between the military and civilian society, aside from some differences. The existence of what in the American debate is referred to as the civil-military gap is therefore comparatively normal when seen in the context of the outlined systems theory approach because, as Ole Holsti (2001) observes, all occupational groups, albeit to different degrees, develop a specific group culture that is different from the culture of society in general. It follows that, regarding the civil-military gap, what matters is not whether it exists but rather *how large* this gap is.

The question of *how large* evidently involves some apprehension, which is based on what Peter Feaver (1996) has called the 'civil-military problematique'. This problem is by no means one of the recent past but has already caught the attention of quite a number of political thinkers, philosophers and politicians. It is rooted in two central and potentially conflicting principles. Firstly, 'the military must be strong enough to prevail in the society's wars' (Feaver, 1996: 151). And secondly, 'just as the military must protect the polity from enemies, it must also conduct its own affairs so as not to destroy the society it is intended to protect' (Feaver, 1996: 152). Armed forces must be effective in performing their function, they must be subordinate to the political authority of the state, and their size and hunger for resources must not place too great a demand on society.

The civil-military problem arises from societal processes of refinement, functional differentiation and specialisation. The trend towards a division of labour as an instrument of social development implies that a society, or the government selected by or imposed upon a given society, delegates the task of defence to some of its members. This segment of society is the armed forces (see also Creveld, 1991). As part of a larger society and as an instrument of a given government, the military has considerable powers that surpass those of the government. This raises the question as to why the armed forces should follow orders issued by civilians. Peter Feaver has referred to this as the civil-military challenge, which lies in the reconciliation of a

> military strong enough to do anything the civilians ask them to with a military subordinate enough to do only what civilians authorize them to do. This is a special problem of political agency: how do you ensure that your agent is doing your will, especially when your agent has guns and therefore may have more coercive power than you do? (Feaver, 1996: 149)

The issue, then, is one of civilian control over the military. Civilian control of armed forces is a fundamental question that all societies with a military face, irrespective of whether the political system or the government is democratic, monarchic, theocratic, autocratic or totalitarian. As civilian control initially says little about a society's degree of democratisation, the more normative term *democratic control* has been suggested for democratic states and states that are moving towards democracy (von Bredow/Kümmel, 2000: 126).

There is a fundamental consensus among democracies that the existence of armed forces requires institutions, mechanisms and instruments of political, democratic and social control of the military so as to prevent it from detaching itself from society and gradually becoming a 'state within the state'. This requires both 'hardware' and 'software', as Douglas Bland (2001: 525) has convincingly argued. According to his approach, the hardware of civilian control over the military includes aspects such as the enactment of pertinent laws, the rule of law, opting for a combined civil-military defence ministry, preferably with a majority of civilian personnel, the establishment of parliamentary control committees, and the appointment of a civilian defence minister.

Providing the hardware is generally quite simple. The software, however, is much more difficult to implement, as it concerns the way people think and may also require a change in established patterns of thinking. In more precise terms, the software of civilian control of the armed forces denotes the acceptance and internalisation of fundamental democratic ideas, values and principles in military environments, in the political culture, and in the defence establishment of a democracy. And this internalisation can only be successful if democratic principles are not only proclaimed but also implemented in everyday life and continuously renewed. Germany and the Bundeswehr are trying to put this into practice with Baudissin's concept of *Innere Führung* (leadership development and civic education), which has recently received harsh criticism from within the armed forces. Other armed forces follow the concept of the *citizen soldier*.

Thus far, civilian control of armed forces has primarily been discussed from a civilian perspective. The military perspective should not be ignored, however. For instance, the armed forces have a strong interest in limiting excessive influence from the civilian sphere, particularly by establishing mechanisms that prevent misuse of the military by political parties. In Michael Howard's (1957: 12) words, this is the problem 'of the control of a government in possession of such force [the armed forces, G.K.]'. In this sense, for example, the control of the Soviet armed forces by politicians would be seen as an unhealthy excess of political control (see Colton/Gustafson, 1989).

What can be said regarding a legitimate amount of civilian control, though, is that it evidently requires the approval and consent of the armed forces in order to be operational and effective. The military's 'voluntary and purposeful adherence to the principle of civilian control' is essential and even a prerequisite for functioning civilian control (Feaver, 1992: 253). This circumstance has also caused some unease because

> the civil authority has legitimacy, but the armed forces have the guns. (...) Even if the idea of civil control is embedded in the officer corps, one cannot avoid the conclusion that it resides there because officers accept it, not because the civil authority has imposed it (Bland, 2001: 529).

Bland therefore uses regime theory to propose that we understand civilian control of the armed forces as a regime of shared responsibility. Shared responsibility is based on the assumption

> that civil control of the military is managed and maintained through the sharing of responsibility for control between civilian leaders and military officers. Specifically, civil authorities are responsible and accountable for some aspects of control and military leaders are responsible and accountable for others. (Bland, 1999: 9)

Bland uses the term *regime* in the traditional sense as it is used by Stephen Krasner. Alternatively, to use the words of James Gow (1992: 27-32), one could also speak of a *social contract* between the soldiers and the socio-political community.

As decision making is a genuinely political undertaking, this also means accepting the armed forces as a political actor. Morris Janowitz (1971: LVI) has questioned the popular image of the military as a politically neutral instrument by referring to it as an 'effective pressure group' in this context. The armed forces expect to be appropriately consulted and to have their expertise taken into consideration, particularly with respect to decisions requiring the use of military force. If this does not happen, the armed forces can become estranged from the political leadership (see also Betts, 1991).

Ultimately, a regime of civil-military relations or, more precisely, of democratic civilian control of the armed forces can only be successful if all actors involved have a sufficient amount of trust and if they have internalised control mechanisms to some extent. However, speaking of trust also implies that uncertainty cannot be completely eliminated (see Luhmann, 1989). It may therefore be sensible to extend Bland's concept of a *regime of shared responsibility* because it primarily refers to the armed forces and civilian political authorities and therefore emphasises the political, administrative and *government* side of civilian control. The regime concept would also have to include society or parts of it (the interested public, the media, etc.), thereby adding a social component to civilian control, as is suggested in the work of James Gow. According to the theory of democracy, the government in a democratic system derives its legitimacy from society. It follows that 'the legitimacy of the military in relation to society (...) depends on societal acceptance of the military's role(s), and the military's ability to fulfil the demands of that role effectively' (Edmunds/Cottey/Forster, 2001: 8). This social acceptance and legitimacy of the military is an important basis for ensuring the success of military operations.

We thus return to the unease about the civil-military gap. Various approaches, instruments and mechanisms have been developed to improve this situation. In simplified terms, they can be assigned to two different schools of thought: The first is concerned about the military effectiveness and combat power of the armed forces, which make it necessary to 'protect' the military from society, as it were. The most prominent advocate of this approach is the American political scientist Samuel P. Huntington, who published his influential book 'The Soldier and the State' in 1957. Concentrating on the officer corps, he highlights the conflict-laden tension between society's desire to control the armed forces and the requirements of military security. He believes that this tension can be mitigated through objective civilian control. The concept of military professionalism with its components of military autonomy, political neutrality and voluntary submission plays an important role in this context.

The second school of thought takes a different approach and asks how society can be protected from the military. This is where the American sociologist Morris Janowitz plays an important role. In his classic work 'The Professional Soldier' (1971), he sees

> civilian control in terms of societal control rather than state or institutional control. State institutions play a secondary role as an extension of society, but societal control, measured in part as integration with society, was Janowitz's normative and empirical focus (Feaver, 1996: 166).

Nevertheless, Janowitz also includes the idea of professionalism in his concept, although unlike Huntington he was prepared to acknowledge a certain degree of inevitable politicisation of the military during the bipolar nuclear age of the international system (Janowitz, 1971: chapter 20). He also sees professional ethics as being dynamic and therefore changeable. The officer, according to Janowitz (1971: 420), is subject to civilian control not merely due to self-imposed professional standards, but also as a result of 'meaningful integration with civilian values'.

The recurring intellectual struggle between these two viewpoints is also visible in Germany. Here, one group is described as 'traditionalists' and the other as 'reformers'. This brings us to the empirical reality of civil-military relations in Germany.

From rejection of war to intervention fatigue: civil-military relations in Germany between 1945/49 and 2012

Following the end of World War II, Germany was at first demilitarised. On account of their participation in the war waged by National Socialist Germany and their involvement in the Holocaust, the German armed forces were held in disrepute in some parts of the population (on this and the following see von Bredow, 2000; Bald, 1994; 2005). Similar to post-war society in Japan, many Germans were drawn to pacifist ideals, so that the term *rejection of war* is an appropriate label for this phase. The rearmament of West Germany was a matter of course for the political leadership under Federal Chancellor Konrad Adenauer. The intention was to return as an (almost) equal member in the concert of the powers, which in turn implied equipping oneself with the appropriate attributes of power, including military assets.

It was ultimately the global political situation and particularly the outbreak of the Korean War that led to the far-reaching realisation of this plan and allowed West Germany to once again maintain regular armed forces by the mid-1950s. West German society found itself divided into two factions. The 'Without Me' movement was strongly opposed to the remilitarisation of Germany. Across society as a whole, there were slightly more opponents than supporters of rearmament. An opinion poll conducted in February 1955 showed that 42% of West Germans were in favour of rearmament, while 39% were opposed to it (Noelle/Neumann, 1956: 366). However, due to the prevailing anti-communist sentiment of the day, the arguments calling for an independent defence capability vis-à-vis the 'Eastern bloc' gained increasing attention. Support for the Bundeswehr grew. While 43% of West Germans were still calling for the disbandment of the Bundeswehr in October 1956, this figure dropped to 30% by February 1957 and to 23% by July 1961 (Noelle/Neumann, 1965: 470). Outside Germany, the notion of a communist threat from the East also convinced the Western powers to approve the creation of one of the largest armies in Europe as well as its membership in the Western European Union and the North Atlantic Treaty Organisation. West Germans, however, remained opposed to the acquisition of nuclear weapons (see Figure 1).

Figure 1: "Should the Bundeswehr have nuclear weapons?"

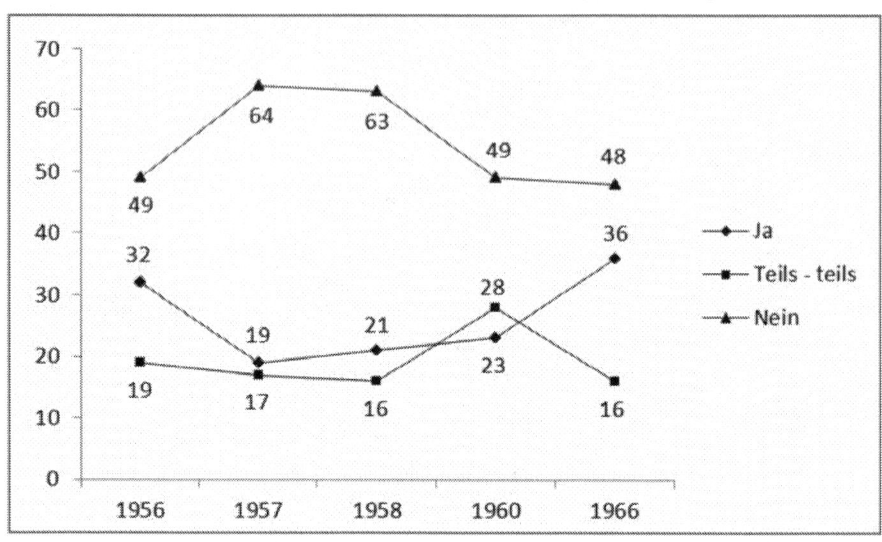

▷ yes ← partly ▲ no

Sources: For the years 1956-1960: Noelle/Neumann, 1965: 471. For the year 1966 with a differently-worded question: Noelle/Neumann, 1967: 300.

The armed forces of West Germany were to be distinctly different from the German military of the past (see Nägler, 2010). They were therefore bound to the constitution as well as to the United Nations Charter. The constitution aimed at establishing political and democratic control of the armed forces and at ensuring their social 'compatibility', a project that was fostered by developments in the 1960s (1968 protests). Institutional measures were taken, such as the creation of the office of the Parliamentary Commissioner for the Armed Forces, in other words a parliamentary ombudsman who acts as a point of contact for every soldier (see Schlaffer, 2006), and the creation of the office of a commissioner for education and training in the Bundeswehr. On the other hand, a conscious decision was made not to introduce military jurisdiction. General Wolf Graf von Baudissin lay the foundations for this reform project with his concept of *Innere Führung* and the principle of the *citizen in uniform, drawing* on early concepts such as the idea of the citizen soldier in the United States and on ideas found in Prussia in the early 19th century which were taken up by military reformers such as Scharnhorst and Gneisenau (Bredow, 2008:124). The Himmelrod Memorandum of October 1950 underlined the necessity to embed the Army within a democratic society, in other words the compatibility of the military with democracy, and the perception of the soldier as a human being with unalienable democratic rights. This led to a more cooperative and less directive-based approach to leadership in the armed forces (Ebeling/Seiffert/Senger, 2002; Dörfler-Dierken, 2005). The concept of Innere Führung is thus rightly considered one of the most innovative and creative developments of the Federal Republic of Germany, the significance of which is comparable to that of the economic and social concept of the social market economy (Bredow, 2008: 125).

The concept of Innere Führung, however, was controversial from the very beginning. While the 'reformers' saw it as the tool to firmly establish the armed forces in the democratic system, the 'traditionalists' feared that this 'corporate philosophy' might ultimately undermine military effectiveness. Disputes over this issue have accompanied the Bundeswehr throughout its history and are still encountered today (see e.g. Linnenkamp/Lutz, 1995; Prüfert, 1998; Opitz, 2001; Wiesendahl, 2005).

Figure 2: Attitudes toward conscientious objection in West Germany

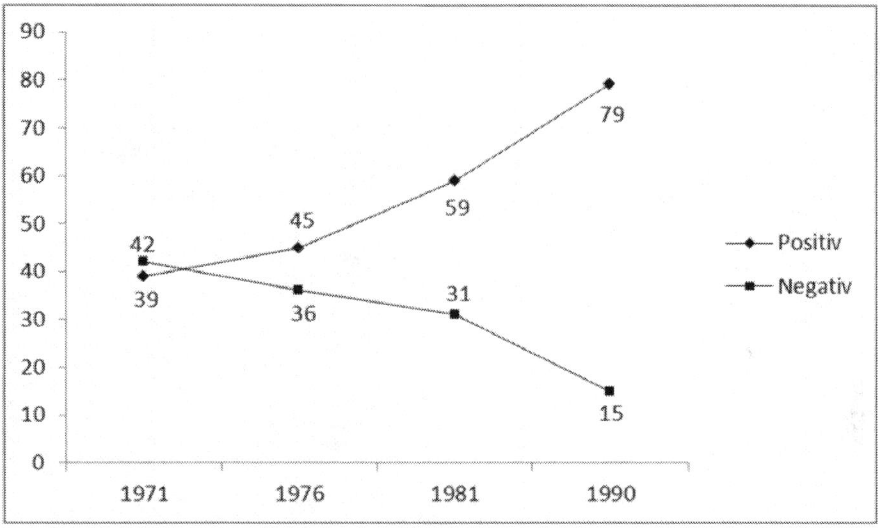

▷ positive ← negative

Source: Noelle-Neumann/Köcher, 1993: 1057.

In addition, mandatory academic studies for officers at Bundeswehr universities in Munich and Hamburg were introduced, as was the institution of conscription, which – because of conscientious objection – was never universal. Although conscientious objection was not acknowledged by society in the beginning (see Noelle/Neumann 1974: 499), the number of applications by conscientious objectors has continuously risen since the 1970s. Shortly after this, German society increasingly began to accept conscientious objection to service involving the use of arms (see Figure 2).

This came about not only because of domestic reasons but also because of developments in the field of security policy and military strategy: NATO's strategy of *massive retaliation* was replaced with a *flexible response* strategy. More flexible military responses, however, led to a pluralisation and diversification of military instruments, i.e. weapons. One of the most important security-policy debates in Germany, in NATO, and in Europe in the late 1970s and early 1980s was about the stationing on European and German soil of American medium-range nuclear missiles (cruise missiles and Pershing II), which would allow for a more flexible response.

Figure 3: Attitudes toward the stationing of cruise missiles and Pershing II missiles in Germany

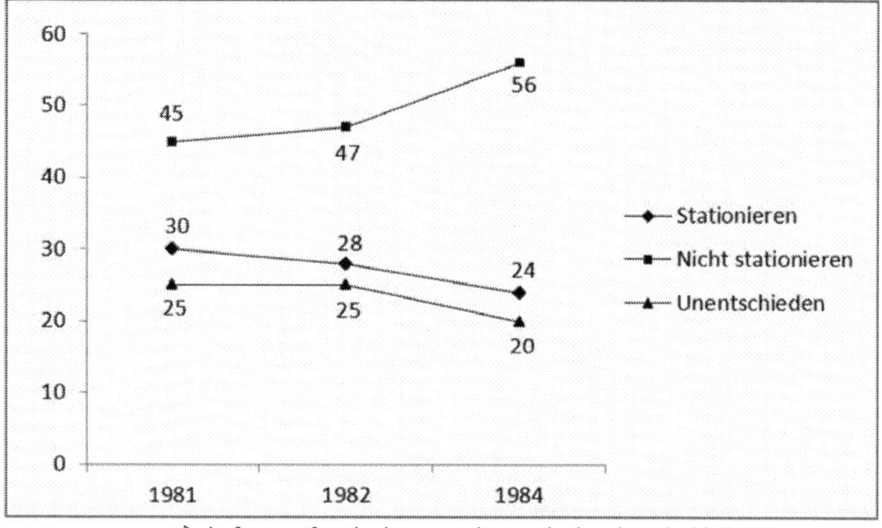

▷ in favour of stationing ← against stationing ▲ undecided

Sources: Noelle-Neumann/Piel, 1983: 633; Noelle-Neumann/Köcher, 1993: 1064.

Since, in a worst-case scenario, the two Germanys would have been a battlefield without a chance of survival, the number of opponents of stationing was twice as large as the number of supporters (see Figure 3). As a result, the peace movement became a relevant political force that staged mass protests, and a new political party (*Die Grünen*) was founded.

Interestingly enough, social opposition was directed primarily against military strategy and nuclear weapons and not so much against the German armed forces. Social acceptance of the Bundeswehr even increased (see Figure 4).

Figure 4: Attitudes toward the Bundeswehr in West Germany

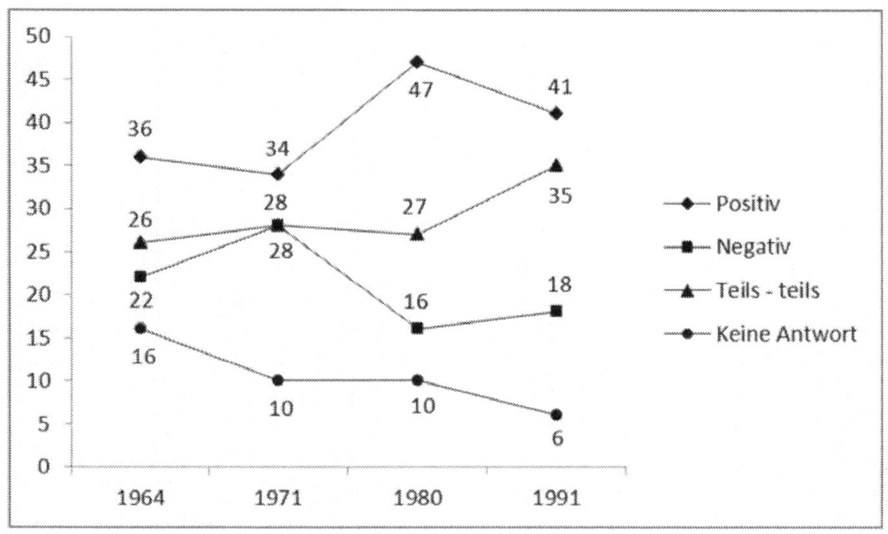

▷ positive ← negative ▲ of divided opinion ↑ did not respond

Source: Noelle-Neumann/Piel, 1983: 325; Noelle-Neumann/Köcher, 1993: 1060.

When Mikhail Gorbachev entered office, relations between the two superpowers relaxed in the 1980s thanks to his policies of *perestroika* and *glasnost*. As a result, no less than 65% of West Germans in 1987 believed that further rapprochement between the US and the Soviet Union was likely (Noelle-Neumann/Köcher, 1993: 1065).

Civil-military relations in Germany were rebalanced following the implosion of the Soviet Union and the connected collapse of the bipolar world order, i.e. the disappearance of the conflict that had long characterised international relations. In addition, the old world order was not replaced by a similarly bipolar and antagonistic one. As a result of these circumstances, Germany was reunited and the National People's Army of East Germany was integrated into the Bundeswehr (see Biehl/Bulmahn/Leonhard, 2003). This alone put the question of civil-military relations onto the agenda in Germany.

In addition, the end of the East-West conflict meant losing the 'enemy' and Ulrich Beck's notion of a 'state without enemies' (1993) was discussed in Germany and abroad. Against this backdrop, countries throughout the world made reductions in their armed forces and in armament programmes. Defence expenditures dropped, bases were closed, and armed forces were reduced (see e.g. IISS, 2003: 335 et seq.). The consequences for civil-military relations are obvious, because this leads to a reduction of what James Burk (2001) referred to as 'the institutional presence' of the military. This means that the presence and visibility of the armed forces for society will decrease across the country. These findings are important today, too, as the Bundeswehr will be dramatically downsized, with bases being closed in large numbers due to reorientation of the Bundeswehr, an almost Herculean task.

This could, however, enlarge the social distance between the armed forces and society, which is accentuated by socio-cultural changes in Western societies and therefore also in Germany. These processes affect the normative structure of these societies. Ronald Inglehart (1977), for instance, argues in his classic study 'The Silent Revolution' that the values of modern societies are changing from materialistic to post-materialistic ones. This corresponds with Ulrich Beck's (1986) analysis of the risk society, which is characterised by long-term processes of individualisation. Gerhard Schulze (1992), however, speaks of an experience-oriented society which is characterised by hedonism and seeks fun. Others, in turn, speak of the creation of a post-modern society with increasingly relativistic leanings (Boëne, 2000: 16).

The effects of these social and cultural changes on the military may be profound, as they go hand in hand with an increasing discrepancy between military and civilian value systems. While armed forces value authority, obedience, duty, community, comradeship, discipline, patriotism and the willingness to give one's life for the community, civilian life emphasises values such as individualism, self-fulfilment, autonomy, cosmopolitanism, and 'taking' instead of 'giving' (Wiesendahl, 1990). In the end, the fear is that this could lead to a growing gap between large parts of society and the armed forces.

International relations after the end of the East-West conflict initially developed in a similar way. The loss of the 'enemy' – 'encircled by friends' – nurtured hopes for a harmonic and peaceful world order under the aegis of the United Nations. In such a world, Germany could act as the prototype of a 'civilian power' (see Kirste/Maull, 1996). It is therefore no coincidence that between 1984 and 1990/1991, the number of people who believed that Germany continued to need armed forces decreased from 75 to 57 per cent (Noelle-Neumann/Köcher, 1993: 1050).

After the fall of the Berlin Wall and the Iron Curtain, however, it quickly became clear that military conflicts and wars would continue to be part of international relations. Since the early 1990s, old conflicts have re-emerged and new ones have developed, some of them violent. With this, war has again become an aspect of everyday life in Western democracies, including in Germany.

With its foreign, security and defence policy, a reunited and now fully sovereign Germany tried to adapt to the changed international environment, and to appropriately respond to the associated risks and challenges, with a more global approach. During this process, four events were of decisive significance: the Gulf war, the war in the Balkans, Somalia, and the attacks of 11 September 2001 (see also Schwab-Trapp, 2003; Florack, 2005).

The conservative-liberal government under Kohl and Genscher did not participate militarily in the US-led Gulf War of 1990/91 against Saddam Hussein's

Iraq; it did, however, bear a large part of the operation's financial cost. Nevertheless, this triggered a discussion about military participation by Germany in international missions. Ethnic cleansing in the Balkans and the precarious human rights situation in Somalia fuelled this debate in German politics and society. In the course of this debate, remarkable changes of opinion have occurred in circles that were previously critical of the military and of operations abroad; both the peace movement and the environmental party the Greens had controversial discussions about the use of force to end violence; many refused to rule this out completely. Opinion polls from these years show that a majority of Germans not only accepted that Germany had to assume more responsibility at an international level but were also increasingly open to the idea of Bundeswehr participation in United Nations missions, for instance to monitor compliance with ceasefire agreements (Juhász, 2001). The terrorist attacks of 11 September 2001 on the Twin Towers and the Pentagon transported war (back) into the supposed 'zones of peace' and underlined how essential armed forces are to any foreign and security policy, and thus also to German foreign and security policy (see Jäger, 2011).

At the end of a tedious process that was often accompanied by intensive social and political discussions, Germany showed its willingness to assume more international responsibility and to play an active role. It would, in other words, modify its 'culture of restraint' (see Duffield, 1998), and this included a willingness to deploy the Bundeswehr in traditional peacekeeping operations and beyond. As a consequence, German soldiers participated not only in the UN mission in Somalia but also in the UN-mandated peace enforcement mission in Bosnia, in the self-mandated NATO peace enforcement mission in Kosovo, and in the ISAF mission in Afghanistan. The relevant constitutional issues (regarding the different positions of the parties on this matter, see Duffield, 1998: 173 et seq.) had been settled by the German Constitutional Court, which confirmed the legality and constitutional conformity of such military participation by Germany.

This development was fostered by the concomitant creation and development of an international community of responsibility based on cosmopolitan ideas and human rights. This community is committed to a – selectively applied – *Responsibility to Protect* (ICISS, 2001) and has a military component as well, namely humanitarian interventions (see Münkler, 2002; Kümmel, 2010b; Jäger/Beckmann, 2011). As a result, the number of soldiers deployed on operations abroad has increased dramatically since the beginning of the 1990s (see Figure 5).

Figure 5: Soldiers deployed on missions abroad, 1980–2002

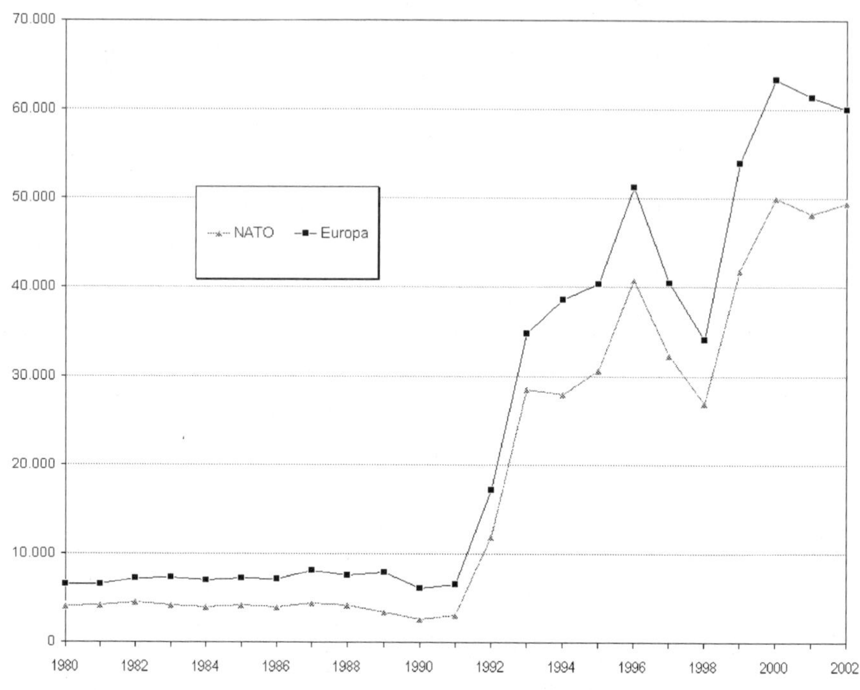

Source: Werkner, 2004: 10.

Nevertheless, the German public still has reservations about the use of military force. While almost two thirds (64%) of Germans in 1993, for example, thought peacekeeping should be a task of the Bundeswehr, only about one third (35%) were in favour of peace enforcement operations (Noelle-Neumann/Köcher, 1993: 1146). The fact that there is more acceptance in German society for humanitarian, peacekeeping and international disaster relief operations than for peacemaking and peace enforcement missions is a stable, coherent trend and is characterised by the amount of kinetic violence encountered in an operation. Table 1 gives a detailed overview of public opinion in 2007.

In this context, it should be mentioned that German public opinion about the mission in Afghanistan, which began as 'robust' and is now even referred to as 'war,' is becoming increasingly critical. The percentage of Germans who consider the mission a success decreased from 39 to 30% from 2007 to 2010 (Bulmahn, 2011b: 56). Opinions between 2008 and 2010 on various associated issues are shown in Table 2.

Table 1: Attitudes towards task areas of the Bundeswehr abroad in 2007

Question: 'What tasks do you think the German armed forces should assume abroad? Do you agree that the Bundeswehr should perform the following tasks, or do you disagree?' (Figures in per cent)				
The German armed forces should be deployed abroad in order…	Agree[1]	Agree in part	Dis-agree in part	Dis-agree[2]
to provide victims of natural disasters with food and medical relief.	83	13	2	2
to evacuate German citizens from crisis areas.	71	21	5	3
to prevent a terrorist attack on Germany.	66	23	7	4
to free German citizens who have been kid-napped.	66	23	6	5
to help a NATO ally that has been attacked.	54	31	9	6
to prevent genocide.	54	30	10	6
to stabilise the security situation in a crisis re-gion in Europe	52	33	10	5
to participate in the fight against international terrorism.	46	31	13	10
to prevent the proliferation of weapons of mass destruction.	45	30	14	11
to ensure Germany's access to energy and raw materials.	45	25	16	14
to monitor and protect international sea transport.	42	36	13	9
to protect free and unimpeded world trade.	39	35	14	12
to prevent countries such as Iran from develop-ing nuclear weapons.	38	24	20	18
to prevent drug cultivation and drug traffick-ing.	33	25	23	19
to assist democratic election processes.	32	33	18	17
to stabilise the security situation in a crisis re-gion in the Middle East.	31	31	10	18
to stabilise the security situation in a crisis re-gion in Africa.	27	34	22	17
to remove a foreign government that has vio-lated human rights.	26	22	23	29

Comments:

1) Percentages of 'Totally agree' and 'Largely agree' have been combined.

2) Percentages of 'Totally disagree' and 'Largely disagree' have been combined.

Source: Bulmahn, 2008: 93.

Table 2: Expected effects of the deployment of the Bundeswehr to Afghanistan 2008–2010

Question: 'In your opinion, how has the participation of the Bundeswehr in the United Nations Security Assistance Force in Afghanistan (ISAF) affected the following areas?' (Figures in per cent)

	2008	2009	2010	Diffe-rence 2008-10
Reputation of Germany in the Western world	65	62	58	-7
Work of international relief organisations in the region controlled by the Bundeswehr	67	60	56	-11
Living conditions of people in the theatre of operations of the Bundeswehr*	61	59	52	-9
Security situation in the theatre of operations of the Bundeswehr in northern Afghanistan**	56	49	45	-11
Stability in the entire region	55	50	44	-11
Reputation of the Bundeswehr in Germany	54	49	43	-11
Fight against international terrorism	47	45	38	-9
Afghanistan's chances to become a free, secure and prosperous country	42	44	35	-7
Fight against the cultivation of drugs in Afghanistan	29	33	27	-2
Germany's reputation in the Islamic*** world	39	33	27	-12
Security situation in Germany	31	27	22	-9

Comments:

*: 2008 and 2009: in the region controlled by the Bundeswehr

**: 2008 and 2009: in the region controlled by the Bundeswehr in northern Afghanistan

***: 2008 and 2009:in the Arab world

Source: Bulmahn 2011b: 55.

In 2010 a clear majority of Germans, i.e. 54%, called for the Bundeswehr to withdraw from Afghanistan immediately (Bulmahn, 2011b: 57) and a certain *intervention fatigue* pervaded Germany, which brings us to the description of the second key element of the time period we are looking at. A similar development can also be observed to a certain extent in other European countries (Biehl et al. 2011).

This has not affected the fact that, on the whole, Germans have a positive attitude towards the Bundeswehr. Almost 90% of respondents to the annual poll by the Bundeswehr Institute of Social Sciences stated in 2009 and 2010 that they in general have faith in the Bundeswehr, thus ranking it second among all public institutions and organisations. The same holds true for the ranking of public institutions and organisations with regard to the fulfilment of tasks (Bulmahn

2011a). Since 1998, between 80 and 86% of Germans have shown a positive attitude towards the Bundeswehr (Figure 6).

Figure 6: Attitudes towards the Bundeswehr, 1997–2010

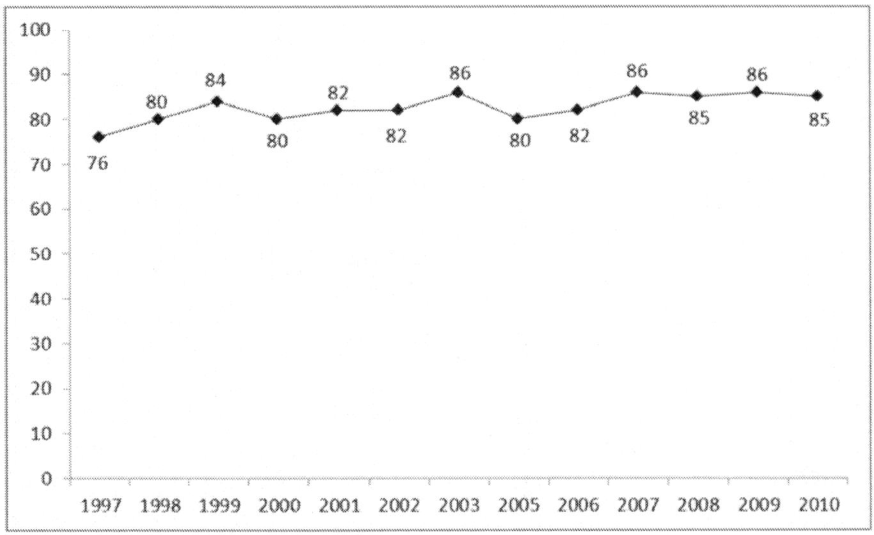

Source: Bulmahn/Fiebig, 2011: 67.

In Germany, too, the trend was thus confirmed that the armed forces are generally appreciated and there is by no means a lack of support in German society for the Bundeswehr and its soldiers (see also Biehl/Fiebig, 2011). At the same time, however, their missions are receiving more critical scrutiny and the willingness of individuals to join the armed forces is receding. Recruitment is thus becoming a central and yet ever more difficult task for the Bundeswehr (see also Bulmahn et al. 2010), also on account of the 'aging' of German society (Apt, 2009) and the suspension of conscription.

Conclusion

Civil-military relations in a country are the result of the interrelationship between the government, society and the armed forces in the context of a given international constellation. If we consider civil-military relations in Germany during the time period studied here, the following can be said:

Firstly, the international context has changed considerably. An antagonistic bipolar world order that was largely determined by state actors has given way to a turbulent world order characterised by globalisation processes in which non-state and transnational actors are becoming more and more important, for better or for worse. As a result, demands on the government, the armed forces and society in Germany have changed.

Secondly, since 1989/90 German political leaders and German society have sufficiently addressed the pros and cons of globalisation in socialisation and learning processes that have not always been easy or straightforward. In principle, they recognise that, in times like these, the defence and security policy of a country like Germany requires a global orientation; that the armed forces do have an important role to play, and that Germany must as a result be a military power (Kümmel, 2005). Amending and reversing what Klaus Naumann (2008) once said, there is in politics and society an acknowledgement of the 'political need for a military'.

Thirdly, a clear change in the function of the German armed forces has taken place as a result of changes in international relations. During the East-West conflict, the Bundeswehr was an armed force that was established, equipped, organised and trained to deter a possible attack by the Eastern Bloc and, if this failed, to defend the country. 'Being prepared for combat so as to avoid needing to fight' was the name of the game. In an age of nuclear weapons, however, we must remember that the threshold from a conventional to a nuclear war could have been crossed quickly. It was thanks to the – at times precarious – functioning of bilateral nuclear deterrence that operations had a theoretical quality for the Bundeswehr until 1989/90. With the collapse of the Soviet Union and the end of the East-West conflict, the image of the enemy lost its clarity and mutated into an amorphous and vague idea of security, which diffused into other areas and finally evolved into a global risk society, with both pre- and post-Westphalian characteristics (Kümmel, 2010b: 166). For the armed forces, this meant transition towards an army geared towards operations abroad ('form follows function') and an extended task spectrum, which Däniker (1992) expressed in his description of the soldier as a '*miles protector*'. Other authors mention non-traditional and hybrid roles of armed forces and their soldiers (Kümmel, 2003; Kutz, 2006; Haltiner/Kümmel, 2009), which armed forces and thus also the Bundeswehr have attempted to reflect in smaller, more flexible and modular high-tech forces of volunteers and professionals (Dandeker, 1999).

Fourthly, this diversification of tasks and roles within the military organisation and with respect to the soldiers themselves also implies a redefinition and rebalancing of the question as to the 'limits of the military' (Hammerich/Hartmann/Rosen, 2010) and the limits of politics (see also Strachan, 2006). Or, to use the words of Klaus Naumann (2010): 'How much political responsibility for the military elite' is appropriate and necessary at present and in the future?

Fifthly, reservations about the Bundeswehr that have existed in large parts of German society since the early years of the Bonn Republic and the attitude described above as a 'rejection of war' have been overcome. The Bundeswehr is now broadly accepted in German society and has thus essentially become part of normal life, as far as this is possible in view of Germany's history. Germans display almost overwhelming approval of the Bundeswehr. It is trusted and perceived as necessary, and Germans are willing to provide the Bundeswehr with at least sufficient resources. Actively taking part in person, however, is usually out of the question for most people. This is what Charles Moskos (2000: 15) means when he describes the position of Western societies towards their armed forces as 'indifferent.'

Finally, the German public has stronger reservations about military operations than about the armed forces as an institution. Now that it has gradually become clear that expectations regarding the deployment of armed forces were exaggerated (see e.g. Geldenhuys, 1998; Jett, 2001), German society is currently experiencing a certain degree of intervention fatigue (see also Kümmel, 2012). There is, however, no reason to complain about this situation. In fact, intervention fatigue can be seen as an expression of a society's democratic maturity because it shows that this society is asking significantly more questions about the reasons for, legitimacy of, and rationale behind military operations.

Bibliography

Apt, Wenke (2009): Trends in Demographie und Gesellschaft: Auswirkungen auf Streitkräfte und militärische Rekrutierung. In: Kümmel (Ed.) (2009): 127-155.

Bald, Detlef (1994): Militär und Gesellschaft 1945-1990. Die Bundeswehr der Bonner Republik. Baden-Baden: Nomos.

Bald, Detlef (2005): Die Bundeswehr. Eine kritische Geschichte 1955-2005. Munich: Beck.

Bebler, Anton A. (Ed.) (1997): Civil-Military Relations in Post-Communist States. Westport/London: Praeger.

Beck, Ulrich (1986): Risikogesellschaft. Auf dem Weg in eine andere Moderne. Frankfurt am Main: Suhrkamp.

Beck, Ulrich (1993): Der feindlose Staat. Militär und Demokratie nach dem Ende des Kalten Krieges. In: Unseld (Ed.) (1993): 106-122.

Betts, Richard (1991): Soldiers, Statesmen, and Cold War Crises. New York: Columbia University Press.

Biehl, Heiko/Bulmahn, Thomas/Leonhard, Nina (2003): Die Bundeswehr als Armee der Einheit: Eine ambivalente Bilanz. In: Kümmel/Collmer (Eds.) (2003): 199-228.

Biehl, Heiko/Fiebig, Rüdiger (2011): Zum Rückhalt der Bundeswehr in der Bevölkerung. Empirische Hinweise zu einer emotional geführten Debatte (SOWI.Thema 01/2011): Strausberg: SOWI.

Biehl, Heiko/Fiebig, Rüdiger/Giegerich, Bastian/Jacobs, Jörg/Jonas, Alexandra (2011): Strategische Kulturen in Europa. Die Bürger Europas und ihre Streitkräfte. Ergebnisse der Bevölkerungsbefragungen in acht europäischen Ländern 2010 des Sozialwissenschaftlichen Instituts der Bundeswehr (SOWI-Forschungsbericht 96): Strausberg: SOWI.

Bland, Douglas L. (1999): A Unified Theory of Civil-Military Relations. Armed Forces & Society, 26: 1, 7-26.

Bland, Douglas L. (2001): Patterns in Liberal Democratic Civil-Military Relations. Armed Forces & Society. 27: 4, 525-540.

Boëne, Bernard (1990): How 'Unique' Should the Military Be? A Review of Representative Literature and Outline of a Synthetic Formulation. European Journal of Sociology. 31, 3-59.

Boëne, Bernard (2000): Post-Cold War Trends in the Civil Control of Armed Forces in the West. In: Kümmel/von Bredow (Eds.) (2000): 11-31.

Boëne, Bernard/Bredow, Wilfried von/Dandeker, Christopher (2000): The Military in Common-Risk Societies. Elements of Comparison among Nine Countries of West, Central, and East Europe. In: Kuhlmann/Callaghan (Eds.) (2000): 305-331.

Böckenförde, Stephan/Gareis, Sven B. (Eds.) (2009): Deutsche Sicherheitspolitik. Herausforderungen, Akteure und Prozesse. Opladen/Farmington Hills: Barbara Budrich.

Bredow, Wilfried von (2000): Demokratie und Streitkräfte. Militär, Staat und Gesellschaft in der Bundesrepublik Deutschland. Wiesbaden: Westdeutscher Verlag.

Bredow, Wilfried von (2008): Militär und Demokratie in Deutschland. Eine Einführung. Wiesbaden: Westdeutscher Verlag.

Bredow, Wilfried von/Kümmel, Gerhard (2000): New Roles for the Armed Forces and the Concept of Democratic Control. In: Kümmel/von Bredow (Eds.) (2000): 109-131.

Bulmahn, Thomas (2008): Aufgabenfelder der Bundeswehr. In: Bulmahn et al. (2008): 89-107.

Bulmahn, Thomas (2011a): Die Bundeswehr im Vergleich: Vertrauen und wahrgenommene Aufgabenerfüllung. In: Bulmahn/Fiebig/Hilpert (2011): 75-79.

Bulmahn, Thomas (2011b): Wahrnehmung und Bewertung des Einsatzes der Bundeswehr in Afghanistan. In: Bulmahn/Fiebig/Hilpert (2011): 51-62.

Bulmahn, Thomas/Fiebig, Rüdiger (2011): Einstellungen zur Bundeswehr und Bewertung der gesellschaftlichen Anerkennung. In: Bulmahn/Fiebig/Hilpert (2011): 67-73.

Bulmahn, Thomas/Fiebig, Rüdiger/Greif, Stefanie/Jonas, Alexandra/Sender, Wolfgang/Wieninger, Victoria (2008): Sicherheits- und verteidigungspolitisches Meinungsklima in der Bundesrepublik Deutschland. Ergebnisse der Bevölkerungsbefragung 2007 des Sozialwissenschaftlichen Instituts der Bundeswehr (SOWI-Forschungsbericht 86): Strausberg: SOWI.

Bulmahn, Thomas/Fiebig, Rüdiger/Hennig, Jana/Wieninger, Victoria (2010): Ergebnisse der Jugendstudie 2008 des Sozialwissenschaftlichen Instituts der Bundeswehr (SOWI-Forschungsbericht 93): Strausberg: SOWI.

Bulmahn, Thomas/Fiebig, Rüdiger/Hilpert, Carolin (2011): Sicherheits- und verteidigungspolitisches Meinungsklima in der Bundesrepublik Deutschland. Ergebnisse der Bevölkerungsbefragung 2010 des Sozialwissenschaftlichen Instituts der Bundeswehr (SOWI-Forschungsbericht 94): Strausberg: SOWI.

Burk, James (2001): The Military's Presence in American Society, 1950-2000. In: Feaver/Kohn (Eds.) (2001): 247-74.

Caforio, Giuseppe (Ed.) (2003): Handbook of the Sociology of the Military. New York et al.: Kluwer Academic/Plenum Publishers.

Caforio, Giuseppe/Dandeker, Christopher/Kümmel, Gerhard (Eds.) (2009): Armed Forces, Soldiers and Civil-Military Relations. Essays in Honor of Jürgen Kuhlmann. Wiesbaden: VS Verlag für Sozialwissenschaften.

Colton, Timothy J./Gustafson, Thane (1989): Soldiers and the Soviet State. Civil-Military Relations from Brezhnev to Gorbachev. Princeton, NJ: Princeton University Press.

Cottey, Andrew/Edmunds, Timothy/Forster, Anthony (Eds.) (2002): Democratic Control of the Military in Postcommunist Europe: Guarding the Guards. Hampshire/New York: Palgrave.

Creveld, Martin van (1991): The Transformation of War. New York: Free Press.

Croissant, Aurel/Kühn, David (2011): Militär und zivile Politik. Munich: Oldenburg Verlag.

Dandeker, Christopher (1999): Flexible Forces for the Twenty-First Century (Facing Uncertainty, Report No. 1): Karlstad: Department of Leadership, Swedish National Defence College.

Dandeker, Christopher (2000): The Military in Democratic Societies: New Times and New Patterns of Civil-Military Relations. In: Kuhlmann/Callaghan (Eds.) (2000): 27-43.

Danopoulos, Constantine/Zirker, Daniel (Eds.) (1998): Military and Society in the Former Soviet Bloc. Boulder, CO: Westview Press.

Däniker, Gustav (1992): Wende Golfkrieg. Vom Wesen und Gebrauch künftiger Streitkräfte. Frankfurt am Main: Huber Frauenfeld.

Dörfler-Dierken, Angelika (2005): Ethische Fundamente der Inneren Führung. Baudissins Leitgedanken: Gewissensgeleitetes Individuum – Verantwortlicher Gehorsam – Konflikt- und friedensfähige Mitmenschlichkeit (SOWI-Forschungsbericht 77). Strausberg: SOWI.

Dörfler-Dierken, Angelika/Portugall, Gerd (Eds.) (2010): Friedensethik und Sicherheitspolitik. Weißbuch 2006 und EKD-Friedensdenkschrift 2007 in der Diskussion. Wiesbaden: VS Verlag für Sozialwissenschaften.

Dörfler-Dierken, Angelika/Kümmel, Gerhard (Eds.) (2010): Identität, Selbstverständnis, Berufsbild. Implikationen der neuen Einsatzrealität für die Bundeswehr. Wiesbaden: VS Verlag für Sozialwissenschaften.

Duffield, John S. (1998): World Power Forsaken. Political Culture, International Institutions, and German Security Policy after Unification. Stanford, CA: Stanford University Press.

Ebeling, Klaus/Seiffert, Anja/Senger, Rainer (2002): Ethische Fundamente der Inneren Führung (SOWI-Arbeitspapier 132). Strausberg: SOWI.

Edmonds, Martin (1990): Armed Services and Society. Boulder, CO/San Francisco, CA: Westview Press.

Edmunds, Timothy/Cottey, Andrew/Forster, Anthony (2001): The Military and Society in Central and Eastern Europe: A Background Paper (http://civil-military.dsd.kcl.ac.uk/TCMR%20Papers/TCMR%201.13.htm; accessed: 19.11.2001):

Everts, Philip/Isernia, Pierangelo (Eds.) (2001): Public Opinion and the International Use of Force. London/New York: Routledge.

Feaver, Peter D. (1992): Guarding the Guardians: Civilian Control of Nuclear Weapons in the United States. Ithaca, NY: Cornell University Press.

Feaver, Peter D. (1996): The Civil-Military Problematique: Huntington, Janowitz, and the Question of Civilian Control. Armed Forces & Society. 23: 2, 149-178.

Feaver, Peter D./Kohn, Richard H. (Eds.) (2001): Soldiers and Civilians. The Civil-Military Gap and American National Security. Cambridge/London: MIT Press.

Finer, Samuel E. (1962): The Man on Horseback. The Role of the Military in Politics. London: Pall Mall Press.

Florack, Martin (2005): Kriegsbegründungen. Sicherheitspolitische Kultur in Deutschland nach dem Kalten Krieg. Marburg: Tectum.

Geldenhuys, Deon (1998): Foreign Political Engagement. Remaking States in the Post-Cold War World. Hampshire: Macmillan.

Giegerich, Bastian/Kümmel, Gerhard (Eds.) (2013): The Armed Forces: Towards a Post-Interventionist Era? Wiesbaden: VS Verlag für Sozialwissenschaften.

Gow, James (1992): Legitimacy and the Military: The Yugoslav Crisis. London: Pinter Publishers.

Greven, Michael Th. (2009): Die politische Gesellschaft: Kontingenz und Dezision als Probleme des Regierens und der Demokratie. 2nd updated edition. Wiesbaden: VS Verlag für Sozialwissenschaften.

Haltiner, Karl W.; Kümmel, Gerhard (2009): The Hybrid Soldier: Identity Changes in the Military. In: Caforio; Dandeker; Kümmel (Eds.) (2009): 75-82.

Hammerich, Helmut R./Hartmann, Uwe/Rosen, Claus von (Eds.) (2010): Die Grenzen des Militärischen. Jahrbuch Innere Führung 2010. Berlin: Carola Hartmann – Miles Verlag.

Holsti, Ole (2001): Of Chasms and Convergences: The Attitudes and Beliefs of Civilians and Military Elites at the Start of a New Millenium. In: Feaver; Kohn (Ed.) (2001): 15-99.

Howard, Michael (1957): Soldiers and Governments: Nine Studies in Civil-Military Relations. London: Eyre & Spottiswoode.

Huntington, Samuel P. (1957): The Soldier and the State. The Theory and Politics of Civil-Military Relations. Cambridge, Mass./London: The Belknap Press of Harvard University Press.

Huntington, Samuel P. (1991): The Third Wave. Democratization in the Late Twentieth Century. Norman, OK: University of Oklahoma Press.

International Commission on Intervention and State Sovereignty (ICISS) (2001): Responsibility to Protect. Ottawa: International Development Research Centre. Online: http://responsibilitytoprotect.org/ICISS%20Report.pdf.

Inglehart, Ronald (1977): The Silent Revolution. Changing Values and Political Styles among Western Publics. Princeton, N.J.: Princeton University Press.

International Institute for Strategic Studies (IISS) (2003): The Military Balance 2003-2004. London: Oxford University Press.

Jäger, Thomas (Eds.) (2011): Die Welt nach 9/11. Auswirkungen des Terrorismus auf Staatenwelt und Gesellschaft (Sonderheft 2 der Zeitschrift für Außen- und Sicherheitspolitik): Wiesbaden: VS Verlag für Sozialwissenschaften.

Jäger, Thomas/Beckmann, Rasmus (Eds.) (2011): Handbuch Kriegstheorien. Wiesbaden: VS Verlag für Sozialwissenschaften.

Jäger, Thomas/Kümmel, Gerhard (Eds.) (2005): Private Military and Security Companies: Chances, Problems, Pitfalls and Prospects. Wiesbaden: VS Verlag für Sozialwissenschaften.

Jäger, Thomas/Kümmel, Gerhard/Lerch, Marika/Noetzel, Thomas (Eds.) (2004): Sicherheit und Freiheit. Außenpolitische, innenpolitische und ideengeschichtliche Perspektiven. Festschrift für Wilfried von Bredow. Baden-Baden: Nomos.

Janowitz, Morris (1971 [1960]): The Professional Soldier. A Social and Political Portrait. New York/London: The Free Press.

Jett, Dennis C. (2001): Why Peacekeeping Fails. New York: St. Martin's Press.

Juhász, Zoltán (2001): German Public Opinion and the Use of Force in the early 1990s. In: Everts; Isernia (Ed.) (2001): 57-85.

Kirste, Knut/Maull, Hanns W. (1996): Zivilmacht und Rollentheorie. Zeitschrift für Internationale Beziehungen, 2, 283-312.

Klein, Paul (2004): Die Integration der Bundeswehr in Staat und Gesellschaft der Bundesrepublik Deutschland. In: Jäger/Kümmel/Lerch/Noetzel (Eds.) (2004): 268-282.

Krämer, Raimund/Kuhn, Armin (2006): Militär und Politik in Süd- und Mittelamerika: Herausforderungen für demokratische Politik. Berlin: Dietz.

Kümmel, Gerhard (2001): Untiefen des Menschenrechts-Diskurses. WeltTrends, 31, 101-117.

Kümmel, Gerhard (2003): A Soldier is a Soldier is a Soldier!? The Military and Its Soldiers in an Era of Globalization. In: Caforio (Ed.) (2003): 417-433.

Kümmel, Gerhard (2005): Es ist, wie es ist: Deutschland ist Militärmacht. WeltTrends, 56, 79-88.

Kümmel, Gerhard (2010a): Auf der Suche nach dem Politischen – Die Friedensdenkschrift, das Weißbuch und das Konzept der Menschlichen Sicherheit. In: Dörfler-Dierken/Portugall (Eds.) (2010): 227-241.

Kümmel, Gerhard (2010b): Das soldatische Subjekt zwischen Weltrisikogesellschaft, Politik, Gesellschaft und Streitkräften. Oder: Vom Schlagen einer Schneise durch den Identitäts-Selbstverständnis-Berufsbild-Dschungel. In: Dörfler-Dierken/Kümmel (Eds.) (2010): 161-184.

Kümmel, Gerhard (2011): Per Anhalter durch die Galaxis – Von Afrika über den Balkan zum ‚Krieg gegen den Terror': Zur Rolle von Privaten Sicherheits- und Militärunternehmen bei militärischen Einsätzen. In: Jäger; Beckmann (Ed.) (2011): 535-552.

Kümmel, Gerhard (2012): Das Ende der Interventionen, wie wir sie kennen? Oder: Auf dem Weg in eine postinterventionistische Ära? if – Zeitschrift für Innere Führung, 56: 3, 5-8.

Kümmel, Gerhard (Ed.) (2009): Streitkräfte unter Anpassungsdruck. Sicherheits- und militärpolitische Herausforderungen Deutschlands in Gegenwart und Zukunft. Baden-Baden: Nomos.

Kümmel, Gerhard/Bredow, Wilfried von (Eds.) (2000): Civil-Military Relations in an Age of Turbulence: Armed Forces and the Problem of Democratic Control (SOWI-Forum International Nr. 21): Strausberg: SOWI.

Kümmel, Gerhard/Collmer, Sabine (Eds.) (2003): Soldat – Militär – Politik – Gesellschaft. Facetten militärbezogener sozialwissenschaftlicher Forschung. Liber amicorum für Paul Klein. Baden-Baden: Nomos.

Kümmel, Gerhard/Giegerich, Bastian (Eds.) (2013): The Armed Forces: Towards a Postinterventionist Era? Wiesbaden: Springer VS. (i.V.).

Kuhlmann, Jürgen/Callaghan, Jean (Eds.) (2000): Military and Society in 21st Century Europe. A Comparative Analysis. Hamburg: Lit.

Kutz, Martin (2006): Deutsche Soldaten. Eine Kultur- und Mentalitätsgeschichte. Darmstadt: Wissenschaftliche Buchgesellschaft.

Lambert, Alexandre (2009): Democratic Civilian Control of Armed Forces in the Post-Cold War Era. Münster: Lit.

Linnenkamp, Hilmar/Lutz, Dieter S. (Eds.) (1995): Innere Führung. Zum Gedenken an Wolf Graf von Baudissin. Baden-Baden: Nomos.

Luhmann, Niklas (1989): Vertrauen. Ein Mechanismus der Reduktion sozialer Komplexität. 3rd revised edition. Stuttgart: Ferdinand Enke.

Luttwak, Edward N. (1979): Coup d'État: A Practical Handbook. Boston, Mass.: Harvard University Press.

Merkel, Wolfgang/Puhle, Hans-Jürgen/Croissant, Aurel/Thiery, Peter (2006): Defekte Demokratie. Band 2: Regionalanalysen. Wiesbaden: VS Verlag für Sozialwissenschaften.

Moskos, Charles C.; Williams, John Allen; Segal, David R. (Eds.) (2000): The Postmodern Military. Armed Forces After the Cold War. New York – Oxford: Oxford University Press.

Münkler, Herfried (2002): Die neuen Kriege. Reinbek bei Hamburg: Rowohlt.

Nägler, Frank (2010): Der gewollte Soldat und sein Wandel. Personelle Rüstung und Innere Führung in den Aufbaujahren der Bundeswehr 1956 bis 1964/65. Munich: R. Oldenbourg Verlag.

Naumann, Klaus (2008): Einsatz ohne Ziel? Die Politikbedürftigkeit des Militärischen. Hamburg: Hamburger Edition.

Naumann, Klaus (2010): Wie viel politische Verantwortung für die Militärelite? In: Hammerich/Hartmann/Rosen (Eds.) (2010): 62-77.

Noelle, Elisabeth/Neumann, Erich Peter (Eds.) (1956): Jahrbuch der öffentlichen Meinung 1947-1955. Allensbach: Verlag für Demoskopie.

Noelle, Elisabeth/Neumann, Erich Peter (Eds.) (1965): Jahrbuch der öffentlichen Meinung 1958-1964. Allensbach/Bonn: Verlag für Demoskopie.

Noelle, Elisabeth/Neumann, Erich Peter (Eds.) (1967): Jahrbuch der öffentlichen Meinung 1965-1967. Allensbach/Bonn: Verlag für Demoskopie.

Noelle, Elisabeth/Neumann, Erich Peter (Eds.) (1974): Jahrbuch der öffentlichen Meinung 1968-1973. Allensbach/Bonn: Verlag für Demoskopie.

Noelle-Neumann, Elisabeth/Köcher, Renate (Eds.) (1993): Allensbacher Jahrbuch der Demoskopie 1984-1992. Allensbach: Verlag für Demoskopie.

Noelle-Neumann, Elisabeth/Piel, Edgar (Eds.) (1983): Allensbacher Jahrbuch der Demoskopie 1978-1983. Munich et al.: K.G. Saur.

Opitz, Eckhardt (Ed.) (2001): Fünfzig Jahre Innere Führung. Von Himmerod (Eifel) nach Pristina (Kosovo) – Geschichte, Probleme und Perspektiven einer Führungsphilosophie. Bremen: Edition Temmen.

Prüfert, Andreas (Ed.) (1998): Innere Führung im Wandel. Zur Debatte um die Führungsphilosophie der Bundeswehr. Baden-Baden: Nomos.

Schlaffer, Rudolf J. (2006): Der Wehrbeauftragte 1951 bis 1985. Aus Sorge um den Soldaten. Munich: R. Oldenbourg Verlag.

Schulze, Gerhard (1992): Die Erlebnisgesellschaft. Kultursoziologie der Gegenwart. Zweite Auflage. Frankfurt am Main – New York: Campus.

Schwab-Trapp, Michael (2002): Kriegsdiskurse. Die politische Kultur des Krieges im Wandel 1991-1999. Opladen: Leske & Budrich.

Seliger, Marco (2013): Auf verlorenem Posten. In: Kümmel; Giegerich (Eds.) (2013) (i.V.).

Strachan, Hew (2006): Making Strategy: Civil-Military Relations after Irak. Survival. 48: 3, 59-82.

Unseld, Siegfried (Ed.) (1993): Politik ohne Projekt? Nachdenken über Deutschland. Frankfurt am Main: Suhrkamp.

Vogt, Wolfgang R. (1986a): Militärische Gewalt und Gesellschaftsentwicklung. Zur Inkompatibilitätsproblematik und Friedenssicherung im Nuklearzeitalter – ein soziologischer Entwurf. In: Vogt (Ed.) (1986b): 37-87.

Vogt, Wolfgang R. (Ed.) (1986b): Militär als Gegenkultur. Streitkräfte im Wandel der Gesellschaft I. Opladen: Leske & Budrich.

Wachtler, Günther (Ed.) (1983): Militär, Krieg, Gesellschaft. Texte zur Militärsoziologie. Frankfurt am Main/New York: Campus.

Werkner, Ines-Jacqueline (2004): Allgemeine Trends und Entwicklungslinien in den europäischen Wehrsystemen (SOWI-Arbeitspapier 134). Strausberg: SOWI.

Wiesendahl, Elmar (1990): Wertewandel und motivationale Kriegsunfähigkeit von Streitkräften. Sicherheit & Frieden. 8: 1, 25-29.

Wiesendahl, Elmar (Ed.) (2005): Neue Bundeswehr – neue Innere Führung? Perspektiven und Rahmenbedingungen für die Weiterentwicklung eines Leitbildes. Baden-Baden: Nomos.

Zentralstelle für Recht und Schutz der Kriegsdienstverweigerer aus Gewissensgründen e.V. (Zentralstelle KDV) (2007): Kurze Chronik der Zentralstelle KDV. Bockhorn: Zentralstelle KDV.

Suspending the conscript system

Sabine Collmer

Introduction

After the end of the Cold War, the conscript army was abolished in a majority of the European Union Member States and beyond. Unlike these countries, Germany maintained the conscript system for its armed forces for some 50 years after the founding of the Federal Republic, and for more than two decades after the end of the Cold War and the unification of the two German states.

When in January 2011 the last cohort of German conscripts entered the Bundeswehr, following a government decision to reform the armed forces, refocus it on new security requirements and remodel it into an all-volunteer force, this move marked the beginning of a dramatic change in policy. Not only had the major political forces in the country for decades refused to discuss any replacement of conscription with a volunteer recruitment system, but so had the German public. For many years after unification, a majority of citizens was not in favour of abolishing the conscript system. Although, politically speaking, the newly-initiated reforms do not completely abolish the conscription process, *suspension* of the military draft means exactly this in terms of consequences – and political observers no longer foresee a *roll-back* to the traditional system.

This chapter explores the root causes of the delayed adaptation to a new recruitment system in Germany. Furthermore, it analyses the more comprehensive reform process in which suspension of the draft is embedded. It also gives an outlook on the issues and challenges that the German armed forces will have to face concerning recruitment and training in the near future.

Background: restructuring the Bundeswehr

The political decisions that led to the suspension of the conscript army system were embedded in a wider reform process, which entailed refocusing on new security demands and streamlining internal processes. Furthermore, reform of the Bundeswehr took place in times of shrinking defence budgets. In spring 2010, the German Federal Minister of Finance announced a strict austerity policy and defence expenditure cuts. This was followed by a cabinet decision in June 2010, which declared a level of ambition for defence cuts of 8.3 bn euros within four years (by 2014). Initiated by then Federal Minister of Defence Karl-Theodor zu

Guttenberg, the government also established a Reform Commission (the so-called *Weise Commission* after its Chairman Frank-Jürgen Weise), with the objective of reviewing the organizational structures and processes within the Bundeswehr and making suggestions for increased efficiency.

The commission identified deficiencies in three broad areas: first, inefficient structures due to excessive size; second, cumbersome procurement processes (especially in armament procurement); and, third, unclear vertical and horizontal responsibilities (Strukturreform-Kommission 2010). These findings were echoed by a report of the European Defence Agency (EDA) in July 2011. In it EDA researchers compared the cost effectiveness of European armed forces. The report pointed out that, from a comparative perspective, the Bundeswehr operated less cost effectively and less efficiently than other European armed forces. Also, it found out that the Bundeswehr had an unfavourable proportion soldiers on deployment compared to support and logistics personnel in the home country. It stated moreover that costs for the deployment of a German soldier on a foreign mission was three times as high compared to the European average – a finding that drew strong criticism from politicians with an interest in defence issues (Welt online 2011).

Experts concluded in a self-critical manner that this report clearly demonstrated the still incomplete status of transformation of the German armed forces from a standing mass army towards highly-mobile intervention forces. In fact, the continuous reform process of the Bundeswehr that had already begun in 1990 with the merger of the two German armed forces, was more or less incremental in nature[1] until the turn of the century. While the unified German armed forces became smaller, they maintained their strictly territorial concept of defence and their traditional three-partite structure[2] of services. They also maintained their traditional equipment and cumbersome procurement and purchasing processes which were – by and large – still geared towards territorial defence. Moreover, while far-reaching changes were heralded by both politicians and the military leadership, this did not trickle down to the rank and file at the time. In fact, it did not initiate a real change of the military mindset, which would have included an adaptation to the new missions (Wiesner 2011: 96).

Substantial change finally came about not due to national reform efforts but through necessity in the form of the participation of German military contingents in two expeditionary missions, both with a strong combat component: These

1 In 1994 the German High court ruled that the ongoing (and already completed) out-of-area missions of the Bundeswehr were not in violation of the constitution. This decision gave certainty to military planners, yet it did not decisively change the military mindset.

2 With the exception that services were swapped and reorganized into newly-created additional services.

were, first, the Kosovo mission in 1999, which sent a clear message to all European allies in NATO to beef up their inefficient military capabilities and, second, the ISAF mission in Afghanistan, which was created in 2001. Then Federal Minister of Defence Peter Struck, who came into office in 2002, coined the famous dictum that the security of Germany is now defended at the Hindu Kush river. The message of this statement can hardly be overestimated in its influence on the reform process. For the first time in German post-war history, it spelled out for a broader public what a refocusing of the threat analysis from block confrontation to a comprehensive security concept actually entailed: due to global security interdependencies, the consequences of crises and conflicts on the periphery and even outside of Europe have become important security concerns for Germany. This in turn demands a more comprehensive risk analysis and a more flexible use of military force in a wide range of environments.

During Struck's time as MoD, first substantial steps were taken towards the reorientation of the armed forces. The key concept of 'transformation' encompassed more than a simple reform process, as it entailed the continuous adaptation of the armed forces to security challenges. The transformation idea was first declared in 2004 in the Konzeption der Bundeswehr (2004) (KdB, Concept of the Bundeswehr). In accordance with the Verteidigungspolitische Richtlinien (VPR, Defence Policy Guidelines) of the previous year, the KdB clearly underlined the importance of deployability of the armed forces on foreign missions.

However, while transformation was an ongoing process across all levels of the German armed forces, and even though foreign missions had become a recurring job requirement for the average soldier, this did not simultaneously trigger a reform of the recruitment system. While a wide range of other European countries in the mid-1990s engaged in a kind of 'second-wave of reform' with force reductions and professionalisation, including the abolishment of conscription (Wyss 2011: 45), in Germany the transition towards all-volunteer forces did not take place. Instead, the country retained the conscript system for another decade. In fact, it was only in 2010 that the popular new Federal Minister of Defence zu Guttenberg came under severe budgetary pressure, at which point he adopted the idea of suspending the outdated and meanwhile dysfunctional conscript system[3]. He advocated not only fundamental cuts in military and civilian armed forces personnel, including at the Federal Ministry of Defence, but also an end to the conscript system. While a complete abolition was quickly discarded, as it necessitates a change in German Basic Law, *suspension* of the draft was considered

3 The last round of conscription comprised some 55,000 conscripts. Within the training system for conscripts, 20,000 military instructors were assigned fixed posts, and therefore not available for foreign deployment. Conscripts were generally not deployed on foreign missions.

feasible. Due to a plagiarism affair, which forced him to resign in 2011, zu Guttenberg did not come to see the last recruited personnel end their obligatory service. The general public however still sees him as the initiator of the most far-reaching change in the recruitment system of the Bundeswehr since its inception (see Keller 2011: 3).

The successor of zu Guttenberg, Federal Minister of Defence Thomas de Maizière, further pursued the transformation agenda. Since entering into office in spring 2011, he made several announcements concerning the *reorientation (Neuausrichtung)* of the German Armed Forces under his leadership. The pillars of his reform concept are a decisive reduction of military and civilian personnel, a funding level in line with the envisioned savings target, a considerably streamlined Federal Ministry of Defence (with the option of closing the Bonn office of the MoD) and a tightened procurement and purchasing process (Steinmann 2011). Concerning the end of conscription, de Maizière used the window of opportunity his predecessor had opened up and continued to press forward politically. On 24 March 2011, the German Bundestag passed a new law, which stated that, after 55 years, starting from July 2011, the conscript system would in fact be suspended.

De Maizière's reform concept set the level of ambition at 5,000 young men and women who would participate in the new format of 'voluntary conscription', with tours of duty lasting between 12 and 23 months. The concept allows for a maximum of an additional 10,000 voluntary conscripts. The opportunity for conscientious objectors to do social work *(Ersatzdienst)* instead of military service ended along with the suspension of conscription. It was replaced by a new service called *Bundesfreiwilligendienst* (Federal Voluntary Service), which would be overseen by the Federal Ministry of Family Affairs, Senior Citizens, Women and Youth.

In June 2012, de Maizière issued a *milestone plan, which set out a* detailed way ahead for the *reorientation* process. The suspension of conscription was given a pivotal position and was named first before other reform projects such as a realignment of the procurement process, the restructuring of the forces, the closing of military bases and the restructuring of the Federal Ministry of Defence.[4]

4 The 2012 milestone plan and other reform documents can be retrieved from http://www.bmvg.de/portal/ (in German only).

Delayed transformation

The transformation process, in which the change of the recruitment system within the German armed forces was embedded, was strongly budget-driven, as has been shown earlier. Had there not been such strong budgetary pressure, that enforced the changes, the Bundeswehr might still be operating its conscript system – no matter how imperfectly it worked during the last decade, with declining *Wehrgerechtigkeit* (justice in the drafting system) and growing numbers of young men, who were not inclined to become involved in military service. On the other hand, the move to change the recruitment system was also prompted by the dramatically changed security environment and post-Cold War threat assessment. It was therefore a necessary and overdue step.

But why did Germany adhere for so long to the conscript system? I argue that the reasons for this can be traced back to a specific combination of historical, security-policy-related, socio-political and military factors (see also: White Paper 1994). First of all, the historical setting needs to be considered: The founding of the Bundeswehr in 1955 took place against the background of the unfolding Cold War and the inclusion of West Germany in a system of collective defence provided by the frameworks of NATO and Western European Union (WEU). In terms of providing manpower for defence purposes, universal conscription was perceived as part of German defence culture. Here, we see a link to more general security-policy considerations in Germany: During Cold War times, the armed forces, with its large number of conscripts, were seen as a factor of stability that contributed to a military equilibrium within an established military-political alliance. Furthermore, drafting a considerable number of young men every year was considered a recruitment system that allowed for a maximum of exchange between the military and wider society. This important factor is acknowledged over and over again in a variety of official papers of the Federal Ministry of Defence up to recent times. The Security White Paper 1994, for example, read (White Paper 1994: 85, own translation):

> Universal conscription firmly establishes the armed forces in society. Through its conscripts, the Bundeswehr remains in close contact with every segment of the population, particularly the young generation. Conscription creates a high degree of social awareness and interest in issues concerning security and the armed forces among policymakers and in society.

From a socio-political standpoint, the establishment of armed forces after World War II was not without controversy. To avoid repeating historical mistakes and to dispel doubts, a unique leadership philosophy, the *Innere Führung*, was established that is valid until today: The concept of Innere Führung regulates the internal conduct among superiors and inferiors within the forces. It spells out their respective legal rights. Also, it entails efficient instruments of checks and balances for the democratic control of the forces, such as the position of the defence commissioner (*Wehrbeauftragter*), who reports to the German parliament. The clear delineation of the Bundeswehr from the Wehrmacht and the implementation of checks and balances via Innere Führung also contributed to the acceptance of a German military that was based on conscription.

Finally, conscription was the preferred recruitment system for military operational reasons: It enabled the Bundeswehr to call up reservists in considerable numbers. This gave the armed forces excellent mobilisation capability and sustainability. It has to be considered that the armed forces recruited around 50% of their regular and temporary-career volunteers from the pool of conscripts (White Paper 1994:85). The same argument is still contained in the current White Paper stemming from 2006: Here, conscripts are characterised as being of "special importance for the operational readiness of the Bundeswehr for operations abroad and during routine duty at home" (White Paper 2006:160). Last, but not least, conscription was also seen as a primary integration mechanism for the former German Democratic Republic (GDR) by "promoting an exchange of views and ideas between young people in the East and the West and helping to complete internal unification" (ibid.).

The above-mentioned factors may not comprehensively list all of the arguments that played a role in the decision-making process to change the recruitment system. However, it illustrates the interwoven nature of historical setting and security-related aspects that led to a specific corporate identity of the Bundeswehr. In hindsight, it is no surprise that the conscript system, established in this unique historical setting and practised for decades, belonged to the core of German strategic culture. Now, more than 20 years after unification, with an entire generation of citizens having grown up without ever having lived in a divided Germany, not only the global security landscape has changed, but also the outlook of the armed forces.

New frontiers: the Bundeswehr without conscripts

With the suspension of the draft, which officially entered into effect on 1 July 2011, the Bundeswehr was seen as entering "a new frontier" (Bundeswehr 2011): for the first time since the founding of the German armed forces, new (male and female) recruits would be exclusively volunteers. From the outset, it was unclear how the process of recruiting volunteers would work – qualitatively and quantitatively. While it may still be too early to conduct a final evaluation of this process, the following paragraphs address the current status of the volunteer recruitment effort and depict the public debate on this issue.

The 2011 reform concept aimed at a target structure of up to 185,000 military personnel, of which 170,000 are regular soldiers (including temporary-career soldiers) and between 5,000 and 15,000 voluntary conscripts. In order to allow for a high level of flexibility, the contract between the volunteer and the Bundeswehr may be terminated within the first six months by both sides, without any indication of reasons. The first cohort of voluntary conscripts was contracted in July 2011. According to official Bundeswehr numbers, 3,459 recruits were admitted (Statista 2011) – a rather modest figure, compared to the number of more than 60,000 conscripted recruits in 2009 (ibid.). In the second round of volunteer draftees in October 2011, the number reached 4,589 (4,437 men and 152 women) and in January 2012, 2,793 recruits entered the Bundeswehr (Bundestagsdrucksache 17/9247).

What worried Bundeswehr officials from the early days of the new concept was the relatively high number of drop-outs. According to official numbers, more than one in four volunteers (28.1% or 972 in absolute numbers) in the first cohort quit the armed forces within the first six months (ibid.). The Federal Ministry of Defence reacted to these developments by announcing an investigation into what motivated these recruits to drop out and at the same time a new "attractiveness programme" was announced (Meyer 2011). In the beginning of 2011, the Federal Ministry of Defence had issued a programme package containing 80 measures through which duty in the German armed forces was to become more attractive. These include improving compatibility of job and family, the transition to more flexible age limits, and better payment for recruits. In addition to this, the Bundeswehr in spring 2011 launched an advertising campaign in which 498,000 young men of the respective age cohorts were contacted via letter, asking them to indicate whether they were generally interested in a job in the armed forces. At that time, the feedback was rather low: Only 0.4% of those contacted showed an interest in the Bundeswehr (Spiegel Online 2011). In order to appeal to the right calibre of recruits, the Federal Minister of Defence in March 2012 reached out to the public by addressing young people who in his view should view voluntary service in the armed forces as a duty that is held in high regard, similar to other volunteer positions (Handelsblatt 2011).

Until the end of 2011, the publicised debate about recruitment of volunteers focused on the apparently low numbers of young people that were attracted by the armed forces. As a counter measure, the current Bundeswehr Commissioner (Wehrbeauftragter), parliamentarian Hellmut Königshaus, suggested integrating more young people of migrant origin into the forces and to offer older enlisted soldiers a prolongation of their contracts (Cicero online 2011). Throughout the year 2011, investigative journalist articles were published that gave insight into the tough business of recruiting fit young men (and women) – mostly including salient details about the low educational standards or naivety of the candidates

(Rosenfeld 2011; Bender 2011). Soon, a well-known argument concerning the recruitment of volunteers surfaced in the debate. With the low initial numbers of interested young people in mind, social scientists warned of a tendency towards a *precariat*[5] within the armed forces or a "two-class army" with an elitist group of well-educated officers on the one hand and a "desperate basis of simple enlisted soldiers" on the other hand (Marguier 2011:3). The parallel occurrence of several incidents of misconduct by supervisors in recruit training units[6] during 2010 and 2011 did not contribute to the vivid image of the Bundeswehr the planners for the post-conscription phase had envisioned.

With the aim of positively influencing public opinion, a large-scale advertising campaign was launched in 2011. It was based on the presentation of a new corporate identity with the motto *Wir. Dienen. Deutschland.* (We. Serve. Germany.). The Bundeswehr continued to send specially-trained youth officers into schools, with the task of informing pupils about military missions. Although youth officers by definition are not meant to inform their audience about job opportunities (this is the task of special recruitment officers), protests by civil society organizations soon followed: Human rights groups accused the armed forces of "systematically and comprehensively urging minors to enter the armed forces", which they saw as a breach of the UN Convention on the Rights of Children. The Bundeswehr reacted to these accusations by clarifying that their explicit goal was to inform the public about the Bundeswehr's mission and work, not to recruit personnel in schools (Trenkamp 2011).

This incident serves as an indicator for the existence of potentially conflicting value systems of the civilian and the military sphere. Here a classic civil-military gap appears: On the one hand, the Bundeswehr has so far produced thousands of soldiers with a deployment background from the missions in which the armed forces participated. Many of these soldiers showed severe problems with acclimatization back at home (if they did not even develop full-fledged posttraumatic stress disorder). On the other hand, there is a population that – by and large – is disinterested in the missions or even disapproves of them (in the case if the ISAF mission in Afghanistan) and that generally does not appreciate the personal sacrifice of deployed soldiers.[7] Moreover, the duty of German soldiers in missions seem to take place under a condition of non-recognition among the wider public,

5 The term *precariat* was coined by French sociologist Pierre Bourdieu and is not part of the English-speaking sociological discourse. It refers to the "working poor" or "new under class", a group of citizens who have to deal with precarious (limited) work contracts and simple working conditions.

6 One female recruit, for example, died on the prestigious sail boat training ship Gorch Fock. This led to the dismissal of the Commander of the ship.

7 These grievances were mentioned, for example, by ISAF veterans on a prime time Sunday night TV talk show in June 2012 (ARD 2012).

which does not draw a connection between soldiers in missions in far-away countries and their own personal security at home.

Here, the question surfaces about the nature of the gap and what it says about current civil-military relations? A recent example from the year 2012 serves to highlight this issue: When the private TV channel ProSieben aired a self-proclaimed "comedy" in April 2012 with the title *Willkommen im Krieg* (Welcome to war) that featured everyday life of German enlisted soldiers in a fantasy country with resemblance to Afghanistan, the online Internet mailbox of that TV station was soon flooded by angry feedback from German ISAF veterans, who felt strongly hurt in their feelings. They articulated that many elements of military life were ridiculed and that the format of a comedy did not pay enough respect to the seriousness and danger of the missions in which they had been deployed nor to those soldiers who had lost their lives in the missions. The TV station itself felt pressed to issue an apology for airing the movie exactly two years after three German ISAF soldiers had died in an ambush in Northern Afghanistan. What had been meant as an "anti-war movie" and an "emotional counterstrike" (ProSieben 2012) in the form of a comedy, was not appreciated at all by this group. The incident may also point to further diverging value systems between the civilian and the military sphere in today's society and to changing civil-military relations in general.

Regardless of the many obstacles the armed forces face in the transition from the traditional conscript system to the new all-volunteer system, a preliminary stocktaking after three cycles of volunteer recruitment shows that the prognosis of a vast shortfall in volunteer candidates for the armed forces was probably premature: As of January 2012, more than 10,000 recruits had actually signed a contract and entered the forces (Löwenstein 2012:2), which is considerably more than the original target number of 5,000. What may have contributed to the relative success of the new recruiting model are attractive payment schemes[8] with special remuneration packages (such as tax exemption and free medical treatment). Critics, however, ask whether financial incentives are a sustainable basis for recruitment and retention of soldiers in the armed forces in the long run.

Furthermore, what is worrisome is the qualitative side of recruitment. Anecdotal evidence suggests that the armed forces are especially attractive today for young men and women who have little or no civilian job alternatives, who have a low educational background and who seek job security in times of general insecurity in the labour market. It is an open question whether or not the Bundeswehr will in future be able to attract the right calibre of recruits, especially for highly sophisticated positions. It may be worthwhile to study the lessons learned of oth-

8 A volunteer in the Bundeswehr earns approximately 1,000 euros per month, compared to the 500 to 800 euro monthly salary of an apprentice metalworker.

er Western countries, which initiated this transition earlier. Already today, it seems clear that with suspension of the conscript system, the Bundeswehr entered into a phase of stronger competition with civilian employers[9] – and the current megatrend of a demographic decrease of successive generations in all Western societies will further aggravate the problem.

Conclusion

The decision to suspend the conscript system in Germany was driven and prompted by budgetary pressure, but it was simultaneously motivated by the altered threat assessment after the end of the Cold War. When looking back at the process of reform in which the move towards all-volunteer forces was embedded, it becomes clear that this process has been considerably delayed, compared to other European countries.

Although several layers of reform were initiated after 1990 by consecutive Federal Ministers of Defence, political observers rate the results as rather incremental in nature. Substantial changes were finally implemented due to the necessity to participate in the international expeditionary missions in Kosovo and Afghanistan around the turn of the millennium. Still, the adapted threat scenarios did not simultaneously trigger the reform of the recruitment system; instead the Federal Republic of Germany adhered to conscription for another decade. It was only in 2010 that the political establishment seriously considered this move. The political decision was then swiftly implemented in mid-2011. The reasons for this late adaptation can be found in a unique combination of historical, security-policy-related, socio-political and military factors.

The end of the draft brought the Bundeswehr to "new frontiers". The newly-established all-volunteer system was closely monitored by journalists. The Federal Ministry of Defence set a rather low level of ambition. In a society in which increasing numbers of young men found ways and means to avoid being drafted or signed up for alternative civil service, willingness for military service was expected to be low. However, the suspected low turn-out did not take place, to the surprise of the wider public. After the initial three rounds of volunteer recruiting, as many as 10,000 volunteers had signed a contract for voluntary service within

9 In an interview in May 2012, the Federal Minister of Defence gave the following numeric example: With a target number of 15,000 recruits per year, in order to be able to choose between candidates, the armed forces require 45,000 applicants. The age cohort of young men each year includes between 310,000 and 320,000. If a number of 10% female applicants is assumed, the number of 350,000 is reached. Out of this basic population every eighth person should apply with the armed forces – a number that was called "unrealistic" by journalists (Bollmann, Lohse 2012).

the armed forces. Yet the picture is somewhat troubled by an alarmingly high number of drop-outs. In any case, it seems to be too early to judge whether the all-volunteer model is a success or not. Doubts stemming from anecdotal evidence remain, whether the right calibre of people from the young generations can be reached – this holds especially true under the conditions of stronger competition with civilian employers and an unfavourable demographic trend.

Meanwhile, concerns about a widening civil-military gap are surfacing – nourished by recent incidents that highlighted the problem of typical post-modern values among civilians, which do not include particular appreciation for military duty or for using the military as a tool in German foreign and security policy. This is pitted against military values held, for example, by war veterans, which cherish sacrifice, duty and comradeship. It seems that the sacrifice war veterans make by risking their lives in violent conflicts takes place under a kind of non-recognition of the wider public. The development of this specific gap under the conditions of an all-volunteer recruitment system should be carefully monitored. Further research into the significance of this gap and the current development of civil-military relations is advisable.

Bibliography

ARD (2012): Trauma Afghanistan – welche Spuren hinterlässt der Krieg? Talk show with Günther Jauch, on 10 June 2012. Online via: http://www.ardmediathek.de/das-erste/guenther-jauch/trauma-afghanistan-welche-spuren-hinterlaesst-der-krieg?documentId=10801830, Retrieved on 11 June 2012.

Bender, Justus (2011): Ein sicherer Job. Die Bundeswehr lockt mit Studien- und Arbeitsplätzen. In: Die Zeit. Zeit Online on 14 November 2011, retrieved on 8 March 2012 via: http://www.zeit.de/2011/06/recruiting-bundeswehr/.

Bollmann, Ralph / Eckart Lohse (2012): Wir brauchen die Besten als Soldaten, Interview mit Verteidigungsminister Thomas de Maiziere. In: Frankfurter Allgemeine. 26.05.2012. Online via: http://www.faz.net/ retrieved on 30.05.2012.

Bundestagsdrucksache 17/9247 (2012): Zahl der Freiwillig Wehrdienstleistenden.

Bundeswehr (2011): Die Reform der Bundeswehr: Ein Überblick. Online document retrieved from www.bundeswehr.de on 12 May 2011.

Cicero Online (2011): Eine Chance für Migranten, Interview mit Hellmut Königshaus. Cicero Magazin für Politische Kultur. 24. June 2011. Online retrieved via: www.cicero.de.

Collmer, Sabine (2011): The Afghanistan Conundrum: Troop Surge or Capacity Building? German Public Opinion towards a Difficult Mission in: Malesic, Marjan; Gerhard Kuemmel (Eds.): Security and the Military between Reality and Perception. Baden-Baden. Nomos.

Handelsblatt (2011): Anti-Guttenberg auf Truppenbesuch, in: HB, 27.03.2011. Online via: www.handelsblatt.com, retrieved on 10.06.2012.

Keller, Patrick: Die strategische Neuausrichtung der Bundeswehr. In: Analysen & Argumente, No 2, June 2011. KAS-Publikationen. Berlin 2011.

Löwenstein, Stephan (2011): Arbeitgeber Bundeswehr. Wer will unter Soldaten? In: Frankfurter Allgemeine. 12.12.2011. Online via: http://www.faz.net/ retrieved on 8.3.2012.

Marguier, Alexander (2011): Streitkraft ohne Strahlkraft. Cicero Magazin für Politische Kultur. 24. June 2011. Online retrieved via: www.cicero.de.

Meyer, Simone (2011): Zehn Sekunden zum Antreten auf dem Kasernenhof, 08.10.11, in: Welt Online, at: http://www.welt-online.de.

ProSieben (2012): Statement zur Ausstrahlung *Willkommen im Krieg*, online via: http://www.prosieben.de/tv/willkommen-im-Krieg/statement-zum-film/ Retrieved on 11 April 2012.

Rosenfeld, Dagmar: Bundeswehr. Sie sind jung und brauchen das Geld, in: Die Zeit. Zeit Online. 05.06.2011. http://www.zeit.de retrieved on 06.06.2012.

SOWI (2009): SOWI Forschungsbericht 90: Sicherheits- und verteidigungspolitisches Meinungsklima in der Bundesrepublik Deutschland. Strausberg 2009.

SOWI (2010): SOWI Forschungsbericht 91: Sicherheits- und verteidigungspolitisches Meinungsklima in der Bundesrepublik Deutschland. Strausberg 2011.

Spiegel online (2011): 21.4.2011.

Statista (2011): Zahl der Einberufenen für den Freiwilligen Wehrdienst im Juli 2011, online via: http://de.Statista.com.

Steinmann, Thomas (2011): Die Baustellen der Bundeswehr, 18.05.2011 in: Financial Times Deutschland, online via: http://www.ftd.de.

Strukturreform-Kommission (2010): Report: Vom Einsatz her Denken. Konzentration, Flexibilität, Effizienz. October 2010. Chaired by Frank-Jürgen Weise. online via: www.ndr.de/info/programm/...und.../reformkommissionsbericht101.pdf

Sturm, Daniel Friedrich: Horst…Warum? Seit einem Jahr schweigt Köhler.In: Welt Online, 31 May 2011, online via: www.welt.de/politik/deutschland/article13403895/.

Trenkamp, Oliver (2011): Nachwuchsmangel bei der Bundeswehr: Freundschaftsanfrage in Flecktarn, in: Spiegel Online 16 May 2011. Online retrieved at http://www.spiegel.de/schulspiegel/0,1518,748434,00.html on 16 May 2011.

Welt Online (2011): Bundeswehr ist teuer und ineffizient. Online at: www.weltonline.de 02.07.2011.

White Paper (1994): Weißbuch zur Sicherheit der Bundesrepublik Deutschland zur Lage und zur Zukunft der Bundeswehr (Weißbuch 1994), Ed.: Bundesministerium der Verteidigung. Berlin. 1994.

White Paper (2006): White Paper 2006 on German Security Policy and the Future of the Bundeswehr. (Engl. Version) Published by the Federal Ministry of Defense. Berlin. October 2006. Online via: www.weissbuch2006.de

Wiesner, Ina (2011): Die Transformation der Bundeswehr in Deutschland, pp.91-106 in: Jäger, Thomas / Ralph Thiele (Eds.): Transformation der Sicherheitspolitik. Deutschland, Österreich, Schweiz im Vergleich. Wiesbaden 2011.

Wyss, Marco: Military Transformation in Europe´s Neutral and Non-Allied States in: RUSI Journal April/May 2011, Vol. 156, No.2, 44-51.

The law on Bundeswehr operations abroad – an overview

Dieter Weingärtner

1. Introduction

Germany's Basic Law, or *Grundgesetz*, defines the Bundeswehr primarily as a defence force. Article 87a (1) stipulates that the Federation shall establish armed forces for purposes of defence. Apart from defence, Article 87a (2) states that the armed forces may be employed only to the extent expressly permitted by this *Grundgesetz*. When lawmakers drew up the constitutional provisions concerning the armed forces in 1956 and amended the *Grundgesetz* in 1968 to take account of emergency legislation, they did not have deployments of German armed forces in international armed missions in mind. Such scenarios were hard to imagine in Germany during the post-war and Cold War eras.

Since then, times have changed. In the Federal Government's 2006 White Paper, international conflict prevention and crisis management, including the fight against international terrorism, are described as the Bundeswehr's main focus. The legal framework for this shift, which was initiated after German reunification, was not created by an amendment to the *Grundgesetz*, but based ultimately on a decision of the Federal Constitutional Court, which held the view that such deployments of the armed forces were covered by the *Grundgesetz* in its present form.[1]

Since then, the Bundeswehr has participated in numerous missions abroad in Europe, Asia, Africa and on the high seas, missions that as a rule have been conducted under the umbrella of the United Nations, NATO or the European Union. The *Grundgesetz* still does not explicitly mention Bundeswehr operations abroad, even though they have been a constitutional reality for 20 years now. Furthermore, very few legal provisions refer to such military operations.

The purpose of this article is to provide an overview of national and international law governing Bundeswehr operations abroad. It is reasonable to distinguish between the law on participation in operations abroad and the legal provisions that are applicable during operations abroad, since these categories are based on the distinction made in international law between *ius ad bellum,* which defines if and under what circumstances the use of military force is permissible, and *ius in bello*, which governs the modalities of permissible warfare.

1 Decision of 12 July 1994, Federal Constitutional Court, 90: 286 et seq.

2. *Legal prerequisites for deployment of the Bundeswehr abroad*

The deployment of German armed forces abroad must be authorised under both international law and the *Grundgesetz*. The Bundeswehr may only participate in such armed missions abroad if these are also legitimised under the *Grundgesetz*. Vice versa, missions authorised by the German constitution must be permissible under international law as well, for otherwise they would constitute a violation of the sovereign rights of the country in which the forces are deployed.

2.1 The international law basis

The vast majority of operations abroad that the Bundeswehr has conducted so far have been authorised under international law by a decision of the United Nations Security Council. Chapter VII of the United Nations Charter provides for action to be taken in the event of threats to peace, breaches of peace and acts of aggression. Under Article 42 of the Charter, the Security Council may employ armed forces to take such action as is necessary to maintain or restore international peace and security. Article 43 of the UN Charter stipulates that the member states are to provide armed forces to the Security Council for this purpose. In practice, however, the Security Council routinely authorises member states or international organisations to carry out peacekeeping operations.

An example of such a Security Council decision is Resolution 1386 of 2001, which, reaffirmed periodically,[2] continues to be the international law basis for participation of German armed forces in the NATO-led mission in Afghanistan. In this resolution, the Security Council authorises the establishment of an International Security Assistance Force (ISAF) to assist the Afghan government in the maintenance of security in the country. It calls upon the member states to contribute personnel, equipment and other resources to ISAF and authorises the member states participating in the International Security Assistance Force to 'take all necessary measures to fulfil its mandate'.

On the other hand, no United Nations Security Council resolution was passed to serve as an international law basis for the participation of the Bundeswehr in the NATO air campaign against the then Federal Republic of Yugoslavia in 1999. To legitimise its participation, the Federal Government referred to NATO's decision to employ armed forces to stop an ongoing humanitarian catastrophe.[3] The Federal Government argued that under the prevailing circumstances, the use of force was necessary to prevent a humanitarian disaster and to put an end to severe human rights violations. There is controversy among legal ex-

2 See also UN Security Council Resolution 2011 (2011) of 12 October 2011.

3 See the Federal Government's motion, Bundestag printed paper No. 13/11469.

perts, however, over whether or not international law permits such humanitarian interventions in response to large-scale, systematic and acute violations of fundamental human rights.

A country's authority to deploy armed forces outside its national territory can also be derived from international agreements other than the UN Charter. The Security Council Resolution to fight piracy off the coast of Somalia[4] explicitly authorises the use of military force in the territorial waters of Somalia. As regards operations on the high seas, it refers to the United Nations Convention on the Law of the Sea. This convention contains authorisations for warships to take action against pirates and armed robbers and thus establishes the international law basis for the participation of the German Navy in the EU-led ATALANTA mission on the high seas off the coast of Somalia.

A right to deploy armed forces abroad under international law can also be derived from the right of individual and collective self-defence laid down in Article 51 of the UN Charter. Following the attacks of 11 September 2001, the United States saw itself in a situation of defence against an armed attack. NATO invoked the mutual defence clause specified in Article 5 of the North Atlantic Treaty. The Bundeswehr's participation in Operation ENDURING FREEDOM was therefore based on the United States' right of self-defence in conjunction with collective defence as defined in the North Atlantic Treaty.[5]

There is controversy over whether the right to self-defence granted by international law also covers the use of military force by a country to rescue its own citizens from a life-threatening situation in another country. This issue is significant, for instance, for the liberation of hostages. The Bundeswehr conducted evacuation operations in Albania in 1997 and in Libya in 2011. In those cases, the Bundeswehr did not invoke the right of self-defence under international law, but referred to the – at least tacit – approval of the states concerned.[6]

This illustrates that request or approval by the government of the country concerned can also legitimise the deployment of forces abroad under international law. The EU-led Operation HARVEST, for example, which took place in Macedonia in 2001 with the participation of Bundeswehr elements, was based on a request from the Macedonian government.[7]

2.2 The national law basis

The deployment of the Bundeswehr abroad must be legitimate not only under international law, but also under the German constitution. Prior to the decision of

4 UN Security Council Resolution 1814 (2008) of 15 May 2008.
5 See Bundestag printed paper No. 14/7296.
6 For details on Albania (Operation Dragonfly), see Bundestag printed paper No. 13/7233.
7 See Bundestag printed paper No. 14/6830.

the Federal Constitutional Court of 12 July 1994[8], it was not clear whether and – if so – on what constitutional basis the Bundeswehr was permitted to conduct operations outside Germany.[9] In these proceedings, parliamentary groups in the German Bundestag had filed a request for the Court to establish that the Federal Government had violated the *Grundgesetz* by having the Bundeswehr participate in NATO military operations in then Yugoslavia and in United Nations operations in Somalia. In its decision, the Federal Constitutional Court did not deal with the question of whether or not Article 87a (2) of the *Grundgesetz*, which requires the employment of armed forces to be expressly authorized in accordance with the constitution, might only apply to military operations within the territory of the Federal Republic. The Court reasoned that Article 24 (2) of the *Grundgesetz* in any event permitted employments of armed forces within systems of mutual collective security. According to the Court, this provision authorises the federation not only to enter into a system of mutual collective security, including the federation's consent to possible such limitations of its sovereignty that this may entail, but also to carry out the typically associated tasks; in such an event the Bundeswehr would be employed within and according to the rules of the collective security system.

In its decision, the Federal Constitutional Court confirmed that the United Nations, NATO and the West European Union are to be considered organisations under Article 24 (2) of the *Grundgesetz*. While scholarly literature on constitutional issues also qualifies the European Union as a system of mutual collective security, the Federal Constitutional Court in an *obiter dictum* remark to its decision on the Lisbon Treaty, raised doubts as to whether the EU already meets the requirements of Article 24 (2) of the *Grundgesetz*.[10] These doubts are apparently not shared by German state practice. The Bundeswehr continues to participate in EU missions abroad, such as Operation ATALANTA off the coast of Somalia.

Nearly all Bundeswehr operations abroad have been conducted under the umbrella of an international organisation. Some people argue that purely national military operations abroad can be justified by the constitutional provisions of the *Grundgesetz* regarding the maintenance of foreign relations (Article 32) or on the primacy of the general rules of international law (Article 25). This opinion has not yet become an accepted view. Unilateral operations such as missions to rescue German citizens can at best be constitutionally legitimised as actions falling under the term "defence" as defined in Article 87a of the *Grundgesetz*. However,

8 See Federal Constitutional Court; 90: 286 et seq.

9 Prior to German reunification, the Bundeswehr only rendered humanitarian assistance abroad in the event of natural disasters; this did not qualify as it being 'employed' as understood under Article 87a (2) of the *Grundgesetz*.

10 Decision of the Federal Constitutional Court of 30 June 2009, Federal Constitutional Court 123: 267 et seq.

there is controversy over whether this constitutional term also covers the defence of individuals.

Some scholars want Article 87a of the *Grundgesetz* to cover not only national and collective defence, but also to allow defence in aid of another state which is being attacked in violation of the UN Charter. So far, however, no such interpretation of the *Grundgesetz* has been used to legally support the deployment of the Bundeswehr outside of the mutual collective security principle.

In its decision of 12 July 1994, the Federal Constitutional Court not only held that Article 24 (2) of the *Grundgesetz* constitutes the legal basis for Bundeswehr operations abroad, but also formulated a central requirement for this process – the constitutive consent of the German Bundestag. The Court based its interpretation on a review of all of the provisions of the *Grundgesetz* that refer to the armed forces and that in its opinion are intended to give parliament a substantial role in the build-up and employment of the armed forces.[11] The Court believed that parliamentary participation applied to the deployment of armed forces in all cases that go beyond the mere provision of relief services abroad. In later decisions, the Court put the term 'deployment of armed forces' in more concrete terms.[12] Under that interpretation, the requirement to obtain parliamentary approval for the deployment of the armed forces applies if, given the operational context and the specific legal and actual circumstances, German military personnel can be clearly expected to become involved in armed activities.

In order to implement this Federal Constitutional Court decision, the German legislators designed a set of rules for the approval process in the Act governing Parliamentary Participation in Decisions on the Deployment of Armed Forces Abroad.[13] The act contains provisions on issues such as the information the Federal Government must include in its motion to parliament, a simplified approval procedure for small-scale operations and subsequent approval in the event of imminent danger.

3. *Applicable legal provisions during operations abroad*

Once the legitimacy of the deployment of German armed forces under international law and the German constitution has been established, the legal provisions that govern the implementation of the mission must be clarified. Certainty regarding compliance with the law is indispensable, for the command of an operation and for every soldier participating in it.

11 See Federal Constitutional Court; 90: 286 et seq., 380.

12 See, for example, the Court's decision of 7 May 2008 (AWACS), Federal Constitutional Court, 121: 135 et seq.

13 Parliamentary Participation Act (*Parlamentsbeteiligungsgesetz*) of 18 March 2005, Federal Law Gazette I: 775.

3.1 The international law level

A detailed set of rules exists that covers the deployment of military personnel abroad in connection with an armed conflict. They particularly include the *Hague Conventions* of 1907, the *Geneva Conventions* of 1949 and their Additional Protocols, to which Germany has acceded, as well as customary international law. International law differentiates between an international armed conflict, an armed conflict between two or more states, and a non-international armed conflict inside a state's territory between the government and a non-state party to the conflict.

In an armed conflict, any military action that is not prohibited by international humanitarian law, including the use of lethal means, is permissible if required for successfully conducting military operations against the opposing party. Specific means and methods of warfare such as weapons that cause unnecessary injury and suffering are prohibited. The principle of distinction, however, matters most: Under this provision, military force may only be used against enemy combatants. Attacks against the civilian population are prohibited. Civilians who do not directly participate in hostilities must be spared and protected both in international and non-international armed conflicts.

So far, most of the deployments of German forces abroad have taken place in support of peacekeeping action underneath the threshold of an armed conflict. The situation was different as regards the action NATO took in 1999 against Yugoslavia and participation in the US operation that was launched in 2001 to oust the Taliban regime in Afghanistan. Yet, concerning the ISAF mission in Afghanistan, only in 2009 did the Federal Government expressly acknowledge that the Bundeswehr was operating in an armed conflict and that the law of armed conflict applied.

The international law provisions for the deployment of armed forces in situations short of armed conflict are fragmentary. Even the Security Council resolutions that serve as the legal basis for such deployments contain hardly any such rules. They merely authorise 'all necessary measures' to be taken to accomplish the mission. The participating nations or international organisations lay down what these measures are and under what circumstances they can be included in plans of operation and rules of engagement. These, however, are merely internal rules and have no external legal effects.

Some international treaties contain more detailed provisions on the conduct of military operations in situations that do not qualify as an armed conflict. These include the *United Nations Convention on the Law of the Sea* and the *United Nations Convention against Torture and Other Cruel, Inhuman or Degrading Treatment or Punishment*. No conclusive answer has yet been found to the question of the extent to which human rights treaties like the *International Covenant on Civil and Political Rights* and the *European Convention of Human Rights* apply to deployments of armed forces abroad. For situations of armed conflict, the specific rules of international humanitarian law take precedence over these treaties. As regards situations short of armed conflict, international human rights apply if the forces deployed exercise effective control. Examinations must be conducted in each case to establish whether or not this is so. Another problem concerning the applicability of human rights is attribution. When reviewing the case of a person arrested during the Kosovo operation, the European Court of Human Rights decided that the action was to be attributed to the international organisation responsible for the operation, the United Nations, and not to the nation whose contingent carried out the action.[14]

3.2 The national law level

Either the law of the country in which foreign armed forces are deployed or the law of the sending state can be considered as the relevant national law. In practice, it is seldom the law of the country in which foreign armed forces are deployed. The law of the receiving state frequently yields to international law, or agreements are concluded with the receiving state which stipulate that his national laws do not apply. So the question remains as to what extent German national law applies to German military personnel deployed abroad.

Firstly, this question has to be answered with regard to the *Grundgesetz*. Under Article 1 (3) of the *Grundgesetz*, the executive branch, which includes the armed forces, is bound by the basic rights as directly applicable law. Meanwhile, the Federal Constitutional Court has ruled that it is admissible and appropriate to modify the extent to which basic rights apply during the exercise of sovereign powers abroad if such modifications are in keeping with international law and have been coordinated with other legal systems.[15] Accordingly, the Federal Government assumes, for example, that Article 104 of the *Grundgesetz*, under which a detained person shall be brought before a judge no later than the day following his arrest, is to be taken to mean that detainees abroad are to be brought before a judge as soon as possible. This interpretation is relevant in the case of the detention of suspected pirates on the high seas.

There is no clear-cut answer to the question of the extent to which other German national laws are applicable to the Bundeswehr during operations abroad. However, there are some explicit rules. Under the Military Penal Code, a soldier who commits a criminal offence during his tour of duty abroad will still be subject to German criminal law, irrespective of the law of the country in which he committed the offence. Other laws like the Military Pensions Act or the Military

14 European Court of Human Rights, 2 May 2007; Europäische Grundrechte Zeitschrift 2007: 522 et seq.

15 Decision of 14 July 1999 *(G -10*, Act on Article 10 of the *Grundgesetz*), Federal Constitutional Court, 100: 313 et seq., 363.

Personnel Representation Act contain their own sets of rules for foreign assignments. In 2004, the Military Counterintelligence Service Act was amended by introducing Section 14, a regulation governing the services' powers during special foreign assignments, which, in principle, are restricted to facilities operated by the Bundeswehr. On the other hand, laws such as the Code of Criminal Procedure or the Act on the Use of Coercive Force by Bundeswehr Personnel do not constitute a basis for infringement of the rights of third parties abroad – as this would violate the sovereignty of the receiving state.

If the wording of a law contains no explicit provision as to whether or not it is applicable abroad, it is particularly important to rely on the presumed intent of the relevant legislators. It is hardly likely that the German legislator intended the principles of waste separation as laid down in the Waste Management Act or the provisions of the Road Traffic Licensing Regulations to be applied to regulate the conduct of German soldiers abroad. These regulations are not applicable in other countries. Bundeswehr personnel can, however, be ordered to observe them when and if this is reasonable.

The situation is different with regard to provisions that govern the relations between the soldier and his employer, the Federal Republic of Germany. The military rights and obligations laid down in the Legal Status of Military Personnel Act also apply abroad, as do the Ministerial Directive Governing Superior-Subordinate Relations, the Military Complaints Regulation and the Military Disciplinary Code. The military disciplinary and complaints courts also base their decisions on this premise.

There has been no comprehensive legal codification of the powers that German soldiers are permitted to exercise in the line of duty during operations abroad. Powers under international law are transferred to the national law level on a case-by-case basis if the German Bundestag approves a Federal Government motion concerning the participation of German armed forces in a mission abroad. These motions and decisions usually only refer to the texts of UN Security Council resolutions that provide authorisation under international law for the use of any measures, including the use of military force, necessary to enforce the mandate. In some cases, they also cite the exercise of the right of individual and collective self-defence and the right to use armed force to help someone in an emergency.

The powers covered by the term 'all necessary measures' are specified for Bundeswehr military personnel not by law, but in internal orders and directives. These contain details on the circumstances under which military force – including firearms – can be used, on other measures that may be taken and enforced and on the standards that are to be observed as regards the principle of proportionality. Measures other than the use of force include the detention of anyone who poses a threat to military personnel or who prevents them from executing their mission. Directives have also been put into effect for these measures, their main purpose being to prescribe the way in which detainees are to be treated.

Each soldier is issued a copy of the directives governing operations abroad in the form of pocket cards.

4. Criminal and civil law aspects of actions by German soldiers abroad

4.1 Criminal law

As was already mentioned, the provisions of German criminal law also apply to actions of German soldiers abroad. This holds true both for military offences under the German Military Penal Code and for general offences under the German Criminal Code. Action in the context of an armed conflict is also subject to the provisions of the German Code of Crimes against International Law, which governs offences such as war crimes and crimes against humanity.

Action taken to ensure mission accomplishment on missions abroad, in particular the use of military force, frequently includes elements of criminal offences such as causing bodily harm, murder or unlawful imprisonment. Such action is not punishable, however, if criminal responsibility is excluded. The first cases in which German public prosecutors investigated the use of firearms by Bundeswehr military personnel in Afghanistan were incidents at checkpoints. Vehicles occupied by Afghan civilians had failed to stop at checkpoints despite being warned to do so, and the German soldiers had expected they would come under attack. Although this assumption was later found to be wrong, the public prosecutors in charge of the investigations ultimately dropped the cases since they were of the opinion that the soldiers, through no fault of their own, had made a judgment error and thereby acted in *imperfect self-defence*.

Meanwhile, legal scholars and practitioners have widely accepted that what military personnel deployed abroad do, irrespective of whether they act in self-defence or in defence of a third party, is justified if it is in compliance with orders and directives, and that such justification rules out criminal liability. Customary international law, for example, permits the use of force against or – as a more moderate measure – the detention of enemy fighters in an armed conflict. For operations in situations short of armed conflict, the mandate under international law, which is implemented in line with a decision of the German Bundestag, provides justification under criminal law by authorising 'all necessary measures'. Military personnel on deployment abroad therefore must not fear criminal prosecution as long as what they do is in compliance with the orders and directives they are issued.

The Federal Prosecutor General is responsible for investigating the actions of German military personnel deployed abroad if the facts suggest that offences have been committed under the German Code of Crimes against International Law. The prerequisite for this, the existence of an armed conflict, was acknowledged by the Federal Prosecutor General for the situation in Afghanistan in 2009. Since then, the Federal Prosecutor General has routinely conducted investigations when actions by German ISAF personnel have caused harm or injury. So far, none of these investigations has led to charges being made in criminal courts, let alone to the conviction of German military personnel for actions they have taken in the line of duty in Afghanistan.

Actions of soldiers in situations short of armed conflict are reviewed by the public prosecutor's office responsible for the region in which the respective soldiers live. In the past, this has led to situations in which a single action involving several soldiers has been reviewed by different public prosecutor's offices, some of which were quite unfamiliar with the conditions in the armed forces and the law applicable during operations abroad. In order to enable public prosecutors' offices and courts to specialise in such cases, the Federal Government has prepared a bill which provides that a single prosecutor's office will have competent jurisdiction.[16] This bill is currently undergoing the legislative process and is expected to become effective in 2013.

4.2 Civil law

With regard to civil law, the most common question concerning Bundeswehr operations abroad is whether people who suffer harm or damage of their property as a result of military actions are entitled to claim compensation from the Federal Republic of Germany.

The law of international armed conflict only recognises compensation between states. Should a violation of the rules of international humanitarian law cause people to be harmed, the right to claim compensation does not rest with the person concerned, but with their home country. The Federal Court of Justice upheld this established principle in 2006 when dealing with a lawsuit filed by two Yugoslav citizens who had suffered damages when NATO aircraft destroyed a bridge during the Kosovo war.[17]

According to prevailing opinion, the exclusion of the right of individuals to claim compensation for damages related to acts of war also rules out the possibility of any claims being raised under national law. Consequently, German law governing the state's liability for any damages caused by officials – including soldiers – to a third party as a result of a culpable violation of their official duty does not apply to actions committed in wars or civil wars. This does not, however, exclude the voluntary provision of financial compensation on humanitarian grounds to people who have suffered from Bundeswehr combat action. If such

16 Bundestag printed paper No. 17/9694.

17 Decision of 2 November 2006 – III ZR 190/05, Federal Court of Justice Bulletin (BGHZ) 169: 348 et seq.

cases arise for example in Afghanistan, the Bundeswehr regularly pays ex gratia compensation.

If damages are caused in peacekeeping operations outside of an armed conflict, German law governing liability for violation of official duty applies in principle. Compensation for damage may be claimed when the prerequisites specified in the German Civil Code are met. Traffic accidents involving Bundeswehr service vehicles are the most common example. Article 34 of the *Grundgesetz* states that if a civil servant or soldier violates his official duty to a third party, the liability for any damage caused rests with the state. In the event of intentional wrongdoing or gross negligence, the state's right of recourse against the individual soldier shall be preserved. However, for the soldiers' benefit, an administrative regulation has been issued to limit the amount that must be paid should such recourse be taken.

5. Practical examples

5.1 Example: The evacuation of German citizens from Libya

In February 2012, the Bundeswehr sent two transport aircraft to Camp Nafura in the south of Libya to evacuate German citizens from the country because their life was endangered by the civil war. In addition to the crews, each aircraft transported six military policemen carrying small arms whose mission was to secure the aircraft after landing and the evacuees during boarding.[18] This Bundeswehr operation is now being reviewed by the Federal Constitutional Court, which was requested by the parliamentary group of Bündnis 90/Die GRÜNEN to establish that by its failure to seek parliamentary approval, the Federal Government had violated the participation clause as established for the deployment of armed forces by the Federal Constitutional Court.

The first point that requires examination is the legitimacy of the Air Force operation under international law and the German constitution. As mentioned, there is controversy in the discourse on international law over whether or not a state is permitted to conduct a military intervention in another country to rescue its own citizens. In this case, however, the Federal Government assumed it was acting with the tacit approval of the Libyan government since its request to conduct an evacuation operation had not been denied. On the other hand, the operation was a purely national effort by the Bundeswehr and thus not justified under Article 24 (2) of the *Grundgesetz*. Therefore, the national legal authorisation can only be

18 For background information, see the Federal Government's response, Bundestag printed paper No. 17/6564.

derived from the Bundeswehr's defence function. This requires the term 'defence' as defined under Article 87a of the *Grundgesetz* to include the protection of German citizens abroad. Furthermore, there is the question of whether or not the operation constituted a 'deployment of armed forces' for which the Federal Government would have had to seek parliamentary approval, something it did not do. The outcome of the proceedings largely depends on the question of whether German military personnel were expected to become involved in armed activities during the mission.

5.2 Example: An airstrike in Afghanistan

In early 2009, a Bundeswehr officer near Kunduz in Afghanistan called in an airstrike against two fuel trucks that had been hijacked by insurgents. This airstrike caused a large number of deaths, with civilians among the victims. The Federal Prosecutor General initiated criminal investigations into the incident.

During the legal review of this incident, the Federal Prosecutor General first noted that the conflict in Afghanistan was a non-international armed conflict and so the German Code of Crimes against International Law was applicable. Under this law, actions are not punishable as war crimes if they are taken within combat action that is permissible under international law. In the view of the Federal Prosecutor General, the order to drop the bombs did not amount to a war crime as this would have required the perpetrator's knowledge that the attack would cause loss of life or injury to civilians which would be clearly excessive in relation to the military advantage anticipated. The defendant, however, had assumed that there were no civilians at the target site at the time of the airstrike. The Federal Prosecutor General furthermore analysed whether a crime under general criminal law had been committed. In his view, the Bundeswehr officer could not be held accountable for murder since his actions were permissible under international law and therefore justified under German criminal law. A breach of internal regulations such as rules of engagement could not make any action that was permissible under international law a criminal act. For these reasons, the Federal Prosecutor General dropped the criminal charges.[19]

5.3 Example: Transfer of a suspected pirate to Kenya

In March 2009, a German Navy frigate taking part in Operation ATALANTA captured and detained nine suspected pirates. Since the suspects were not intend-

19 Order for withdrawal of prosecution of 16 April 2010 – 3 BJs 6/10-4, German version available under www.generalbundesanwalt.de.

ed to be tried in German courts, they were transferred to the Kenyan authorities for prosecution. One of the suspects filed an action with the Cologne administrative court in which he requested that the court decide on whether or not his arrest by the German soldiers, his detention aboard the German warship and his transfer to Kenyan prosecuting authorities were against the law.

The Court did not object to the arrest of the plaintiff. In its view, the action was justified under Article 105 of the United Nations Convention on the Law of the Sea. The prerequisites, in particular the suspicion of piracy, had been met. The Court further argued that the detention aboard the frigate had not been unlawful either and, in particular, had not violated the requirements of Article 104 of the *Grundgesetz*, according to which a detainee must be brought before a judge no later than the day following his arrest. As regards naval operations on the high seas, this fundamental procedural right – so the court – could be interpreted in the sense of bringing a detainee before a judge as soon as possible under the prevailing circumstances. The German soldiers were not found guilty of a culpable delay. The plaintiff's legal action was successful, however, as regards his transfer to the Kenyan authorities. The court was of the view that this did not qualify as an EU measure, but rather was an exercise of German sovereign power. That action had been against the law because at the time there was concern as to whether the conditions in the Kenyan prison and the treatment of the suspected pirate would be in keeping with minimum standards required under international law. The judgement of the Cologne administrative court is not, as of yet, final and non-appealable.[20]

20 Judgement of 11 November 2011 – 25 K 4280/09, Neue Zeitschrift für Wehrrecht 2012: 84 et seq.

Pooling and Sharing in the EU and NATO

Christian Mölling

Like a magnifying glass, NATO's mission in Libya revealed serious flaws in European defence.[1] Not only is Europe's defence capability chronically underdeveloped and US support dwindling; the resources that could be used by European states to work on these deficits are also shrinking dramatically. Tight budgets are having strategic consequences. Unlike the "normal" underfunding of European defence establishments in the past decade, it is abruptly changing the military policy objectives and the means available to attain them, and the effect will be felt for a long time. If Europe does not stop reducing its rapidly dwindling defence resources, it will fundamentally change the structure of the armed forces in Europe and have serious implications for the defence industry. The Europe that will be left at the end of this process will be one that is unable to defend its strategic interests beyond its borders.

In joint communiqués on defence, NATO and the EU state that *Pooling and Sharing* (P&S) is currently considered a technocratic wonder weapon for combating this threatening military incapacity. It seems plausible that European states would benefit economically from the pooling of military capabilities. What remains unclear, however, is how the associated limitation of state sovereignty in defence issues is to be dealt with. The success achieved by the initiatives launched so far has been accordingly scant. In addition, P&S substitutes neither the investments required for the procurement of military capabilities nor the political setting that defines the intended uses of these capabilities. Instead of always looking for new individual projects to undertake, European states must address these difficult issues. At the moment, Europe risks talking to death another sensible possibility for maintaining its defence capability.

Europe without defence

On 6 July 2011, Italy made war history. It ordered its aircraft carrier to withdraw from NATO's mission in Libya for economic reasons. This was the first time a state withdrew war materiel from an ongoing operation due to a lack of money. The rationale behind this is a new paradigm in Europe's defence policy: the defence-economic imperative, i.e. the absolute priority of saving money. Military budgets are being subjected to quick, drastic and permanent cuts, and this has

1 This chapter is based on two earlier articles (Mölling, 2011, 2012).

become a strategic factor. Apart from security interests and risks, this is already determining not only what amounts and kinds of resources are available, but also what military objectives European states are able to pursue. Europe is therefore faced with a choice: It can either organise its defence more effectively or it can abandon its defence capability (Whitney, 2011).

Ailing capability development

Each state continues to insist on deciding itself what equipment its armed forces are to have and how they are to be organised. This, however, is thwarting efforts by the EU and NATO to make up dwindling resources by increasing efficiency, e.g. by intensifying defence cooperation. Such national conceit has caused three chronic problems (Mölling/Brune, 2011):

Firstly, it is true that initiatives and mechanisms of the EU and NATO states (NATO Capability Initiative, EU Headline Goal) have created an awareness of capability gaps, as far as the provision of capabilities is concerned. However, states have only rarely been able to agree on what additional resources are required to fill new gaps.

Secondly, the EU and NATO have almost no influence on armament production. Armament production is guided by national technological, industrial and structural considerations instead of being geared to meet common defence objectives.

The third problem is at the same time the greatest deficit – it is a fact that the provision of capabilities is largely separate from armament. Although Europe's armies regularly use the same capabilities in joint operations, i.e. under identical operational conditions, those capabilities are mostly developed and produced nationally. Armament institutions such as OCCAR (Organisation Conjointe de Coopération en matière d'Armement) are only poorly connected with the EU or NATO and have diverging concepts with regard to capability development and armament. This is also why government funds for capabilities are not invested effectively.

NATO's mission in Libya reveals capability gaps

NATO's mission in Libya in 2011 is only the most recent example of the permanent flaws referred to in this chapter. The dependence of Europe on the US that became apparent in the course of the mission gives a first impression of the situation that will exist when the US shifts its security focus to Asia and is no longer available to deal with European security issues.

In Libya, for instance, there was a shortage of reconnaissance assets and aircraft. Poland and the Baltic states were not even able to take part in the operation because they did not have the necessary equipment. Above all, Europe did not have an adequate C4ISTAR capability. C4ISTAR stands for *command, control, communications, computers, intelligence, surveillance, and reconnaissance* and comprises systems that combine all mission-relevant information and connect weapon systems. Without this capability, which currently only the US has to a sufficient extent, Europe is largely blind and deaf in military terms. Some 90% of military action in Libya would not have been possible without help from Washington.

Colliding problems and a paradigm shift

Europe's loss of its defence capability is therefore rather imminent. Not one European state, nor Europe as a whole, would currently be able to assert its interests with military power at a distance of approx. 1,000 kilometres.

In what is already a disastrous condition, Europe's defence capability is now colliding with the effects of the financial crisis. It is possible to see what this means, just three years after the beginning of the crisis, when one looks at the drastic reduction of capabilities. In contrast, the long-term consequences have yet to be identified.

The initial throes of the financial crisis in 2009/2010 quickly took away vast resources from the defence sectors of many European countries. The largest cuts, going up to 30%, are above all being made by small states such as Bulgaria. Most medium-sized states are cutting their budgets by 10 to 15%, while large states such as Germany and the United Kingdom have so far cut their budgets by less than 8%. There are, however, exceptions, such as Sweden or France, whose military budgets have so far been given a reprieve (Mölling/Brune, 2011).

In the medium term, no state will be able to shield its defence sector from funding cuts, because the liabilities of the European public budgets are an enormous long-term burden. What is more, borrowing is increasing as a result of the crisis. This is increasing the risk of excessive indebtedness for states and financial systems. A further reduction of debt is therefore absolutely necessary.

The European Commission estimates that, to permanently reduce debt to the level it was at before the financial crisis in 2008, the EU states would have to spend 1% of their GDP on redemption alone over the next 20 years. Currently, that would be 120 billion euros a year. Funding cuts would need to take effect immediately, and these projections are based on the crisis not getting any worse (EU Commission, 2011).

However, the forecasts for the coming years give reason to fear that growth will be too weak. The money for servicing existing debts and reducing further debt will thus have to be generated through further budget cuts. Due to contractual obligations, however, only minor savings can be made in the armament and personnel sectors in the short term. Both sectors must be funded by new debt or at the expense of the other national budgets. Demographic change and the low public opinion on the armed forces will in the medium term increase pressure to take funds out of the defence budget and to distribute these to other areas.

The initial effect: reduction of military capabilities at a rapid pace

The budget cuts that defence ministers have agreed on in the past 12 months already go beyond the "normal" underfunding of the defence establishments. The United Kingdom and Germany, two of the three largest European troop-contributing nations, have lowered their defence ambitions and will in future keep significantly fewer forces ready for action. France will follow suit in 2012. The traditional maritime power United Kingdom is doing such things as decommissioning its aircraft carrier overnight and scrapping brand-new maritime reconnaissance aircraft just shortly after they have been fielded. The Netherlands are decommissioning battle tanks they have only just upgraded.

Risk: a defenceless Europe

A further weakening of the capabilities as well as larger gaps can already be foreseen. If Europe continues to ignore the consequences of the defence-economic imperative, it runs the risk of losing its capacity to take military action due to uncontrolled structural changes in the armed forces and the defence industry.

Initially, European states wanted to use the financial crisis as a chance to rid the armed forces of some of the "excess weight" they had put on during the Cold War, with the aim of strengthening Europe's military muscles. However, they responded to the crisis in the usual way: by making reductions in their national forces and without consulting their allies. The trouble is that these responses are no longer helpful; in fact, they are harmful. The states are merely thinning out their equipment, but they are not downsizing the task spectrum they want to cover, i.e. their role specialisation. This is weakening the military muscles, and there are some areas, such as fighter aircraft, that are even gaining fat.

Structural reduction in three waves

Europe's defence capability will be hit by three waves of sustained reductions. Firstly, military capabilities will be reduced, then defence industry capacities, and finally technological competence. The first signs of this can already be seen. The more obvious the plight becomes, the less able Europe will be to take countermeasures. Events in the next three to five years will therefore determine what military capabilities Europe will possess in 20 years' time. By then, Europe might have saved so much that cooperation is no longer possible due to a lack of things to cooperate on.

The first wave: 27 bonsai armies

The first wave will cause 27 bonsai armies to be formed in Europe over the next five years. Due to national austerity efforts, the existing military forces will first be downsized, followed by their capability spectrums. In Germany, France and the United Kingdom, miniature armies will be formed that will cover virtually the entire capability spectrum, but will have little in the way of military punch. The small and medium-sized states, however, are already caught up in a race to the bottom. They are unilaterally abandoning entire capability areas and relying on the partners who still possess these capabilities when it comes to taking on tasks in the EU or NATO. This unintended role specialisation is more likely to widen existing capability gaps rather than close them.

Besides that, a modernisation gap is opening up. While the large states are slowly but steadily modernising their armies, many medium-sized and small countries are being forced to postpone work on further developing their armed forces. Many states are therefore only able to make marginal contributions to joint EU or NATO operations. This is reducing their possibilities of playing an active role in security decisions and thus in shaping common security policy through military involvement. Capability and modernisation gaps are hence also eroding solidarity.

The second wave: exodus of the defence industry

The second wave, within five to ten years' time, will cause the defence industry to leave Europe. Budget cuts will prevent the states of Europe from embarking on large new defence projects. However, while the European market is shrinking, all the other markets, in particular Asia and South America, will grow. The industries that are based in Europe will therefore attempt to gain access to these new markets via cooperation, exports and the movement of production to other countries (Anderson, 2011).

European companies will then be part of a globalised defence production industry, and competition between them will be even fiercer than it is today. This will increase dependence on partners and suppliers from outside Europe. In comparison, the national concern about security of supply for defence materiel within Europe will become a secondary issue. The preliminary stages of this development can already be observed: states are cancelling orders for defence articles that have already been placed. Not only is the export of such goods to the new markets on the rise, but also the transfer of technology. European companies are increasingly buying into these non-European markets.

The third wave: second-class in technology

The third wave, in ten to 20 years' time, will bring consequences in research and development (R&D). Europe will have to abandon its leading position in technology little by little, because fewer and fewer new technologies will be developed for use in the defence industry. Unlike money for armament or personnel, R&D investments are not tied up on a long-term basis in the future defence budgets. This is why they are more likely to fall victim to budgetary constraints that arise at short notice.

Pooling and Sharing – the ideal way to go?

The EU capitals are currently presenting Pooling and Sharing as the ideal way out of the defence crisis. This concept comprises various forms of defence cooperation (Maulny, 2008).

In the case of sharing, one or more countries make available a capability or equipment (such as cargo airplanes) to partners, or take on a task for others. If this is a permanent arrangement, the partners can save acquiring this capability themselves. Germany, for example, monitors the maritime space over the North Sea and therefore relieves the Netherlands of the need to do so. NATO countries take turns in policing the airspace over the Baltic states (Air Policing), meaning that the Baltic states can save the costs that go with having air forces of their own.

National capabilities are also made available to others in the case of pooling. A multinational structure is being established especially for pooling such contributions and coordinating their use, one example being the European Air Transport Command. Pooling can take place in the development, procurement and subsequent operation of joint items of equipment. This either allows items of equipment to be produced in larger numbers or a capability that no one state would be able to provide on its own due to the high cost involved to be acquired jointly. The AWACS flying radar systems or the NATO command structures are examples of joint procurement and operation (Zandee, 2010).

P&S: defence cooperation "reloaded"

In their Council Decision of December 2010, the EU states declared Pooling and Sharing the solution they wanted to adopt in order to cut costs and increase the military efficiency of their defence assets. NATO is pursuing similar goals under the label of "smart defence".

P&S is at present only a new catchword for the long-standing defence cooperation between EU and NATO states. There are currently some 100 projects. About 20 per cent of these are bilateral cooperation projects; 60 per cent of them concern five or less partners.

This patchwork results from the fact that the states have different ideas about what P&S can mean. Cutting costs, however, has seldom been the reason for projects. Their purpose has been to make joint use of equipment (e.g. tanks) or to close a specific capability gap, something that could only be done in a joint effort, as in the case of air transport.

Other factors must come into it. For example, the countries concerned must have similar strategic cultures, be in proximity with each other, be of a similar size themselves and have armed forces of a similar size, have the same understanding of the cooperation objectives, and have defence industries that must be able to compete on the same terms. There must also be a spirit of trust and solidarity among the partners (Valasek, 2010).

New activism, modest results

Since 2010, bilateral and multilateral P&S initiatives among the EU states have been experiencing a renaissance. The most important initiatives are the Anglo-French Defence Treaty, the cooperation between the Visegrád states of Hungary, Poland, Slovakia and the Czech Republic (the Visegrád Group), the Weimar Triangle (Germany, France, Poland) and the Gent Process. The only real novelty is the Gent Process, in which all EU states are participating.

These initiatives have so far painted a disparate picture, because the objectives and the number of participants vary widely. In spite of a few rays of hope, one being the capability of aerial refuelling, the results have been unsatisfactory and inadequate when the sizes of the problems are considered. In addition, the activities often do not serve the purpose of maintaining a common European defence capability, but are aimed at achieving national objectives. The debate is consequently confined to just a small number of military capabilities.

Some initiatives even duplicate or block each other. The Anglo-French Defence Pact, for example, duplicates a European Defence Agency (EDA) mine countermeasures project. To avoid endangering this pact, Paris is withdrawing from the EU Headquarters project, whereas Italy, in response to the same pact, is concluding a bilateral agreement with Germany in order to enable its industry to keep up with developments in the field of Unmanned Aerial Vehicles.

Neglected aspects

Three issues are being systematically excluded: role specialisation, defence industry, and additional investments (Major/Mölling/Valasek, 2012).

Role specialisation requires countries to give up certain capabilities and to focus on just a few. Many European states decline to do so for fear of becoming dependent on others. Nevertheless, this role specialisation is already taking place – involuntarily, in an uncoordinated manner and with considerable consequences for all partners' capacity to take action. When the Netherlands disposed of its battle tanks in 2011, it was not the only country to specialise. Germany and France, too, have involuntarily become role specialists because they are the only countries that possess significant arsenals of battle tanks.

In the medium term, pooling in the field of materiel procurement may initiate a reduction in redundant and costly industrial structures. This reduction, however, must be steered in order to avoid involuntary specialisation, as in the case of capabilities, which would result in the loss of critical or rare industrial capabilities. P&S might not be able to halt the deterioration of existing assets. But you can only share what you have. Gaps that can be found everywhere in Europe, for example in reconnaissance, can only be closed by making additional investments. NATO's mission in Libya in 2011 highlighted just how large these gaps are.

Sovereignty or effectiveness?

The decisive difference between the defence cooperation that states have practised to date and P&S as it is propagated now lies in the requirement that the main purpose of P&S is to help cut costs. However, the states are preventing a higher degree of economic efficiency and military effectiveness to be achieved by continuing to stick to their demand of deciding alone on matters concerning their armed forces.

All partners worry about doing more things jointly because they are afraid of three "multilateralism traps", i.e. being left on their own in a mission because a partner withdraws his troops; being unable to go on a mission because a partner with key capabilities is not participating in it; and being part of a community and thereby giving a free ride to countries that do not make any contributions of their own to security.

However, these worries are partly used as a pretext. The EU and NATO have been sitting in these "traps" for twenty years and have come to terms with them. The Balkans, Afghanistan, Libya – no single state would have been able to carry out any of these missions alone. Cooperation is meanwhile working in spite of national caveats and a lack of common strategic ground, as is so frequently asserted.

A comprehensive approach to P&S

P&S is not a panacea, but a necessary pillar of future European defence. Supporting measures are required in order to shape developments in such a way that the role specialisation that is under way and the additional investment in acquisition of capabilities that are lacking will enable the states to maintain a European defence capability (Major/Mölling/Valasek, 2012).

P&S can only contribute to solutions if European states are prepared to reconsider the idea of political sovereignty taking precedence over military effectiveness and economic efficiency. To be specific, they must address three questions with respect to future P&S projects: Under what circumstances are they willing to trust a cooperation partner, and to what extent are they able to give up their right to making decisions alone, in the interest of the defence requirements of others? Is cooperation effective in military terms? Does it generate savings? In addition, European states must provide a common framework for the counter-productive diversity of cooperation projects in order to bring the economic added value of P&S initiatives to bear.

Firstly, a permanent European Council for defence issues should be established for this purpose. Europe must also determine what its defence capability should look like and what industrial base will be needed to acquire the desired capability. As we can expect to see more joint European military activities in the next twenty years, the focus of current national reforms, plans and P&S projects should be on joint operations. The aim must therefore be to establish efficient European armed forces – instead of giving preference to national plans, as is the case at present (Dickow/Linnenkamp/Mölling, 2012). Only the heads of state and government can set these priorities, by agreeing to commit their defence, foreign, and finance ministers to pursuing firm objectives. The success achieved would have to be monitored on an annual basis.

Secondly, a common capability grid should be drawn up as a basis for role specialisation and cooperation. A European capability grid that provides information on how to sensibly increase and reduce capabilities can be derived from the priorities set by the heads of state and government. This and preventive coordination could help Europe prevent further erosion of capabilities.

Thirdly, the current distrust must be overcome. There are two ways in which to overcome a lack of trust. The states can conclude legally binding treaties on the provision of capabilities, is the case with the Anglo-French Defence Treaty. Or they can make up for the possibility of a partner dropping out of a project by permitting redundancy in their military capabilities. The lack or withdrawal of a number of aircraft, for example, must not lead to the collapse of Europe's air transport capability. Partners who withdraw from projects could make up for their absence by committing themselves to taking over routine tasks with their machinery. In doing so, they would lessen the burden on those who want to deploy their aircraft.

Fourthly, price tags should be made transparent. Anyone who wants to save must first know how much they are spending. Most cost-saving success attributed to P&S cannot be verified. It is also difficult to estimate the costs of non-cooperation. Every service provided in or by European armed forces must therefore have a price tag. Pricing may be difficult, but it is not impossible. NATO has already presented a list of savings that have been achieved through P&S projects.

Fifthly, better use should be made of the potential for savings offered by industry. The projects implemented to date have mainly been aimed at achieving quick successes with P&S so as to create a positive general image. The real savings effects, however, lie in long-term engagement and jointness. To achieve them, European states must coordinate the development of their capabilities with the armament process. This coordination should start with research and development activities, which are sharply decreasing, and must be followed by the joint purchasing of the same equipment. This would generate and harness significant economies of scale in Europe's defence industries. On the other hand, the strengths and specialisations of the individual national producers and suppliers provide starting points for future industrial work-sharing in Europe.

Sixthly, joint (re-)investment pools could be an incentive for cooperative savings. To offer an incentive for finding European solutions to the issue of how to close common gaps, the EU finance and defence ministers should set up a common investment pool, or fund, that is filled with saved defence resources. This pool should be available to the states for joint projects – but they should only be able to draw resources from it on the condition that they contribute an equal share themselves and that the projects yield savings. Compared to individual procurements, the EU defence ministers would then have double the amount at their disposal. This means, however, that they would need to agree on joint procurements. The savings from these projects should flow back into the pool; the states would profit from greater efficiency in industrial operations. This long-term increase in efficiency in the use of defence budgets could serve as an argument for getting the finance ministers to authorise appropriate funds. The seed capital should be advanced as an interest-free loan by those states that particularly stand to profit from the investment pool in political and military-industrial terms: Germany, France and the United Kingdom

The defence-economic imperative is forcing European states to radically reassess the interrelationship between political sovereignty, military effectiveness and economic efficiency. A mandate to carry out such a systematic and joint revision should be issued by the heads of state and government, a mandate that commits not only themselves, but also their foreign, defence and finance ministers. If they do not manage to change course, the finance ministers will take over armies from the defence ministers in a few years – as bankruptcy property.

Bibliography

Anderson, Guy (2011): Major Defence Markets in an Age of Austerity – Trends and Developments. IHS Jane's Report.

Biscop, Sven, Coelmont, Jo (2011): Pooling & Sharing: From Slow March to Quick March? In: The Security Policy Brief No.23. Egmont Royal Institute for International Relations. Brussels.

Dickow, Marcel/Linnenkamp, Hilmar/Mölling, Christian (2012): Für einen europäischen Defence Review. In: SWP-Aktuell 40. Berlin.

European Commission (2011): Annual Growth Survey. Macro Economic Report Annex 2 Brussels, 12.01.2011 COM 11 final.

Major, Claudia/Mölling, Christian/Valasek, Tomas (2012): Smart but too Cautious: How NATO Can Improve Its Fight Against Defence Austerity. In: Policy Brief, CFER. London.

Maulny, Jean-Pierre (2008): Pooling of EU member state assets in the implementation of ESDP. In: Subcommittee on Security and Defence. European Parliament. Brussels.

Mölling, Christian (2012): Pooling and Sharing in the EU and NATO: European Defence Needs Political Commitment rather than Technocratic Solutions, SWP Comments 2012/C 18.06.2012.

Mölling, Christian (2011): Europe without Defence. The States of Europe Have to Re-evaluate the Interrelationship between Political Sovereignty, Military Effectiveness and Economic Efficiency. SWP Comments 2011/C 38. November 2011.

Mölling, Christian/Brune, Sophie-Charlotte (2011): The impact of the financial crisis on European defence. In: Subcommittee on Security and Defence. European Parliament. Brussels.

Valasek, Tomas (2011): Surviving Austerity: The Case for a New Approach to EU Military Collaboration. In: Center for European Reform. London.

Withney, Nick (2011): How to Stop the Demilitarization of Europe. In: Policy Brief, CFER. London.

Zandee, Dick (2010): How governments should compensate for defence spending cuts. In: Europe's World.

Part V

Conclusion

German defence politics – a view from abroad

Tom Dyson

Introduction: German defence politics and burden-sharing

Germany lags behind its main European partners – Britain and France – across three key dimensions of defence reform: force structures, military capabilities and doctrine (Breuer, 2006: 206-20; Dyson, 2010: 47-60). These deficiencies raise important implications, not only for Germany's ability to wield power and influence in the international system, but also for the future of the Atlantic Alliance (Spiegel, 2012). The full participation of Europe's most sizeable and prosperous nation is central to NATO's success in meeting contemporary security challenges. Germany's 2011 Defence Policy Guidelines boldly emphasise the status of the Atlantic Alliance as the 'centrepiece' of its defence and security policy and recognise the imperative of burden-sharing: 'making a reliable and credible contribution to the Alliance is part of Germany's raison d'état' (VPR, 2011: 6). However, as this chapter will highlight, this statement appears insubstantial given the relatively restricted capacity of the *Bundeswehr* to burden-share within the Alliance. Similarly, for CSDP to be a credible organisation it must be in a position to pick up the security burden left by a US that is increasingly focused on the Middle East and Asia, by tackling security problems arising from the EU's geopolitical neighbourhood. Both CSDP and NATO require a strong German contribution, not only to civilian crisis-management capabilities, but also investment in strategic and tactical lift capabilities and command, control, intelligence, surveillance and reconnaissance (C4ISR) capabilities to facilitate participation in networked operations across the conflict spectrum.

This chapter will contextualise German defence politics by drawing comparisons with the defence politics of Western Europe's other Great Powers: Britain and France. In so doing, it sheds new light on the dynamics of German defence policy and politics. The majority of scholarship on post-Cold War German defence policy and politics emphasises the impact of Germany's anti-militaristic 'strategic culture' on the willingness and ability of actors within the defence and security policy-making community to sanction an expanded role for the *Bundeswehr* and develop the military structures, capabilities and doctrine necessary to permit full-spectrum operations (Dalgaard-Nielsen, 2006; Longhurst, 2004). However, this chapter will argue that Germany's laggard defence reform is, to a great extent, a result of the institutional structures of German defence politics, which create incentives amongst both the political elite and the military to manage the temporality of reform. It posits that poor civilian control over management of military input to defence planning and a federal system that incentivises the prioritisation of domestic political interests over convergence with international security imperatives, have left Germany at risk of remaining a relative consumer of security and of playing a backseat role in multinational deployments.

At the heart of the chapter lies the issue of the appropriate balance that should be struck between 'top-down' civilian and 'bottom-up' military input to effective defence planning. The topic of civil-military relations in defence planning is highly contested. While civilian control over the military is paramount in democracies, excessive civilian control can also act to the detriment of efficient military adaptation. As Huntington (1957: 57) notes, particular areas of defence planning processes require a strong degree of military autonomy: 'The fact that war has its own grammar requires that the military professionals be permitted to develop their expertise at this grammar without extraneous interference'.

The chapter finds that in areas where militaries should be permitted a significant level of autonomy to develop expertise, notably in military doctrine, the *Bundeswehr* has been subject to heavy-handed and inappropriate levels of civilian intervention. This intervention has stunted the capacity of the *Bundeswehr* to conform to military 'best practice', as illustrated by the slow adaptation of doctrine and training to operational exigencies under KFOR and ISAF (Dyson, 2012; Matlary, 2009: 151). Yet, in other crucial areas, such as defence procurement, where a stronger level of civilian oversight is necessary in order to align procurement plans with strategic priorities, the military has been able to exert excessive influence, leading to a lack of coherence in procurement. Furthermore, the chapter highlights that civilian intervention has not promoted an atmosphere of sufficient critical reflection and intellectual dynamism within the military. The chapter finds that the reform processes which have been set in place by Defence Ministers Karl-Theodor zu Guttenberg (2009-11) and Thomas de Maizière (2011-present) will go some way to rectifying these problems. However, the institutional structures of German defence politics, both within the military and broader political system, continue to suffer from deficits which impede the *Bundeswehr* from convergence with the model of military 'best practice' that has emerged in post-Cold War Europe.

The chapter begins by outlining the state of German defence policy and politics. It briefly describes the selective emulation[1] of the Revolution in Military

1 Waltz (1979: 127) argues that states *emulate* the military practises of the dominant state in the international system. However, this chapter concurs with the insights of Resende-Santos (2007: 58-61) who posits that secondary states in a unipolar international system (such as the European Great Powers), will seek to minimise the risks associated with

Affairs (RMA) that has formed the basis of European states' defence reforms and assesses Germany's progress across three key areas: force structures; military capabilities; concepts, doctrine and the capacity to learn lessons from operations.[2] Each of these three sections undertakes an analysis of the impact of the institutional structures of the BMVg and *Bundeswehr* upon these areas of policy. These sections also examine the proposals of the Weise Commission[3] and the subsequent reform enacted by de Maizière in April 2012 on the deficiencies identified in the institutional structures of the BMVg and *Bundeswehr*. The chapter then turns to the impact of the broader German political system on German defence reform and analyses the role that the German federal system has played in incentivising ineffective civilian oversight of military input to defence planning.

The state of German defence policy and the institutional structures of the Defence Ministry

British and French defence reforms have involved a partial and selective emulation of the RMA. This emulation has three main characteristics. Firstly the restructuring of command structures and development of joint, expeditionary forces, a process that began in France in 1995/96 and in Britain in 1997/98. Secondly, during the early-mid 2000s, the development of a Network-Enabled Capability (NEC) that seeks to exploit technology's tactical and operational advantages, but is more wary than US 'Network Centric Warfare' about networking's potential to transform the nature of warfare and deliver strategic effects (Farrell, 2008: 786-7). NEC has a technical dimension (the procurement of C4ISTAR systems) and a doctrinal dimension (the reconfiguration of thinking on command and control and military organisation in the context of the introduction of these new technologies).

their self-help efforts by emulating on the basis of proven effectiveness in conflict, rather than aggregate capabilities.

2 A frequently-cited definition of the RMA is provided by Krepinevic (1994: 30): 'It is what occurs when the application of new technologies into a significant number of military systems combines with innovative operational concepts and organisational adaptation in a way that fundamentally alters the character and conduct of conflict. It does so by producing a dramatic increase – often an order of magnitude or greater – in the combat potential or military effectiveness of armed forces.'

3 The Weise Commission was an independent Commission chaired by Frank-Jürgen Weise. It was established by the Cabinet to propose measures to streamline the *Bundeswehr's* command and administrative structures and delivered its report in October 2010

British and French doctrinal development in the context of the RMA has also cohered around the Effects-Based Approach to Operations (EBAO). In contrast to US Effects-Based Operations (EBO), which focus on the application of largely kinetic effects against near-peer competitors, EBAO recognises that it is not military operations themselves which have changed in character, but the approach to operations. It is conceived of as an approach that, embedded within the Comprehensive Approach (a multi-agency, cross- government approach to the planning and execution of operations), can facilitate the integration of all agencies of government in the delivery of both kinetic and non-kinetic effects (JD 7/06). Since EBO were stripped from US Joint Doctrine in 2008, UK EBAO has given way to an emphasis on 'Effects-Based Thinking' that shuns EBAO's determinism, while recognising EBAO's utility in targeting 'closed systems'. In addition, following operational experience in Africa, the Balkans and Afghanistan/Iraq, UK and French defence reform has also focused on doctrine and training for Stabilisation and Counterinsurgency operations and the appropriate role of networked capabilities within these operational contexts (Alderson, 2009; De Durand, 2009).

German emulation of the RMA has been threefold. Firstly, through reforms to command structures, it has focused upon improving the *Bundeswehr's* jointness, deployability and interoperability. German defence reform has also been characterised by C2ISR capability investment to facilitate networked operations, as well as investment in the capabilities required to project power within and outside of Europe's geopolitical neighbourhood. Thirdly, reform has involved doctrinal development around the implications of networking for Command and Control and, to a limited extent, on EBAO (Dyson, 2010: 47-56). Doctrinal development has also cohered around the development of Stabilisation doctrine (Noetzel/Schreer 2009). In this regard German defence reforms represent a case of convergence with those of its closest European partners (Dyson, 2010: 28-60).

However, German emulation of the RMA and the development of Stabilisation/Counterinsurgency doctrine have taken place at a slow pace. The British (in 1997/98) and French (in 1994) abandoned territorial defence in favour of expeditionary crisis-management operations of varying intensity (Irondelle, 2003: 162; McInnes, 1998; 833-36). Yet it was only in 2003 that Germany placed crisis-management at the heart of its defence policy (Dalgaard-Nielsen, 2006: 123-26). As the following sections highlight, this delay in changes to policy objectives has been matched by deficiencies in force structures, military capabilities, doctrine, as well as the capacity of the military to learn lessons from operations, which weaken Germany's capacity to undertake expeditionary operations. These deficiencies derive, to a great extent, from the dysfunctional management of military input to defence planning; a problem that has only been partially addressed by the reform of de Maizière.

Force structures: gradually enhancing deployability and jointness

The 1996 establishment of the Permanent Joint Headquarters formed an important step by the British military in the establishment of joint, interoperable command structures and rapidly deployable forces; a development that was given greater embeddedness in the 1997/98 SDR (McInnes, 1998: 837). The reconfiguring of French command structures to facilitate the generation of joint, modular forces also took place in the mid 1990s (1996). In contrast, it was only after the turn of the Century that deployability and jointness was placed centre-stage in German defence reform, notably through the 2001 creation of the Operations Command and Response Forces Operations Command. Since 2004 the Leadership Academy's Advanced Joint Staff Course has also played an important role in reinforcing the principle of jointness throughout the services (Interviews, Führungsakademie, 2010).

However, problems remain, most notably in the capacity of the *Bundeswehr* to deploy significant numbers of troops overseas. Although the 2006 Defence White Paper (DWP) outlined the intention to develop the capacity to deploy 14,000 troops abroad (from a total force of 245,000) in support of complex crisis-management operations, the *Bundeswehr* is currently struggling to maintain the approximately 7,100 troops currently deployed overseas (Brune et al, 2010: 2). Despite the tight fiscal constraints on British defence spending, these modest goals contrast markedly with the UK's ambitions in the 2010 Strategic Defence and Security Review (SDSR). The SDSR plans to develop the capacity to deploy a one-off intervention force of 30,000 from a total force of 154,000 troops. Alternatively it proposes the capacity to undertake (concurrently) a long-term stabilisation operation of 6,500, a short-term complex intervention of up to 2,000 personnel as well as a short-term simple intervention of up to 1,000 troops (SDSR: 2010: 19). Furthermore, French defence planning assumptions aim (from 225,000 troops) to simultaneously deploy up to 30,000 troops in a major expeditionary operation for up to one year (FWP, 2008: 11).

The *Bundeswehr's* poor deployability is highlighted by the level of support required by each individual combat solider when compared with the UK and France. As Hodge (2012) notes: 'Its tooth-to-tail ratio requires 35 uniformed and 15 civil personnel to support each solider in combat duty, while France gets by with a ratio of 1:8:2 and Britain with 1:9:4'. Moreover the separation between initial entry and stabilisation forces has undermined the capacity of the *Bundeswehr* to act effectively in complex crisis-management operations where the intensity of conflict can vary at speed. Germany's ability to undertake expeditionary operations has also been hampered by the persistence of conscription until 2010 (Dyson, 2007: 74).

The current reform process makes two key changes for German force structures. Crucially a reduction of the *Bundeswehr* to 185,000 troops will take place, accompanied by the suspension of conscription and the introduction of a voluntary, up to 23 month, civil-service that will enable young people to undertake either community service or serve in the *Bundeswehr* (a maximum of 15,000 posts in the *Bundeswehr*) (Weise, 2010: 28). Secondly, in recognition of the tendency of operations to vary in intensity, the separation between attack, stabilisation and support forces will be abolished (Weise, 2010: 31).

The reforms will also make significant reforms to command structures to reduce their complexity and enhance the efficiency of operational leadership. The Weise Commission had recommended strengthening the role of the *Generalinspekteur* (General Inspector) by placing the *Generalinspekteur* on the same level as the Permanent State Secretaries. This would have embedded the *Generalinspekteur* firmly within the executive group of the Ministry (Weise, 2010: 31). The proposal was rejected by de Maizière, due to the fear of vesting too much power in a single military actor (Siebert, 2012: 65). Nevertheless, the position of the *Generalinspekteur* has been strengthened, as he will now take ultimate responsibility for all aspects of the planning, preparation, leadership and follow-up of military operations (Siebert, 2012: 64-5).

The Weise Commission's recommendations to reduce the levels of hierarchy across the *Bundeswehr* in order to increase the transparency, simplicity and speed of decision-making processes have also been adopted (Weise, 2010: 31). The Commission included proposals to avoid overlapping responsibilities between the services by bringing together the civil and military sections of the Ministry on the basis of function, through a reduction of the ministry from 3,000 to 1,500 posts and moving all sections of the BMVg to Berlin, thereby reducing the number of departments in the Ministry by seven (Weise, 2010: 35). De Maizière has proved unwilling to challenge the division of the Defence Ministry between Berlin and Bonn, reflecting the political and bureaucratic difficulties in overcoming the *Berlin-Bonn Gesetz* that stipulated the distribution of government departments following reunification (Interview, SWP, 2012; Interview, BMVg, 2012).

However, de Maizière's reform has adopted the Commission's proposals to overcome duplication within the Ministry of Defence. The simplified Ministerial structures will include eight Departments: Politics; Budget; Law; Planning; Forces Leadership; Personnel; Armament and IT and Infrastructure. This is an important development, as it abolishes the division between civilian and military staff in the Defence Ministry that has existed since the creation of the *Bundeswehr* in 1955 and has fostered unnecessary complexity in policy planning and implementation (Siebert, 2012: 65). Finally, in order to reduce the complexity of operational leadership, the role of the services' leadership commands in international and national operations will also be diminished by further strengthening the Operations Command in Potsdam that will be placed under the direct leadership of the *Generalinspekteur* (Weise, 2010: 35). In short, these reforms to command structures are a very positive step towards enhancing the deployability and jointness of the *Bundeswehr* by reducing duplication, simplifying operational leadership and fostering a stronger *Generalinspekteur* who is able to overcome the more parochial concerns of the single services.

Military capabilities: the politics of procurement

Since 2003 a set of major C2ISR investment programmes have been instigated, which have put in place the foundations for a network-enabled *Bundeswehr*. The first key area of investment is the development of networkable radio equipment in order to boost C2 capabilities and interoperability with EU and NATO partners (Adams/Ben-Ari, 2006: 55-8; Dyson, 2010: 52-3). Secondly, investment has cohered around the creation of an intelligence, surveillance and reconnaissance network (ISR) including space-based reconnaissance systems, as well as Unmanned Aerial Vehicles (Adams/Ben-Ari, 2006: 56-7; Flournoy/Smith, 2005: 91-3).

Despite these acquisitions, the *Bundeswehr* continues to lag behind its key NATO partners in networked capabilities. NEC is composed of three stages: an initial stage, where links between existing equipment are enhanced; a transitional phase where the integration of systems is improved and finally, a mature state in which all possible military equipment is synchronised. By 2007 British and French forces reached an initial networked capability (Dyson, 2010: 40-43). A demonstrator exercise had been planned for late 2013 to test the *Bundeswehr's* initial network-enabled capability, but in late 2011 this exercise was postponed indefinitely. As the following section will demonstrate, this postponement is a consequence of doctrinal disagreement between the individual services over the implications of networking for command and control as well as the need to integrate the lessons of participation in the Afghan Mission Network (ISAF's C4ISR network).

However, it is also the result of technical problems in interoperability between the command and control systems of the services as too little consideration was given to jointness and interoperability in procurement. The individual services have developed their own C2 systems which are unable to properly communicate with each other (Interview, BTC, 2012). Indeed, of the *Bundeswehr's* 70 procurement programmes in 2010 only 6 were network-ready, 11 had limited NCW capability, while the remaining programmes were not network-ready (Wiesner, 2011: 15). Yet, as Wiesner (2011: 15) highlights: 'the identification of these problems did not result in a refocusing of command-and-control systems projects. Quite the contrary, service-specific communication platforms (...) continue to be funded'. In addition to problems in C2ISR acquisition, until recently Germany has continued to invest too heavily in capabilities more suitable for Cold War conflict scenarios than for expeditionary warfare (Dyson, 2011).

The lack of responsiveness and incoherence of the weapons acquisition system is a result of three deficits in the acquisition process. The first problem is the structuring of military input to defence planning. The *Bundeswehr's* Budgetary and Armament Departments are composed of a significant number of civilian personnel who stay in post for several years. This allows civilian personnel to develop expertise and endows them with the capacity to challenge the proposals of military personnel, whose tenure in these Departments is usually no longer than two years (Interview, SWP, 2012). However, until de Maizière's reform, the key organs responsible for decisions on changes and additions to the *Bundeswehr's* acquisition programme were dominated by military input (Dyson, 2011: 261-64). These organs include the Integrated Working Group for Capability Analysis (responsible for translating the broader direction on capabilities provided by the 2006 DWP into decisions on force structures, doctrine and capability procurement), and the Military Advisory Board (that has ultimate decision-making authority on major projects). The *Generalinspekteure* of the individual services have therefore been able to trade-off support for their key projects. As a consequence, weapon systems can be purchased without significant consideration for the implications for the overall capability profile of the *Bundeswehr* (Dyson, 2011: 261-64; Interviews, BTC, 2009).

Secondly, the performance of the German procurement programme is undermined by the weak role of the German SAI. While the SAI is mandated to oversee procurement, it is only able to devote a small pool of manpower to the task (Dyson, 2011: 261-64). Finally, although the *Bundestag* enjoys the power to approve projects costing over €25 million, its capacity to hold the Defence Minister to account for delays and cost over-runs is limited. A culture of secrecy surrounds defence policy that undermines the ability of actors from civil society and Government institutions to properly sanction the *Bundeswehr* for the mismanagement of defence capability acquisition. There is, for example, no information available in the public realm from either the SAI or the *Bundeswehr's* Armament Division on time-slippages and budget over-runs on major defence capability procurement programmes (Dyson, 2011: 261-64).

Poor civilian oversight of defence planning on military capabilities is not confined to Germany. The 2009 Independent Review of Acquisition conducted by Bernard Gray points to significant deficiencies in UK procurement, concluding that the costs of programmes are on average 40 per cent greater than planned and delivered 80 per cent later than estimated (Gray, 2009: 16). The report emphasises the urgent need to reform the acquisition process to allow civilian actors to exert greater control over the services' procurement plans (Gray, 2006: 9). Combined with the poor management of relations with industry, these deficits in the structuring of military input to defence planning in the UK have reduced the responsiveness of the procurement programme to ongoing operations by leaving a deficit of £36 Billion in the defence budget.

However, the Report of Lord Levene (who was mandated by the UK Government with developing reform proposals for the MoD's procurement structures) of June 2011, outlines a number of reforms to the institutional structures of capability procurement. Changes include removing the single service chiefs from the Defence Board (the key decision-making organ on defence procurement) and replacing them with the Chief of Defence Staff (Levene, 2011: 4). In addition, military and civilian personnel will stay in post for longer at Defence Equipment and Support (the MoD's procurement and support organisation). This will allow civilian staff to develop the expertise to challenge military opinion and give military staff the opportunity to focus on delivering capabilities, rather than individual weapon systems for their services (Levene, 2011: 4). Furthermore, by creating the Joint Forces Command (JFC) that will be overseen by a four star General, the reform also enhances jointness in procurement. The JFC is mandated with strengthening joint warfare development by acting as a 'service-agnostic' institution that ensures lessons learned from operations are fed more effectively into high-level decision-making on procurement (Levene, 2011: 4).

France enjoys a more efficient system of procurement. The French acquisition programme suffers from an average delay of only 1.5 months per year, compared to the average delay of 6 months per year in the UK, and is also subject to lower cost over-runs that the UK (Gray, 2009: 215). In contrast to Germany and the UK, decision-making on capability acquisition is highly-centralised and streamlined. Three staff work under the Defence Minister's direct authority on acquisition: the Chief of the Defence Staff, the Chief Executive of the French Armament Agency (DGA) and the General Secretary of the Administration (Gray, 2009: 220-23).The Defence Minister takes full responsibility for project delivery that is coordinated through the Ministerial Investment Board (MIB). While the single services are represented on the MIB, the Minister must balance the services' competing perspectives (Gray, 2009: 220-23). Finally, in contrast to the UK and Germany, the French National Assembly enjoys strong oversight powers on the defence budget through the Military Programme Law (LPM). The LPM establishes the military budget and major capability investment projects over a six year period and the Defence Minister must provide annual reports to parliament on the cost, timing and performance of projects (Gray, 2009: 220-23).

The reform proposals of de Maizière make a number of important changes to the process of procurement. Firstly, the reform establishes a central purchasing organisation to foster a clear delineation of responsibility in acquisition by abolishing the overlapping structures of the BMVg's Armament Division, Federal Office of Defence Technology and Procurement and the IT Division (Weise, 2010: 37). Furthermore, procurement process will be optimised by avoiding maximalist project specifications and through the use of off-the-shelf technology wherever possible to avoid the complexities associated with new projects (Weise, 2010: 37).

In addition, by making the *Generalinspekteur* responsible for combat readiness, the reform appears to provide an opportunity to foster greater coherence in procurement. While the *Generalinspekteur* previously only had a decisive decision-making role on the Military Advisory Board in cases where the services could not reach agreement, he now enjoys veto power (Interview, BMVg, 2012). Finally, the creation of the *Planungsamt* (that will work under the *Bundeswehr's* new Political Division) will help ensure that jointness infuses the development of concepts and procurement. The reform process establishes a new Integrated Planning Process (IPP) that aims to ensure that fewer, but more coherent procurement plans are put forward to the upper echelons of the Ministry for approval. The IPP will be led by the *Planungsamt* who will exert strong centralised control and ensure that greater consideration is given to impact of procurement decisions for the overall capability profile of the *Bundeswehr*. As the single service commands are now located outside the structures of the Defence Ministry, all their input to capability development must be routed through the *Planungsamt.* Furthermore, the *Planungsamt* will be composed of a significant number of civilian personnel. This will not only permit the development of a greater level of knowledge and 'institutional memory', but will also ensure a higher level of impartiality in procurement.

However, problems remain. Firstly, the coordinative power of the *Generalinspekteur* may be stymied by his reliance on the services for information. Although the number of civilian staff dealing with procurement will increase, the military staff of the *Planungsamt* will consist of officers from the services whose tenure will only last two years. During these years they will be expected to act primarily in the interests of their service. Failure to do so would be likely to result in reduced promotion prospects (Interview, SWP, 2012). Secondly, in contrast to the high-level of civilian control exhibited by the French procurement process, the reform fails to strengthen the capacity of external actors, like the *Bundestag* and the SAI, to hold the BMVg to account for time slippages and cost-over-runs. Finally, while the Weise Commission recognised the need focus on off-the-shelf solutions and acknowledges the necessity for fundamental change in cooperation between the *Bundeswehr* and industry, the Commission and the reform do not propose specific measures which will allow the BMVg to exert greater control over industry when projects are not delivered on time and to cost.

Concepts, doctrine and learning from operations

Germany exhibits highly-reactive doctrinal development, undermining Germany's performance in operations and reducing its capacity to burden-share in CSDP and the NATO. As the introductory section highlighted, British and French thinking on concepts and doctrine associated with the RMA is highly developed. Both countries have converged around the 'Effects Based Approach to Operations' (EBAO) and more recently, 'Effects-Based Thinking'. Significant conceptual development has also take place around NEC (Dyson, 2010: 28-47). German thinking on NEC has taken the form of *Vernetzte Operationsführung* (Networked Operational Command, Doctrine *NetOpFü*). The selective emulation of the RMA undertaken by Britain and France that focused on the adaptation of RMA technologies to deliver kinetic and non-kinetic effects, provided a strong indication of 'best practice' in networking (Dyson, 2010: 50-1). Hence while initial thinking on networking cohered closely with that of the US, these observations of Alliance partners have combined with Germany's experiences in the Balkans and Afghanistan to ensure that *NetOpFü* emphasises the capacity of RMA technologies to facilitate the speedy, efficient application of military action across the conflict spectrum. There is also a broad consensus across that the principle of 'Mission Command' should stand at the heart of *NetOpFü* (Interview, BTC, 2012). However, significant contestation remains about EBAO and *NetOpFü*. Indeed, the 2009 Common Shield experiment, that formed an early test of the *Bundeswehr's* networking capabilities, identified the lack of a common position on *NetOpFü* between the services as a major problem (Heitmüller 2009).

The *Bundeswehr* also suffers from deficits in Stabilisation and Counterinsurgency (COIN) doctrine. In the UK and France, doctrine provides a detailed account of how to undertake Stabilisation and COIN operations (Alderson, 2010: 28-40; De Durand, 2010: 11-28). Crucially, British and French army doctrine has, since 1997, recognised that expeditionary crisis-management operations are characterised by conflict of rapidly varying intensity (Dyson, 2010: 34-47). Yet, until its revision in 2007, German Army doctrine (*Truppenführung von Landstreitkräften*) categorised fighting, peace-support and humanitarian aid into distinct conflict categories (Noetzel/Schreer, 2009: 16-22). Doctrine was updated in 2005 to include Guidelines for Operations against Irregular Forces; however it did not properly integrate the kinetic and non-kinetic dimensions of military operations (Noetzel/Schreer, 2009: 16-22). Hence the *Bundeswehr* lacks a comprehensive COIN doctrine suitable for the north of Afghanistan. In the words of a leading figure at the German Army Office, the absence of explicit COIN doctrine has 'fostered a lack of COIN mindset within the Army' (Interviews, Heeresamt, 2011).

Doctrinal adaptation has been hampered by the institutional structures of the BMVg, notably by the delay in the establishment of a formalised process of lesson evaluation and implementation following operations ('lessons-learned'). The British and French adopted a digitised lessons-learned system in the late 1990s. Yet it was only in 2004 that Germany established an IT system to support lessons-learned (*InfoSysEEBw*) at the Operations Command (Interviews, Heeresamt, 2011). The Operations Command acts as a 'service agnostic' institution coordinating lesson identification and implementation, deciding which service should take the lead on the analysis of an issue and checking follow up through *InfoSysEEBw* (Interview, BMVg 2010). The Operational Staff and its section for Operational Assessment have also played an important role in enhancing the *Bundeswehr's* capacity to adapt doctrine to the operational environment. It has allowed the military to more fully exploit *InfoSysEEBw* by more effectively identifying and disseminating lessons (Interview, BMVg, 2010). The work of the Operational Staff has been supplemented by the *Bundeswehr's* Institute of Social Sciences that, on behalf of the Operational Staff, prepares questionnaires for commanders to be completed before, during and after deployment and organises workshops for commanders (Interview, BMVg, 2010). The 2004 establishment of the *Bundeswehr* Transformation Centre (BTC) as a 'think-tank' on issues of force structures, doctrine, military capabilities and concept development and experimentation (CD&E) also had a positive, albeit rather limited, impact on the *Bundeswehr's* capacity to identify military 'best-practice'.

While the creation of the Operations Staff has improved joint lessons learned, it has had negative implications for the lessons-learned processes within the individual services. In the UK, the services have the capacity to attend to issues which do not have implications for jointness and interoperability. However the Operations Command has the power to decide whether a single service issue enters into *InfoSysEEBw*. This control over lessons-learned is convenient for the core executive as it ensures that changes do not take place which may cause political difficulties (Dyson, 2012: 47-8) Yet it slows military adaptation and has led the Army Command to work outside the formal lessons-learned process to enact necessary changes to training, doctrine and procurement (Dyson, 2012: 41-2).

In addition, despite the establishment of the Working Group on Joint and Combined Operations (AGJACOP) at the Leadership Academy and the creation of the BTC, Germany has lacked a central body like the UK's Development, Concepts and Doctrine Centre (DCDC) and France's Centre for Concept Development, Doctrine and Experimentation (CICDE) that can lead the development of joint doctrine. The implementation of doctrinal change involves a complex process of consultation that reduces the *Bundeswehr's* ability to decisively respond to operational challenges and slows the speed with which changes are integrated into training (Dyson, 2012: 39-44). This problem has not only slowed the development of COIN doctrine, but has also reduced the capacity of the services to develop a consensus position on *NetOpFü* and EBAO.

Furthermore, the identification of lessons-learned in the Comprehensive Approach (known as 'Networked Security' in Germany) has been undermined by poor communication between the Foreign Ministry (AA) and BMVg. The lack of institutionalised dialogue between the two ministries has been particularly evident following cooperation in Provincial Reconstruction Teams in Afghanistan (Interview, BMVg, 2010). The 2006 DWP contained two pages detailing the centrality of the Networked Security to German security policy (DWP, 2006: 22-24). However, the document was written by the BMVg and approved by the Cabinet without full AA 'buy in' (Interview, BTC, 2011). Networked Security is viewed by the AA as a concept that is 'owned' by the BMVg and a tool to allow it to accrue competencies from other ministries (Interview, SWP, 2012). Consequently, the AA is very reluctant to cede competencies to the BMVg in this area (Interview, SWP, 2012). In addition, the Interior Ministry and Police broadly continue to view overseas missions as outside their traditional areas of responsibility (Interview, BMVg, 2012).

Moreover, whilst in the UK and France the military is permitted significant autonomy in doctrinal development and implementation, German doctrine is subject to strong civilian control (Aust/Vashakmadze, 2008: 2223-36). The *Bundestag* enjoys constitutionally-mandated powers over operational issues, including rules of engagement, command and control and risk-assessment. In contrast, the oversight powers of the UK Parliament extend only to the approval of a mission's mandate and the right to visit troops on deployment, while the French National Assembly enjoys the right to vote on troop deployments, but only four months after the initiation of an operation (Aust/Vashakmadze, 2008: 2225). The high-level of *Bundestag* control has been matched by preoccupation of the core executive and BMVg political leadership with doctrinal development and tactical and operational issues (Dyson, 2012: 48). Strong civilian control not only complicates the process of doctrinal development, but also allows party-political concerns to cloud doctrinal decision-making, fostering stagnation. This stagnation has been evident in the development of an explicit German COIN doctrine that has proved a particularly sensitive political issue (Dyson, 2012; Noetzel/Schreer, 2009; Noetzel, 2011). Finally, German doctrine remains classified and doctrinal development is surrounded by a culture of secrecy. Classification limits the military's ability to call upon expertise from academia and civil society. Hence despite the steps taken by the BTC to foster a more open environment to doctrinal and conceptual development within the *Bundeswehr*, it was less successful in engaging with external actors (Interview, BTC, 2011).

The changes to command structures outlined earlier in this section have been welcomed by key figures within the *Bundeswehr* responsible for coordinating the 'lessons-learned' process as an important step in enhancing the implementation of lessons-learned. It is anticipated that these changes will lead to a reduction in the number of veto-points to enacting change and that they will enhance ability of the *Generalinspekteur* to ensure greater coherence in the process of military transformation (Interview, BMVg, 2010; Interview, BMVg, 2012). Zu Guttenberg had also given consideration to proposals to bring together the work of the Leadership Academy, Centre for Inner Leadership, *Bundeswehr* Universities, the Academy for Information and Communication, Institute for German Military History, BTC and *Bundeswehr* Institute for Social Sciences to create a single Defence Academy (Interview, BTC, 2011; Interview, BMVg, 2012; Interview, SWP, 2012). Had this restructuring been enacted, it would not only have led to a reduction in costs, but would also have helped to streamline the analysis and follow up of lessons-learned and the identification of doctrinal 'best-practice' from observation of the experiences of Alliance partners. However, following vociferous opposition from the Academy for Information and Communication, Institute for Social Sciences and Centre for Inner Leadership, these proposals were dropped (Interview, SWP, 2012).

Nevertheless, de Maizière's proposals offer hope of improvement in the intellectual dynamism of the *Bundeswehr*, notably through the creation of the *Planungsamt*. The *Planungsamt* will incorporate staff from AGJACOP as well as the Transformation Centre and create an organisation with the power to take a lead role on doctrine and conceptual development. This development is likely to have a positive impact by allowing greater centralised control in conceptual and doctrinal development. It will, for example, allow a stronger level of coordination to be exerted in conceptual development on *NetOpFü*. A single actor will be aware of all the activities – technical, organisational and conceptual – which are taking place within the single services and various sections of the Ministry on *NetOpFü*. The Division for *NetOpFü* within the *Planungsamt* will have the power to intervene in these processes and enjoy similar powers to the UK's NEC Programme Office that was established at the UK MoD in 2007 and has enjoyed relative success in overseeing and directing the concept development and implementation of NEC (Wiesner, 2011).

The reform proposals are, however, silent on the problem of excessive civilian interference in doctrine that has fostered doctrinal inertia. In addition, the reform fails to address the lack of openness to critical reflection that derives from the classification of doctrine. Finally, the reform process does little to attend to deficiencies in cross-government cooperation under 'Networked Security'. In particular, the reform missed an opportunity to establish an organisation akin to the UK's Stabilisation Unit (jointly owned by the Foreign Office, Defence Ministry and Department for International Development) that could help to mediate cross-government collaboration more effectively.

In summary, the analysis presented in the above sub-sections highlight the negative impact of the institutional structures of the *Bundeswehr* and BMVg and poor civil-military relations in defence planning processes on the German defence reform process. However, the following section will demonstrate that these deficiencies in defence planning processes are a symptom of a wider set of problems which beset German defence politics at the macro-political level.

The German political system and impediments to the effective structuring of military input to defence planning

The majority of the literature on German defence policy posits that German strategic culture – rooted in the moral and military defeat of WW2 and characterised by anti-militarism and a reflexive commitment to multilateralism – is an important determinant, not only of the content of German defence policy, but also the nature of defence politics (Dalgaard-Nielsen, 2006; Longhurst, 2004). The concept of strategic culture emphasises the role played by cognitive paradigms within societies and the key institutions of defence and security policy-making in 'predisposing societies in general and political elites in particular to certain actions and policies over others' (Duffield, 1998: 27). According to this scholarship, the retention of conscription for the first two decades of the post-Cold War era and concern about the need for a high-level of civilian control over rules of engagement and military doctrine are a consequence of the legacy of Germany's past. Our attention should, however, not be focused so much on the impact of strategic culture, but on the federal political system. The institutional structure of the German state and particular linkages between defence, budgetary and social policy has narrowed the autonomy of the core executive to make far-reaching changes to the content of German defence policy and by extension, to the institutional structures of German defence politics.

Firstly, the federal system has created a preoccupation amongst successive defence ministers with the politics of base closures. Military bases can sustain thousands of jobs and directly affect the political interests of *Länder* politicians, engaging in particular the interest of *Länder* Chancelleries and Economies Ministries (Dyson, 2007). In the UK and France, the unitary state provides significant windows of opportunity to push through politically-unpalatable large-scale base closures. However, the regular regional elections of the German federal system and power of the *Länder* through the *Bundesrat* has created a greater degree of sensitivity to regional concerns (Dyson, 2007). Hence the difficulty of managing the electoral fall-out of base closures affected the willingness of Defence Ministers to propose large-scale force reductions, including the conscription's abolition. It also led to the political targeting of base closures, whereby bases were not closed on the basis of a sober assessment of military requirements, but national and *Länder* electoral cycles and the extent to which *Länder* contributed to the policy success of the governing coalition (Dyson, 2007: 64-65).

Secondly, the autonomy of the core executive in defence is also restricted by the impact of the German federal system on the capacity of political elites to mobilise the public on behalf of contemporary security challenges. German public opinion is sensitive to the development of a more assertive military doctrine and the use of the *Bundeswehr* for higher-intensity operations. However, to locate this sensitivity solely within the German security culture and the 'culture of anti-militarism' that took root during the post-war era neglects the malleability of culture that is a resource as well as constraint in the mobilisation of society on behalf of defence, foreign and security policy goals (Dyson, 2007: 165-73).

During the Cold War anti-militarism and multilateralism formed the central pillars of German defence and security policy. These principles formed a logical response to Germany's security environment after the end of WW2. The restrictions on German sovereignty which were imposed following WW2 restricted the *Bundeswehr* to the defence of German territory. The principles of anti-militarism and embedding German defence and security policy within multilateral frameworks were vital mechanisms in managing German rehabilitation into the international community and in ensuring international support for reunification (Cole, 2001: 6-12). By the early 1990s these imperatives had taken on a significant level of ideological rigidity. However, the post-Cold War era presented new imperatives, notably the need to deploy high-intensity expeditionary military force as part of coalitions of the willing. As a result, the narratives which had been deployed to legitimate German adherence to the dictates of Cold War security exigencies needed radical reshaping.

The British and French unitary political systems provide substantial windows of opportunity to take unpopular decisions about expeditionary troop deployment and to make fundamental changes to long-standing tenets of their defence and security policies. For example, upon his election in 2007 without the constraints of cohabitation, French President Nicolas Sarkozy enjoyed the opportunity to refashion nationalism and ideology by using Gaullist principles were used in a controversial and 'hollowed-out' form to justify reintegration to NATO's integrated command structures. Sarkozy claimed that reintegration was as a 'break with the method, but not the principles' of Gaullism and was a means with which to ensure French 'independence' (France 24: 2009). In contrast, regular elections at the *Länder* level complicate the process of reshaping the discursive narratives underpinning German defence and security policy (Interview, AA, 2012). During the post-Cold War era German policy-makers have, therefore, been forced to undertake a 'salami-slicing' approach to redefining the role of military power in German defence policy that involved regular, but limited, changes to policy (Dyson, 2007: 69-71).

The linkages between defence, budgetary and social policy in Germany have also had an important impact upon the temporality of German defence reform and have had a particularly strong impact on German force structures. Germany's well-established system of conscientious objection provided cheap labour for the German social system throughout the post-Cold War era. Each year between 80,000-130,000 young men worked in the social system at a third of the cost of professionals. Hence the Federal Finance Ministry was highly-reluctant to abolish conscription, for fear of the negative impact on the process of budget consolidation (Dyson, 2007). In contrast, the sudden abolition of conscription by President Jacques Chirac in 1996 was facilitated by a system of conscientious objection that did not permit extensive social work and the large window of opportunity afforded by a seven-year term in office. It was only in 2010, once the utility of conscripts in contemporary military operations had become unequivocally clear, that zu Guttenberg suspended conscription.

These three factors have played a significant role in creating the dysfunctional model of civil-military relations in defence planning outlined in the above section. The incentive provided by low executive autonomy in defence to manage the pace of defence reform has led Defence Ministers to block 'bottom-up' learning from operations. Hence Ministers have failed to enhance the *Bundeswehr's* intellectual dynamism, not only on questions of force structures, but also in doctrine, where low executive autonomy has had a very detrimental impact. 'Bottom-up' learning processes about the implications of operations for doctrine had the potential to upset the 'salami-tactic'. As a consequence, civilian policy-leaders have played an active role in hindering the ability of the *Bundeswehr* to tackle any lessons from theatre that sit uncomfortably with perceived electoral imperatives, not least the development of an explicit COIN doctrine (Dyson, 2012: 39-44). This situation contrasts markedly to the UK, where under conditions of high executive autonomy in defence, the military is allocated a great deal of freedom to facilitate adherence with doctrinal best practice (Dyson, 2012: 34-39). Civilian intervention in doctrinal development in the UK and France has not focused upon dictating the content of doctrine. Instead civilians have sought to create institutional structures, such as the DCDC and CICDE, which can promote objectivity in joint doctrinal development (Dyson, 2012: 34-39; Dyson, 2010: 153-57).

Furthermore, restrictions in executive autonomy have also hampered the responsiveness of the German procurement programme. The previous section has highlighted the impact of organisational politics between the single services and dysfunctional civil-military relations in defence procurement planning processes. However, these problems are, to a great extent, a consequence of the way the federal political system sensitises Defence Ministers to job losses in the German defence industry. As a source within the BMVg noted: 'The presence of powerful regional politicians makes it very difficult to push through a radical reform to capability acquisition or force postures' (Interviews, BTC, 2009). This lack of political will to reform the acquisition process fosters an inappropriately low level of civilian interference in defence planning processes. It reduces the capacity of the *Bundestag* to scrutinise the utility of the procurement programme in the context of changing security exigencies and also limits the ability of 'service agnostic' organisations to foster greater objectivity in conceptual development and procurement. The UK's high levels of executive autonomy are not matched by an efficient system of defence capability procurement, due to poor civilian management of decision-making processes surrounding defence acquisition. However, in France, high executive autonomy, married with astute political leadership on the institutional structures of procurement has fostered a particularly adaptable and efficient system of acquisition.

Conclusions: overcoming low executive autonomy

Driven by the imperatives of contemporary security challenges, Germany is undergoing a slow process of 'normalisation' in the attitude of the general public and political elites to the use of military force. As a source in the CDU/CSU noted: 'In the light of the reduced ambitions of the British and potential for cuts in the French armed forces, Germany is going to have to begin to fully translate its economic power into military power in order to pick up a greater share of the security burden in Europe' (Interview, CDU, 2012). The recent reforms set in place by de Maizière have taken some important steps to achieving this goal by increasing the pace of German convergence with the defence reforms of her key European partners in the areas of force structures, military capabilities and doctrine.

Yet, as this chapter has highlighted, a number of deficiencies remain in the transmission belt linking changes in the international system with changes to force structures, military capabilities and doctrine. These deficiencies are a result of problems in the 'internal' politics of the BMVg, whose institutional structures fail to properly mitigate the negative impact of inter-service rivalry on defence policy and do not provide a sufficiently critical and dynamic intellectual environment. However, it is the low autonomy of the core executive in defence policy that has incentivised politicians to develop ineffective oversight mechanisms in defence. As a consequence, Germany exhibits a rather dysfunctional model of civil-military relations in defence planning, whereby civilian intervention is excessive in doctrine and more laissez-faire in capability procurement. There are, however, signs that this disabling context of low executive autonomy can be overcome in certain areas of defence reform.

Changing public attitudes to the use of military force and the need to enhance military adaptability are likely, over time, to foster a more effective model of civil-military relations in doctrine development through the allocation of greater freedom to the military in tactical and lower-operational level doctrine. However, the constitutionally-enshrined division of competencies between Ministries acts as a fundamental impediment to the development of greater cross-government collaboration as part of Networked Security at the higher-operational level. Furthermore, despite the positive changes which will be delivered by the Integrated Planning Process, the presence of powerful regional politicians with an interest in sustaining jobs in the German defence industry is likely to continue to de-incentivise greater transparency and the development of effective civilian oversight mechanisms in procurement.

Bibliography

Adams, Gordon/Ben-Ari, Guy (2006): Transforming European Militaries: Coalition Operations and the Technology Gap. Abingdon: Routledge.

Alderson, Alexander (2010): 'Britain'. In: Rid/Keaney (Eds.) (2010): 28-40.

Aust, Helmut/Vashakmadze, Mindia (2008): Parliamentary Consent to the Use of German Armed Forces Abroad. The 2008 Decision of the Federal Constitutional Court in the AWACS-Turkey Case. In: German Law Journal, 9, 2223-36.

Breuer, Fabian (2006): Between Ambitions and Financial Constraints. The Reform of the German Armed Forces. In: German Politics. 15:2, 206-20.

Brune, Sophie-Charlotte/Cameron, Alastair/Maulny, Jean-Pierre/Terlikowski, Marcin (2010): Restructuring Europe's Armed Forces in Times of Austerity. Berlin: SWP Comments. 28.

Cole, Alistair (2001): Franco-German Relations. Harlow: Pearson.

Dalgaard-Nielsen, Anja (2006): Germany Pacifism and Peace-Enforcement. Manchester: Manchester University Press.

De Durand, Etienne (2010): France. In: Rid/Keaney (Eds.) (2010): 11-28.

Duffield, John (1998): World Power Forsaken. Political Power, International Institutions and German Security Policy after Unification. Stanford: Stanford University Press.

DWP (2006): White Paper on German Security Policy and the Future of the Bundeswehr. Berlin: Bundesministerium der Verteidigung.

Dyson, Tom (2007): The Politics of German Defence and Security: Policy Leadership and Military Reform in the post-Cold War Era. New York: Berghahn.

Dyson, Tom (2010): Neoclassical Realism and Defence Reform in post-Cold War Europe. Basingstoke: Palgrave.

Dyson, Tom (2011): Managing Convergence. German Military Doctrine and Capabilities in the 21st Century. In: Defence Studies. 11:2, 244-70.

Dyson, Tom (2012): Organising for Counterinsurgency: The Adaptation of British and German Military Doctrine in Afghanistan. In: Contemporary Security Policy. 33:1, 27-58.

Farrell, Theo (2008): The Dynamics of British Military Transformation. In: International Affairs. 84:4, 777-807.

Flournoy, Michelle/Smith, Julianne (2005): European Defence Integration. Bridging the Gap Between Strategy and Capabilities. Washington: Centre for Strategic and International Studies.

France 24 (2009): Sarkozy Unveils Plan for French Return to NATO Command. http://www.france24.com/en/20090311-france-nato-commandstructure-wider-role-troops-charles-de-gaulle, date accessed 29.05.2012.

FWP (2008): The French White Paper on National Security. Paris: Odilie Jacob.

Gray, Bernard (2009): Review of Acquisition for the Secretary of State for Defence. London: HMSO.

Heitmüller, Ulrike (2009): Common Shield: Die Bundeswehr testet neue Technologien. In: Die Welt, 13.02.2009.

Hodge, Carl Cavanagh (2012): Rebalancing Priorities: America, Europe and Defence Austerity. In: e-International Relations. 05.03.2012. http://www.e-ir.info/2012/03/05/rebalancing-priorities-america-europe-and-defence-austerity/, accessed 05.03.2012.

Huntington, Samuel (1957): The Soldier and the State. Cambridge, MA. Harvard University Press.

Interview SWP (2012): Interview, Working Group on International Security, Stiftung Wissenschaft und Politik, Berlin, 27.02.2012.

Interview, AA (2012): Interview, German Federal Foreign Ministry; Defence and Security Policy Division, 09.03.2012.

Interview, BMVg (2010): Interview, German Ministry of Defence, Berlin, 16.10.2010.

Interview, BMVg (2012): Interview, German Ministry of Defence, Berlin, 24.02.2012.

Interview, BTC (2011): Interview, Bundeswehr Transformation Centre, Strausberg, 19.12.2011

Interview, BTC (2012): Interview, Bundeswehr Transformation Centre, Strausberg, 15.06.2012.

Interview, CDU (2012): Interview, CDU/CSU Bundestagsfraktion, Arbeitsgruppe Verteidigung, Berlin, 17.02.2012.

Interview, FES (2012): Interview, Friedrich Ebert Stiftung, Berlin, 18.05.2012.

Interview, Führungsakademie (2010): Interviews, Führungsakademie der Bundeswehr, Hamburg, 08.12.2010.

Interviews, BTC (2009): Interviews, Bundeswehr Transformation Centre, Strausberg, 26.11.2009.

Interviews, Heeresamt (2011): Interviews, Division 1 (Army Development); Division 2 (Training) and Department for Coordination of Lessons-Learned, Heeresamt, Cologne, 18.05.2011.

Irondelle, Bastien (2003): Civil-Military Relations and the End of Conscription in France. In: Security Studies. 12:3, 157-87.

JD 7/06 (2006). Incorporating and Extending the UK Military Effects-Based Approach, Joint Doctrine 7/06. Shrivenham: Development Concepts and Doctrine Centre.

Krepinevic, Andrew 1994: Cavalry to Computer: The Pattern of Military Revolutions. In: The National Interest. 37, Fall 1994.

Levene, Lord Peter (2011): Defence Reform: An Independent Report into the Structure and Management of the Ministry of Defence. London: HMSO.

Longhurst, Kerry (2004): Germany and the Use of Force: The Evolution of German Security Policy 1989-2003. Manchester: Manchester University Press.

Matlary, Janne-Haaland (2009): European Union Security Dynamics. Basingstoke: Palgrave.

Noetzel, Timo (2011): The German Politics of War. In: International Affairs. 82: 2, 397-417.

Noetzel, Timo/Schreer, Benjamin (2009): Missing Links: The Evolution of German Counter-insurgency Thinking. In: RUSI Journal. 154: 1, 16-22.

Resende-Santos, Joao (2007): Neorealism, the State and the Modern Mass Army. Cambridge: Cambridge University Press.

Rid, Thomas/Keaney, Thomas (Eds.) (2010). Understanding Counter-insurgency. Abingdon: Routledge.

SDSR (2010): The Strategic Defence and Security Review. Norwich: HMSO.

Siebert, Bjoern (2012): A Quiet Revolution. The RUSI Journal. 157: 1, 60-9.

Spiegel (2012): Unreliable Partners? http://www.spiegel.de/international/world/criticism-of-germany-s-military-role-in-the-nato-alliance-a-833503.html date accessed 21.06.2012.

VPR (2011): Defence Policy Guidelines. Berlin: BMVg.

Wiesner, Ina (2011): The Paradoxical Ally. Germany's Decoupling Strategy in the Adoption of NCW. Paper presented at the 2011 ISA Convention, Montreal, March 2011.

Weise (2010): Report of the Structural Commission of the Bundeswehr. Berlin: BMVg.

About the authors

Dr Stefan Bayer teaches economics and ecology in every course offered at the Bundeswehr Command and Staff College. He also regularly teaches economics at the Faculty of Economics and Social Sciences of the University of Tübingen and at Helmut Schmidt University/Bundeswehr University in Hamburg. His preferred fields of research are military economics, environmental economics, and applied finance issues related to security and the environment.

Ulf Bednarz has a degree in law and joined the Bundeswehr in 1998, his initial post being that of a legal adviser at the Army Forces Command. In 2003, while working as a lecturer of law at the Bundeswehr Leadership Development and Civic Education Centre, with a focus on international law, he took part in the KFOR mission in Kosovo, serving as a legal adviser with the 6th German Contingent of Multinational Brigade Southwest. After working at the Armed Forces Office and the Legal Affairs Directorate of the Federal Ministry of Defence, he moved to the Organisation Staff of the Ministry and was a member of the FMOD Organisation project group.

Dr Stephan Böckenförde studied political science (M.A. and PhD) and German philology (M.A.) in Münster and Seattle. He has taught at the Free University of Berlin, Humboldt University in Berlin, Dresden University of Technology and the University of Greifswald. In 2008/2009, he worked as a substitute professor at the University of Marburg. He has been a research assistant at the Bundeswehr Academy for Information and Communication in Strausberg since 2005. His publications focus on German and US security policy. He also co-published the textbook *Deutsche Sicherheitspolitik: Herausforderungen, Akteure und Prozesse*, the second edition of which is currently in preparation.

Dr Sabine Collmer is a social scientist currently serving as Professor of International Security Studies at the College of the George C. Marshall European Center for Security Studies in Garmisch-Partenkirchen, Germany. She has researched and published in the fields of defence transformation and civil-military relations after the Cold War and on changing security dynamics in Eurasia. Currently, she is working on the impact of the changed military recruitment system on German civil-military relations.

Dr Tom Dyson is a lecturer in politics and international relations at Royal Holloway, University of London. He has published three monographs: *The Politics of German Defence and Security* (Berghahn, 2007); *Neoclassical Realism and Defence Reform in post Cold War Europe* (Palgrave, 2010) and *European Defence Cooperation in EU Law and IR Theory* (Palgrave, 2012/13, with Theodore Konstadinides). Dyson has also published articles on issues of British, French and German security and defence policy in *The British Journal of Politics and IR*, *Contemporary British History*, *Contemporary Security Policy*, *Defence Studies, European Security* and *German Politics and Security Studies*.

Manfred Engelhardt, a lieutenant general, joined the Bundeswehr in 1969. An armour officer, he underwent general staff officer training at the Bundeswehr Command and Staff College from 1980 to 1982. In 1985 and 1999, he attended courses at the British Army Staff College in Camberley and at the Royal College for Defence Studies in London, respectively. Besides field assignments as a battalion, brigade and division commander, he completed several assignments at the Federal Ministry of Defence, including in the FMOD Policy Planning Staff, as a branch chief in the Military Policy Division, as Deputy Chief of Staff for Bundeswehr Operations and as Director of the Armed Forces Staff before becoming the Commander of the Joint Support Command in 2008.

Prof. Dr Sven Bernhard Gareis is the German deputy dean at the George C. Marshall European Center for Security Studies in Garmisch-Partenkirchen, as well as a professor of political science at the University of Münster. His major fields of research and teaching are German foreign, security and defence policy, Chinese politics, and United Nations peacekeeping.

Dieter Heuer joined the Federal Defence Administration – Office of Defence Administration, Military District VI, Munich, in 1980, after passing the First and Second State Examinations in law (University of Munich / State Law Examination Office of Bavaria). Following numerous assignments in almost all fields of defence administration and after working as an assistant branch chief at the FMOD, where his primarily focus was on organisation and infrastructure issues, he is currently in charge of the personnel accounting department at the Munich branch of Military District Administrative Office South. He is also the permanent deputy to the head of the Munich branch office.

Helmuth Heumann joined the armament organisation of the Federal Defence Administration after graduating in aeronautical engineering. He has held posts at the FMOD, the Federal Office of Defence Technology and Procurement as well as at the former German space agency DARA and is also a graduate of the NATO Defence College in Rome. Before becoming president of the Federal

Academy of Defence Administration and Technology (BAkWVT), he was general manager of the NATO Helicopter Management Agency (NAHEMA).

Dr Jörg Jacobs studied political science at the University of Bamberg, focusing on empirical social research methods and economics. He obtained his doctorate at Viadrina European University with a paper entitled *Tücken der Demokratie – Antisystemeinstellungen und ihre Determinanten in sieben postkommunistischen Transformationsländern* (The pitfalls of democracy – Anti-system attitudes and their determinants in seven post-communist transition countries). In 2007, he was a visiting professor for European Studies at the University of Texas in Austin. Since June 2007, he has worked in the research and development section of the Bundeswehr Academy for Information and Communication. He has published on subjects such as public opinion and security policy, comparative cultural studies as well as media and political communication.

Dietmar Klos, a retired German Army colonel, was a career officer until the end of 2005. He completed numerous command and staff assignments in the mechanised infantry and infantry and as a general staff officer both in the Bundeswehr and NATO, most recently as a branch chief at the FMOD – Army Staff, being responsible for national territorial tasks (until 2001) and German Army operations and operational tasks (1998 – 2005). Dietmar Klos is a special correspondent on land forces for the magazine *Europäische Sicherheit & Technik* (Mittler Report Verlag GmbH), focusing on issues of security and defence policy, comprehensive security as well as German and NATO/EU land forces.

Dr Gerhard Kümmel is a scientific director at the Bundeswehr Centre for Military History and Social Sciences, Potsdam, chairman of the Military and Social Sciences Working Group (AMS), president of the Research Committee 01: Armed Forces & Conflict Resolution of the International Sociological Association (ISA) and lecturer in the Military Studies Master's degree programme at the University of Potsdam.

Dr Heiner Möllers, a lieutenant colonel, has been the project manager for the history of the Bundeswehr at the Bundeswehr Centre for Military History and Social Sciences in Potsdam since 2008. His research focuses on military history from the 19th to the 21st century.

Dr Christian Mölling studied social sciences, economics and history in Duisburg and at Warwick University in the UK. He obtained his doctorate under Professor Daase at the University of Munich. In 2009, he joined the German Institute for International and Security Affairs (*Stiftung Wissenschaft und Politik – SWP*) as a research assistant, focusing on the development of the armed forces, armament policy and the defence industry in Germany and in Europe. Before that, he worked at the Centre for Security of the ETH Zurich (2008-09) and at the Institute for Peace Research and Security Policy (IFSH), Hamburg. He was also a guest researcher at the *Fondation pour la Recherche Stratégique* in Paris, the Royal United Services Institute in London, and the European Union Institute for Security Studies in Paris.

Armin Müller, a graduate in engineering, M.A., is a reserve lieutenant commander in the German Navy and currently works as a research assistant for the chair of modern history at the University of Marburg. As a freelancer, he is furthermore involved in "The Bundeswehr as an Army engaged in Operations" project at the Bundeswehr Centre for Military History and Social Sciences in Potsdam, working on a project about the Bundeswehr reserve after 1990. His research interests are modern military history and the history of the intelligence services.

Christoph Reifferscheid has a degree in physics and, after completing a two-year period of preparatory service, passed the Second State Examination in defence technology in 1987, subsequently holding several assignments at the Federal Ministry of Defence and its subordinate agencies in the areas of armament, basic and follow-on training and organisation and, in 2011 the FMOD Organisation project. Since January 2013, he has been President of the Bundeswehr Educational Centre *(Bildungszentrum der Bundeswehr)* in Mannheim.

Dr Gregor Richter studied sociology, economics and statistics at the University of Munich and obtained his doctorate at the Bundeswehr University in Munich in 2002. He currently works as a project manager at the Bundeswehr Centre for Military History and Social Sciences, Potsdam. His work focuses on administrative studies as well as organisational and personnel research.

Dieter Stockfisch is a retired German Navy captain whose assignments included those of a frigate commander and a squadron commander. He underwent admiral/general staff training, served at the NATO Headquarters AFNORTH/Norway and was both an assistant to a state secretary and a branch chief at the FMoD (Naval Staff). He now works as an editor for security policy and naval forces for the magazine *Europäische Sicherheit & Technik.*

Dr Dieter Weingärtner studied administrative law before working in the administration of the German Bundestag, at the Ministry of the Environment of Baden-Württemberg and at the Federal Ministry of Justice (Head of the Executive Staff, Chief of the Criminal Law Division). He has been the director of the Legal Affairs Directorate of the Federal Ministry of Defence since 2002. He is the chairman of the German Society for Military Law and International Humanitarian Law.

Hans-Werner Wiermann, a graduate in engineering and brigadier general, studied electrical engineering before joining the Bundeswehr in 1976. Between 1988 and 1990, he underwent general staff officer training at the Bundeswehr Command and Staff College in Hamburg. In 1993, he attended a course at the British Army Staff College. He was an aide-de-camp to the Chief of Staff of the Bundeswehr, deputy director of the Military Policy Directorate and later chief of the Security Policy Division of the Federal Ministry of Defence.

Dr Ina Wiesner studied political and social sciences in Potsdam, Berlin and Aarhus, Denmark. In 2011, she obtained her doctorate at the European University Institute in Florence, Italy. Since then, she has been working as a research fellow at the Bundeswehr Academy for Information and Communication in Strausberg near Berlin.